UNDER THE GENERAL EDITORSHIP OF

JESSE W. MARKHAM

PRINCETON UNIVERSITY

HOUGHTON MIFFLIN ADVISER IN ECONOMICS

INTERNATIONAL

CONOMICS AND BUSINESS

.... SELECTED READINGS

WALTER KRAUSE · THE UNIVERSITY OF IOWA

F. JOHN MATHIS · UNIVERSITY OF ILLINOIS

HOUGHTON MIFFLIN COMPANY · BOSTON

NEW YORK   ATLANTA   GENEVA, ILL.   DALLAS   PALO ALTO

EDITOR'S INTRODUCTION ....

It is highly doubtful that the traditional dichotomy between international *economics* (mainly concerned with the activities of national governments that bear upon their patterns of trade), and international *business* (mainly concerned with the international activities of private business enterprises) has been fullly consistent with the facts of the international economy. For, private companies began to grow in size, number, and economic importance in the sixteenth century; and the course of, say, Great Britain's economy surely has been steered as much by her manufacturing corporations (not to mention the Bank of England — a private bank until after World War II) as by her Minister of External Affairs.

If the traditional separation of international business and international economics has been of dubious validity, to continue to treat them as separate and essentially independent disciplines would be fatuous. The recency of the term "multi-national corporation" can be ascribed in part to a cultural lag, but the rapidity with which the term has gained currency dramatically attests to the rising importance of the large modern corporation as an international institution. Since the gross sales — even the value added — of some of the larger corporations exceed the gross national product of over half the members of the United Nations, it is apparent that their decisions not only affect, in a significant way, the economic activities carried on in and among nations, but the nations themselves.

Professors Krause and Mathis have designed this volume of readings for the purpose of giving explicit recognition to the fusion of international economics and international business, and to the interactions among governments and international business enterprises. In doing so, they have included the best of the most recent scholarly works by authors also seeking to integrate international economics with international business. In addition, the selections are addressed to problems and institutions that comprise the contemporary international economy — common markets and custom unions, the position of the underdeveloped countries, balance of payments, international liquidity, United States business investment abroad, and a host of other timely and related topics. The result is a volume that should be extremely useful to both teachers and practitioners of international economics and business.

JESSE W. MARKHAM
Princeton University

PREFACE ....

Traditionally, the subject of international economics headlines the role of government — in the "Kennedy Round," in GATT, in the European Common Market. The international economy is, however, in fact (and in action), a composite of the role played by government and the role played by business. Government and business share in decision-making authority and in the operations that flow from it — and, thus, share in creating the overall international environment. Indeed, international economics, as a subject, does not exist independently of international business; international business does not exist independently of international economics.

International Economics and Business: Selected Readings seeks to integrate, in a "pioneering" way, the two approaches. It presents a careful choice of newsworthy and timeworthy articles and documents. And it introduces, at strategic points, editorial commentary which relates one selection to another and which focuses all of the selections within an overview of international economics and business.

Part One of the book describes the international economy — its nature, participants, trends. Part Two views it from the standpoint of the United States. And Part Three discusses it in relation to policy formulations of the United States. With Part Four, the involvement of U.S. business is approached directly (as Raymond Vernon asks "Foreign Trade or Foreign Investment?," as Donald A. Wells considers "Attitudes Toward Foreign Investors"). Part Five treats some special "problem areas." Finally, Part Six is devoted to speculation about the future (for instance, Simon Kuznets assesses "The Forces of World Change: Diversity and Interdependence," Raùl Prebisch tells us about the "Attack on the Old Order").

The integrated approach of *International Economics and Business* qualifies it for use in international economics courses taught primarily in economics departments and for use in the fast-growing international business courses taught in business schools. Beyond the classroom, the book's broad coverage of topics qualifies it as a general and ready reference source.

In the course of editing *International Economics and Business,* our indebtedness to others mounted. We want to express our appreciation to those who commented helpfully on the book's basic framework — to, especially, Professor Jesse W. Markham of Princeton University and to Professor Ernest V. Zuber of the University of Iowa. Also, we want to thank Mr. Christopher Garbacz of the University of Iowa for research assistance, Mrs. Betty Gray of Houghton Mifflin Company for editorial assistance, and Miss Marie Smith for superior secretarial service.

WALTER KRAUSE
The University of Iowa

F. JOHN MATHIS
University of Illinois

CONTENTS ....

ix

INTERNATIONAL ECONOMICS
AND BUSINESS
..... SELECTED READINGS

PART ONE ....

THE INTERNATIONAL ECONOMY

Economic theorists long ago extolled the merits of an international economy: according to the law of comparative advantage, any country — through specialization in production, followed by trade — could gain economically. Policy-makers of a later day were concerned with freeing trade, in the interests of a greater flow, from inhibitive restrictions. Although completely free trade never has become a reality, other pro-internationalist activities *have* been realized — for instance, the international movement of investment capital applied on behalf of production itself.

Recent decades have seen a markedly stepped-up tempo of activity in the international economy — with world trade increasing eight-fold and United States trade increasing ten-fold (both in dollar value) over the last thirty years and with a new high in overall foreign investment. Indeed, recent decades have seen a markedly stepped-up tempo of activity on the international scene in general: tourism is "up"; improved news media bring us more and more information on far-away places and events; the rising costs of our foreign participation boost tax levies. And, as our earlier isolation, both physical and emotional, has lessened, our national concern and action result in programs of foreign aid, the setting up of international agencies, the calling of international conferences.

It is tempting to conclude that growing internationalism equals progress; that it is all for the "good." But we must be aware of the problems — greater perhaps than ever before in history — that confront us and realize that if the "good" comprises the woof, so to speak, of growing internationalism, they comprise the warp. Among these problems, two are paramount. The first pertains to technology; the second to political (and economic) ideology.

As we have noted, the law of comparative advantage specifies specialization; only through specialization can the diversity on which trade is based be secured. Of course, economic diversity always has been present — if only because of varying circumstances of resource distribution and climate. However, during the course of modern history, the advent and

1

application of man-made technology had the effect of accentuating diversity. And, as we know, with the coming of the Industrial Revolution and with the subsequent refinement and intensification of technology, countries began to "pull apart" in terms of their production patterns.

Thus, we have moved to a world environment of "rich" and "poor" countries — the developed and the underdeveloped. And the gap between them, the productivity and income gap, has been widening. Yet, to hark back to a point made earlier, the same revolution in technology that triggered this widening economic schism also provided the basis for closer contact between countries — more trade and investment, better communication, and so forth. And brought about today's world of (a) greater and greater diversity and (b) greater and greater interdependence.

Diversity and interdependence are two forces that can meet in harmonious complementarity, but that, alternatively, can cause an explosion. Indeed, explosion becomes a real possibility when, as now, the man-in-the-street, almost everywhere, is conscious of what goes on in his own and other countries and when an active ideological rivalry — both political and economic — constitutes, in large part, what does go on. Today's world is dominated by the Communist Bloc(s) versus the so-called "Free World." And so to the divisive potential of disparate technological progress is added the divisive (and destructive) potential of technology's application to the furtherance of ideological competition.

Other problems, too, contribute to the possibility of explosion. Let us cite a few. The number of sovereign states is increasing (under one hundred a few years ago; over one hundred and thirty today) and, at the same time, groups of these countries consider regional economic amalgamation. Are there too many countries? Should such amalgamation be encouraged? Both individual governments and private entrepreneurs are displaying more and more interest in matters of international trade and investment. What policy posture should governments adopt? What is the proper role of the entrepreneurs? Internationally, the competitive position of the United States has weakened (or so our recent balance-of-payments deficits suggest). Is the United States still competitive internationally? Or what must it do to be, or remain, competitive in the years ahead?

In Part One, we raise some of the foregoing problems and questions as we look at the background of the international economy — at the bases of disunity (and also at possible avenues of reconciliation); at the identity of the major international decision-makers; and, briefly, at the history of present-day international trade.

A..... A Disunited World

Disunity is, as we have seen, a paramount feature of the present-day world: it is grounded in disparate technological progress and amplified, increasingly, by an ideological rivalry of political-economic scope.

Professor Horowitz, in our first selection, speaks not of "one world," but *three*. He offers a capsule description of the economic environment of each: (a) the "First World" of Western Europe and the United States — rich, developed, and growing; (b) the "Second World" of Eastern Europe and Mainland China — uneven as to income and advancement, but sharing a commitment to the Communist way of life; (c) the "Third World" of the underdeveloped countries — the most populous of all, poverty-ridden, imbued with new expectations, and torn between the courses offered by West and East.

Professor Johnson, in our second selection, considers current areas of international conflict among these "worlds," — for instance, the clash between the trade aspirations of underdeveloped countries, premised on avowed developmental goals, and the trade institutions and policies of the developed countries. He goes on to point out that conflicts exist *within* the individual "worlds," too — for instance, the policy goals of the Common Market area of Western Europe and of the United States no longer meet as harmoniously as in an earlier day.

1..... Not "One World," But Three[*]

IRVING LOUIS HOROWITZ

Washington University

First World

Dominated by the United States, including allies in Western Europe and satellites in Latin America and elsewhere.

Economy

Capitalist system; based on private ownership in a free market; development of corporate wealth and strong tendencies toward monopolistic controls of large private power blocs. The typical economy is middle class; based on individual entrepreneurial initiative, with little centralized planning (generally only in social welfare sectors). Emphasis on services and consumer goods production. Open internal market; high international integration created by financial and commodity markets, with slight regulation. Savings policies are individual-voluntary and/or based on democratic tax system. Investment is private, unrestricted, unco-ordinated. Source of funds is variable; based on decisions taken by household, business, bank credit, and international capital market. Currencies are stable. Terms of trade favorable. Growth rates are low, but generally balanced for needs of industrial society. Agricultural sector 5 to 20 per cent of GNP, and 5 per cent of labor force; contraction of this sector is aided by international competition (market forces) and by government subsidy. Industrial level of development is high; growth rate has plateaued off. Consumption orientation, encouraged as necessary stimulus for growth; restricted by market fluctuations and private savings. Labor unions strong, highly organized, constituting an economic force.

Second World

Dominated by the Soviet Union, including allies and/or satellites in Eastern Europe and parts of Asia.

[*] Abridged from *Three Worlds of Development* by Irving Louis Horowitz, pp. 39–42, 44–45. Copyright © 1966 by Irving Louis Horowitz. Reprinted by permission of Oxford University Press, Inc.

Economy

Socialist system; based on public (state) ownership in a strictly controlled internal and external market; centralization of all sectors of the economy by political elites; based on total planning. The typical economy is geared to proletarian values. Emphasis is on heavy industrial production. Highly regulated internal and external markets, determined primarily by economic considerations. Trade agreements are largely within Eastern bloc countries; not subject to severe trade fluctuations. Savings policies are non-voluntary; state determined and government controlled. Investment is through the public sector; highly restricted and co-ordinated. Source of funds is stable; based on internal budgeting. Currencies are generally stable. Growth rates are high; imbalances controlled through economic regulation. Agricultural section 15 to 30 per cent of GNP, 40 per cent of labor force; contraction due to prohibition of individual private agriculture. The factors making for land speculation are strictly regulated in order to release resources and increase output at a rate integrated to industrial expansion. Industrial level of development is high, and growth rates have just begun to plateau off. Direct and manifold controls on production and distribution of consumer goods; discouraged as deterrent to industrial development. Labor unions perceived as part of state directorate, worker councils play minor role.

Third World

Non-aligned and non-satellitic nations with a general tendency toward clustering in Africa, Asia, and Latin America — a spectrum conventionally covering Algeria to Yugoslavia in economy and India and China in polity.

Economy

Mixed economy; with both private and public sectors, but moving toward some form of socialism. Economy reveals conflict between desire for integration based on self-sufficiency, and need for aid in development. There is a dilemma between strong internal regulation (foreign/internal investment ratio) and moderate external regulation (freedom of bloc trading) and ability to implement development schemes. Decline in terms of trade; balance of payments problem. Variety of planning techniques (total, national flow, national budget, project, labor, etc.). The typical economy is based on the peasant sector; basic level of economic production is agricultural; although emphasis is on basic industry. Desire for contraction of primary sector: mechanization of agriculture, overwhelming push factors, and imposed plans (rate of collectivization is presently reducing); agriculture often neglected in favor of emphasis on basic industrial development (the highest premium is placed on heavy industry whatever the costs in terms of man-hours) to create import substitute mechanisms. Successful integration of shift from agricultural to industrial sector is therefore uncertain, and dependent upon national planners' ability to control. Compounded by "demonstration effect," which government often tries to dampen through inflationary policies. Source of funds is variable and generally short term; foreign aid and investment supplement domestic savings (which are mitigated by unstable currency). Savings policies mostly voluntary and due to inability to control. Growth rates are high; attempted control of imbalances through political regulation. Short-run private-sector gains often vitiate effects of long-run public-sector planning. Labor unions are radical and unstable, with little economic role.

2..... International Conflicts of Interest*

HARRY G. JOHNSON
University of Chicago

The past two years have been characterized by a great deal of activity in the field of international economic relations. In September 1963 the Board of Directors of the International Monetary Fund, and the representatives of the so-called "Group of Ten" participants in the General Arrangements to Borrow, inaugurated separately studies into ways of strengthening the international monetary system, studies whose results formed the background of the Annual Meeting of the International Monetary Fund held in Tokyo in September 1964. From March until June of 1964, the United Nations Conference on Trade and Development (UNCTAD) — the first such conference to be convened — was in session in Geneva. And since early 1963 the representatives of the nations belonging to the General Agreement on Tariffs and Trade (GATT) have been carrying on negotiations for the "Kennedy Round" of bargaining for multilateral tariff reductions, which was formally initiated in November 1964.

What is important about all this activity on the international front is not so much the fact that it has been going on, as the fact that it has emphasized and brought to public view serious and sharp divisions among the major countries or groups of countries in the world economy with respect to the direction in which the present system of international economic organization should evolve. These divisions are based on the dissatisfaction of important members of the world economy, with the present system of international economic organization, and the international institutions in which that system is incorporated. The international economic system referred to is, of course, the system prevailing among the nations of what is commonly described — with some degree of euphe-

* From *The World Economy at the Crossroads* by Harry G. Johnson, pp. 1–6. © 1965 by Oxford University Press. Reprinted by permission.

mism — as the "free world," and not of the countries of the Communist *bloc.* The divisions among these nations imply that the present system of international economic organization, built with so much careful thought by the Bretton Woods Agreements, must either evolve in new directions to accommodate the dissatisfied, or run the risk of disintegration. Since the international institutions under which the system is organized have in fact been evolving fairly rapidly in recent years in adaptation to their changing environment and the changing demands made upon them, the problem for the future might perhaps be more accurately described as whether the emerging dissatisfactions can be adequately dealt with by further and accelerated evolution of these institutions, or will require a radical change in the whole framework of international economic organization. In either case, it is clear that the international economic system has arrived at a crossroads; and that which direction it now takes is a vital matter for the future of the world economy.

The basic lines of cleavage among the members of the international system are essentially political, in the broad sense of the term, and involve a division into three major groups: the Anglo-Saxon group led by the United States, the European Common Market countries led by France, and the less-developed countries, led largely by the ideas of one man, Dr. Raúl Prebisch. Dr. Prebisch has dominated the Economic Commission for Latin America for most of the post-war period, held the key post of Secretary-General of UNCTAD, and wrote the basic document for the Conference; and his ideas largely shaped the Conference's proceedings and Final Act. The Conference symbolized and also cemented the emergence of the developing countries — and the change of terminology, from "underdeveloped" to "less developed" to "developing," is itself symbolic — as a new and potentially powerful influence in international economic relations. The emergence of this new influence, in turn, has complicated and exacerbated the cleavages between the other two groups that had already been precipitated by the formation of the Common Market.

Broadly speaking, the Anglo-Saxon group stands for the existing international institutions and system of international economic institutions and system of international economic organization, which are indeed largely of its own creation, and takes the position that any apparent problems can be handled by modification and adjustment of the present framework. The Common Market group, on the other hand, is primarily concerned with building up the Common Market as an economic and political force in world affairs. It tends to regard the present international institutions with suspicion, viewing them as instruments for preserving the political and economic dominance in world affairs of the United States, or of the United States and United Kingdom combined, and to prefer to meet emerging problems by superimposing new arrangements in which it has a controlling influence on top of the existing arrangements, instead of by modification of the latter. This has been specially so in the sphere of international monetary organization. There is a rather facile tendency on the part of the United States to attribute this, as well as other awkward obstinacies of European behaviour, to the "third force" ambitions of General de Gaulle; but European suspicion of the existing international institutions has deeper roots in the experience of the immediate post-war period, when the United States did call the international tune because it alone was paying the piper. In addition, as the formation of the Common Market itself bears witness, the European attitude towards a variety of important problems in the government of international trade is radically at variance with the Anglo-Saxon attitude, not only over the central issue of multilateralism and the most-favoured-nation principle versus preferential trading arrangements, but also and more fundamentally in taking an essentially political rather than economic view of the nature of competition in international trade and of the objectives of governmental intervention in it.

Again speaking broadly, the less-developed countries as a collectivity are all suspicious of and hostile to the present institutions of international economic organization, but for a rather different reason. They believe, or like to believe, that these institutions are instruments designed to foster the further development of the already-advanced countries and to impede or prevent their own economic development. Especially in Latin America, the International Monetary Fund has frequently appeared as the stern enforcer of orthodoxy in fiscal and monetary policy, and the resolute opponent of the inflationary policies that in many less-developed countries are regarded as the *sine qua non* of rapid economic growth. The World Bank has been persistently criticized for its attachment to specific-purpose commercially sound loans, when what these countries want is general-purpose finance on the easiest possible terms. In the trade field GATT and its principles appear to these countries as an arrangement by which the rich get richer at the expense of the poor: not only does the whole apparatus of bargaining for reciprocal tariff reductions appear unfair — both because they have little trade to bargain with, and because bargaining with it would entail sacrificing the protectionist policies on which they believe their growth depends — but the exemption of agricultural products from GATT rules enables the advanced countries (as the less-developed countries see it) to solve their agricultural problems at the expense of the export earnings of the less-developed countries. Underlying all this aversion to the existing institutions of international economic organization is the strong and highly moralistic conviction that the advanced countries are responsible for their less-developed condition, and owe them redress on a massive scale, this redress to be rendered through the unilateral tender of both unencumbered development assistance and special advantages in international trade. This is a political claim on the advanced countries, and to enforce it the less-developed countries have resorted to the one international institution in which nations appear as political equals rather than as economic unequals, and which they can control by force of numbers, the United Nations.

These, then, are the basic lines of cleavage among the nations of the international economy, which must somehow be resolved in the future evolution — or dissolved in the possible future breakdown — of the international economic order; and they are basically of political origin. The foregoing description of them is intended, of course, to be only the briefest of thumbnail sketches; it has necessarily glossed over important divergences of opinion among the members of the various groups — for example, between the United States on the one hand and the United Kingdom or Canada on the other, between France and Italy on the one hand and Germany and the Benelux countries on the other, and among the less-developed countries between net-exporters and net-importers of foodstuffs. . . .

B..... Avenues of Resolution

At all global levels, between different sections of the world or within given sections, there is a basis for conflict. But countries and areas must deal with one another — or try to find a way to do so. Indeed, much of what transpires internationally is in the nature of an attempt to deal with — indeed, to resolve — essentially antagonistic situations. Here, we look at some of the potential *avenues* of resolution.

Dr. Black, long-time head of the International Bank for Reconstruction and Development, looks at international aid for the developmental aspirations of the still underdeveloped countries. He speaks of "development diplomacy" — assistance given by the richer, more-advanced countries to the efforts of poor countries to better their lot, with such assistance provided on terms, and to an extent, consonant with the lessening of one form of world tension.

Next, the conduct of international business comprises an important avenue of contact, one in which the governments and peoples of the businessman's home country and of the country in which business is done have a clear interest. According to a growing view, private business (including American business) has an obligation in its international dealings that goes well beyond the economic theorist's favorite equilibrating consideration, the maximization of profits. Under the heading of "international business responsibility," Professor Blough refers to businessmen as "ambassadors" who, in the course of their operations, can do much good, or harm, for the image of their country and for international relations generally.

3..... The Diplomacy of International Development*

EUGENE R. BLACK
Formerly, President, World Bank

. . . [The] division of the world [into rich and poor, East and West] is made important largely through the spread of science and technology. It is said that science and technology have shrunk the world, and indeed they have. But they have also enlarged the world's problems out of all proportion with the past. Science and technology have forced the societies of the human race into an intimacy never before shared in history. At the same time, . . . the first and foremost effect of the spread of science and technology has been to infuse humanity with an immense increase in the sense of human power — man's power over nature and over his fellow man. The combination of greater intimacy and an immensely increased sense of human power has heightened the Babel of differences among the societies of mankind so that the degree of danger and discomfort in which we live together today is unique in modern history.

To the usual tasks of diplomacy these facts of modern life add a whole new dimension. To the age-old task of maintaining the balance of power must now be added the task of maintaining the balance of hope — hope in the proposition that the underdeveloped societies of the world can take science and technology into their lives without in the process denying the values of freedom and tolerance. It is to this problem that development diplomacy addresses itself.

Cooperation in economic development can be the most hopeful means, perhaps the only really important means, of maintaining this balance of hope. But the real advantages of such a cooperation must be separated from the false ones.

. . .

* Reprinted by permission of the publishers from Eugene R. Black, *The Diplomacy of Economic Development*, Cambridge, Mass.: Harvard University Press, Copyright, 1960, by The Fletcher School of Law and Diplomacy, Tufts University, Medford, Massachusetts, pp. 3–4, 47–53, 58.

There have been some occasions, not necessarily connected directly with the Cold War, when I have been tempted to believe that development diplomacy has no status at all in the strategy of the Western powers. Economic aid has been used all too frequently in recent years in an effort to bring about some temporary accommodation in conventional diplomacy — as a reward for military alliance or a diplomatic concession, or as a last-ditch attempt to retrieve a diplomatic miscalculation. . . .

I will not attempt to judge whether the price of using aid in this way has been worth it or not. It is enough to say that from the point of view of development the price has been very high, especially where aid bestowed for some narrow political end has abetted and perpetuated policies which make growth impossible. This cost must be figured into the cost of any temporary accommodation which the diplomatists and military strategists may have secured.

In contrast, if economic aid is accorded a separate and distinct status in national policy, development diplomacy can help conventional diplomacy. In so far as it brings about a more durable contact between the Western nations and the underdeveloped nations — the kind of contact which may remain open when conventional diplomacy breaks down — then it offers the hope that there may be less need for expensive and often self-defeating temporary accommodations.

And there is still a great deal of unexplored territory in development diplomacy. Over the long run it is, I am confident, through exploring this territory that the Western nations can best serve their political interests in the underdeveloped world. It is by giving development diplomacy a separate and distinct status in national policy — a status apart from the tactical problems posed by the existence of Communism as a world force and apart from other narrow political and military interests — that the West can best influence the course of events in the underdeveloped world in directions compatible with liberty and tolerance. I do not say that development diplomacy should ignore the problems which concern conventional diplomacy; I do say that it should hold out the hope of continued constructive contact in spite of them.

· · ·

What is true of the political interest of the old nations of the free world is also true of the economic interest of these nations. Expanding trade and investment between these parts of the world depends now on a quite fundamental break with past attitudes and practices. Where a trader's outlook sufficed in the past, an investor's outlook is needed now. And again this boils down to recognizing the status of development diplomacy.

This is particularly true for trade. The simple idea of "growth through trade" no longer satisfies the underdeveloped world today as it did, by and large, even a generation ago. This is not true for all countries; but it is true for those countries that are trying to push their development along under forced draft. And as more countries undertake to do this, the problem of maintaining conditions for a healthy and expanding trade is likely to be even more difficult than it is now.

Why is it going to be more difficult? It is because all too often the governments of these countries are defeatist, if not actively hostile, towards exporting. Wide fluctuations from year to year in income from key commodity exports harden many politicians in their belief that one prime objective of development is to achieve total economic "independence" from the rest of the world. This desire for economic self-sufficiency runs deep. Since so many export enterprises in the underdeveloped world were the creation of foreign entrepreneurs and are even now owned and operated by foreigners, exporting tends to be regarded as a business for somebody else, if not a reminder of a hated colonial past. At the same time restrictive trade practices and attitudes in the older nations — particularly hostility toward imports of manufactured and semimanufactured goods from the new nations — often discourage governments from channeling investment into new export lines in order to relieve their dependence on one commodity and earn more foreign exchange for their own development.

The trader is in no position to overcome this defeatism and animosity. His concern is naturally for his order book, not for the balance of payments or the political suspicions of the governments in his customers' countries. At the same time the long-term prospects for trade between the West and the underdeveloped countries clearly depend on the capacity and the willingness of the new nations to develop their purchasing power through building up their exports. Therefore the governments of the trading nations in the West, in so far as they are concerned with a rising volume of trade with the new nations, must concern themselves with the export potential of the new nations as well as of their own nations.

Unfortunately all too many of the devices used to promote exports from the industrialized countries reflect no such concern; in fact, they often make matters worse. Loans tied to purchases in the lending country, easy credit terms which run out in a few years and long before the life of the product sold, restrictions against lending for projects in the new nations which might some day provide competition for domestic manufacturers or their exports — all of these devices make the job of creating the right conditions for growth through trade even more difficult. . . .

These devices are usually justified on balance-of-payments grounds, and I do not mean to make light of the problem which the industrialized nations face in maintaining external equilibrium. This is a very real problem. . . . But the demands of development diplomacy should be given a hearing in solving this problem. Such a hearing is often lacking now; development aid does not have that separate and distinct status which would allow its contribution to be weighed in the decision.

The future of trade between the West and the underdeveloped world depends primarily on what happens, not in the West, but in the under-developed countries. It depends on the kind of balance that is struck in these countries between the desire for autarky and the desire for more rapid growth. The desire for autarky will not be tempered until there is more awareness of how, by underemphasizing exports, the leaders of these nations are prolonging the poverty of their people. This is one of the kinds of choices development diplomacy is supposed to "illuminate." Inasmuch as the future of trade and investment between the West and the underdeveloped world is at stake in this matter, would it not seem wise to grant development diplomacy a chance to do its work?

Economic aid should be a very great help to trade, as is often said. But to be a help, aid must be a means of promoting "the right kinds of decisions" in terms of development, not just a means of rewarding traders. Aid can never be a true substitute for trade — not for the underdeveloped countries, nor for the industrialized countries either.

. . .

It seems clear to me that only by granting development diplomacy a separate status — not an overriding status but a clear and distinct status — in national policy can the stated political and economic interests of the Western nations in the underdeveloped world be served. . . .

One way or another, the Western nations will have to live intimately with the historic transformation going on in the underdeveloped world. The question is, will these nations also live constructively with that trans-formation or will they merely seek to insulate themselves from the effects of historical forces which they themselves are so largely responsible for having loosed? Development diplomacy is one logical means to a hopeful modus vivendi; there may in fact be no other means that is both so logical and so hopeful.

4..... Business Activity and International Relations*

ROY BLOUGH

Columbia University

The Directions of Change

The [foregoing] discussion . . . reflects the belief that international business in general and the multinational corporation in particular will become increasingly important factors in economic life. Support for this belief is found both in recent trends and in the dynamic forces of our times.

This is an age in which man has greatly increased his mastery of the secrets of economic growth. In all parts of the world there is recognition of the possibilities of improving human welfare and insistence on progressing as fast as possible in that direction. Rapid advances in technology, implemented with capital and entrepreneurship, have brought into use new products and more efficient production methods. Perhaps the most important developments for international business have been instantaneous mass communication and very rapid transportation. These advances in communication and transportation, together with striking progress in the science and practice of management, have made it possible to bring increasingly numerous and complex business operations under effective unified control. The outlook is for continuing, perhaps accelerating, advance throughout the technological spectrum.

These factors are promoting the enlargement of markets from local to national and from national to regional and worldwide scope. The spread of industrialization to many countries seems assured, although it certainly will be slower and more painful than optimists thought a generation ago. The rigid conception of the economic world as made up of complemen-

* From *International Business: Environment and Adaptation* by Roy Blough, pp. 331–332, 338–339. Copyright, 1966, by McGraw-Hill, Inc. McGraw-Hill Book Company. Used by permission.

tary manufacturing and primary producing countries is being undermined. It is clear that efficient manufacturing can be carried on almost anywhere, given the capital and technology and after a period of learning and experience. Moreover, the markets for many primary products continue to be eroded, relatively if not absolutely, by the substitution of manufactured synthetic materials. These developments in themselves point to a slower increase in international trade than in world production. However, there is another side. Economies of scale within manufacturing are being realized through national specialization in particular products or components. The strengthening and spread of this tendency could give us a world having less national complementarity based on resources and climate but with growing trade based on economies of scale. The extent of the development of such trade depends in part on the costs of transportation (including the time factor as part of cost) in relation to the costs of production, since transportation costs are a barrier to trade.

Whether or not trade develops in these directions, the demands for foreign investment and other international movements of capital may be expected to increase for many years to come, in view of the present geographical concentration of capital. Such investment is the basis for a rising volume of business, which in the case of United States companies taken as a group already has substantially outstripped the volume of their exports. This trend may be expected to continue with the growth in their accumulated foreign investment.

The major uncertainties regarding the future size and configuration of international business lie in the area of governmental policy. Many aspects of such uncertainty . . . [can be cited] — for example, future relations with the communist world; the ability and willingness of countries to stem the rising tide of population; whether and on what terms the industrial countries will make large sums of capital available to developing countries and will buy the products of these countries; the extent of the acceptance of large foreign corporations by national governments, of pressures for local participation in the control of those corporations, and of insistence that they establish research laboratories along with their factories in order to promote indigenous technological progress — these and many other uncertain factors that have a bearing on the future of international business merit greater study and analysis for the determination of business and national policy.

The most immediate policy problem of important concern to international business perhaps is the direction to be taken by trade policy. Since the war, there has been substantial progress toward nondiscriminatory tariffs and freer movement of goods and capital. It is by no means clear that this progress will continue. A competing philosophy, that of regional trade preferences, . . . has some support as a principle of world economic organization. . . .

International Business Responsibility

. . . Accepting the realistic view that corporations recognize responsibilities to the governments and publics of the countries in which they make their profits, the international corporation's responsibility presents a difficult problem of balance. Since its profits are dependent on activities in two or more countries, it has dual or multiple loyalties. Clearly, the opportunity to operate profitably within a foreign country carries with it loyalty obligations to that country, both to obey its laws and to promote its welfare. The corporation also has loyalty obligations to its home government. Let us take, for example, companies based in the United States. The company expects as a matter of course to receive all the governmental aids that the law provides or that have been established through practice. This involves not only information, financial aid, and trade facilities but also assistance in dealing with host governments to secure favorable arrangements or to forestall unfavorable treatment. Businesses differ widely in their dependence on their home government. Some are highly dependent on it for aid in negotiating with foreign countries for permission to operate within their borders, while others require relatively little, if any, direct service. None, however, could be sure of lasting long overseas without the presence at least in the background of the strong arm of the United States.

Thus it is inescapable that the businessman abroad has some responsibility to the United States government. Whether they wish it or not, businesses and their managers are an important part of the face which the United States turns toward the world. The businessman is an ambassador and can do his country much harm or good in foreign eyes. The question of how far his responsibilities to the home government extend in the light of his other responsibilities, however, is the subject of continuing debate. Presumably the United States government is entitled to expect that the business will behave well in its relations with other countries. . . .

C..... The Primary Participants

As we have seen, the two primary participants on the international scene are governments and businesses. Both make decisions; both take action. While government may well claim the greater power (by virtue of sheer size and inherent right of authority, if for no other reasons), neither can afford to proceed independently of the other. The normal situation between them, in fact, is one of complementarity and cooperation, along with a certain "competitiveness."

To begin, Professor Benoit examines some current trends in international business. Foreign investment is being substituted more and more for traditional foreign trade; more goods are being produced close to ultimate markets, rather than shipped in from afar. Know-how and technology are assuming increased importance as international "commodities," helping to modify the tradition of basing comparative-cost calculations on raw materials and labor as *the* crucial resources. Finally, private enterprise is proving highly adaptable in relationships in which government is dominant — a fact evidenced by new international partnership arrangements between private foreign companies and the state-directed economies of Eastern Europe.

While Professor Benoit alludes (albeit within a special context) to a new measure of cooperation between business and government, Professor Kronstein outlines a problem relative to their cooperation. What is the proper role of each (viewed from the United States' standpoint)? How should they play their roles to achieve maximum advantage? He suggests that, as matters stand, the answers are unclear and even haphazard — a situation detrimental to all concerned.

5..... International Economic Relations: Participants and Practices*

EMILE BENOIT
Columbia University

We now live in a world in which all men are so close that only a few minutes' communicating, orbiting, or shooting time separates them — a world which is only a tiny footstool for the beginning of man's exploration of the universe. Yet we are still trying to make do with a system of international relations based on a much earlier order, one that could accommodate scores of "independent" self-centered nation-states. . . .

The tension between these two worlds — the vast one of petty "independent" quarreling human groups, and the small one inextricably linked for good or for ill by modern technology — is the central drama of our era; it is unimaginable that these two concepts of the world can coexist for long. One or the other — or both — must go. It is the writer's belief that the universe of seemingly sovereign political entities will gradually disappear as mankind grows to understand the basic facts of its interdependence and learns to fashion political tools more consistent with them. This interdependence is both military and nonmilitary. The first variety has been accorded greater publicity, but . . .

An End to Polarity

. . . [The] improvements being made both in the market economies and in the centrally planned economies are gradually drawing the two systems together. In essence this "depolarization" may be characterized as a

* Taken and adapted from "Interdependence on a Small Planet," *Columbia Journal of World Business,* Spring 1966, pp. 9, 12–16. The original selection appears also in *Disarmament and World Economic Interdependence,* Universitetsforlaget–Oslo and Columbia University Press–New York, London.

movement toward centralization in the west, and away from it in the east. . . .

With convergence arises a greater possibility of fruitful economic cooperation. . . .

Investment Displacing Trade

But the process of convergence will not merely enhance the possibility of routine economic cooperation; of perhaps even greater significance, it will open vast geographic areas to a relatively new type of business association — one that is proving increasingly valuable in the west. Hopes of improved economic cooperation among western nations had hitherto centered mainly on the possibility of a balanced expansion of commodity imports and exports. I would like to register my conviction, however, that trade in the conventional sense of a balanced two-way flow of goods is now being displaced in importance by a different, though little noticed, mode of economic cooperation.

Essentially, what seems to be happening is that conventional international trade, involving autonomous "untied" exchange of exports and imports, has been rapidly losing in importance to a type of international economic activity dependent on private or public investment or grants. Thus, of the $21.9 billion of U.S. nonmilitary exports in 1963, a third were either financed by government loans or grants ($2.7 billion) or involved sales to U.S. foreign affiliates (estimated at $5 billion) and were thus to a degree dependent on earlier investment. Only $14.2 billion were balanced exports of the conventional autonomous sort, not the result of prior investment or aid-giving decisions.

Moreover, even the total export figure is completely dwarfed by *production abroad by American-owned enterprises*. U.S.-owned foreign manufacturing enterprises alone showed sales of $31.3 billion for 1963. My own rough estimate (based on the ratio of foreign investment and earnings in manufacturing to total foreign investment and earnings) suggests that total 1963 sales of goods and services produced abroad by American-controlled companies were of the order of $60–$70 billion, which is about the size of the national income of France, the United Kingdom, or Germany. (Value added by these companies would, of course, be less than sales. On the other hand, a substantial additional amount of output was obtained as a result of technical and managerial assistance by U.S. companies under licensing and management contract agreements, and is not reflected in the above foreign investment and earnings estimates.) Incidentally, this foreign production of American-owned companies is not only much larger than U.S. exports, but seems to be growing twice as fast.

Why is this so? What has happened to give such growing emphasis to producing abroad in place of exporting? I suspect that this trend reflects a fundamental change now occurring in the determinants of comparative advantage and specialization. Conventional economic analysis lays great stress on differences in factor endowments as the source of international division of labor. Particularly emphasized were gross geographic differences of climate, soil and mineral or other natural resources. The tropics would, in this view, export tropical fruits, coffee and tea, petroleum, rubber, silk, tin, etc., because their climate and raw material endowments gave them a unique ability to produce such items at low cost. Similarly, it was thought that the industrial countries had the capacity to produce and export steel because of the availability, in close proximity, of high quality deposits of coal and iron ore.

Manufacturing Dominating Commerce

While this concept may have been adequate to explain trade patterns in agriculture or basic metals, it never shed much light on the pattern of trade in manufactures. It could not, for example, explain why the three leading producers and exporters of machinery, the U.S., U.K., and Germany, also bought such a large quantity of machinery *from each other*. It is becoming even less useful as manufactures grow to constitute a far larger share of world trade. This process is the inevitable result of the displacement by synthetics of tree rubber, silk, wood and other natural products, as well as continued technical improvements reducing the amount of raw materials per unit of output and permitting the use of lower-grade material. The industrialized countries have also insisted on developing their own agriculture and reserves of oil, gas and other natural resources, even when adequate imported supplies at low cost were available. Thus, the explanation of trade in terms of gross geographic advantage applies satisfactorily to an ever smaller part of the world's commerce.

Triumph of the Superior Firm

Competitive advantage in manufactures is only indirectly and partially dependent on possession of the required raw materials or other strictly geographic advantage. Rather it is now primarily an attribute of *particular firms, or even particular product lines*. It rests on the capability of a given company, establishment or production unit to produce a superior bundle of goods and services — including such services as speedy delivery, favorable terms of payment, availability of spare parts, technical advice on using the product and technical servicing to keep it operating efficiently during its normal life period. Such advantage is the fruit of superior technical knowledge, new products, and better product specification resulting from past research and development activities, and from greater efficiency in meeting the varied needs of customers. Sometimes, this is accompanied by lower prices, but often it is not, since the buyer may be more concerned with the dependability of the product, or the quality of the services provided, than with marginal savings on the original price.

To provide such services reliably, a company must command resources that will enable it to extend meaningful service guarantees far into the future and a vast organization which can offer a variety of personnel opportunities for a lifetime career. Such enormous, virtually permanent, world-wide organizations as General Motors, Jersey Standard, Unilever, Philips' Gloeilampen, etc., with assets and life expectations paralleling those of nation-states, completely transcend the competitive-market assumptions of classical economics.

As the key competitive advantages become essentially matters of skill, knowledge and organization rather than of climate or natural resource location, the economies of scale are altered. It becomes less advantageous to complete a production operation in one central place and ship bulky goods for long distances to where they will be used. Opportunities will increasingly be found to sell or rent the superior knowledge or skills and ideas that convey the crucial competitive advantages. Alternatively, efforts will be made to establish new production affiliates close to where the goods and services will eventually be utilized and where the particular needs and desires of the user can be given consideration, and the essential servicing provided in a reliable and economical manner. In effect what is now being demonstrated is that the long-run cost of transferring ideas, skills, and organizational patterns from one place to another is far lower than the cost of continuously transporting merchandise.

Cash Is Secondary

People not in international business rarely understand the extent to which international direct investment today involves such a transfer rather than the mere migration of surplus capital. Much of the capital from U.S. direct investment in recent years has come from local and other non-U.S. sources: local investors and suppliers, banks, governments, and international agencies. The American investor's most valuable contribution hasn't been cash but know-how and management skill. Moreover, as restrictions on capital exports diminish, European, Japanese and other non-U.S. investors are beginning to emulate U.S. companies, with parallel benefits to the economies in which their investments are made. The U.S. has, of course, no monopoly on advanced technology and management, and will itself benefit from direct investments made by European and other foreign companies in this country. An interesting example of such reverse flow of technology and management is offered by the acquisition, reorganization and modernization of The Underwood Typewriter Company in the U.S. by the pioneering Italian firm of Olivetti.

Abstract But Compelling

It is thus not amiss to argue that the increasingly abstract character of competitive advantage is the chief reason that international investment tends to displace exports in importance. While such investment also creates further opportunities for the export of components, raw materials, supplementary models, etc., the relative importance of overseas production steadily increases.

What benefits have foreign countries gotten out of the supplementation of management, skill and technology represented by the over $40 billion (by 1963) of U.S. investment in foreign enterprises? First, an enormous increase in production — as indicated, perhaps $60–$70 billion per year, including wages and salaries paid almost entirely to workers and employees of the host countries. Secondly, substantial interest and profit payments to local lenders and equity investors participating in the projects. Third, $1.5 billion of reinvested U.S. profits in 1963, representing new savings and investment. Fourth, a large volume of profits taxes collected, which could easily have totaled around $1.5 billion, or even more, in that year. Fifth, and crucially important, an enormous contribution to foreign exchange earnings: these came to $4.7 billion from exports of manufactures alone generated by these investments. Adding the exports generated by mining and petroleum would easily double this figure. Furthermore, that part of overseas production which was not sent out of the country may be regarded as in some sense a substitute for imports that the host country would otherwise have had to purchase. The cost to the host country for all this was $4.5 billion of U.S. profits, of which, as we have noted, only $3 billion was withdrawn. Moreover, nearly $2 billion of this $3 billion was offset by new U.S. direct investment.

Private Investment in Public Enterprise

Demonstrably, international investment is a fruitful source of cooperation for economic progress among western nations. But of what relevance is this to countries where the means of production are not privately owned? Certainly, communist society would appear to provide little place for foreign private investment. However, if we remember that the essential aspect of such investment may be viewed as a transfer of skills, ideas, and techniques — to be paid for with fees or royalties —rather than primarily as a migration of capital — to be remunerated by a dividend or an interest payment — it is possible to discern a basis for east-west collaboration. Such a basis already underlies many joint-venture situations. Here, the foreign investment process is looked upon as an export of equipment paid for in installments over an extended period, plus royalty payments for the licensing of new technology, know-how or trademarks, and management fees for the costs of advising and administering the new operation, transferring the new technology, etc. Comparable arrangements can also be made between east and west. Alternatively, one can avoid the need for an agreement in financial terms altogether by simply deciding to divide the physical output of the joint venture in agreed proportions, with the private-enterprise partner free to retain the foreign exchange proceeds from the foreign marketing of his share of the output. There are a number of other formulas that will serve equally well.

This mechanism has come to be called "co-production." Such an arrangement usually involves the use of advanced western technology, equipment and management by a productive enterprise in an East European country in a partnership arrangement with a capitalist production unit. The East European partner normally contributes the labor, the raw materials, and the plant — and often some of the components. The western partner supplies advanced equipment and know-how, product design, often at least part of the management, and — what is extremely important — international marketing channels.

This concept is certainly rather a startling one. Not only is it hard to see how a communist society could accept private foreign investment, it is equally difficult to understand how western managers could participate in running a unit of a centrally planned economy which would presumably issue directives to the enterprise inconsistent with the profit-maximization objectives of western entrepreneurs. Yet surprising or unbelievable as the idea of co-production may seem, the fact is that such ventures actually exist, that they are increasing in number, and that many more are currently being explored as possibilities, or are in the stage of active negotiation. Let me mention a few examples.

Curious Combinations

The West German firm of Rheinstahl has entered into a joint venture with the Hungarian Ministry of Machine Building for the construction in Hungary of quarrying equipment, machine tools, and other steel products, utilizing Hungarian as well as German semifinished components. The Austrian firm of Simmering-Graz-Pauker has a joint venture with the Hungarian group called Komplex to build power plants in India, financed through Hungarian-Indian bilateral clearing arrangements. IKEA, a Swedish furniture company, supplies machinery and designs for the semimanufacture of furniture in Poland under its own technical control. The semimanufactures are shipped to Sweden for finishing and marketing. The British firm of Walmsley (Bury) Group Ltd. has agreed with Poland's Metalexport to supply paper-making machinery to Poland (and thereafter to sell it to other Soviet bloc countries) which will after a time contain components made in Poland with Walmsley technical assistance. The British firm of Callaghan & Son, Ltd., and the Czech firm of Kdynske Strojirny have an agreement to manufacture jointly a line of automatic textile machinery, and to market and service the machinery throughout the world on a prearranged basis. A great many other examples could be cited.

It is important to be clear about the economic bases of such ventures. What is in it for each side? For the east the answer is obvious. The eastern partner is enabled to produce the sort of items for which there already exists a large demand in western markets, to reach and maintain the necessary quality standards, and to make and service the goods as they must be manufactured and serviced to win and hold western customers. But what offsetting special advantages can be offered by the eastern countries to the western partners? Why bother to produce in Eastern Europe items to be sold in the west?

Surprisingly, the most important advantage offered is the eastern labor force. Overfull employment in Germany, Switzerland, and other countries of Western Europe has generated severe manpower shortages, relieved only by expensive importation and on-the-job training of foreign workers, with considerable social dislocation and expensive new requirements for housing, schools, etc. The Eastern European countries, on the other hand, still have considerable labor surpluses in agriculture, or even inefficiently employed in industry, owing to the requirement that enterprise directors find employment for a given work force whether they really need them or not. (Of late, the growing freedom granted to managers to disregard such considerations has begun to create overt unemployment, especially in Poland.) . . .

6..... Business and Government: Cooperation or Conflict?*

HEINRICH KRONSTEIN

Georgetown University

In examining the relationship between political government and private power (private corporations or trade unions), it seems to be agreed that an order should be re-established which would assure the domination of political power in the field of government, while maintaining the autonomy of private organization in trade and industry. In this new order private power should be brought into line with the "public interest."

This all sounds very well, but experience has shown that without the aid of *workable standards* government cannot effectively promote an alleged public interest, nor can corporations be blamed if they should happen to violate that interest. . . .

Behind this controversy there is a basic question: Is there an existing American order into which American corporations have to be integrated? . . . The problem, of course, is a part of the fundamental issue of what the proper relationship is not only between government and corporations in foreign trade but between government and corporations in general.

. . . To this purpose I will offer some observations on the present international trade situation. I hope my examples will indicate to what extent both government and corporations today fail to serve those functions in society which have been entrusted to them and how, as a result, the balance of our social forces is fast disappearing. Perhaps these examples may show what can be done to re-establish the balance between corporations and government and to clarify the functions of each. For without some such clarification it is impossible to define the "public interest" that is to be assured by "some type of planning agency" of government.

The following three propositions, which are examples of the complete

* Excerpts reprinted from "Government and Business in International Trade," September 1961, with the permission of the Center for the Study of Democratic Institutions.

dichotomy between American private and public power in the area of international trade, will serve as materials for discussion of the question of how public and private interests can be reconciled under a common denominator. From this it will then be possible to proceed into the larger issue of the present relations between corporations and government in the United States.

Proposition One

The American private corporation, the powerhouse of American technology and economic experience, is being deterred from the mainstream of activity in new underdeveloped countries.

During recent years the United States developed, or at least accepted, a fresh approach to American activity in the new countries. The government has conducted economic relations through its different agencies, or jointly with other governments, usually through the United Nations or an institution established under the auspices of the United Nations. In turn, the recently sovereign nations have entered into economic relations through *their* governments. As a result, private enterprise has to a large extent lost its role as instigator, planner, and executor of development in these new lands. Adaptation of private policy to the needs of the countries or to American needs in foreign markets has declined. Many governments not in the Communist bloc have excluded private enterprise as a participant in important industrial fields or have created difficulties that amount to practical exclusion.

A number of more or less settled practices has developed, such as making outright gifts of military and other technical materials, offering governmental long-term loans, and guaranteeing through governmental agencies credit which is made available as corporate loans.

The combination of military and economic aid by the same organization, the United States government, is a clear example of the confusion of social functions. The Executive and the Congress, formulating one budget, make basic decisions on military, technical, and economic aid, even though these are administered by different agencies. Compare for a moment the coincidence between the development of military dictatorships in new underdeveloped countries and the concentration of aid in their centralized governmental agencies.

Corporations have more or less accepted this policy. Today they are active in the new countries only insofar as the government will assume the risk. One reason for this is undoubtedly the rule of international law that local governments may nationalize commercial enterprises and other forms of foreign investment at any time. The expropriations in Cuba are recent examples, as is the expropriation of the Belgian-owned street-car system in Cairo, which was carried out without any previous conflict or warning. Since even old underdeveloped countries may behave in this way, the governments of new countries may be expected to follow suit as soon as enough private investment has accumulated to make so-called nationalization attractive.

American corporations do not really fight this situation. They are satisfied with receiving guarantees by the government through the channel of a semi-governmental bank which amount to 90 per cent of the possible losses, provided the contemplated transaction conforms to the rules and limitations established by the American government. This means that the transaction must be acceptable to and supported by the friendly sovereign government of the other country. Therefore, there is no room for any careful autonomous planning by American experts with a view toward a long-term program. As a result, the initiative is left in the hands of the new nations and their governments. . . .

Perhaps a nineteenth-century company would have concentrated on only one particular country or one particular line of business, but it would have involved itself in some way in this potential development in spite of risks. For the contemporary American corporation, however, the philosophy of safety has taken over and deprived management of business initiative. . . .

Proposition Two

The American corporation, which has invested substantial funds, especially in the old underdeveloped countries, is not treated as a part of the economy when American trade policy is being formulated.

Among the American enterprises most active in foreign countries, irrespective of government guarantees, are the omnipresent oil companies. Like other corporations, they have not always put the interests of their own country first, but recently their actions have begun to show an intention to help the United States and the local countries.

Our special problem can be best illustrated in the transformation of Venezuela by the American oil companies from a poor agricultural economy into a country with a mixed economy, to a certain extent modern and effective, in other respects still at the economic level of the fourteenth century. Then, a few years ago, the American steel industry, having acquired highly valuable iron ore deposits in Venezuela, became the second great United States investor there. This further revolutionized life in Venezuela. Only the lethargic remained unmoved, and no one's aspirations stayed the same. A modern industrial life, a modern capitalistic spirit, was forced on the nation.

No one can be surprised that investments of this scope should lead to social upheaval. The farming population, living at the lowest possible level, met American luxury and a standard of living they had never even imagined. Many people left their farms and tried to get jobs in the oil and steel industries. Some of them succeeded. Those who did not, and who are now living in the cities under conditions worse than those they had left, threaten the public order in Venezuela.

Now if relatively open market conditions had been maintained within the United States, the ups and downs of business cycles would not have brought about the dangers of a revolt in Venezuela. Iron ore deposits developed by American enterprise would have led the country further away from its undesirable monolithic economy. But at a time when Venezuela had a weekly income of about $25 million from oil, and could expect and hope for development of its large resources of minerals and cheap power, the United States government, led by the Congress, accepted a new type of isolationist policy. The American oil industry had gone to Venezuela in the light of forecasts that the end of our own oil supply was imminent. But our statisticians and planners proved to be wrong. The United States did not enter a period of shortage of energy. Local coal interests and independent oil producers persuaded Congress and the Executive to act in their sole interest. The Johnson Oil Import Bill authorized the President to establish quotas on oil imports into the United States.

American politicians did not consider what would happen to Venezuela and to the American investor there. Not only did Venezuela suffer from the new legislation; the American consumer, especially in New England, was forced to pay higher gasoline prices. Venezuelan oil was forced to look for substitute markets, and turned to Western Europe. Near-East oil, which to a large extent is under the control of American firms, had its principal markets there. United States coal also had an important market in Europe, at least for a time. Now we find the American coal corporations attempting to persuade Europe to keep out Venezuelan oil by fixing import quotas. Such attempts show our lack of a clear trade policy. We deal with expediencies, ignoring the interdependencies of corporate and public interests.

Other cases point up the degree of confusion existing in our international economic relations. For example, in the same week the American government was making a drastic demand in Bonn for foreign aid not tied in any way to the buying of German goods, the president of the United Mine Workers submitted a paper to a committee of the House of Representatives strongly recommending that foreign aid be given only to those nations purchasing their coal supply in the United States. This proposal was supposed to be a remedy for unemployment in the American coal industry. We may well ask whether it would not be cheaper to grant temporary unemployment benefits in the coal industry than to enact an import quota of this kind.

Proposition Three

The United States government has no influence on investments made by American private corporations in other industrial countries, such as England, Australia, Western Europe, or Japan.

The American public has suddenly found itself confronted with a crisis in the balance of payments. For years it was common to speak of the dollar gap of the industrial European nations. Recently, however, the newspapers reported on the same day a request for German aid to the United States, and a new dollar investment by Ford in shares of its English subsidiary. The American government appeared to be without any controlling influence over investment in Western Europe. Besides the undesirable results that this could have for the United States, the European governments themselves are unhappy with the extent of present investment in Europe by American firms and private individuals. These investments have an inflationary effect and constitute an element of insecurity, especially in dangerous political and social situations. . . .

American industry, whether admitting it or not, is vitally interested in collecting and using all modern technology. Obviously, one of the most effective ways to maintain a continuous access to new technology is to keep a strong financial interest in European corporations that are themselves doing research.

Up to now European trade with new or old underdeveloped territories has been easier and more profitable than American trade, partly because of the different price levels, partly because there are fewer bureaucratic entanglements. How do we define the governmental or public interest with respect to this fact? Has the public enough material to reach a considered judgment? The fact is that misinformation is especially rampant about American interests in foreign technology. Just as he did in the Twenties, the man in the street believes that the United States is technologically self-sufficient and that a corporation making investments in other industrial countries is a kind of traitor to America.

I hope that these brief references show the lack of any fixed policy into which the acts of our government and our corporations may be integrated. How can we find a clear line of policy?

. . .

It is understandable that some people want to overcome these difficulties by setting up a public planning group of one or another kind. Indeed, something like this is necessary. But how would such an agency determine what is actually in the public interest? And could such an agency operate in a democratic society?

The economic order functions only as long as all participants, public and private, preserve an order within the social order. This is equally true for the special order of international trade. Under the nineteenth century European idea of social order, the state, whether organized on a democratic or an autocratic order, had the exclusive legal and sociological role in setting up the principles of the social order. Today in Europe, whatever pluralistic tendencies may exist, the concept of the state as standing over society in each of its elements remains the prevailing idea. This distinction is felt especially in the relations between government and corporations. But whatever the present character of society in the United States may be in practice, the original concept of a pluralistic society remains the controlling force in America. The social groups composing American society are not coordinated, but each of them — labor, farmers, industrialists — must be directed to a set of unified goals. It should be the special function of the President of the United States by his moral force to set the pattern of American society.

. . .

By now it should be clear that the needs of American trade in the international field are sufficient to form the basis for national policy. Such a policy would assure the use of our advanced technology in building up that of our neighbors and a movement toward a balanced market which would insure an open exchange of opportunities for individual industries to exploit their talents. Under the conditions of the American system, standards cannot be established by mere legislation but must be the natural product of cooperation among the various social forces, especially those of government and corporations. . . .

Corporations engaged in the foreign trade of the United States can only be coordinated with the public interest after some basic decisions have been made. We have to resolve whether we want to see a new mercantilistic trade policy in which the test of any decision is its effect on the public and private treasury of the United States, or an open market within the family of industrial nations. Once this determination is made, it will be possible for a public agency to decide whether or not specified acts of corporations in foreign trade are in the public interest. And it will be possible for our corporations to determine what is in the public interest.

We must also decide whether we would like to retain, or, better yet, to rebuild a free enterprise economy in which corporations and other private business organizations have control of technology and of commercial and economic machinery. There are not enough people to do both — to develop and administer this technology in all fields on both a governmental and a private basis. Nor do we have enough capital for such duplication of work. Furthermore, experience shows that this type of mixed economy will not work in our system. We must give corporations both the power and the responsibility to make a large part of the American contribution to the development of new countries. Governmental coordination should consist of devices for public support such as tax exemptions, tax credits, and investment insurance.

I realize that this calls for something foreign to the American scene — a decision to establish a long-term political international trade program. . . .

D..... Some Basic Trends

The present section, intended to round out the introductory materials of Part One, is devoted to the pattern of world trade and development. (Since our primary concern relates to the integration of international economics and international business, we focus on observable trends in trade and development, accepting as a "given" the postulates and analyses of the pure theory of international trade. The latter, of course, comprises an extensive, though specialized, literature in its own right.)

Professor Ingram, in our first selection, refers to a dual long-range trend: (a) growing world trade (with some of this trade rooted in forces aimed at international development), and (b) a lagging share of the total for poorer (underdeveloped) countries. While the world may be getting better off in general (at least in terms of one test), all portions of it are not moving ahead evenly.

In a follow-up selection, the Council of Economic Advisers assesses what has been occurring recently — during the 1960's. We see that the current era essentially carries forward the basic long-range trend: production and global trade are growing, but, since the poorer countries lag behind, growing at an uneven pace.

To state that the foregoing situation poses a problem seems, if anything, an understatement. And it is a problem to which we shall return, time and again, in succeeding sections.

7..... Patterns of Trade and Development*

JAMES C. INGRAM

University of North Carolina

Ever since the Age of Exploration, the underdeveloped world has been engaged in trade with the more advanced industrial nations of the West. Indeed, the desire for trade was an important aspect of the outward thrust of European civilization from the 16th to the 19th centuries. Trade was a vehicle through which scientific advances, social change, and economic progress could be transmitted from leading to lagging regions and thereby disseminated throughout the world. In D. H. Robertson's phrase, trade was a marvelous "engine of growth."

In addition to its role as an agent of change, trade also increased income directly through the gains from specialization based on comparative advantage. . . . The clear conclusion, according to this traditional view, is that international trade stimulates and fosters economic development; hence, underdeveloped countries should adopt a policy of free trade and specialize in those lines of production in which they have a comparative advantage.

Although trade was never fully free of tariffs and other restrictions, most of the underdeveloped world did engage in active trade with industrial countries, and they still do. They specialized in primary products (food and raw materials), exporting these in exchange for a wide variety of manufactured goods. Thus, a pattern of trade developed between the two broad groups of countries. Despite this active trade and the close economic intercourse between advanced and underdeveloped countries, the income gap between the two groups steadily widened. The actual level of economic well-being in 1750 was probably not much, if any, higher in Europe than in China or India. Indeed, the early travelers from the West were dazzled by the wealth of the Orient! During the 19th and 20th centuries the income gap steadily widened, and underdeveloped

* Taken and adapted from *International Economic Problems,* New York: John Wiley & Sons, Inc., 1966, pp. 78–87.

countries began to suspect that the benefits of trade were unequally divided, and that "free trade" was a clever Western ruse to keep them in a subordinate position. This suspicion and hostility toward trade became intermingled with attitudes toward colonialism and economic exploitation. One of the legacies of the fight against colonialism is a continuing suspicion that trade and other forms of economic intercourse may operate to the disadvantage of underdeveloped countries.

The Network of Trade

Dividing the world between advanced countries (A) and underdeveloped countries (U), we find that the major flow of trade is among the A countries themselves. A smaller but still very large amount of trade flows between A and U, but only a small amount of trade takes place among the U countries themselves. Table 1 contains actual figures for 1963. We see that trade among U countries amounted to only $6.6 billion, or 5.2% of total trade, while trade among A countries amounted to $74.6 billion (60%), and trade *between* A and U countries amounted to $45.2 billion (34.8%). It is clear that U countries do not trade very much among themselves. Their exports go largely to A countries, and their imports come from A countries.[1]

The Composition of Trade

When merchandise trade is divided into primary products and manufactures, we find that U-country exports consist largely of primary products and U-country imports consist largely of manufactures. Table 1 also shows this division. U countries exported $22.9 billion to A countries, of which $19.6 billion was made up of primary products and only $3.3 billion of manufactures. (One half of these "manufactures" consisted of semiprocessed base metals.) On the other hand, U-country imports from A countries included $17.7 billion of manufactures and only $4.6 billion of primary products. (Of these primary product imports, $3.0 billion consisted of food.)

Primary products are also dominant in trade among U countries. Three quarters of such trade in 1963 consisted of primary products.

These trade patterns have existed for a long time. Similar estimates have been made for 1913, 1928, 1938, and for many recent years. The general pattern is the same. If anything, the contrasts are sharpening; trade among A countries is rising faster than the other categories. From 1953 to 1963, for example, trade among A countries more than doubled, while trade between A and U countries rose only 50%, and trade among

[1] Remember that we are omitting trade with the Soviet bloc. Such trade is quite small, however. In 1963, U countries exported $1.9 billion to the Soviet bloc and imported $2.3 billion — only 8% of their trade with A countries.

TABLE 1

Trade Within and Between Advanced
and Underdeveloped Countries, 1963 (Billions of Dollars)

Exports[a] from: ＼ Imports of:	A Countries[b]	U Countries[b]	Total
Advanced Countries			
Primary products[c]	24.9	4.6	29.5
Manufactures	49.7	17.7	67.4
Total	74.6	22.3	96.9
Underdeveloped Countries			
Primary products	19.6	5.1	24.7
Manufactures	3.3	1.5	4.8
Total	22.9	6.6	29.5
Total			
Primary Products	44.5	9.7	54.2
Manufactures	53.0	19.2	72.2
	97.5	28.9	126.4

Source: United Nations, *Monthly Bulletin of Statistics*, March 1965.
a Exports are valued F.O.B.
b A countries include Western Europe, North America, Japan, Australia and New Zealand.
U countries include the rest of the world outside the Soviet bloc.
c Primary products are categories 0, 1, 2, 3, and 4 in the Standard International Trade
Classification.

U countries rose only 30%. It is a striking fact that the greatest expansion
of trade has occurred among the industrial nations whose economies have
been growing more similar.

It is also significant that the degree of U-country specialization in primary products has not lessened. Despite their efforts to diversify and
develop manufacturing industries, U-country exports remain almost
wholly concentrated in primary products. These countries are increasingly dissatisfied with the role assigned to them by the world trading
system.

Concentration of Export Trade

Exports of U countries are highly concentrated. In 40 countries, a single
product accounts for over one half of the total exports. In 70 countries,
three principal products account for 60%, or more, of the total exports.
See Table 2 for a tabulation indicating the dependence of countries on
certain exports. Of the 70 countries depending on 3 principal exports
for over 60% of their export proceeds, only *1* is an A country — New
Zealand.

Instability of Export Proceeds

Such a high degree of export concentration in U countries makes these countries vulnerable to fluctuations in market prices and in supply. A fall in demand — or a poor crop — can cause a large drop in export proceeds. Since exports generate a large part of national income in many U countries, big changes in export proceeds are a major disruptive influence in their domestic economies.

From 1900 to 1950, the export proceeds of underdeveloped countries were highly unstable. For 18 major commodities, the *average* fluctuation from one year to another was 22%, up or down.[2] For rubber alone, it was 36%. In the same period, the average change in price from one year to another was 14.5% for 22 major commodities. Instability of prices and export proceeds has lessened in recent years, but it is still great for individual commodities and for the countries dependent upon them. Figure 1 shows the behavior of coffee and rubber prices (monthly averages) from 1947 to 1965. Since coffee is the major export of several Latin American countries, these big changes in price have powerful political effects.

Export prices and proceeds of advanced countries have been much stabler than those of underdeveloped countries, which is another reason why U countries believe that the cards are stacked against them in international trade.

The Terms of Trade

The final characteristic of trade between A and U countries is much more difficult to establish than the previous four. It is often argued that the terms of trade have turned against underdeveloped countries during the last 100 years — that the prices of their exports relative to the prices of their imports have declined.[3] Such a long-run decline in their terms of trade would mean that U countries were receiving a smaller and smaller amount of imported goods for a given volume of exports.

Hundreds of economists and statisticians have made millions of calculations, but they are still unable to settle this matter conclusively. The difficulties are conceptual, not just computational, so bigger and faster computers will not necessarily permit a definite answer. One major problem is that proper allowance cannot be made in the price indexes for new products and for changes in quality. Since these changes affect the imports of U countries more than their exports, to omit them is to exaggerate the rise in import prices and thus make the index of terms of trade

[2] *Instability in Export Markets of Underdeveloped Countries* (New York: United Nations, 1952), pp. 39–40.

[3] We refer to the commodity terms of trade, defined as index of export prices ÷ index of import prices. For example, from 1958 to 1963, Brazil's export price index fell from 100 to 83, her import price index rose from 100 to 104; the Brazilian terms of trade therefore declined from 100 to 80 (= 83/104).

TABLE 2

Concentration of Exports of Underdeveloped Countries: Percentage of Total Exports Accounted for by three Principal Products, 1962

COUNTRY	PERCENTAGE 0 25 50 75 100	PRINCIPAL EXPORT COMMODITIES
Somalia	99.0	Cattle, skins
Venezuela	98.1	Petroleum, iron ore, coffee
Gambia	98.0	Peanuts, palm kernel
Libya	97.9	Petroleum, peanuts, olive oil
Neth. Antilles	97.7	Petroleum and products
Mauritius	97.6	Sugar
Réunion	97.4	Sugar, essential oil, rum
Iraq	97.4	Petroleum, dates, barley
Brunei	97.0	Petroleum, natural rubber
Guadeloupe	97.0	Sugar and honey, banana, rum
New Hebrides	94.9	Copra, fish, magnesium ore
Papua	94.6	Rubber, copra, crocodile skin
Panama	92.1	Banana, petroleum, fish
Trinidad and Tobago	91.6	Petroleum, sugar
Fiji	91.1	Sugar, coconut oil, copra
Liberia	90.5	Iron ore, rubber, palm kernel
Colombia	89.6	Coffee, petroleum, cotton
Iran	89.6	Petroleum and products, cotton
Surinam	89.5	Bauxite, rice, plywood
Sudan	88.7	Cotton, oil seeds, gum
Sierra Leone	88.6	Diamond, iron ore, palm kernel
Costa Rica	87.5	Coffee, banana, cocoa
Ecuador	87.5	Banana, coffee, cocoa
Ceylon	87.2	Tea, rubber, coconut oil
El Salvador	86.5	Coffee, cotton, shellfish
Uganda	85.4	Coffee, cotton, copper
Ivory Coast	84.4	Coffee, wood
Zanzibar	84.3	Clove, copra, coconut oil
Viet Nam	83.8	Rubber, rice, tea
Ghana	83.5	Cocoa, wood, diamond
Chile	82.4	Copper, iron ore, saltpeter
Chad	82.0	Cotton, cattle, petroleum
Central Afr. Rep.	82.0	Cotton, coffee, diamond
Guatemala	81.7	Coffee, cotton, banana

COUNTRY	PERCENTAGE 0 25 50 75 100	PRINCIPAL EXPORT COMMODITIES
Burma	81.6	Rice, wood, oil-seed cake
Barbados	81.5	Sugar, molasses, rum
Indonesia	81.0	Rubber, petroleum, tin
Malaya	81.0	Rubber, tin, iron ore
Rhodesia	79.1	Copper, tobacco, asbestos
Cambodia	79.1	Rubber, rice, corn
Iceland	79.0	Fish, animal oil, hides
Senegal	77.9	Peanuts, peanut oil, oil-seed cake
Gabon	77.7	Wood, petroleum, uranium ore
Tunisia	77.2	Olive oil, alcoholic beverage, fertilizer
Ethiopia-Erit.	77.2	Coffee, hides, oil seeds
Niger	75.9	Peanut, cattle, vegetable
New Zealand	75.4	Wool, meat, butter
Bolivia	74.9	Tin, silver, lead
Mali	72.9	Peanuts, fish, cattle
Togo	72.9	Coffee, cocoa, oil seed
Jamaica	72.2	Bauxite, sugar, aluminum
Dominican Rep.	70.0	Sugar, coffee, banana
Honduras	69.9	Bananas, coffee, wood
Egypt	69.6	Cotton, petroleum, cotton yarn
New Guinea	68.8	Copra, copra oil, cocoa
Brazil	68.1	Coffee, cotton, iron ore
Uruguay	66.9	Wool, beef, hides
Syria	66.5	Cotton, barley, wheat
Angola	66.4	Coffee, diamond, sisal
Cameroon	66.3	Cocoa, aluminum, coffee
Nicaragua	65.6	Cotton, coffee, meat
Thailand	65.2	Rice, rubber, tin
Algeria	65.0	Wine, citrus fruits, iron ore
Philippines	63.3	Sugar, copra, wood
Haiti	62.6	Coffee, sisal, sugar
Aden	61.8	Gas, diesel, and other fuel oil, lamp oil, etc.
Afghanistan	61.0	Caracul, dried fruits, carpets
Mauritania	60.4	Fish, aircraft, road motor vehicle
Cyprus	60.0	Copper ore, potatoes, fruits

Source: United Nations, *Yearbook of International Trade Statistics.*

FIGURE 1

Monthly Averages of Coffee and Rubber Prices from 1949 to 1965 (The range of fluctuation in daily prices is much greater than in these monthly averages.)

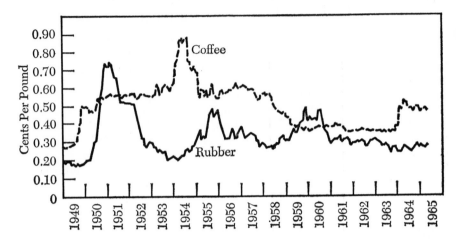

(Source: *International Financial Statistics*, International Monetary Fund.)

appear less favorable than it should be. For example, a country exporting coffee and importing adding machines may find that each adding machine in 1965 can do 10 times as much work as a 1920 model. Therefore, if the price of adding machines has risen twice as much as the price of coffee, the terms of trade are highly favorable to the coffee exporter even though the statistical computation would show the opposite.

Another major problem is that changes in the commodity terms of trade do not necessarily indicate whether a country's *welfare* has improved. To determine the effect on welfare, a much more complicated calculation is required: one that can take account of changes in productivity of labor and other factors. This point can best be illustrated by reference to the problem of "fair prices" for the farmer, or what we call "parity prices." The parity-price ratio compares the prices that farmers receive with the prices that they pay, and is therefore the same thing as the commodity terms of trade. However, we recognize that improvements in machinery, seeds, fertilizers, and insecticides make it possible for a farmer to produce several times as much output (for instance, wheat) as he could produce with the same land and labor in the years 1910 to 1914. Therefore, even if the parity ratio is well below 100 (the terms of trade have turned against agriculture), the farmer is far better off than he was in the years 1910 to 1914. Exactly the same problem exists when we calculate the terms of trade of primary-producing countries and try to use the trend in the terms of trade as an indicator of the benefits derived from trade.

Other difficulties concern the methods to be used in weighting the commodities included in the index, methods of valuing imports and exports,[4] and choice of the base year.

Despite all of these statistical and conceptual problems, spokesmen for underdeveloped countries are firmly convinced that there is a chronic tendency for their terms of trade to worsen. They also believe that the adverse terms of trade are harmful to their economies, and that most or all of the "gains from trade" have accrued to advanced countries.

In recent years, especially since the underdeveloped countries have won their independence, they have challenged with increasing vehemence the traditional view of the beneficence of trade. They are profoundly skeptical and suspicious of trade and of the working of the world market system. They no longer accept the pattern of specialization and trade that seems indicated by the market, and their search for a "new trade policy" has become a crucially important issue in world affairs.

---

[4] Treatment of shipping charges makes a substantial difference. Much of the long-term deterioration in U-country terms of trade disappears when allowance is made for the great reduction in ocean transport rates from 1870 to 1900. See P. T. Ellsworth, "The Terms of Trade between Primary Producing and Industrial Countries," *Inter-American Economic Affairs*, Summer 1956.

8..... Trade and Development in the Sixties*

COUNCIL OF ECONOMIC ADVISERS

World economic expansion in the first half of the 1960's has been sustained and rapid. The pace has probably been surpassed only during the period of recovery from World War II. Moreover, since the end of the war, the extreme fluctuations of earlier years have not been repeated.

But continued economic progress is not assured. Many problems remain. The most difficult and important is that of overcoming poverty in many of the less developed countries of Africa, Asia, and Latin America. A major problem for the developed countries is to cope with international financial imbalances in ways which do not inhibit sound economic growth. . . .

Two quantitative goals for economic growth in the 1960's have been fixed by international organizations:

> The United Nations has set 5 per cent a year as the minimum growth rate for the less developed countries over the 1960's, calling this the "Development Decade."
>
> The Organization for Economic Cooperation and Development (OECD), which includes the countries of Western Europe, the United States, Canada, and Japan, has called for an increase in aggregate output of all member countries combined, amounting to 50 per cent over the decade or an average annual growth rate of 4.1 per cent.

As can be seen from Table 1, the expansion of real output in the less developed countries, estimated at 4½ per cent a year, so far has fallen somewhat short of the UN target on average, and far below it in several of the largest of these countries. However, the table also shows that output in the OECD countries has been exceeding the growth rate of the OECD target.

* Taken and adapted from *Economic Report of the President,* January 1967, pp. 170–175.

TABLE 1

Changes in Total and Per Capita Real GNP in OECD
and Less Developed Countries Since 1955

	Share of total output (per cent)[1]	Percentage increase per year			
		Total real GNP		Per capita real GNP	
		1955 to 1960	1960 to 1965	1955 to 1960	1960 to 1965
OECD countries: Total	100.0	3.2	5.0	2.0	3.7
United States	53.3	2.2	4.7	.4	3.2
Total excluding United States	46.7	5.0	5.3	3.7	4.2
Germany	8.6	[2]6.3	[3]4.8	[2]5.1	[3]3.5
United Kingdom	7.7	2.8	3.3	2.2	2.6
France	7.3	4.6	5.1	3.7	3.7
Japan	5.4	9.7	9.7	8.8	8.5
Italy	4.1	5.5	5.1	4.9	4.3
Spain	1.4	4.3	9.2	3.4	8.3
Greece	.4	5.4	8.7	4.3	8.1
Less developed countries: Total	100.0	[4]4.5	4.6	[4]2.2	2.2
Africa	12.5	[5]	3.3	[5]	1.1
Nigeria	1.3	[5]	5.0	[5]	3.0
Ghana	.7	6.1	4.0	3.5	1.3
Latin America	50.1	4.8	4.4	2.0	1.5
Brazil	11.6	5.8	3.3	2.7	.2
Argentina	10.7	2.6	3.0	.9	1.3
Mexico	10.7	6.1	5.9	3.0	2.8
Asia	37.4	4.5	3.9	2.4	1.5
Middle East	6.4	6.1	6.1	3.7	3.7
Other Asia	31.0	4.2	3.4	2.1	1.0
India	16.3	4.4	2.9	2.3	.4
Pakistan	3.7	3.5	5.4	1.2	2.8

Sources: Organization for Economic Cooperation and Development (OECD), Agency for International Development (AID), and Council of Economic Advisers.
1 Share in 1963 for OECD countries and in 1960 for less developed countries.
2 Excludes Saar and West Berlin.
3 Includes Saar and West Berlin.
4 Estimates.
5 Not available.
Note. — Totals include countries not shown separately. Detail will not necessarily add to totals because of rounding.

Developed Countries

In the first half of the 1960's, real output in Western Europe and Japan increased by more than 5 per cent a year. Contributing to the rapid expansion were government policies directed toward achieving and maintaining high levels of employment with reasonable price stability, stimulating the movement of labor from low to high productivity employment, reducing barriers to foreign trade, and encouraging the more efficient utilization of resources in other ways.

A high rate of capital formation helped to achieve this rapid growth. Investment averaged 18 per cent of gross national product (GNP) in the OECD countries other than the United States; it ranged from almost 30 per cent in Japan to less than 14 per cent in the United Kingdom. While much of the increase in output comes from investment in physical capital and from the incorporation of technological advances, a good deal also comes from investment in human capital — in raising the education, skills, and health of the population.

The growth of output is also benefiting from the movement of labor out of activities of low productivity to those of higher productivity. There has been a large-scale movement of labor from Southern Europe to Northwestern Europe — from areas of low productivity, low incomes, and high unemployment to areas where productivity and incomes are high and unemployment low. Within countries, the major shift has been out of employment in agriculture. The OECD estimates that this latter shift alone accounted for between 10 and 15 per cent of the increase in productivity during the first half of the 1960's in France, Germany, Italy, and Japan. The United Kingdom, which by 1960 already had only a small agricultural sector, did not have this source of expanding productivity.

Internal shifts of labor have been stimulated and facilitated by the expansion of foreign trade, which has far exceeded the growth of output. The rapid growth of trade has resulted, in part, from the reduction of trade barriers, especially within the two regional groupings — the European Economic Community (EEC) and the European Free Trade Association (EFTA).

For a number of European countries and Japan, a rapid rise in exports has also directly stimulated the growth of GNP. In addition, when domestic expansion is led by export growth, the resulting rise in imports can be readily financed; there is less chance that the government will need to apply the brakes to reverse a developing balance of payments deficit.

Less Developed Countries

The achievement of an adequate rate of self-sustaining growth in the less developed countries remains an urgent world economic problem. Over half of the 4½ per cent annual growth of total output for the less developed areas has been needed just to maintain their low level of living, since their populations have been rising by 2½ per cent annually. The yearly increase in per capita output has been only 2 per cent, or barely $3 a person.

Achieving rapid and sustainable growth in these countries is by no means a hopeless task, however. Self-sustaining growth has been attained in certain less developed countries — including Israel, Malaysia, Mexico, Taiwan, Venezuela, and some Central American countries. Others — such as Pakistan, South Korea, Thailand, and Turkey — are approaching that objective.

But the problems are formidable. Further efforts by both the developed and the less developed countries are required. The rapid growth of population in many less developed countries, already over-populated in relation to their economic resources, must be slowed. A number of these nations have adopted measures to induce their citizens to limit the size of their families. Some of these programs — in Hong Kong, Singapore, and Taiwan — have already shown signs of success. Nevertheless, the growth rate of population in the less developed countries as a group is still rising.

Another major problem area is agriculture. Agricultural output has grown so slowly that food output per person in many countries is below pre-World War II levels. Unless a vigorous effort is made to redress the situation, it is likely to deteriorate further as population and need for food continue to grow rapidly. . . .

The developed countries can do much to help by providing technical assistance, food, fertilizers, agricultural equipment, and financing. But the basic responsibility rests on the less developed countries themselves. They must, among other things, improve the incentives for farmers to increase output.

Education also is a major field in which improvement is essential. Economic progress requires literacy. A modern and expanding economy needs much more — people trained to operate farm machinery, run a lathe, operate a retail store, and keep accounts. In recognition of the importance of education, the less developed countries have in recent years increased their education budgets by 15 per cent annually. This effort has long been supported by the United States. . . .

The Need for Capital

The developing countries also need capital. About one-fourth of their domestic investment is financed by capital imports. From 1961 to 1965, the net amount of this capital inflow rose by only 5 per cent a year in money terms and less in real terms. Some increase continued into 1966. Since 1963, the entire increase from abroad has been in private capital flows.

This investment, to be sure, benefits the recipient countries, and the

United States has taken steps to encourage it. But it has gone mainly to the extractive industries, particularly oil. Thus, it is unevenly distributed among countries. Further, investment in technologically advanced, sometimes highly automated, extractive processes does not have the same stimulating effects on general economic activity as does investment in local manufacturing. It does, however, provide much needed foreign exchange and technological know-how for those countries fortunate enough to be well-endowed with minerals.

For many developing nations, a growing burden of interest and amortization payments on external debt absorbs a large and rising proportion of gross aid receipts. In 1960, debt service charges amounted to 13 per cent of the official bilateral aid receipts of less developed countries; today the figure is 19 per cent. India's debt service charges on government assistance for the period of its Third Plan amounted to 26 per cent of its foreign aid. In Turkey, debt service during 1963–66 was more than half as large as gross foreign aid.

For the net inflow of aid merely to remain constant, the gross inflow must rise to cover growing debt service. In fact, the gross flow of government aid from the developed countries has been rising just enough to keep net aid inflow on a plateau since 1963. Future prospects are even less encouraging. Bilateral aid commitments — pledges of actual aid disbursements to be made in the future — declined in 1965. This could foreshadow a decline in net and even in gross official aid disbursements in the years to come.

The stagnation in the net flow of official capital to the less developed countries has come at the very time that the industrial countries have reached new heights of prosperity. And it comes at a time when the pace of economic expansion achieved by the less developed countries as a group is encouraging. They are developing the skills required for a modern economy. They are capable of using more capital than they can raise domestically or borrow abroad on commercial terms. For this and other reasons, foreign aid, both bilateral and multilateral, should have a high priority claim on the resources of high-income countries. . . .

Foreign aid and private foreign investment finance only one-fifth of the foreign exchange expenditures of the developing countries. The remaining four-fifths is financed by their own export earnings. After near stagnation in the late 1950's, these earnings rose by about 6 per cent a year during the first half of the 1960's. The increase was produced by many factors, including strengthened prices for many primary commodities, the growing ability of the less developed countries to supply these commodities, and the rapidly expanding markets in the United States, Western Europe, and Japan. Only with continued vigorous growth in the developed world and improved access to its markets can the less developed countries earn the foreign exchange needed to support their own continuing growth.

Trade Policies

The less developed countries obviously have much to gain from reductions in tariffs, quotas, and other barriers to trade in primary products, since such products constitute 85 per cent of their exports. Over the longer run, satisfactory growth in the export earnings of the less developed countries will require relatively less reliance on sales of primary products and continuation of the sharp expansion in exports of manufactured goods. Such diversification will also be important for their internal growth. Reductions in tariffs and other trade barriers in developed countries can contribute much to the needed growth of manufactured exports from developing countries.

In most of the less developed countries, internal markets are too small to support efficient modern industrial plants. It is not geographic size or population but effective purchasing power that determines the size of a market. Regional cooperation can create larger markets so that the enterprises of the developing countries can benefit from the economies of scale and of specialization on which growth and efficiency depend.

Encouraging progress toward regional integration is being made in a number of areas. The Latin American Free Trade Association, despite handicaps, can form the basis for a true Latin American common market. Particular progress has been made in the Central American Common Market. The United States supports outward-looking regional integration.

The importance of trade expansion as a factor in economic growth in all countries argues strongly for more rapid trade liberalization. This proposition is effectively demonstrated by the recent experience in the new free-trade areas of Europe, just as it was earlier demonstrated in the great common market of the United States. Thus, it is essential that success be achieved in the current multilateral trade negotiations, by far the most comprehensive in history. . . .

PART TWO ....

THE UNITED STATES

IN THE INTERNATIONAL ECONOMY

As noted in Part One, the international economy is growing: trade and investment reach new levels; acceptance of an "internationalist" attitude widens. But what of the United States? How, precisely, does it fit into the international economy?

Great Britain, not so long ago, was the "number one" country in the international economy; this rank now belongs to the United States. Essentially, the transition can be explained as the product of two diverse, though interacting, sets of circumstances: (a) an era of enormous wealth-creation in the young, vibrant, richly-endowed American economy and (b) the adverse impact of two world wars upon the older, less-favorably-situated British economy.

The United States today is, by far, the world's richest country, generating regularly about one-third of global GNP. It stands first on other scores, too. It is the world's foremost trader (measured in aggregate dollar volume, though not in terms of trade as a proportion of GNP). And it is the world's foremost lender, as well as foremost provider of foreign aid. To be sure, all these "firsts" — trade, investment, aid — derive, in part, from the country's sheer size and wealth. To a considerable extent, though, more is involved. Economic power readily finds a counterpart in economic (and political) influence; and the United States is a source of potent influence on the world scene. The country holds, for itself, a national interpretation of the posture appropriate for the "international leader" — an interpretation currently reflected, at least in some degree, in the investment and aid components.

Because the United States clearly is *the* "economic giant" on the world scene (and, coincidentally, occupies a leadership position assigned it by the events of history), the rest of the world has reason to watch what goes on here. For foreign producers, the American economy represents a market outlet, or a source of competition. For capital-short areas abroad, the American economy represents a source of funds. For foreign consumers, the American economy represents a big supermarket. For friendly governments, stability in the American economy adds hope for like circumstances at home. For governments of antagonistic ideology, prosperity in the American economy looms as bad news. For the international financial community, a viable balance of payments for this country underscores confidence. And so it goes. Without question, the American presence is far-reaching in its implications.

Just as the rest of the world is much affected by what occurs in the United States, the United States is much affected by international factors. Quite apart from the impact on the domestic economy of, say, heavy defense outlays, the course of international trade has an impact, too — on income and employment. Though United States exports typically total only 5% of GNP, and imports only 4%, these are not the relevant percentages for *particular* products, industries, or locales. A far higher percentage of the output of some products enters export channels — roughly one-third of all wheat and cotton, and roughly that proportion of some categories of machinery output. In such instances, the economic well-being of the regions or industries of product origin is intimately dependent upon export health. Conversely, large and favored as the United States is, the country cannot practice self-sufficiency without a considerable sacrifice in income and comfort. Plainly, both the smooth-functioning of the industrial process and the caliber of daily life depend upon access to external supplies not otherwise available.

In its position as a giant economy and major power, affecting other countries, and, in turn, affected by them, the United States looks out upon a world characterized, as we discussed in Part One, as "disunited." Essentially, this country finds itself dealing with three widely diverse regions: Western Europe, the underdeveloped countries, and the Communist Bloc(s).

The first, Western Europe, has a long history in world economic affairs — having served as the initial base of the Industrial Revolution and as the undisputed "core" of the global economy. Subsequently, the area suffered relative economic retrogression as younger regions advanced and as involvement in destructive wars took its toll, but, post-World War II, it recovered and moved on to achieve new levels of production and world trade. Spearheading the area's remarkable recovery has been a "common market" organization under which six continental countries pool resources and markets. As Western Europe strengthened its economic position internationally, the United States began, virtually concurrently, to experience troublesome balance-of-payments deficits — a fact frequently cited as firm evidence of Europe's success.

The second major external region, that comprised of underdeveloped countries, has moved increasingly into the limelight during recent years. Remaining poor while some other countries have progressed, the underdeveloped countries recently "awakened" in the sense of suddenly wanting development. Implications for the United States of the new development-urge have included (a) the "awakened" countries' expectation of economic assistance to help spur rapid progress and/or, (b) in the face of inconclusive gains, their frustration — which makes them into ready pawns in the world-wide struggle of ideology.

The countries of the Communist Bloc(s), the third major external region, consist in the main of the U.S.S.R. and its Eastern European satellites, plus Communist China and its satellites. These countries are distinguished by adherence to a political (and economic) ideology that casts them in fundamental disharmony with the United States. Partly developed and partly underdeveloped, they desire more development for themselves, even while they support the development aspirations of other, non-aligned underdeveloped countries. Thus, aid is added to trade to form the battleground in a basic East-West economic conflict.

Viewed from the standpoint of the American economy, then, the external world is divided; each of the three major areas that we have indicated is unique, each giving rise to a special set of "problems." Among these "problems" (to approach them functionally rather than areally, since some do cut across geographic lines), two loom with special prominence before the United States. First, the American balance-of-payments position has changed. Persistent deficits are now the rule, not surpluses or oscillating balance. In fact, following several years of heavy deficit, even the role of the dollar, traditionally a "key" currency in international finance, is being questioned. Second, there is the matter of commodity status. At issue is whether or not an exchange of raw materials for manufactures can prove "fair" — whether or not underdeveloped countries, as specialized suppliers of raw materials, can possibly prosper. If the answer is "no," so a common argument runs, the very basis for a healthy international-trade environment is lacking — as is then the basis, also, for a true global complementarity on other scores.

In Part Two, we survey background materials relative to each of the three major external regions that confront the United States, approaching each in terms of the materials relevant to the United States: (a) Europe and the Common Market, (b) the underdeveloped countries and development, and (c) the Communist Bloc(s) and ideological rivalry. Thereafter, we turn to some problems of special concern to the United States in the course of its external contact. These problems, treated here because of their gravity and their ramifications, include (a) the United States' balance-of-payments position, (b) international liquidity, and (c) commodity status.

A..... Europe and the Common Market

The European Common Market — or European Economic Community (EEC), the more formal designation — came into being in 1957 under terms of the Treaty of Rome (which, in a sense, is a constitution for the Community). Comprised initially of six continental countries (France, West Germany, Italy, and the Benelux countries: Belgium, the Netherlands, and Luxembourg), and joined thereafter by several associate members, the EEC was intended to promote a "common market" area. Achievement of the desired regional economic integration was premised on two-fold action: (a) the removal, step by step, of all barriers to trade among the member countries, and (b) the standardization of barriers to trade between members and all nonmembers. By the end of a transition period culminating in roughly 1970, free trade was to prevail *within* the common market area, while uniformity was to characterize trade restrictions *between* the area and the rest of the world.

The rationale for the program of integration was that the region would be strengthened economically — as measured in terms of production and income internally and of balance-of-payments position externally (relative to the rest of the world). The hope was that, through integration, resources available to the region might be employed more advantageously, inviting greater production at lower cost and expanded trade — thereby enhancing real income per capita. The rationale was regarded as in no way novel; it had, in fact, sufficed as the prompting force for earlier post-World War II actions toward economic integration — as in the case of the European Coal and Steel Community (ECSC), aimed at a pooling of the coal and iron resources (and markets) of the six countries, and of the European Payments Union (EPU), aimed at clearing payments regionally in order to facilitate intra-regional trade (at a time of widespread currency inconvertibility). Indeed, the EEC arrangement, at the time of its initiation, represented merely the latest, though by far the most ambitious, of a series of regional integration measures.

The Common Market arrangement, viewed a decade later, has proven itself a success. First, the creation of EEC (or the *promise* that seemed inherent in its creation) triggered a second regional arrangement within Western Europe, the European Free Trade Association (EFTA) —consisting of the United Kingdom, along with Austria, Denmark, Norway, Portugal, Sweden, and Switzerland. Though intended as an "answer" to EEC, the EFTA arrangement constituted a far looser type of organization and at no time entertained goals, or measures, of the boldness characteristic of EEC.

Second, implementation of integration measures under the EEC arrangement has proceeded steadily, even ahead of schedule. Intra-regional impediments to trade, capital movements (and investment), and even labor shifts have been largely removed. Agreement on a common (uniform) external tariff has come somewhat less readily, since protectionist sentiments on behalf of domestic agriculture in one or two member countries have proved a stumbling block. All in all, however, the initial target of free trade within the EEC area and of common (uniform) restrictions against imports from outside the area has well-nigh been reached.

Third, and most important, production and income have risen markedly within the region. The "growth rate" of the Common Market area has consistently exceeded that of the United States. And, while the people of the region have experienced a new high in economic prosperity, the region has become a powerful trading force in the world. Goods in unprecedented volume have begun to flow from the Common Market area, flowing, in large part, in fact, straight into the United States market.

As the United States looks out at the world about it, Western Europe, highlighted by its booming Common Market area, merits major consideration. What the United States sees is a concentration of great and growing productive capacity and output — with much of the area, in addition, now organized to act *in unison*. The implications for the United States, both directly and indirectly, are bound to be enormous.

Also, full of implications for the United States is the urge on the part of other European countries, not now within the Common Market area, to join — ostensibly in order to share in expected future benefits. For example, Great Britain periodically debates whether or not to seek membership, and, if so, on what conditions. If Great Britain does gain membership, interesting questions arise as to the status of traditional Commonwealth ties, the overall strength of Western Europe, and the relationship of outside regions vis-à-vis Western Europe. Perhaps all of Europe is well on its way to unification.

Meanwhile, the countries of the underdeveloped world have a direct stake in what is happening in Western Europe, which comprises a big and growing market, actual or potential, for them. The EEC currently extends special preferential treatment to products originating in "associated territories" in Africa (ex-colonies of particular EEC members) — with the result that commercial (and investment) ties are forged between these territories and the Common Market. And with the further result that other underdeveloped countries, producing products competitive with the African territories (mostly raw materials), are put at a comparative disadvantage in dealing with the Common Market area. The impact, current and prospective, is basically adverse for Latin America and Asia. All the while, the underdeveloped countries of these continents want development too — and, in order to push development, need the proceeds of a thriving export trade.

While the United States has an interest in the implications of possible territorial expansion of the Common Market within Europe and of the disparate treatment accorded underdeveloped regions by the Common Market, it has, above all, a direct and immediate interest in its own bilateral relationship with the Common Market. The Common Market countries comprise a *single* trade bloc for the United States; trade (tariff) and other economic concessions sought by government are negotiated with the bloc, not country-by-country. United States producers face new and rigorous competition from Common Market exports, both in the home market and in third-country markets. And because the market represented by the Common Market area is big and growing (yet, by virtue of a new uniform set of trade restrictions, increasingly difficult to service from outside), United States producers have an incentive to invest *inside* the Common Market area — producing a flow of investment instead of a flow of goods.

In short, the "new Europe," with its Common Market, poses a challenge for the United States — for the economy, for government, and for producers. Here, we examine some important facets of this challenge. The focus in the first selection — by Lawrence B. Krause — is on how the Common Market has affected, and seems likely to affect, United States trade, both bilaterally and via third-country relationships.

Next, Professor Balassa directs attention to the impact, current and probable, of the Common Market on underdeveloped countries. His analysis points to possible gains for parts of Africa, paralleled by serious competitive problems internationally for Latin American and Asian countries — especially for most of the Latin American countries.

In a third selection, Professor Kindleberger examines the "corporate structure" aspects that hold special relevance for external companies — say, American companies — desirous of entering into operations inside the Common Market area.

In a final selection, Professor Kravis presents an overview of the impact of the Common Market. To long-run forces working against the United States' global trade position, the presence of the Common Market, he suggests, adds further complexity: some factors favorable to this country's trade, others unfavorable.

9..... The European Common Market and the United States*

LAWRENCE B. KRAUSE

Brookings Institution

For the second time in the twentieth century, a new area is dominating international trade. Just as the United States eclipsed Great Britain as the world's largest trading nation in the early part of the century, so is the European Economic Community outpacing the United States today. The exports and imports of the Common Market represent 24 per cent of world trade (including intra-Community trade) while the U.S. percentage is only 16 per cent. The members of the European Economic Community maintain their separate political identities, but for questions of international commerce they must be treated as a single unit, since they make unified decisions with respect to commercial policy. If all the countries currently applying for membership in the EEC were to be accepted, then the United States would be relatively small by comparison.

The formation of the European Economic Community has not only redefined trade statistics, it has and is changing the patterns of world trade. In 1958, the last year before tariff preferences were begun, less than 30 per cent of the imports of the member countries originated in other member countries. In 1961, just three years later, 36 per cent of the imports of the member countries came from other members. Looked at from the other side, exports of the EEC countries to nonmembers increased by only 29 per cent between 1958 and 1961 while their exports to each other increased by 73 per cent.

The economic success of the Common Market has been demonstrated, not only by the remarkable increases in trade, but also by the fact that the dismantling of internal restrictions to trade has been appreciably ac-

* Taken and adapted from "European Economic Integration and the United States," *American Economic Review*, May 1963, pp. 185, 187–196.

celerated. With the reaching of an agreement on the beginning of a common agricultural policy, the EEC has moved into the second transitional stage of the Rome Treaty. Because of the very success of the Common Market in its economic objectives, it has become even more necessary to evaluate the EEC as to its effects on nonmember countries. . . .

Economic Implications of the EEC for the United States

The importance of the political bias against the economic interest of nonmember countries depends in part on what effects the Community is likely to have on excluded countries. For the United States, this question can be analyzed by looking at the consequences of the EEC on the bilateral trade between the U.S. and the EEC and also at its consequences on our trade with third countries. For this purpose, United States exports to the Common Market can be divided into three groups: industrial products, agricultural products, and nonagricultural raw materials.

U.S. Exports of Industrial Products

Unlike trade in agricultural products, the Common Market has made relatively few changes in the institutional system whereby industrial goods are imported into member countries. A tariff is levied on industrial products when imported from nonmembers, but this has always been the case. The new element arises from the fact that goods coming from other member countries will not have to pay a tariff or be restricted in any way, and the tariff barrier to the outside world will be uniform regardless of which member country the import is sent.[1] The consequences of this system for nonmembers depend on how much protection the external tariff wall provides as compared to the previously existing national tariffs. The common external tariff was calculated by taking an unweighted average of the French, German, Italian, and Benelux tariffs (with some exceptions).[2] The protectiveness of the tariff cannot be determined by merely comparing the resulting increases and decreases in tariffs required to reach the calculated level. For a producer within the Community that was previously protected by a high tariff, the most serious challenge to its competitive position will come from low-cost producers within the Community against which it will have no tariff protection. Unless the

[1] During the transitional period, existing barriers on intra-Community trade will be gradually reduced and finally eliminated.

[2] This average led to tariffs somewhat on the high side because of the unweighted feature and also because the national tariffs used in the calculation were above those actually in force on January 1, 1958. The German tariff which was averaged excluded the 25 per cent tariff reduction of August, 1957. The rate chosen for Italy excluded the tariff reductions of 1951. Also a Benelux tariff on most chemicals of 12 per cent was average in, although no such tariff was in force. Rome Treaty, Article 19(2), Article 19(3) (d) and List E.

high-cost producers can bring their prices (and costs) down to the level of the low-cost producers within the EEC, they cannot stay in business. The essence of economic integration depends on this type of competition taking place. The prices of the large, low-cost producers within the Community will set the competitive level for the entire market. The common external tariff will be protective only to the extent that it protects the firms that can survive the internal competitive struggle.

An analysis of the protectiveness of the external tariff was made by estimating the amount of protection it affords the dominant low-cost suppliers within the EEC. The dominant suppliers were identified by looking at the trade flows among the member countries before the establishment of the Community. It was assumed that the dominant suppliers of a particular product class are to be found in the country which had the largest share of intra-Community trade in that product class. We can compare the level of the external tariff for each commodity class with the former national tariff of the country with the largest share of intra-Community trade. If the new tariff rate is higher than the old national rate, then the amount of protection it affords is greater than the rate needed to protect the industry previously. If the rate is the same as previously or lower, then we can say that the amount of protection has not been increased. We cannot definitely state that a reduced tariff will undermine a previously existing level of protection without knowing whether there was excess protection under the old national tariff rate.

Two further assumptions are required to make the comparison meaningful. It must be assumed that if the high-cost firms cannot meet the competition within the Community, then the low-cost producers can expand output without significantly changing their average costs. Further, it must be assumed that changes in the tariffs on imported raw materials will not greatly affect the competitive position of the dominant supplier. . . .

A comparison of the new EEC tariff for each of sixty-one three-digit SITC commodity classes with the former national tariff protecting the dominant suppliers gives the vivid impression that the protectiveness of the new tariff is much greater than that previously existing (Table 1). Our analysis shows that 75 per cent of all manufactured products will have their protection raised and by large amounts. The size of the tariff reduction required to bring the new tariff down to the level of the old national tariff of the dominant supplier is over 50 per cent for twenty-one out of the sixty-one classes, 26 per cent to 50 per cent for sixteen classes and less than 25 per cent for only nine classes. Furthermore, for half of the ten classes for which tariff protection has been reduced, other methods of trade restrictions are commonly employed.

The impact of these higher EEC tariffs upon United States exports may well be substantial. Most of the industrial products which the United States exports to the EEC are concentrated in twenty-two of the sixty-one

TABLE 1

Comparison of the New External Tariff Rate of the EEC
on Selected Products with the Old National Tariff
of the Dominant Supplier of Each Product*

Types of Products	Total	Tariff Comparisons†		
		Plus	Even	Minus
Chemicals	12	10	0	2
Textile Products	7	3	1	3
Manufactured products, classified by material, other	19	14	3	2
Machinery and transport	11	11	0	0
Other manufactured products	12	8	1	3
Total	61	46	5	10

Source: "Post-Geneva Weighted Average *Ad Valorem* Equivalent of Duties," prepared by International Trade Analysis Division, U.S. Department of Commerce, March, 1962, P.E.P. *Atlantic Tariffs and Trade.*
* Figures refer to number of products in category.
† Plus: tariff increased. Even: tariff unchanged. Minus: tariff declined.

SITC classes analyzed (Table 2). Substantial tariff reductions on these product classes will be required to bring the level of protection down to that previously granted to the dominant supplier. Up to now, the United States has benefited greatly from the rapid growth of the European economies and the pressures put on the German engineering industry in particular. We have been the residual supplier making the most of excess demand. However, this may not continue.

If Great Britain should join the Common Market, further difficulties will be created for American exports. As desirable as the union may be on other grounds, it will cause a twofold increase in the troubles facing U.S. exporters. In the first place, as British exports cease to feel the discrimination of the EEC, an easy target for market dislodgment by the EEC and U.S. producers will be removed. Furthermore, the British themselves then may well become a serious competitor for existing American shares of the EEC market. In all the twenty-two product groups in which U.S. exports are concentrated, with the exception of paper and paperboard, the British also have a substantial position. In seven groups, the British share of the EEC market exceeds our own, and it is well above 5 per cent for most of the others. This means that the British have a substantial base for expanding their exports if their competitive position improves. The competitive pressures arising from membership in the EEC and the tariff preferences gained thereby may be enough to transform the British into a fierce competitor. United States exports would become the prime target under such circumstances and maintaining our market position in industrial products would not be easy.

TABLE 2

Imports of Manufactured Products by the EEC
from the United States, 1961*

Products	Value of Imports (Million Dollars)	U.S. Share of EEC Imports	Reduction of EEC Tariff Required to Maintain Protection
Inorganic chemicals	47	19.7%	49%
Organic chemicals	142	31.8	50
Paints	9	13.6	48
Medicinal and pharmaceutical products	37	22.3	25
Miscellaneous chemicals	130	26.0	63
Paper, paperboard	31	6.9	10
Yarn and thread	21	4.9	20
Processed gems	14	7.1	0
Iron and steel	63	3.4	36
Manufactures of metals, n.e.c.	35	8.1	42
Power machines	104	27.1	68
Agricultural machinery	23	10.6	65
Office machines	79	28.2	4
Metal-working machinery	99	28.0	65
Miscellaneous machinery	301	21.8	67
Electric machinery	199	16.2	48
Road motor vehicles	61	7.1	35
Aircraft	190	62.5	100 (if applied)
Apparel (non-fur)	13	3.7	0
Instruments	54	26.2	55
Musical instruments	13	11.9	26
Manufactured goods, n.e.s.	22	9.2	40
Total	1,687		

Source: U.N. *Commodity Trade Statistics* (1961).
* Values will differ from U.S. exports of these items to the EEC because of the inclusion of transport costs and differences in accounting periods.

U.S. Agricultural Exports to the European Economic Community[3]

The most serious challenge to United States exports arises from the adoption this year [1962] by the EEC of a common agricultural policy. While many important aspects of the policy are yet to be determined, the major impact of the policy can be inferred from the mechanism that has been created. This development is of particular concern to the United

---

[3] A more extensive treatment of this subject can be found in my paper published by the Joint Economic Committee, *Factors Affecting the United States Balance of Payments*, Part 2, The Common Market: New Challenges to U.S. Exports, 1962.

States because Western Europe is such a large purchaser of U.S. agricultural products. During recent years the EEC countries alone absorbed over 20 per cent of our agricultural exports and close to one-third of all such exports sold for hard currencies. The addition of the U.K. to the Common Market would increase the latter percentage to one-half and amounts to $1.5 billion.

The agricultural agreement of January 14, 1962, provides the initial steps for the integration of the agricultural sector of the EEC. The regulations found in the agreement differ substantially among the various products, but there are some common features. Existing restrictions of all kinds on imports are to be replaced by variable levies designed to offset the differences in market prices (after adjusting for transportation costs) in the EEC country importing and in the country of origin. The levies on imports from other EEC countries are to be gradually reduced until 1970, when a one-price system will emerge. The levies on imports from non-EEC countries are to be sufficiently high to ensure preference for imports from other EEC countries; they will not be reduced over time and might be increased if Community and world prices diverge further.

This system of variable levies will work in such a way that a chain of preference will be set up. Demands for agricultural products in any EEC country will be met first by domestic production. Should these supplies prove insufficient at existing support prices, then products from other EEC countries will be allowed into the market. Only if aggregate production within the Community is insufficient will imports be allowed from non-EEC countries, regardless of how competitively priced these goods may be.

Provision is also made in the agreement for export subsidies designed to offset differences in market prices which will enable a member country with an exportable surplus to export to another member country needing imports but having a lower price level. Subsidies on intra-Community trade will disappear by 1970. However, similar provisions are made for export subsidies in the event that the Community as a whole experiences an exportable surplus to enable its products to compete in world markets and these provisions will not end with the transition period.

With imports determined solely as a residual between production and consumption of agricultural products within the Common Market, evaluation of the consequences of this policy depends on these magnitudes. Since the target level of price supports has not yet been agreed upon (nor pricing criteria), production cannot be estimated with certainty. The eventual agreement on price level will result from a compromise of the political requirements within the member countries. So far the West Germans have been particularly unwilling to consider a lowering of their price supports and German prices are the highest in the Community. In all likelihood, agreement can only be reached by substantially raising the average level of prices within the Community.

The implications for EEC imports of agricultural products from non-member countries are quite clear. With rising average prices, increases in production will exceed increases in consumption and an accelerated movement toward self-sufficiency for a wide range of products will occur. U.S. exports of wheat, coarse grains, and meat will be endangered, and these products make up a substantial portion of our exports. Some other U.S. exports will be undermined by the granting of tariff preferences to the products of the Associated Overseas Countries; namely, fats and oils and to a lesser extent tobacco and cotton.

Even with this over-all pessimistic expectation, the United States will probably fare better than most third country exporters of agricultural products because of the structure of our comparative advantage. The U.S. exports mainly coarse grains to Europe rather than wheat, poultry rather than beef or lamb, and oil seeds, cotton, and tobacco, rather than cocoa, coffee, and sugar. The prospects are that other countries whose product structure is concentrated in the latter categories will be in a much worse position than the U.S.

The aggregate of unfortunate consequences for nonmember countries of the common agricultural policy is greater than the sum of the losses in individual product markets. The agreement essentially removes the agricultural sector of the EEC from the resource allocating mechanism of world-market forces. If the EEC policy is pursued without moderation, bargaining for trade liberalization will be almost impossible because the mechanism ensures an absolute level of protection.

Exports of Nonagricultural Raw Materials

While the United States exports a considerable amount of nonagricultural crude materials to the Common Market ($750 million in 1960), the common external tariff is unlikely to interfere very greatly with this trade. Only for two commodity groups, petroleum products and aluminum, is the United States likely to suffer a trade loss. The loss may arise from the expansion of capacity that is induced by the tariff shelter. For most other products in this category, the external tariff is either zero or very low.

Trade Effects of the EEC via Third Countries

The commerce of the United States can be further affected by the Common Market even though American goods are not directly involved. If countries which normally spend a substantial portion of their foreign exchange earnings in the United States have their exports curtailed, then our balance of payments will subsequently suffer. This may well come about through tariff preferences granted the Associated Overseas Countries by the EEC.

The former French colonial areas of Africa are already substantial exporters of most tropical-zone agricultural products, and these compete with Latin-American exports to Europe. The common external tariff levied on Latin-American goods plus the marketing privileges offered African products gives a distinct competitive edge to the African suppliers. If there were a net shortage or balance of world supplies relative to demand at ruling prices, then the diversion of African supplies to Europe would leave other markets open to Latin America. Since, however, there are more than sufficient world supplies of coffee, cocoa, sugar, and tropical fruit (the principal products involved), the losses to Latin America of sales to Europe as a result of tariff discrimination cannot be made up elsewhere and are likely to lead to a substantial loss in foreign exchange for the Latin-Americans. Since the Latin-American countries buy from 48 to 64 per cent of their total imports from the United States while the African countries buy only 4 per cent of the total imports from us, the net loss to United States exports from the preferential position which the EEC affords African supplies could be substantial.

A further problem is created for the United States because another good customer of ours, Japan, is prevented from exporting to the EEC. All of the member countries discriminate against Japanese goods either by refusing to grant most-favored-nations treatment or by more devious methods. This affects us in two ways. The Japanese are denied foreign exchange, a major part of which would have been spent in the United States, and the Japanese are forced to send a disproportionate share of their output to the U.S. because we have the only market that is even partially open to them. The problem promises to be more serious as Japanese development continues. Even though discriminations against the Japanese predate the Rome Treaty, they are aggravated by the EEC because the freedom of transshipment of goods within the EEC will limit the liberalization of their restrictions to the pace of the least liberal country. Since the EEC countries must liberalize jointly, the speed of the liberalization measures will be much slower than the pace some countries were prepared to undertake in its absence.

Offset: Higher Rates of Growth of the EEC Countries

In discussions of the external impact of economic integration, the point is always made that the unfavorable impact of the formation of a customs union on nonmember country exports will be offset in whole or in part by the increase in member country growth rates stimulated by the establishment of internal free trade. If the EEC has had or is likely to have a growth-stimulating effect, then it must be recognized that the beneficial consequences of this growth on the trade positions on nonmember countries is not as great as one might expect at first glance. Since this growth is likely to be of an import-replacing character, the natural consequence of stimulating growth via exports induced by preferential tariffs, the quantity of additional imports demanded from nonmember countries is likely to be less per unit of growth in income than could have been expected from past behavior. It is not enough for the growth of income merely to lead to a slight increase in imports from nonmembers if the Community's extra exports to the rest of the world per unit of growth of income are not declining sufficiently fast to maintain balance.

In order to make the point somewhat differently, consider the EEC as if it were a single country. The character of the growth of this country is such that it is progressively requiring less imports per unit of output. If at the same time, the exports of the country are not also declining fast enough in relation to GNP, then other countries' balances of payments will be put under pressure. Merely to maintain the existing balance-of-payments positions of third countries, outsiders will have to improve their competitive position vis-à-vis the Common Market. Rapid growth within the EEC has not so far led to a deterioration in their competitive positions in third markets; in fact, the contrary may be true. As a result, rapid growth of the EEC has been combined with balance-of-payments surpluses.

Summary and Conclusions

As indicated previously, the consequences of the Common Market for nonmember countries will depend as much or more on subsequent policy decisions of the Community as on the provisions of the Rome Treaty. This analysis suggests that at present nonmember countries have been put in a disadvantageous position. Future developments will depend in a large measure on the willingness of the EEC to recognize the interests of nonmembers in their deliberations or, to use the standard phraseology, whether the Common Market will be outward or inward looking. There is some evidence to indicate that up to now the Community has been looking a little in both directions.

One can get some comfort in the belief that the Common Market will be outward looking from the Rome Treaty itself. Article 110 indicates that the interests of the Community lie in expanding world trade. Furthermore, the influential leaders of the Commission of the EEC . . . have continually supported this belief in public statements. Nor has the liberalism of the Common Market been confined to words alone. The first two internal tariff reductions were generalized to nonmember countries (as long as the resulting tariff did not fall below the external target rate). Also, the Common Market was willing to enter negotiations through GATT in the so-called "Dillon round" and eventually reached agreements with other countries through which their external tariff was reduced by almost 20 per cent.

There is some indication, however, of less liberal tendencies within the EEC. The tariff reductions made so far by the Common Market have been relatively painless in that they have merely removed some but not most of the excess protection created by the common external tariff. The common agricultural policy, however, has not only raised new barriers to trade, it has established a system that guarantees perfect protection. This policy can only be considered as extremely protectionist from the point of view of agricultural exporting countries.

Policy formation within the Common Market, of course, is not created in a vacuum. If the United States moves toward greater trade restrictions . . . , then we strengthen the protectionist forces within the EEC and bring forth retaliatory restrictions. . . . With the passage of the Trade Expansion Act, the United States has taken the first step toward leadership in the liberal direction. It is now up to the Common Market to indicate its willingness to proceed along this road.

Unfortunately, the immediate response in Europe to the American overture seems far from enthusiastic. While there is little question as to the willingness of the EEC to take part in another tariff negotiation, the hoped for major reduction in tariffs that is possible under the American law has little chance of acceptance according to some EEC spokesmen.[4] If a negotiated tariff reduction seems difficult, then a unilateral reduction by the EEC of their tariffs seems remote indeed. Yet according to this analysis, a unilateral reduction by the EEC is called for to satisfy the spirit, if not the letter, of the GATT requirement that protection not be increased through the formation of a customs union.

The economic size and power of the European Economic Community has cast it in a leadership role in the world. This power, unfortunately, can be used to further the narrow self-interest of the member countries as they conceive it to be. A continuance of existing political institutions almost assures that the power will be used in this way. On the other hand, responsible exercise of this power is possible with the development of greater political unity. Many difficult decisions would have to be made in exercising enlightened leadership, such as inducing major shifts of resources out of agriculture, and this is possible only with a strong sense of unity among the members.

---

[4] Speech by M. Couve de Murville on February 20, 1962, before the American Club of Paris; speech by Valery Giscard d'Estaing on March 27, 1962, at the opening of the Lyon Trade Fair; and speech by Michel Maurice Bokanowski on October 25, 1962, to the American Chamber of Commerce in Paris.

10..... The European Common Market and the Under- developed Countries*

BELA BALASSA

Yale University

The main purpose of economic integration in Europe is to accelerate the growth of the participating economies. The creation of the European Economic Community (EEC) was geared to this objective; it was not intended to facilitate (or hinder) economic development in nonindustrial countries, though special provisions were made for associated overseas countries and territories (colonies and former colonies of EEC countries). Still, integration in Europe cannot fail to cause repercussions in other areas of the world, including the less developed countries.

These repercussions can be classified as "preference effects" and "growth effects." Trade diversion (the substitution of commodities produced in member countries for the products of nonparticipating nations) falls in the first category. The "growth effects" refer to the increase in imports resulting from the accelerated growth of Common Market countries.

Some trade diversion will no doubt occur after the removal of tariff barriers within the Common Market. For example, while Belgium used to import most of her oranges from Spain (the cheapest source), she will, in the future, increase her imports from Italy, a fellow member of EEC. Should production costs be 15 per cent higher in Italy than in Spain, Italian oranges will still be able to undersell oranges from Spain, since the Common Market tariff has been set at 15 to 20 per cent.

Thus, it is clear that the "preference effect" leads to a reduction of exports to the Common Market on the part of nonparticipating countries. These countries will, however, benefit from the "growth effect," for, as integration accelerates economic growth in the Community, member

* Reprinted from *Challenge, The Magazine of Economic Affairs,* a publication of Challenge Communications, Inc., May 1962, pp. 30–34.

countries will spend more on goods from abroad. It is difficult to tell in advance which of the two effects will be stronger. Still, a discussion of expected changes in regard to various commodities can indicate the possible lines of future development. In the following, we will examine the prospects in tropical agricultural products, in Temperate Zone agricultural products, in minerals and in industrial products.

. . .

Tariff preferences granted by the industrial countries of the Temperate Zone to each other have no effect whatsoever on imports of tropical agricultural products. (Sugar and tobacco, which can grow in temperate climates, are exceptions.) Trade in tropical crops is affected, however, as a result of the preferential treatment accorded to the Common Market's associated overseas countries and territories.

At the insistence of the French negotiators, special provisions on the status of the overseas territories of the member countries were included in the treaty establishing the European Economic Community. The treaty and the implementing convention did not spell out what should happen once a dependent territory achieved independence. But, in the absence of a stipulation to the contrary, EEC authorities have taken the position that these territories can maintain their status in the Community, even after their political ties with member nations are loosened or cut off entirely. As a result, all former French colonies — including Mali, Senegal, Upper Volta, Gabon and Guinea — as well as the former Belgian Congo, still enjoy preferential treatment.

But what does preferential treatment amount to? First, development assistance; second, free entry to the market of the Community; and, third, the privilege of retaining or establishing tariffs on the imports of industrial products from the Common Market.

Development assistance is handled through a development fund provided for in the treaty. But, so far, the fund's impact has not been great. If we consider that the U.S. alone gave Ghana $133 million for the Volta Dam project, the $100 million per year the development fund allocates among the Common Market's overseas territories looks small by comparison.

. . .

It appears, therefore, that the main benefit these countries derive from association with the Community is the duty-free entry of their exports to the markets of the European members. This privilege not only gives them an important advantage in selling traditional export products, but can also stimulate their industrialization since they will find market outlets in the Common Market countries for processed food and light industrial products manufactured with cheap labor.

After the completion of the transitional period, the associated countries will enjoy a margin of preference equal to the tariff paid by outsiders.

Nonassociated producers of bananas, for example, will have to pay a 20 per cent tariff on exports to the Common Market. Therefore, their competitors in associated countries will have a 20 per cent advantage over them. In the case of sugar, an associated producer will have an 80 per cent advantage, in the case of tea, 18 per cent, etc. But, in a number of instances, the commodities produced by the two groups of countries are not identical. Coffee, bananas and tobacco are examples.

Coffee, the most important tropical import, appears in two main varieties on the European market — *arabica* and *robusta*. The former, though more expensive, is more popular in Europe (with the exception of France). Hence, though several robusta-producing countries will have tariff preferences in the Common Market, they are not likely to make significant inroads into arabica sales there.

Since climatic and geographical conditions in the associated areas are not favorable to the production of arabica, the coffee producers of Latin America, Kenya, Ethiopia and Tanganyika stand to lose very little of their trade with Common Market countries. But imports of robusta coffee from African countries not associated with EEC are expected to decline.

. . .

Quality differences are of importance in the case of bananas, too. In Germany and the Benelux countries (Belgium, the Netherlands, Luxembourg) the predominant variety consumed is the more expensive Gros Michel, which is grown chiefly in Latin America and the Canary Islands. On the other hand, the African Cavendish banana is imported to France and Italy from their respective overseas territories. But the Gros Michel has been grown successfully in the Belgian Congo, and British consumption has recently shifted to a variety of the Cavendish banana. And, although Germany's traditional sources of supply still have the benefit of a duty-free quota, this quota will be progressively reduced. Consequently, we can expect the "preference effect" to reduce not only the banana exports of the nonassociated African countries, but also those of Latin America.

In the case of tobacco, since the common tariff of EEC is calculated as a percentage of the value of imports rather than as a flat rate, the greatest burden falls on high-quality products. As a result, dark tobacco produced in the former Belgian Congo, the Malagasy Republic and the French Cameroons will replace some imports from Nyasaland and Rhodesia.

Similar consequences are expected to follow as a result of the preferences accorded to Greek tobacco and the possibility of the expansion of tobacco production in the Common Market countries themselves. On the other hand, the cigar leaf exporters of Indonesia, Brazil, the Dominican Republic and Cuba have little to fear from direct competition. Substitution may take place on the consumption side, however, if cigarettes replace cigars to a greater extent.

Quality differences are less important in the case of cocoa; hence the Common Market tariff is bound to affect the patterns of cocoa trade. Before the Common Market was established, about half of the cocoa imports of member countries came from the French, Belgian and Dutch overseas territories. Now this share is expected to increase, while the share of Ghana, Nigeria and Brazil will fall proportionately.

The situation in sugar is akin to that in cocoa, since it makes little difference to the consumer whether he uses beet or cane sugar. But in the case of sugar, the Common Market countries themselves, rather than the overseas territories, are the most dangerous competitors to outside countries. Behind the high tariff wall, domestic sugar producers (especially Italian) will be able to expand their production at the expense of producers in Haiti, Brazil, the Dominican Republic and Cuba.

. . .

To what extent are the preferential advantages accorded to producers in associated countries greater than those enjoyed before integration took place? In the case of the former Belgian Congo and Ruanda-Urundi, tariff preferences under Belgian rule did not amount to much, affecting only banana imports. Since the Common Market tariff on bananas is five per cent above the old Belgian tariff, the position of producers in the Congo and Ruanda-Urundi will improve. The new tariffs on other commodities, such as tobacco and tropical timber, will also serve as an advantage to these areas. On the other hand, the former Italian Somaliland will actually suffer, since its bananas will no longer be sheltered by the higher Italian tariffs and by the Italian state monopoly.

The position of the former French colonies is more complicated. The exports of these countries to France are exempt from customs duties. In addition, they have received preferential treatment in the form of special marketing arrangements. These arrangements have often brought producers in these areas prices considerably above the world market figures. In recent years, coffee, oilseeds, vegetable oils and bananas from French territories have sold in the French market at prices about one-third above world market price.

The treaty does not expressly state that France should do away with her special marketing arrangements, but they are clearly incompatible with the spirit of the treaty. Assuming that these special arrangements will be discontinued, the preferential treatment many producers in these countries will receive in EEC may actually be less advantageous to them than their privileged position in the French market. This will be true for the producers of coffee, bananas, sugar and groundnuts, but not for producers of cocoa, tea and tropical wood. Consequently, coffee and banana production in the former Belgian colonies will benefit and the losses suffered by the nonparticipating countries will be reduced.

. . .

Given the fact that producers in the associated territories will receive higher prices than other producers, we must consider the extent to which these territories are likely to expand production. In the short run, the prospects for expansion are limited. Most tropical products are yearly crops and many require a number of years from planting to harvesting. Output can be increased to some extent through more careful harvesting, better care of crops during the growing season, and the use of fertilizers. But such measures can only have a limited impact.

The short-run impact of the Common Market in the case of most tropical commodities will be to promote a shift in trade patterns. The associated territories will sell more to the Common Market countries and less to outsiders, while other African as well as Latin American countries will redirect part of their exports from the Community to, say, the United States. Still, the producers of nonassociated countries will suffer a loss since they will now receive lower prices and hence their export earnings will decline. In addition, there will be a decline, in absolute terms, in their exports of commodities such as coffee and sugar, which are in oversupply on the world market.

The possibilities of expanding the production of tropical commodities are greater over the long run. But even then expansion is restricted by the availability of land, labor and capital. A significant increase in the production of any one commodity will necessarily entail a smaller rise in the output of another; at the same time, moves toward industrialization will draw labor and capital away from tropical agriculture.

Still, on the basis of available evidence, we may expect that the output of tropical products will double over a 15- to 20-year period. Expansion at this rate would not reduce Common Market imports from nonassociated countries in absolute terms, but it would reduce them in *relative* terms. Also, the growth of the exports of these areas would likely be inhibited.

Some modification of these conclusions will be required if European integration accelerates the economic growth of member countries as it is expected to do. At a higher level of GNP, these countries would import more tropical foodstuffs, for consumption of these products increases considerably in response to increases in income. Thus, EEC's effect on growth should roughly compensate nonassociated producers of tropical products for the losses suffered because of tariff discrimination.

This conclusion, however, does not hold for all commodities. Sugar consumption, for example, increases but little as income rises, and, furthermore, a large expansion of sugar production is expected to take place within the European Common Market countries. Some of the rise in the consumption of tobacco will also be taken up by the expansion of domestic production.

· · ·

The example of sugar and tobacco indicates the problems faced in the case of Temperate Zone products. The recently adopted common agricultural policy of EEC appears to be directed toward self-sufficiency. Although the new support prices have not yet been established, it is expected that they will be low enough to freeze out inefficient, marginal farmers, but high enough to give a stimulus to the expansion of agricultural production, especially in France and Italy. The goal of self-sufficiency will be furthered by the establishment of an agricultural fund designed to assist farmers in buying modern equipment and to subsidize exports of excess agricultural products.

Cotton and soybeans will be the only nontropical agricultural products to enter the Common Market duty-free. Other commodities will have to pay tariffs equaling the difference between the world market price and the EEC support price. This regulation ensures that no imports will be admitted as long as home output, produced at costs equal to or lower than the support price, can satisfy the demand. The new agricultural policy of the Common Market will affect primarily the producers of cereals, beef and poultry, and it is also likely to have some effect on trade in hides, skins and wool.

There will be no increase in the Common Market's demand for bread grains as incomes go up. In fact, human consumption of bread grains may actually fall. And, though a larger proportion of grain will be fed to cattle, the anticipated expansion in domestic production is likely to take care of this need. As EEC attains self-sufficiency in grain production, some grain-exporting areas will suffer — primarily Argentina, and to a lesser extent, Australia and the Middle East.

Somewhat better are the prospects for the outside producers of rice, since Italy presently does not grow the preferred long-grain variety. But plans for a shift toward the production of long-grained rice in Italy, if realized, would adversely affect the position of Thailand and Burma. Italy will also be the chief beneficiary of increases in the consumption of citrus fruits, although outside producers may maintain their relative share in the market by reason of such increases in consumption.

Under the new agricultural policy, France is making strong efforts to increase beef production and some expansion is expected also in Germany and in Italy. As a result, imports of beef are bound to fall, despite the fact that the consumption of beef increases as incomes rise. Argentina, Australia, New Zealand and Uruguay are likely to be hit hardest by these developments.

The picture is quite different in respect to minerals and fuels. The accelerated growth of incomes in the Community will benefit producers of these commodities, for — with the exception of low duties on lead, zinc, aluminum and manganese — minerals and fuels are not subject to duty in the Common Market. And the anticipated increase in manufacturing will lead to a rising demand for them.

What about the ability of developing countries to bring manufactured goods — especially processed food and light industrial products — into the European Community? The establishment of EEC will have a two-fold effect in this regard. First, trade between individual Common Market countries will increase at the expense of EEC's trade with the outside. In addition, assistance given to the associated territories in their efforts to establish light industry and food-processing plants will be prejudicial to similar efforts made by the nonmember countries. A good example is the manufacturing of cocoa powder and butter. The Common Market duty of about 25 per cent will benefit the former French and Belgian colonies at the expense of Ghana and Nigeria.

· · ·

It appears, then, that the establishment of the European Economic Community will have wide-ranging repercussions on the developing countries. Exporters of minerals, fuels and some tropical products will certainly benefit. But a number of nonparticipating countries are likely to be adversely affected. In Africa, the cocoa and coffee producers of Ghana, Kenya, Uganda and Tanganyika appear to be in a vulnerable position. For Latin America, competition from the European members of the Common Market in products grown in temperate climates presents the greatest danger. Finally, in Asia, the exporters of tea, rubber, hides and skins will see their earnings decline while there will be few changes in exports of cotton and jute.

This picture will be modified if the United Kingdom and Denmark join the Community. Denmark's participation would further dim the export prospects of countries in Latin America's Temperate Zone. In addition, preferences given to the [British] Commonwealth countries could be prejudicial to the interest of outside producers in both the Temperate and Tropical Zones. For example, there are strong possibilities that coffee production will be expanded in Kenya — a development which would threaten the coffee industry in Brazil and other Latin American countries. Finally, the outsiders would suffer further if some kind of preferential agreement should be reached between the U.S. and the Common Market countries.

These considerations clearly bring into focus an important economic and political problem that the industrial countries of the West will have to face. Their self-interest dictates that they should reduce tariff barriers that presently interfere with economic intercourse among them. But every reduction of tariffs unaccompanied by concessions to the developing countries amounts to discrimination against the latter. Thus, the establishment of an Atlantic Community can easily have the side-effect of endangering Temperate Zone agriculture in the nonparticipating countries and obstructing their plans for industrialization.

Furthermore, there is no reason why some developing countries should receive preferential treatment while others are discriminated against merely on the basis of their former relationships with Europe. Preferential treatment of the Congo over Ghana, of Somaliland over Ethiopia, or of Upper Volta over Liberia, is not likely to contribute to harmonious relationships between an Atlantic Community and the nations of Africa. And if most of Africa receives advantages in one form or the other, can we expect Latin America to approve?

These are matters that the industrial countries of the West — both inside and outside EEC — cannot afford to ignore.

11..... The European Common Market and the International Corporation*

CHARLES P. KINDLEBERGER

Massachusetts Institute of Technology

My thesis is that economic integration cannot be achieved by customs unions alone, but requires factor movements, and that factor movements on an adequate scale to achieve or closely approach integration require institutions beyond those normal to factor markets.[1]

In particular, to make substantial progress toward economic integration probably necessitates the development of corporations that are equally at home in the various political entities party to the integration attempt. Ideally in the European integration contemplated by the Rome Treaty, it would be a European corporation, reconstituted under European charter, or resulting from mergers that transcended national lines to create a truly European, not a national, decision-making entity. Or the effective institution might be an international corporation with a home base outside the Common Market, and therefore indifferent in its dealings with one or another country of the Six. At the moment, when provision for European incorporation in the European Economic Community has been tabled, it looks as though the international corporation, typically that with headquarters in the United States, is the leading prospect for the effective instrument of European integration. If the Common Market repulses the American giant corporation, and fails to establish European incorporation, the European movement may fall short of real integration.

But it is necessary to proceed more systematically. Permit me to discuss the two substantives in the title of this article separately before I

* Taken and adapted from "European Integration and the International Corporation," *Columbia Journal of World Business*, Winter 1966, pp. 65–73.

[1] Based on the Ascher Isaacs Memorial Lecture in International Economics, delivered at the University of Pittsburgh on April 1, 1965.

73

develop the connection. Economic integration I define as factor-price equalization, that is, the equalization of wages, interest and profits. This definition is more far-reaching than those which emphasize merely the elimination of restrictions on the movement of goods. It makes integration a standard, like absolute zero in temperature, which can be approached or moved away from, but is seldom if ever reached.

Factor Movements Essential

Of course, freedom-of-goods movement is an important ingredient of integration, as the factor-price-equalization theorem suggests. If two countries produce goods in the same way, equalization of goods-prices will result in equalization of the prices of factor inputs — land, labor and capital — provided certain rather restrictive assumptions are met about the unimportance of transport costs, the identification of certain goods with certain factors, the production of every good in all the countries, perfect competition, constant returns to scale, etc. So restrictive are the assumptions, however, that few economists believe that goods-movements alone can produce economic integration as here defined. It probably requires as well the movement of factors, which the classic economists thought did not occur in international, as contrasted with domestic, trade.

The Rome Treaty establishing the European Economic Community provided for freedom of factor movements. Yet large-scale movements of capital have not taken place within the Common Market. To the extent that the capital markets of Europe are joined, it was, before the announcement that the President would seek passage of an Interest Equalization Tax in July, 1963, principally by means of New York. European borrowers would sell bonds in New York, and European lenders would buy bonds. Some of the bonds were identical, i.e., bought by Europeans from Europeans in New York. . . .

Another institution for moving capital from one national money or capital market in the EEC to another is the large American bank with branches in the separate countries. This device is not available for integration in the United States, since branch banking is forbidden in most states. Nor has it gone far elsewhere. But it is interesting to observe that there are no European-wide commercial banks except the Chase Manhattan, the First National City, the Bank of America, and the Morgan Guaranty. French, German, Italian, Dutch and Belgian commercial banks cooperate, and regularly participate in consortia for successive loans; but the identity of interest is limited. A new decision is made each time for each operation; there is no mechanism for borrowing in one market and lending in another automatically, such as occurs in the single bank which receives deposits here and makes loans there.

Integration through factor movements also takes place by means of movements of labor, and these, too, operate in Europe largely by outside mechanisms. It is true that Italy has provided the largest number of foreign workers for Germany, France and Belgium (leaving out Switzerland which has half a million Italians but is not a member of the Common Market). But the numbers of border workers who cross from Belgium into France, or The Netherlands and France into Germany, are trivial compared to the large inflow from Eastern Germany to the west, from North Africa to France, and from Portugal, Spain, Greece and Turkey into Germany, France and Belgium.

Strange Intermediaries

Moreover, the outsiders with no roots are more mobile than Bretons are in France or East Bavarians in Germany and far more mobile than nationals between the separate countries. It has been noted that wage equalization is taking place between Southern and Northern Italy by means of Switzerland and Germany. Southern Italians go to Switzerland and Germany at the same time that Italian employers are recruiting Italian workers in those countries to bring them to Northern Italy. Similarly, 12,000 Moroccans leaving Northern France for the Ruhr when their contracts in the French coal mines are up raise wages in France and lower them in Germany, a step in the direction of wage equalization.

But the tendency toward equalization of factor prices does not always occur through organized markets — for goods or for labor and capital. In the United States an important contribution to integration has been the national corporation. This borrows in New York and invests where it can assemble materials and labor in least-cost combinations, relative to market outlets. . . . The economic historian, Alfred Chandler, dates the rise of the national corporation in the United States at the 1890's, and observes, interestingly, that with the change of scale and horizon, there was also a change in behavior, as the national corporation took marketing back from wholesalers and discharged the function itself. A national corporation that shuts down production in a high-cost and expands in a low-cost location provides a mechanism of integration connected with but significantly differentiated from the markets for goods and factors.

Jet-age Flowering

The rise of the international corporation is more difficult to date. Some American companies "went international" shortly after becoming national, at the turn of the century. By 1929 there was a sizable list. But it was not until the development of the aircraft, and especially the jet aircraft, that the international corporation came into its own. As Stephen Hymer has pointed out,[2] international operations are expensive. They require face-

---

[2] "The International Operations of National Firms: A Study of Direct Investment," unpublished doctoral dissertation, MIT, 1960.

to-face contact, expensive communication by telegram and telephone. They involve misunderstandings and loss. They can be undertaken, therefore, only when they offer a particularly high return. Hymer's point is that direct investment is not simple capital movement. That could take place more cheaply through capital markets. Direct investment implies coordination of company operations to take advantage of super-profits. The basis of the higher-than-normal profits may be a monopoly in technology, or access to extra large amounts of capital, or capacity to coordinate operations in several parts of the world in ways which cannot be managed through the free play of market forces.

A few further remarks about the international corporation before coming to grips with the connections between it and European integration. There is a theorem set out by Irving Brecher and S. S. Reisman that since people in the same position trying to maximize profits will necessarily behave in identical fashion, it makes no difference whether a given company in Canada is Canadian or American: the economic result will be the same. I doubt this. Two decision-making units trying to maximize profits within the same horizon, spatially and through time, will behave in the same fashion — assuming equal intelligence and managerial capacity — but if one is a national corporation and the other an international one, their horizons will differ, and so may their behavior. The international corporation will be keeping an eye on profit opportunities, governmental intervention, political pressures, and so on all over the world. To meet a local demand, the local company will expand in the local area. The international corporation might well supply the demand from abroad. Moreover, if demand contracts in the market, the local corporation is likely to cut production and dig in. The international corporation may close down altogether. . . .

The differences between the national and the international corporations explain why joint ventures are such failures as an answer to the problem of direct investment — one partner wants income and the other wants capital gains, or one partner wants profits from refining and distribution and the other wants profits from selling the basic material. They also explain why the international corporation's answer to the demand for local participation — why don't you buy shares in the parent corporation? — usually falls on deaf ears. . . . Local capital is limited to a local horizon. It sees a local profitable enterprise owned abroad, and it wants a piece of it, including the wealth that comes from capitalizing the super-profits from the particular operation. On Hymer's principle of the need to overcome costs of foreign operations, direct investment must earn not only a higher return than the company could earn at home, but also a higher return — owing to the monopoly — than a local company can make in the host country. Since they operate with different horizons, the international corporation and the local investor or government have a hard time agreeing on what constitutes optimal behavior.

Dim Outlook for Continental Corporation

Now to join up European integration and the international corporation. As previously noted, my hypothesis is that if European integration is really to be achieved, there must develop European corporations, maximizing profits over some appropriate time profile, within the geographical limits of the Common Market. I do not see such corporations coming into being. . . . To the extent that international corporations operate in the Common Market, the bulk of them will be American, with most of their interests outside. But I doubt that there will be enough American corporations operating in the Common Market to achieve much of the indicated integration by this mechanism.

There are some European corporations, to be sure. The 1964 merger of Agfa and Gevaert in the photographic-film field, a German corporation and a Belgian, was viewed by some as the beginning. But the two firms maintain separate identities for their products, separate boards of directors, separate bodies for decision-making. It is said that they will start by merging their distribution facilities, and move on after that to research. The test of a merger, however, is whether there is finally one decision-making unit, and whether the decision can be taken to close out an activity in one location (read country) when it is found less efficient than in another location where operations can be expanded. Cooperation between two locations that are both maintained stops short of integration in the sense I mean it. The forms of integration may be adopted without the substance. . . .

Cartels Are the Norm

The fact is that the European tradition calls not for merger but for business agreement, or cartels. The Rome Treaty forbids cartels, but the European Economic Commission, in the course of applying the provisions of the Treaty, has chosen to distinguish between good agreements and bad ones. In the early period of the Common Market a number of agreements between national firms were made in the interests of rationalization. One company would make this product, and the other that. The need to maintain a complete line behind a tariff wall gave way to specialization and exchange within the Common Market, with large economies of scale, according to observers like Herbert Giersch, arising from rationalization cartels. But when Nordhoff of Volkswagen publicly proposed that the various national companies of Europe specialize by model size[3] as a means of meeting American competition, he was indignantly refused. Professor Valetta, of Fiat, who had earlier suggested an agreement of the European producers for pricing, purchasing (especially steel) and selling as a means of heading off American competition, but was turned down be-

[3] *Le Monde,* July 26–27, 1964.

cause his scheme was obviously in contravention of the Rome Treaty, rejected the Nordhoff proposal. Fiat has a full line of cars, and Volkswagen has specialized. The Volkswagen proposal for specialization patently favors Volkswagen and hurts producers with a more balanced set of models.

Four in U.S.; Forty in Europe

The automobile industry furnishes an excellent example of the problem. The United States, with a single market of 194 million consumers, has three or possibly four producers. Europe, with more than 200 million consumers, has had forty altogether and possibly fifteen to twenty substantial producers, but is surely going to find itself reduced to a smaller number. A semimerger took place in France between Citroen and Peugeot, which formed a special company, a fifty-fifty subsidiary to produce parts common to both, including certain transmissions and truck engines.[4] Volkswagen originally bought up DKW but has since sold it to Mercedes-Benz. It is significant that these are national mergers. Italian, French and even German interests are fearful of American "monsters," but the answer to them seems thus far to have been merger at the national level rather than the development of the European corporation. Apart from the Citroen interest in Wankel with NSU and Henschel-Berliet in trucks, there have been no international mergers.

Contrast the position of the American Big Three. General Motors has the fast-rising Opel in Germany and Vauxhall in Britain, and has announced a $100 million expansion of its Belgian assembly plant in Antwerp. Ford is well established in Germany and England with local models, with a new plant in Belgium. Chrysler has acquired interests in Simca in France, Rootes in England, and a Spanish subsidiary, and is said to be looking for a suitable company to buy in Germany. These firms are already in position to adjust production internationally.

Europe generally is made unhappy by the size of American corporations. It is pointed out that General Motors alone grosses as much as the thirteen largest German companies, and that this is 10% larger than the gross national product of The Netherlands; or that General Motors' profit has been larger than Renault's turnover. This was in 1963, before its record $1.75 billion profit in 1964. Among the world's sixty biggest corporations, forty-nine are American and only eleven European,[5] and of the 100 top firms in turnover in 1962 Germany placed only thirteen, with its largest, Volkswagen, thirty-fifth on the list.[6] Of the giant companies of the world, the Americans listed an average five times larger in size than

4 *France Actuelle*, November 15, 1964.
5 *New York Times*, July 28, 1964.
6 German Embassy, *The Bulletin*, September 22, 1964.

the leading British or German corporations in their field, and ten times larger than the French companies.[7]

But these figures, as economists know, are not only difficult to interpret, depending upon whether one chooses assets, net worth, turnover, profits, or cash flow; they are also of doubtful relevance. The amount of funds which an American company will invest in Europe is limited, and it is this limited portion of assets, profits, sales, cash flow or whatever which should be compared with European companies. Even so, the comparison is frightening for Europe.

Specific Objections . . .

France objects to the American companies on more than mere size. These companies, it is held, can frustrate the French Plan. The plan is implemented to a considerable degree through the control which the Commissariat du Plan exercises over the flow of government funds and public savings. With an underdeveloped capital market, savings move from household to French business largely through government institutions. This is especially true when profits are squeezed by rising costs so that investment depends more on outside and less on internal funds. Foreign corporations with access to outside sources of capital can escape governmental control.

The other concern of the French is that the technological fallout of international corporations will occur outside of France. When General Electric buys Machines Bull and parts of Olivetti, the research will be done in Schenectady rather than in Paris or Ivrea. . . .

. . . and a General Unreadiness

Neither of these objections is very compelling. As to the first, the plan has thus far been a success because it pushed for expansion. To worry that investment may occur which is not wanted is to anticipate a shift in the thrust of planning to restraint, higher prices, less growth. There have been symptoms of this attitude in France from time to time, but happily they have been fleeting. If American companies want to invest their own money or money borrowed outside France, they are sensible or foolish. If they are sensible, France benefits, as well as the company; if foolish, it is their money which is lost, not French, unless their expansion leads to intense competition and losses for other manufacturers.

The more fundamental reason, it seems to me, is that the French are unwilling yet to be truly international, nor even, as I shall suggest in more detail shortly, truly European in their economic life. This attitude is not solely French, by any means. Industrial associations in Germany last

[7] *France Actuelle, op. cit.*

winter were studying whether European industry should be delivered to United States capital power. The great German banker, Herman Abs, is said to be restive under the threat of United States direct selling of securities by American brokers to Europeans, instead of through German banks, and German banks dislike the international corporation because it weakens their monopoly on capital by providing the firm with access to credit abroad. The Dutch are regarded as international and maintain strong ties to Britain and the United States, but this sometimes appears less as a positive attitude of faith in internationalism than a counterpoise to the domination of Germany and France in the Common Market. There are times, exemplified by their attitude toward Mediterranean labor, to which they have not extended a warm welcome, when they seem slightly nationalistic too. But the French are outstanding in independence of trans-Channel or trans-Atlantic suggestion or leadership, and we can use them to illustrate the vestigial importance of national life in the Common Market.

The French opposition to the international (read American) corporation is partly its freedom from capital control, and partly the fact of technological fallout abroad. But fundamentally the trouble with these corporations is that they are not French. The French want a French and not an international technology, just as they want a French and not an international deterrent. This is true in atomic energy, in supersonic aircraft, in computer technology and everything else. It is widely believed by American officials in Europe that the French opposition to American "monsters" is a smokescreen under which the Conseil du Patronat Francais hopes to soften up the Community's antimerger and anticartel actions. But this is too subtle. The point is that the French are not ready for the European corporation, much less for the international corporation.

Fragmented Firms

This can be demonstrated partly by the absence of international mergers in Europe involving French and partner companies. It is also mirrored in the actions of others. Take the attitude of American corporations. When the Common Market was initially organized, it was believed that American firms operating in the separate markets would rationalize their operations. IBM, for example, was said to have maintained plants in separate countries assembling separate machines, the components of which were produced in several other countries. This layout was believed to minimize the danger of nationalization, since no country taking over a plant would acquire an integrated operation. When the Common Market took effect, this rather expensive arrangement could be abandoned for a more efficient organization of production. Or in the case of companies making a single line, scale economies might make it sensible to substitute one plant for five after the internal protective tariffs were eliminated.

The notions of investment creation and investment diversion were evolved to parallel (verbally, though not analytically) trade creation and trade diversion in the economic analysis of customs unions. Investment creation was the response by the outside producer to the stimulus of trade diversion. Unable to lick them, he joined them, establishing a plant inside the Common Market to fill the market from which discrimination cut him off. This was the widespread American response to the Rome Treaty and is completely analogous to a tariff factory — that is, a manufacturing operation called into being by a tariff on finished products. Much of the effect of the Common Market in attracting United States investment was not investment creation in the sense that investments in Europe which were not profitable with internal tariffs separating the four countries and the Belgian-Luxembourg customs union became profitable when these were removed. It came from the attention which the Common Market drew to investment opportunities in Europe which had previously passed unnoticed, having lain beyond the horizon of the American businessman still preoccupied after the war with the American market.

Investment diversion, as contrasted with investment creation, was to stem from the anticipated reorganization of the European investment of outside companies that were already established in Europe to take advantage of newly arisen opportunities for economies of scale and specialization. The creation and the diversion effects could be intermingled. The Common Market could lead to both expansion and reorganization. But investment diversion, so far as is observable from the outside, is negligible. American companies seem to have decided that the anticipated opportunity to rationalize was illusory. It was put to me once in 1964: "To sell in France, build a factory in France." General Motors Frigidaire incurred the displeasure of the French government when it closed down its small plant at Gennevilliers in 1962. This was required by the force of Italian competition in automatic refrigerators. If the cause had been company rationalization, the indignation would doubtless have been greater. It is true that there is considerable interplant exchange between Ford of Limburg in Belgium and Ford of Cologne — enough, it is said, to have increased the ratio of Belgian foreign trade to national income in recent years (without affecting the balance of trade). The General Motors investment in Antwerp may be more than a mere duplication of Opel and Vauxhall facilities in Germany and Britain, respectively. But investment diversion by American plants does not seem to have been significant.

It is not only the international companies of American origin which encounter problems in France. The rebuff to Shell and Badische Anilin has been mentioned. At the time of the General Electric purchase into Machines Bull of France, it is said that a private banker had tried to interest Siemens and Philips, separately, in the venture. These two companies, like General Electric, have need of a ready-made entry into the computer field, where they have fallen behind. Capital problems may have contributed to the decision not to pursue the matter, but it is said that each company lacked the assurance that it would be treated in the long run as a national in France.

Trade discrimination is possible under GATT because the world has made provision within the most-favored-nation clause for customs unions and free-trade areas, to bridge the gap between free trade (in the national market) and tariffs. In the corporate field, no such discrimination has been possible. The standard here is national treatment, in which foreign corporations are treated like national corporations.

No Right in Law

For example, national treatment of each other's corporations is provided by the Franco-American Convention of Commerce, Friendship and Navigation, the latest of which was signed in November, 1959, even though the French have disregarded it in announcing restrictions on foreign investment in April, 1965. Foreign corporations can be discriminated against as a class by legislation or by administrative action. But while it is possible *administratively* to favor corporations from some foreign countries over those of others, there has been in the past no recognized right *in law* to discriminate in favor of the corporations of one nation over those of another. This right is now claimed by Article 52 of the Treaty of Rome which grants national treatment to the companies of partner countries, but not to those of outsiders, a claim which has still to be tested in diplomacy and in international law. If it is successfully defended, and if the conditions for establishing corporations are made uniform in the Community, as had been sought but tabled in 1961, there would be created in effect a European corporation.

Note that the concept of a European corporation presupposes the development of a corps of European executives who are mobile from Catania to Friesland. The European bureaucrat has been developed, ready for quick relocation to Brussels, Paris, Geneva and, with less grace, Luxembourg and Strasbourg, but the European executive is less inclined to pull up stakes — and far less inclined than the business school graduate in the middle rank of executives in the United States, who is prepared to transplant his family and chattels from San Diego or Miami to Seattle or even Calais.

Waiting on National Treatment

Yet despite the readiness of American executives to follow orders from the vice president in charge of foreign operations, unless the international corporation is assured of national treatment over a wide area, it can have no greater mobility than the single domestic company. If risks attach to the mobility, rather than extra profits, the international corporation will operate a series of separate foreign investments rather than a single efficient and factor-price-equalizing one.

Would the United States object to discrimination in the Common Market in favor of Common Market corporations? The subject is evidently complex and involves legal considerations of a sort that a mere economist hesitates to contemplate. There are those who think retrospectively that this country made a mistake in encouraging the Common Market with its trade discrimination against United States exports. They, and doubtless others, would insist that while the goal is national treatment for foreign-owned corporations, there must be at minimum nondiscriminatory treatment of foreign-owned corporations. This would make the European corporation wait until there was a European sovereignty. The question is academic in view of French hesitation to take a European rather than a French view of economic, social and political life in the Common Market. But it may not remain so.

12..... Impact of the European Common Market: An Overview*

IRVING B. KRAVIS

University of Pennsylvania

. . . [Long-run] forces working against the U.S. trade position . . . arise fundamentally from changes in the technology of transportation and communications and from basic changes in the economic structure of Western Europe. Western Europe has been the chief beneficiary of the enhanced geographical mobility of the elements that historically have been primarily sources of American advantage in international trade. Furthermore, Western Europe proceeds toward Americanization from an internal dynamic as well as from external effects flowing from the United States. As incomes rise, costly and high quality products begin to find domestic markets. Domestic industries arise to cater to these demands, and supplying industries develop to produce the improved materials and the new machines necessary to make the new goods.

These changes were flowing at full tide before the advent of the Common Market at the beginning of 1958, and the new organization has probably added to them only marginally. It is easy to exaggerate the purely economic impact of the Common Market upon its members. The Six were growing rapidly before they joined together as well as afterwards; indeed in the 4 years preceding the Common Market (1953–57) industrial production in the six countries combined expanded by 40 per cent and their trade with one another by 78 per cent, while in the 4 ensuing years (1957–61) the corresponding percentages were 30 and 64, respectively. The real threat posed by the organization of the Common Market for the trade position of the United States is the greater concentration of economic and political power than had previously existed,

* Taken and adapted from "Factors Affecting the U.S. Balance of Payments" (The United States Trade Position and the Common Market), *Hearings Before the Joint Economic Committee*, 87th Congress, 2nd Session, 1962, pp. 96–100.

particularly since there are built-in factors that may cause this power to be used in ways that will be harmful to American exports.

Before turning to these political aspects, however, let us examine briefly the respects in which the advent of the Common Market brings or accelerates economic changes that weaken the U.S. trade position.

In the first place, the Common Market institutions may have had some effect in producing more rational practices with respect to certain raw materials than might otherwise have been followed. The complete elimination of tariffs and other restrictions on intracommunity trade in coal and steel, achieved under the European Coal and Steel Community (ECSC), reduced transport costs by rationalizing channels of distribution. In coal, for example, mines near national boundaries began to serve areas determined by economic rather than political factors. There are some signs also that the European Communities (i.e., the ECSC, EEC, and Euratom) aided by pressure from the Italians (who have no coal and depend upon cheap oil from external sources), will hasten the process of relaxing restrictions against the import of oil so as to obtain cheap energy supplies despite unfavorable effects on coal. Belgium has surely gone farther in closing down high cost coal mines than she would have been able to do without the political and economic support of the ECSC. Of course, there are some offsetting policies which tend to raise material costs, but these affect mainly tropical products from French-associated areas in Africa and are probably less important in their overall impact upon materials costs than the policies relating to coal and steel.

Secondly, the Common Market has dramatized the European market and made it more attractive to American capital and enterprise. The Common Market thus has tended to accelerate the process by which American enterprise, technology, and capital rather than American goods move across the ocean.

Third, the formation of the Common Market seems to have provided a stimulus to the growth of large size firms. A wave of mergers, affiliations, and understandings has probably led to larger size and lower cost plants, and has increased the degree of product specialization in plants of a given size. It has led also to larger firms which are more strongly placed with respect to research, finance, and foreign marketing than the smaller ones they replaced. The extent and significance of merger movement in the Common Market are difficult to assess. It is conceivable that what is going on is merely an adjustment by business to the new situation created by the prospect of free trade within the Community. If so, the policy of live and let live, which seems to have characterized Western European business psychology to a greater degree than that of the United States, may soon reassert itself. It is possible that this attitude was as responsible as the inherent limitations of a market of the size of, say, England or France or Germany for the existence of smaller scale plants than in America. Of course, the EEC has taken steps to implement the anticartel provisions of the Rome Treaty, but whether European business will become imbued with a new competitive spirit either through self- or official-inspiration is far from clear. In any case, at the moment there has been a clear gain in efficiency from the rationalization movement that has taken place.

Fourth, the formation of the Common Market has made a contribution to the rate of growth, and thus created a greater market and a greater opportunity for the mass production of standard items and for the large scale production of more costly goods that were almost an American monopoly. In TV and radio, for example, the European market is already on a par with that of the United States in the quality of the product which it can absorb; in most other consumer durables, however, it is 10 to 30 years behind the United States. Of course, the expansion of the European market has been a boon to American exports thus far; it has offset any tendency for trade diversion to hurt U.S. exports. Indeed, U.S. exports to the Common Market have expanded more rapidly than U.S. exports as a whole since 1957 or 1958. However, the European boom can hardly last forever, and when the domestic absorption of European output slackens, U.S. producers may feel the full impact of the new capacities of European firms to produce goods in varieties, qualities, and quantities which formerly could be obtained only in the United States. Many American businessmen fear just this. They feel that their European competitors have been satisfied to follow the price leadership of American firms in the American and sometimes in other markets; this enables European firms, in view of their lower costs, to enjoy high profit margins on their foreign business at a time when their plants are occupied with domestic orders anyway. Of course, if the European countries succeed in maintaining full employment economies with only mild and infrequent recessions[1] further European inroads on markets held by the United States will depend upon the longer run growth of European capacity.

Finally, the agricultural policy of the Common Market threatens to increase the degree of self-sufficiency of the area by stimulating the expansion of internal production. New export surpluses such as French wheat have already appeared, and if high internal prices are added to the system of variable levies giving preference to Community products, the United States which has been exporting over $1 billion of agricultural products to the Common Market may find itself reduced to the position of a residual supplier especially for grains. Unlike the other factors we have listed, this one involves competition between United States and European producers only for the markets of the Community itself. To the extent that it will affect competition for other markets, it will be unfavorable to the EEC because it will tend to raise the level of costs.

With the possible exception of the last factor, the adverse influences fact that their quantitative restrictions against American goods were still

---

[1] See the paper by Milton Gilbert and the discussion by Walter Salant in the May 1962 *American Economic Review.*

upon U.S. trade that we have discussed thus far have stemmed from economic changes. The most important consequences of the Common Market for the U.S. trade position are, however, likely to flow from a new political fact: For the first time in many decades the United States is faced in the Western World with an almost equal aggregation of economic and political power. The uncoordinated, sometimes conflicting, and often offsetting policies pursued by six governments are being replaced by coordinated decisions reached in Brussels. Even without the addition of new members, the decisions are taken on behalf of countries whose combined importance in world trade already equals or exceeds that of the United States and who provide a significant fraction of the U.S. export surplus.[2] The bargaining power of the Common Market, already substantial, will of course be further increased if Great Britain and other new members and associates are admitted. As the geographical scope of the Common Market is expanded, it will embrace an increasingly diversified area and will become more self-sufficient and less dependent upon external trade than the individual member countries have been. Thus, like the United States, the new entity will have considerable leeway for deciding upon more or less liberal policies.

How will this power be used? Some parts of the answer seem clear. In the first place, the power of the Common Market is likely to be used to retaliate promptly and fully in response to any adverse actions taken in trade matters by another country, including the United States. This has recently been illustrated by the action of the Council of Ministers of the EEC in raising the common external tariff on a half dozen product groups in reprisal for U.S. increases under the GATT escape clause in the duties on carpets and glass. This type of response may be expected not only because of the natural tendency for partners to support an aggrieved member (Belgium, in the carpet and glass case) against an outsider, but also because of the psychology underlying commercial policy in Western Europe. In the latter connection, it is not much of an exaggeration to describe the postwar history of the dismantlement of trade barriers in Western Europe as a story of careful horsetrading in which no concession was given without extracting one of equal value.[3] In the past, however, retaliatory action by European countries against American protective measures has been infrequent and never so prompt and forthright; countries almost always awaited the negotiation of compensatory concession from the United States to replace the ones that had been withdrawn. The past patience of European countries may, of course, be attributable to the in effect, and as long as this was the case they could not feel quite so ill treated by U.S. actions. However, it may also have been due in part to

[2] In 1961, for example, U.S. exports to the Six were $3.5 billion and imports from them were $2.2 billion, while the overall U.S. trade surplus was $5.3 billion. OECDE, "Foreign Trade," series A, April 1962.

[3] Perhaps this helps to explain the poor record — relative to that of the United States — of most of the Western European countries in opening their markets to the "low-wage" countries.

the absence of a mechanism such as the Common Market which has the power to retaliate effectively and without the fear of the consequences that a small country acting alone would have.

A second factor affecting the use of the power that the EEC has is the inherent tendency of any large area composed of diverse interests to reconcile conflicts over the resolution of domestic difficulties by shifting as much of the burden of adjustment to outsiders as possible. This is evident in U.S. commercial policy. For example, the extensive protection accorded by the United States to its textile industry, including high tariffs and new legislation authorizing the establishment of import quotas, reflects pressures arising from the failure of domestic consumption of textile products to expand as rapidly as productivity, with the result that employment levels have been declining. In the short history of the Common Market, there are already a number of illustrations of this tendency to resolve difficulties by cutting off the outsider. These include instances of troubles caused by shortages as well as those caused by surpluses. The most important case involving a surplus, which related to coal, developed in the late 1950's. The desirability of a reduction in imports from the United States and other third countries was virtually the only point on which the Six could agree in their prolonged and difficult negotiations. . . . Analogous action was taken in a number of cases involving shortages; for example, . . . [recently] the European Commission recommended to the Dutch Government that it permit the normal volume of potato exports to member countries and restrict exports to third countries.

Even if it seems reasonable to suppose that the Common Market will retaliate when the occasion arises and shift the burden of adjustments to third countries when internal difficulties develop, there remains a large and important area of doubt about the way in which the Community will wield the great power which its size and importance confers upon it. Although the Rome Treaty contains a clause stating that the member countries intend to follow a liberal commercial policy (art. 110), the commitment is quite general and could conceivably be subordinated to other objectives of the Six. At the risk of some oversimplification, one might say that there are two schools of thought within the Community on this matter. One school, for which the French are the spokesmen on many issues, takes the view that the Community represents, among other things, a club for the mutual benefit of the member countries at the expense of outsiders. This position has been generally opposed by the Dutch and also by the Germans, both of whom tend to prefer more liberal trading policies for the Community. Of course, the difference is one of degree, albeit an important one, because some element of tariff discrimination in favor of fellow members is the essence of a customs union. While it is true that the conception of the EEC goes far beyond a mere customs union, it is also true that the most immediate practical attraction of the EEC to participants and would-be participants is its customs union feature. . . .

B ..... The Underdeveloped Regions and Development

The underdeveloped countries constitute the second major economic grouping confronting the United States in its external dealings. Scattered through Asia, Africa, and Latin America, the underdeveloped countries include some two-thirds of all countries — with some two-thirds of the world's population. They have in common heavy production in raw materials, often decidedly export-oriented; low productivity, reflecting a poor utilization of available labor; and levels of per-capita income and material well-being, the end rewards of the prevailing production-and-trade order, which are vastly inferior to those in the developed countries.

The underdeveloped countries have at least one further thing in common: an urge for "economic development." There is within these countries a widely-held desire to shake free of the prevailing underdevelopment (and from the distasteful attributes associated) — to achieve with dispatch the degree of development that can assure a more rewarding existence.

This desire for economic development — frequently referred to as "the great awakening" — is fairly recent, dating from World War II days or thereabouts. It is not that vast numbers of people suddenly realized that they lived in poverty (this fact had been brutally apparent for centuries), but that they suddenly determined to do something to *change* the status quo.

Why did "the great awakening" come about when it did, not earlier and not later? The answer appears to be that a set of circumstances, all intertwined, came to a head during World War II days. Improved technology, communications, and news media brought a greater awareness of other places, other people, and other modes of life; and, with such awareness, came growing discontent with what prevailed. The events of World War II set the stage for an ending of an increasingly unpopular colonialism; new countries appeared, free to act on their own in the pursuit of national aspirations. The Soviet example — from feudalism to Sputnik in literally half a life span — drove home the point that economic gains are possible, here and now; and, indeed, Soviet advisers often seemed to be on hand in many locales to explain the point.

"The great awakening" had its parallel force, "the revolution of rising expectations." Popular discontent was now matched with positive expectation. Governments felt pressed to respond — to act as instruments for change. A flurry of "planning" was set in motion: identify the problem, devise a course of attack, and set in motion the implementation.

In all this, the United States had a direct interest. Coming out of World War II as the acknowledged leader of the Free World, this country felt compelled, if not inspired, to help build a better world. The needs of the domestic economy dictated that this country concern itself about markets, sources of supply, and outlets for capital. And, by way of coercive inducement, the presence of a Soviet influence stood ever ready to turn unmet aspirations to its own advantage. Accordingly, the United States acted — with a swiftness and intensity that in retrospect seem unprecedented — to spearhead a massive program of foreign aid on behalf of the development-conscious underdeveloped regions.

Our present section is devoted to the status of the underdeveloped countries and to their aspirations for development — all of which the United States (government and business) must recognize in its external dealings. To begin, our first selection, by the late Ragnar Nurkse, makes the point that raw-materials-producing countries (primary-producing countries — synonymous, for all practical purposes, with underdeveloped countries) have been experiencing lagging exports. This depressant on primary products poses a serious problem for underdeveloped countries, both because it induces low and/or lagging income and because it denies adequate access to the foreign exchange needed to promote the development upon which improvement depends.

Raúl Prebisch, in our second selection, gives us an explanation for this weakness in the position of raw-materials-producing countries. Prebisch's "message," of course, is that development is imperative — which, to him, means the acquisition of a goodly amount of new industry.

W. W. Rostow, in excerpts from his much-referred-to book, *The Stages of Economic Growth,* goes on to explain the development process in terms of a sequence of "stages"; as the study of history reveals, he says, countries move upward toward and to "stage five": the age of high mass-consumption. A particularly crucial point for them is "stage three," the "take-off" — a phase few present-day underdeveloped countries have as yet entered.

A usual view in underdeveloped countries is that development occurs faster, and more surely, if given helping nudges. To this end, underdeveloped countries are prone to plan, rather than leave their developmental fates to chance (i.e., to the whim of free market forces). Indeed, much literature exists on *how* to plan. A selection authored by Albert Waterston — a foremost authority on planning, long associated with the World Bank — undertakes to assess the record of planning effort. According to him, much of on-going planning is amiss in its insufficient attention to implementation aspects; targets mean little in the absence of the means for their attainment. Waterston then offers some concrete suggestions on how to strengthen planning effort.

In planning, certain initial decisions on basic developmental policy need to be made. For instance, how are relatively limited means to be applied? Roughly across-the-board? Or in extra-heavy doses at points presumed to be strategic? The issue alluded to involves "balanced growth" *versus* "unbalanced growth," the subject of the selection authored by Professor Baldwin.

Developmental effort along regional lines — the planning of developmental actions on a multi-country basis within particular regions — is a new and growing trend in underdeveloped countries. A final selection examines the regional approach to economic development — its rationale, application, problems, and implications for the United States.

13..... The Export Lag of Primary
Producing Countries*

RAGNAR NURKSE
Columbia University

. . . [As shown by a recent GATT report.[1]] world trade as a whole has . . . lagged behind the growth in world production. From 1928 to 1957 the proportional increase in world exports (58 per cent) has been only half as great as that of world production, which has increased by well over 100 per cent. Moreover, the available data for 1957 suggest that the exports of primary producing countries have lagged behind those of industrialized countries, though according to the quantum indices this lag appears only recently.

If next, however, we look at the exports of primary products by major categories, the rise of petroleum stands out far above everything else. Excluding petroleum, the quantum index of primary commodity exports in 1955 as compared with 1928 shows a percentage increase which is only half as great as that of the exports from industrial countries. The blame for this lies heavily on the group of nontropical foodstuffs.

There can be no doubt that *agricultural* products as a whole have been lagging far behind manufactured articles in the growth of international trade. The report cites figures (on p. 44) showing that from 1913 to 1955 the volume of world trade in agricultural products increased by only 27 per cent, in contrast to an 85 per cent expansion in that of manufactured goods. There is no comparable index for trade in mineral raw materials and fuels as a whole, but the indices . . . suggest that the trade expansion in minerals other than petroleum has not been exceptionally great.

Although the terms of trade of primary producing countries in general,

---

* Taken and adapted from "Trends in World Trade," *Kyklos*, Vol. XII, 1959, Fasc. 1, pp. 11–20.

[1] GATT, *Trends in International Trade* (A Report by a Panel of Experts), Geneva, October 1958.

after deteriorating sharply in the 1930's, have by now reverted to approximately the 1928 level, changes in price relationships nevertheless limit the significance of the quantum indices . . . in the appraisal of trends in trade. What has been the share of the non-industrial countries in the total value of world trade? The figures are presented in Table 1; and in view of the exceptional career of petroleum they are first shown with, and then without, the main oil exporting countries.

TABLE 1

Percentage Share of Non-Industrial Countries
in Value of World Trade*

	1928	*1937–38*	*1953*	*1955*	*1957*
Including oil-exporting countries:					
Exports	32.8	34.0	36.4	34.6	31.8
Imports	27.6	28.1	34.5	34.9	35.2
Excluding oil-exporting countries:					
Exports	31.2	31.2	30.4	27.8	25.0
Imports	26.5	27.8	30.7	31.0	30.7

* Excl. Soviet area.

Whether or not we include the oil exporters, the less developed countries are seen to have increased the share of their imports in the total value of world trade, from 1928 to 1953, though not in later years. On the export side, if the oil exporters are left out, there appears a very marked drop in the percentage share of the non-industrial countries between 1928 and 1957, though most of it has occurred since 1953. The inclusion of the oil countries greatly moderates this drop but does not entirely eliminate it, if we compare the latest year with 1928.

Why exclude the oil countries at all, if what we are after is the position in world trade of the less developed countries as a whole? It may seem invidious indeed to leave aside the group of countries that have done particularly well and then to point to a lag in exports of the other non-industrial countries, whose percentage share in world exports has certainly declined. If these others are lagging, we may be tempted to ask, echoing Marie-Antoinette: then why don't they export oil?

The writer hopes to be excused for his pedantry in pointing out that oil deposits are unevenly distributed gifts of nature, and that if a country does not happen to have any, it can do nothing in response to the rise in world demand for the favored commodity. The countries that have no petroleum to export (or have not found any yet, or refuse to let it be extracted — there are a few of those!) account for more than nine-tenths of the total population of the less developed countries.[2] In these circum-

---

[2] See the last E.C.E. report, *Economic Survey of Europe in 1957* (United Nations, Geneva, 1958), Chap. V, Chart I on p. 23, which indicates that in 1956 the *agricul-*

stances it does seem defensible to segregate the oil countries, as is done in the GATT report, and on occasion to exclude them from the trade accounts of the less developed countries as a group. What are the nine-tenths in this group to do if the expansion of world demand tends to pass them by? But first a word about the causes of the lag in their exports.

Let us run through a list of seven . . . factors, of which the first three, though covered in earlier GATT studies, are not mentioned in the present report:

(1) The rise in the share of the United States in world manufacturing output since 1928 seems to be one factor responsible for the lag of total world exports behind world production as well as for the lag in exports of non-industrial countries in particular. In short, production in the non-Soviet world has expanded heavily in an area relatively little dependent on trade in general and on imports of primary commodities in particular. Even if the United States had maintained its own, relatively low, ratio of imports to national production (in fact, this ratio declined), its increased weight in world output would have tended to reduce the ratio of world trade to world production. This may look like a mere statistical matter of weighting, but it is a point of substantive importance. The fact that industrial activity has increased particularly in an area with vast natural resources of its own is less favorable to the primary producing countries than if that increase had occurred elsewhere, for instance in Britain.

(2) In all industrial areas there has been a shift from light to heavy industries, especially to engineering and chemical industries, in which the raw material content of output is relatively low and the imported raw material content lower still. This very marked change in the composition of industrial output has tended to prevent the trade in raw materials from rising as much as world manufacturing activity.[3] Again we have here a change in "weighting" which would have caused a trade lag in primary products even if each industry had continued its methods of production unchanged.

(3) The establishment of textile industries in cotton growing areas is a specific factor responsible for a decline in demand for raw material imports into certain industrialized countries. It will be noticed that this shift, which has been much in evidence within the United States, need not at all involve a decline in raw cotton production in the cotton growing areas. Here is a fall in raw material exports directly due to industrialization in

---

tural exporters among the less developed countries outside the Soviet area accounted for about 87 per cent of the total population of underdeveloped countries, but only for some 67 per cent of the total value of exports shipped from these countries to the industrial areas. There are in addition some countries (Bolivia, Chile, some African territories, etc.) exporting minerals other than petroleum. The oil countries happen to be, on the whole, particularly sparsely populated.

[3] This point along with others in our list is stressed in the UN *World Economic Survey 1955* (New York, 1956), Chap. 2, as well as in *International Trade 1955* (GATT, Geneva, 1956).

economically backward areas, but it does not quite conform to the standard model in which industrialization draws away labor and other resources from primary production. This shift in the location of textile manufactures may to some extent be a "natural" development, just as it is within the United States. We may think of it as an example of the change noted under (2). Yet in part it has been merely a special instance of the next point on the list, namely:

(4) Industrialization policies in primary producing countries, which *may* undoubtedly cut down the *supply* of primary products on the world market, but which can also, in some cases plausibly, be interpreted as reactions to adverse changes in world *demand* for such products. Speaking of a group of eight "semi-industrialized" countries,[4] the GATT report attributes the lag in their primary commodity exports "not necessarily . . . to industrialization policies as such, but to certain forms of such policies which carry with them an anti-export bias" (pp. 24–26). . . .

It is true that "the protection of manufacturing industries in non-industrial countries may have diverted resources from primary production" (p. 42). But is it very likely to happen where labor is in excess supply or where the total labor force is rapidly increasing through growth of population? Have India's primary export staples — tea, pepper, jute, hides, indigo[5] — been hurt by domestic industrialization policies with an anti-export bias? Have they not rather suffered from a low income elasticity of foreign demand (for the first two) and from the development of substitutes (for the last three)?

(5) The low income elasticity of demand for some primary products is a well-known factor and is duly mentioned in the report, with special reference to the demand for foodstuffs, on which some interesting evidence is provided. It seems right to limit the concept to consumer goods, for when applied to raw materials it may come to include the effects of technical changes, which are a separate factor.

(6) In addition, agricultural protectionism in industrial countries, particularly in Western Europe, has adversely affected the demand for certain foodstuffs exported by less developed countries. . . .

(7) Last but by no means least, there have been important technological changes in industrial countries leading to the displacement of natural raw materials by synthetic and other man-made substitutes or

---

[4] The reviewer is not happy with this group, which includes a truly industrialized country like Australia, with only 17 per cent of its active population engaged in farming pursuits, side by side with a country like India, where 71 per cent of the people are in agriculture and only 11 per cent in industry (including handicrafts). The contrast between Argentina and Brazil, also included in this group, is only a little less marked. It is true that despite her high degree of industrialization Australia's exports consist mostly of primary products while India's exports are now largely manufactured or semi-manufactured goods. The reasons for this are interesting, but in any case it is clear that a country's exports need not reflect at all closely the character of its national economy.

[5] Indigo is one of the earliest examples of a natural product almost totally displaced by chemical substitutes.

at any rate to drastic economies in the use of crude materials. According to figures cited in the report (p. 43) the volume of "manufactured" — as opposed to natural — raw materials used in industrial areas has increased about seven-fold between 1938 and 1954. There is also some evidence about the total input of materials lagging behind the growth of manufacturing activity, though no attempt is made to determine to what extent this has been due to the change in composition of industrial output, which is already taken into account under (2) above.

Some readers may feel that a long list such as this, which even so is not complete, tends to over-explain the lag in trade in primary products. But if we keep in mind the extent to which world output, especially industrial output, has grown, and the fact that there are commodities other than petroleum that have greatly increased in demand (e.g. bauxite and uranium), the facts as presented in the GATT report appear roughly in line with expectations derived from a survey of causal factors.

It seems fairly clear that most of these factors operate on the side of demand for primary commodities emanating from the great industrial consumers, though limitations on the supply side in the producing countries have doubtless been effective in certain cases. Besides, there may be factors that cannot easily be classified as working on either the demand or the supply side. The writer sometimes feels a certain difficulty, for instance, in deciding whether to think of item (3) as a demand or a supply factor.

If, then, there is such a thing as a lag in exports of primary products from the less developed countries, and if we think we can explain the reasons for it, we still have to ask what, if any, significance it has. To put it as briefly as possible, its significance lies in reflecting the extent to which the present-day world economy provides — or fails to provide — the less developed countries with opportunities for growth through trade. A question might be raised, however, as to whether for this purpose it really matters very much whether the exports of the non-industrial countries are expanding faster or more slowly than those of the industrial areas. Since at the back of it all lies the concern over the growing discrepancies in average income levels, perhaps a better criterion is whether demand for the export staples of the less developed countries is expanding more or less in step with the growth of output and income in the world's industrial centers. The answer is that on this criterion, too, there has been a lag. It has been estimated that, since the late 1920's, exports from the primary producing countries to the United States and Western Europe have fallen from about 3½ per cent to rather less than 3 per cent of the combined gross national product of these two areas.[6] If again we exclude

---

[6] E.C.E., *Economic Survey of Europe in 1957* (op. cit.), Chap. IV, p. 6. Needless to say, such calculations are inevitably somewhat rough and hazardous because of the difficulties of combining the national income estimates of different countries and especially of measuring them in terms of a common monetary unit.

petroleum exports, the fall would be from about 3½ per cent to rather less than 2½ per cent. This means that over the last three decades most primary producing countries have suffered a marked shrinkage in the importance of their exports in relation to the output and income of the industrial world.

We have, however, fastened our attention, perhaps unduly, on the exports of the less developed countries and have so far almost entirely ignored the import side of the picture. . . . As was shown in Table 1, the imports of these countries now constitute a considerably higher share of world trade than they did 30 years ago. If the export and import sides of the picture are combined, as would seem necessary for any comprehensive appraisal, there can no longer be any question of a lag in the trade of non-industrial countries (if the lag is defined by comparison with the industrial countries' trade). The lag is on the export side only and is counterbalanced by a "lead" on the import side. When the Contracting Parties . . . spoke of "the failure of the trade of less developed countries to develop as rapidly as that of industrialized countries", it is now clear, from facts set out . . . , that the word "export" should have been inserted between "the" and "trade".

Does this mean that all is well after all? It would be rash to jump to any such conclusion. . . . The export lag is troublesome enough, even when matched by an "import lead" in the consolidated trade accounts. The wide discrepancy which has emerged between the export share and the import share of the less developed countries in world trade reflects the transfer of private investment and governmental aid to these countries, from the more prosperous industrial areas. Now, is not the export lag, just as much as the import lead, to be interpreted simply as part of the mechanism whereby the real transfer of this capital flow is accomplished? In the conventional theory of capital movements it has often been explained that the transfer can occur through a fall in the borrowing country's exports as well as a rise in its imports.

But this is merely the arithmetic, not necessarily the economics of the problem. A rise in a country's exports in response to growing external demand can be extremely useful as an *inducement* for private capital to flow into that country. Thus a recent reinterpretation of the Canadian borrowing experience prior to 1914 points to the growth of Canadian exports, which was "wrong" from the standpoint of transfer arithmetic, as the essential incentive and object of the capital inflow into Canada.[7] Conventional transfer theory has, sometimes deliberately, tended to abstract from the phenomena of economic growth. The 19th-century world economy centering on Great Britain's rapidly growing import needs provided splendid opportunities for growth through trade, at any rate to the "new" countries, and, on top of this, for growth through private inter-

[7] James C. Ingram, "Growth in Capacity and Canada's Balance of Payments," *American Economic Review*, March 1957.

national investment fundamentally if not directly induced by the growth in demand for primary products.

In the mid-twentieth century such conditions are no longer quite so characteristic — except in the remarkable case of petroleum, for which world demand has rapidly expanded and which consequently has been able to attract the lion's share of private international investment in spite of all the risks involved in international investment.

It would have been clearly more appropriate to the international economic circumstances of the less developed countries if the transfer of capital to them could have been effected chiefly through an increase in their import share rather than largely through a fall in their export share in world trade. They have a large and growing need for imports of capital goods, for giving productive employment to their growing populations and merely for keeping in step with the advance of the industrial areas, to say nothing about catching up with them. What is more, the fact that the expansion of their exports has been relatively sluggish has undoubtedly helped to cause a general lack of incentive for private international investment. In place of private capital movements, governmental grants and loans have been called upon to fill the gap. . . .

14..... Reasons for the Weakness of Primary Producing Countries*

RAÙL PREBISCH
Secretary-General, UNCTAD;
formerly with ECLA

The Factors Underlying Peripheral Weakness

Ever since the ECLA secretariat issued its first studies, the importance of the deterioration in the terms of trade has been stressed, and attempts have been made to analyse the forces that were tending to cause it. Perhaps because of the piecemeal nature of these explanations, our ideas have not always been correctly interpreted. It may be well to set them out afresh in the form of an elucidatory synthesis, since the deterioration, which has been so clearly marked in the last ten years,[1] may persist in future and have serious repercussions on economic development, even if there is no further decline from its present level.

The origin of this phenomenon is to be found in the relatively slow rate at which world demand for primary commodities grows in comparison with that for industrial products. The disparity need not necessarily bring about any decline in primary prices so long as production adjusts itself

---

* Taken and adapted from UN, *Towards a Dynamic Development Policy for Latin America,* New York, 1963, pp. 78–88.

[1] If the average terms of trade for the period 1950–54 are selected as a yardstick, the effect of the deterioration in 1955–60 can be estimated at 7,400 million dollars. In other words, more than 60 per cent of the annual increment in exports was wiped out by the deterioration. The net inflow of foreign capital in 1955–60 is estimated to have been about 7,700 million dollars (at 1950–54 prices), which means that the repercussions of the terms-of-trade position nullified the additional purchasing power achieved by the Latin American countries on the basis of that capital. It should be noted that relative prices were favourable in 1950–54, even though the level prevailing before the world depression was not fully recovered.

continually and easily to the tempo of demand. But for this to be possible, three conditions which are not observed in practice would have to be satisfied:

(a) The redundant proportion of the increment in the economically active population in primary activities would have to be displaced, so that production could expand at a rate not exceeding the rate of growth of demand. Other factors being equal, the more productivity in primary activities was stepped up, the more displacement would have to be intensified;

(b) The manpower thus displaced would have to be employed in industry and other labour-absorbing activities . . . ; and

(c) The manpower in question would have to be absorbed quickly and completely enough for the real wages of workers in primary activities to rise and advantage to be taken of the increment in the productivity of the latter.

As a rule, the wage level in primary activities is lower than in urban labour-absorbing activities. If absorption is intensive, wages in primary production may mount to the urban level, which will rise little by little in keeping with the increase in productivity in labour-absorbing activities. Beyond this level, the increment in primary productivity will not be retained by the wage increase, even if the three conditions stipulated above are complied with.

If they are not, and the level of wages in primary activities fails to rise to the extent permitted by the increase in productivity, the latter will be transmuted into a profit gain and will go to stimulate the growth of production beyond the tempo imposed by the growth of demand, thereby forcing down the relative prices of primary commodities as compared with those of industrial goods.

The phenomenon of deterioration is to be found as much in primary production for domestic consumption as in production for export. In the former case, it simply means that the benefits of the increase in productivity are transferred internally. In the latter, there is a loss of income which the expansion in the volume of export trade can do relatively little to offset in comparison with the improvement that would have to take place in order to keep pace with demand.

To put the idea in a nutshell, deterioration is caused by the lack of dynamism in development, which hinders or precludes absorption of the surplus manpower resulting from the sluggish growth of demand and higher productivity in primary activities. The same factor is instrumental in preventing the wages of workers in primary activities from rising on a par with the increase in productivity, and to the extent that they fail to do so, primary production loses all or part of the benefits of its technical progress.

Such is the nature of the deterioration phenomenon. It presupposes that the rate of expansion of production may outstrip that imposed by the relatively slow growth of demand, on the basis of availability of land and other natural resources and of manpower. Otherwise, if production were to lag behind demand, relative prices would tend to improve. Whether this improvement is entirely expressed in terms of an increase in income from the land or is also shared to some extent by the workers depends — as in the former case — on the effect produced by labour absorption in urban activities on the real level of wages in primary production.

What grounds are there for hoping that conditions favouring an improvement in the terms of trade will prevail during these next ten or fifteen years that will be decisive for Latin America's economic development? There are no visible signs that they will. On the contrary, the effort to quicken the slow growth of exports is becoming increasingly apparent in both the Latin American countries and the other countries in process of development that are competing with them in respect of production. And it is natural that in order to accomplish this aim efforts should be made to increase productivity. Moreover, these efforts will have to be extended to the whole of agricultural production if it is to meet the increasing claims of domestic demand. The manpower thus displaced by technical progress will present a serious absorption problem which, if not solved, will curb the rise in wages that technical progress itself might make possible in primary export activities.

The Impossibility of Treating the Deterioration as an Isolated Problem

The absorption problem is not confined to particular producer countries but is common to all alike. If one country succeeds in making development sufficiently dynamic and creating suitable conditions for the retention of the benefits of technical progress in primary activities through a rise in wages, this does not mean that they can actually be retained, since unless other producer countries succeed in remedying the lack of dynamism also, their production will continue to expand at a rate faster than that dictated by the income-elasticity of demand, and relative prices will decline. The first country will obviously have to follow the same trend in order to be able to compete on the world market. And to the extent that wages in its primary activities have undergone an improvement it will have to resort to subsidizing exports or devaluating the currency; in either case it will inevitably lose all or part of the fruits of its technical progress.

By protection, of course, the level of nominal wages can be raised in conjunction with internal prices. This would contribute towards the retention of the benefits in question, provided that adequate manpower-absorption took place. But in this case again the other competitors would have to be in a position to do the same in order to prevent deterioration. And this is not a state of affairs that occurs in practice.

The same applies to taxes. If the State were to tax exports commensurately with the increase in productivity in export activities, the benefits could be retained just as if wages had been raised; but all the producer countries would have to adopt the same measure.

Thus, it is clear that the problem of deterioration will not solve itself of its own accord, so long as the developing countries fail to remedy their dynamic weakness — which will take a very long time — or if difficulties supervene that cannot be dealt with by technical advances in the development of primary production.

Differences Between Central and Peripheral Countries

So far the phenomenon of deterioration has been considered in relation to the peripheral countries. The next question is whether forces are not also to be found in the great centres whereby the fruits of their technical progress tend to be shifted abroad. It may be argued that such transfers do, in fact, take place, and that any deterioration in the terms of trade for the export activities of the peripheral countries is due to the fact that technical progress there has been more marked than in the industrial export activities of the great centres.[2] In other words, the behaviour of the terms of trade in the past was attributable to the relative increase in productivity as between primary commodities and industrial goods.

This argument might be admissible in a world in which every country had reached the same stage of development, but not while the disparities that are now apparent between the great centres and the peripheral countries still persist. From the standpoint of the terms of trade, the fundamental differences are as follows.

First and foremost, the essentially industrial nature of exports from the great centres. Industrial goods usually have a very high income-elasticity of demand, and as soon as demand for certain products shows signs of becoming saturated with the passage of time, new products or new types

[2] This seems to have been the argument put forward by Lincoln Gordon, economist and United States Ambassador to Brazil, in his speech to the Brazilian National Economic Council on 29 January 1963, when he stated: "There have long been conflicting general theories about inherent long-range trends in the terms of trade. One old theory, now discredited, held that agricultural prices were bound to improve in relation to industrial prices because an increasing world population on a limited surface of arable land would be constantly bidding up food prices, whereas industrial output was indefinitely expansible. This disregarded the effects of the technological advance in agriculture, which have increased productivity even more rapidly than in industry, at least in the free world. For some years, the ECLA secretariat was arguing the contrary thesis, namely that the long-term trend was necessarily unfavourable to agriculture, but this argument was based largely on nineteenth-century British data which did not allow for reductions in shipping costs or for inherent difficulties in any long-term measurement of comparative prices for manufactured goods. The nature of industrial products changes completely from decade to decade as new inventions are made, and they are also subject to constant improvements in quality. As a result, most serious scholars today are very skeptical as to the validity of any long-term generalizations about inherent trends in the terms of trade." *FYI News Digest*, United States Information Service, 63/7, Santiago, Chile, 4 April 1963.

of existing products appear which act as a continual stimulus to industrial demand. Labour is displaced from one industry to another, but industrial activity as a whole absorbs an increasing proportion of the increment in the economically active population, at least up to a certain limit, beyond which this function is progressively transferred to other labour-absorbing activities. In primary production the reverse takes place; demand for existing products is relatively slow in expanding, and new products or new varieties of products do not appear except in rare instances. Even when this occurs, it does not take place on a large enough scale to counteract the tendency of the labour force to shift to urban activities.

The second basic disparity is that in the big industrial countries the absorption of labour from primary production and other labour-expelling activities has made great strides, a relatively small proportion of the economically active population remaining in those activities. For instance, the proportion in agriculture is 7 per cent in the United States and about 15 per cent in the major industrialized countries of Western Europe. This is highly significant, since the same increment in productivity in Latin American agriculture — where the average proportion is 45 per cent — represents a relatively much greater displacement of labour than in the advanced centres. If the large proportion of the economically active population is still to be found in artisan activities and unskilled personal services is also taken into account, together with its tendency to shift to labour-absorbing activities, the full extent of the difference will be grasped. To put it another way, in the great centres a large proportion of the economically active population is found in the labour-absorbing activities and a very small proportion is found in those that are labour-expelling, while the reverse occurs in the peripheral countries.

Consequently, the pressure exerted by the displaced population on the level of wages in the labour-absorbing activities is relatively weak in the advanced centres and relatively heavy in the countries on the periphery. This is undoubtedly one of the reasons why trade unions in the former have acquired an increasing ability to keep wages rising on a par with or even faster than the increase in productivity. What is more, in countries which are also manifestly lacking in dynamic force, the trade unions succeed in raising the level of wages in spite of unemployment.

In the peripheral countries, on the other hand, the relatively strong pressure applied by labour that is displaced or seeks to move elsewhere is a heavy handicap to trade union action. In so far as Latin America is concerned, it is only in exceptional cases that the trade unions have succeeded in getting wages raised in certain export activities irrespective of the general level in the region. But even if trade union action were effective in the case of export activities by virtue of the increase in productivity and notwithstanding the dynamic weakness of the economy, the real wage increments could not be maintained for long unless they were matched by increments in other exporter countries that had likewise stepped up their productivity.

In other words, it is not the relative differences in productivity increments in the primary export activities of the peripheral countries as
compared with industrial activities in the great centres that are responsible
for the trend of the terms of trade. Generally speaking, it is rather the
differences between productivity in the centres, on the one hand, and in
the peripheral countries, on the other, that have not been absorbed by
the respective increases in wage rates. The ability to raise wages is very
marked in the great centres, at least to the extent that the productivity of
industrial activities improves, and only those industries whose productivity increment is above the average tend to transfer the balance abroad.
In the peripheral countries, on the contrary, the fact that it is difficult to
raise wages in export activities — and primary production in general —
means that they are constantly in danger of losing all or part of the
average productivity increment in the activities concerned. Moreover,
if technical progress has been greater in some countries than in others,
the decline in prices brought about by the former may deprive the latter
of a larger proportion of income than would correspond to their particular
productivity increment.

The favourable trend of the terms of trade in the distant past may have
been due to the fact that, as the capacity of the industrial centres to raise
the level of wages was then far less pronounced, the course of events
was much the same as that now occurring in the peripheral countries.
There may also have been difficulties in increasing primary production,
whereas later this became easier because of the rise in productivity as a
result of land reclamation and the utilization of new natural resources, as
well as of improved transport facilities.

Deterioration in the Great Industrial Centres

At all events, everything would seem to suggest that this inherent in-
capacity of the peripheral regions to retain the benefits of their technical
progress will persist for a long time yet. The very situation of agricultural
production in the large industrial centres, despite the advanced stage of
development reached, affords striking evidence of this fact. There too
relative prices are following a downward trend, which is not incompatible
with the tendency of industrial wages to appropriate the increases in
productivity to the detriment of the primary activities.

In the great centres no one has attempted to deny the existence of this
trend, or to belittle its importance on the grounds that have been adduced
in connexion with the corresponding deterioration in the peripheral regions, namely, that statistics do not reflect the improvement in the quality
of industrial products, or that the ratio cannot be accurately calculated on
the basis of price indices. Perhaps this is because the reasons for the
decline have become obvious. In the United States a technological
revolution has taken place in agriculture which is now spreading to

Western Europe, with similar consequences; there too the tempo of production is tending to outstrip the rate of growth of demand. A further population shift from the rural areas would be necessary — small as is the proportion of the active population still living there — and people are unwilling to migrate to the towns; they do not want to abandon their land, even in countries where the intensive absorption of manpower in industry and other activities is attracting labour from abroad.

To defend the internal terms of trade, recourse is had to various procedures: in the United States, to internal support prices which maintain a variable parity with the prices of the industrial goods purchased by agricultural workers, and to subsidies for exports to the internal market; in Western Europe, to the tightening of restrictions on imports of agricultural commodities, as a means of broadening the market for the region's own production and supporting high internal prices. Another possibility contemplated is that of subsidizing exports to the world market if and when surpluses exist.

These measures to defend agricultural relative prices on the home market — understandable as they are from the standpoint of the great centres — imply a still further aggravation of the consequences of the slow growth of demand for agricultural exports from the peripheral countries. However, they have the merit of affording a concrete demonstration of the importance attached by the world centres to the decline in the prices of primary commodities, and at the same time indicate a possible way of solving the problem at the international level.

Possibility of International Retransfer of Income

Strictly speaking, what do these forms of intervention signify? Simply the recognition that market forces do not provide an equitable solution for the problem in question. The technical progress achieved in industrial activities in the world centres had left agricultural production lagging in the rear. But as agriculture manages to make up its leeway, the effects of its technical progress tend to be passed on to the rest of the community. The solution is therefore of a moral and political character: to retransfer to agricultural producers whatever income they may have lost through the operation of market forces whose action has been preventing the levelling-up of their income with that of the urban sectors. In the long run, every income redistribution measure is essentially of this nature.

Viewed from this angle, the process of remedying the deterioration of the terms of trade in the peripheral countries becomes one vast problem of international redistribution of income, as a measure dictated not only by justice, but by the great policy design of helping the developing countries to cure their congenital weakness, acquire the ability to retain the benefits of their technical progress and accelerate their economic and social development. But this involves something more than international co-operation. It would be impossible to adduce valid arguments based on international equity unless a serious effort were made to tackle the problem of internal equity, and the savings potential of the higher income groups were thoroughly exploited with the same end in view — that of speeding up the rate of development.

Consequently, the international retransfer of income to compensate the peripheral countries for the deterioration of their terms of trade could not be an automatic measure, but would have to be closely linked to their development plans, and to the economic and social effectiveness of the plans in question.

This idea of retransfer really represents the more detailed working out of a suggestion put forward in 1954 at the Quintandinha session. In the report presented by the ECLA secretariat[3] at the request of OAS, the agency sponsoring the conference, it was proposed that the countries which were consumers of primary commodities might establish an import duty equivalent in amount to the decrease in prices, and that the revenue accruing from this duty should be passed back to the producer countries.

The results of a measure of this kind would be similar to those that might be obtained by the producer countries if they reached agreements to defend their prices not only against periodical fluctuations, but also against a persistent downward trend. The complexity of such procedures is undeniable, as is the fact that if prices were stabilized at relatively high levels, the expansion of production would be encouraged, with the consequent aggravation of the price decline. . . .

In any case, the retransfer of income to primary-producing countries represents a very simple solution, since the resultant inflow of international resources would be used to increase capital formation, as a means of helping to remedy the lack of dynamism in the development process. Investment in rural areas would, of course, have to be assigned a high priority. The retransferred income would therefore not be used to compensate the decline in internal prices, except when they had reached a level so critically low as to discourage production.

The scope of this idea should be clearly understood. Most of the rural workers fall within that half of the Latin American population whose income levels are extremely low. Would the application of international resources to economic development rather than to prices be effected at the expense of the effort to improve their standard of living? Obviously not. This latter aim would be served, however, by direct action to influence workers' income levels rather than prices, for export activities constitute only a fraction of the whole group of primary activities, and the income of workers employed in them could not be higher — save in exceptional cases — than the level prevailing in the primary activities in general. As has already been shown, the solution of this problem lies in

[3] See *International Co-operation in a Latin American Development Policy*, op. cit.

remedying the lack of dynamism in the development process, without prejudice to the pursuit of a wage policy reflecting the primary activities' increase in productivity. It is true that competition from other countries which did not follow a similar policy would adversely affect export prices in the way described elsewhere. Critical situations would thus arise, as a result of which part of the international resources would have to be used for supporting a domestic price level commensurate with the increase in the real income of rural workers. We would stress that these are general ideas rather than concrete suggestions, and that they are presented here as a basis for the discussion of this vital problem of relative prices.

External Bottleneck and Contribution of International Resources

The present chapter . . . has been devoted to an explanation of the persistent trend towards an external bottleneck in the Latin American countries and the essential need to combat it on two convergent fronts: (a) by promoting industrial exports to the rest of the world, especially to the great centres, without neglecting to encourage traditional exports to existing and new markets; and (b) by safeguarding the terms of trade. . . .

The contribution of international resources is not in itself an alternative solution to the bottleneck problem. Such resources are certainly of vital importance, but as a means of enabling structural changes to be introduced in foreign trade so that this problem can be attacked at the root. Unless the causes of the situation are thus extirpated, external contributions will be required indefinitely and in increasing volume.

The consequences of this steady piling-up of external debt, under the present trade régime, have already made themselves manifest. The slow growth of exports and the downward trend of prices on the one hand, and the increasing service payments on foreign capital on the other, are progressively weakening the capacity to import, vis-à-vis the growing import requirements in respect of essential goods which are needed without delay and for which it is increasingly difficult to substitute domestic production.

A more and more serious incompatibility between services and imports thus arises, and is frequently aggravated by the shortness of loan maturity periods, which entails excessively heavy amortization payments.[4] And as imports cannot easily be reduced, the only way out is to obtain further international resources to defray service payments, even when such contributions are not absolutely essential to fill the gaps in external capital

---

[4] It would be desirable to overhaul this burdensome amortization system — as is already being done in some cases — in order to secure some immediate relief in respect of external payments.

formation. What can prevent the recurrence of this phenomenon if the structure of foreign trade is not remodelled?

Certainly not exhortations to financial good conduct; this will no longer suffice as a preventive. It might have been enough in the nineteenth century. There was then a clear and logical link between externally-geared development and foreign loans and investment. The latter were primarily applied, in one way or another, to the expansion of exports. And this expansion made it relatively easy to defray the similarly growing service payments, without the necessity for international contributions to be increased, as is now the case for reasons of external disequilibrium and shortage of capital. What is more, in several instances the expansion of exports permitted the gradual repatriation of the external capital received, so that the burden of services was lightened. If difficulties supervened, they were due to financial ill-conduct, generally internal, but also, in some instances, external, for there was a little of everything in those vanished days.

Within the logic of externally-geared development, the granting of financial favours had no place. Foreign loans and investment were a straightforward expression of mutual interest. Nor did the connotation of "assistance" exist on which emphasis is naturally laid during the periodical development crises. Loan operations in this way often become politically vulnerable in certain respects, both for the givers of the loans and for the receivers.

Basically, the problem does not lie in inability to meet service payments — which might increase without representing an intolerable burden — but in the transfer difficulties which the bottleneck creates. Longer-term loans and a rapid expansion of exports would also make the burden in question very easy to carry, as far as external accounts were concerned. There would then be plenty of scope for good advice to bear fruit; and moreover, a deaf ear could be turned to those admonitions — uttered from a monetary standpoint — which often suggest a false dilemma in relation to stability and development, for if the external sector were restored to prosperity in a new pattern very different from that at present followed, our countries would be released from harassing pressures, and would acquire the essential freedom of choice. And only when the structural obstacles that now make choice inevitable had been surmounted, would the alternatives present themselves in their proper terms: external co-operation to accelerate development, or a more thoroughgoing internal effort to do so.

15..... The Stages of Economic Growth*

W. W. ROSTOW

*Massachusetts Institute of Technology
and U.S. Government*

It is possible to identify all societies, in their economic dimensions, as lying within one of five categories: the traditional society, the preconditions for take-off, the take-off, the drive to maturity, and the age of high mass-consumption.

The Traditional Society

First, the traditional society. A traditional society is one whose structure is developed within limited production functions, based on pre-Newtonian science and technology, and on pre-Newtonian attitudes towards the physical world. Newton is here used as a symbol for that watershed in history when men came widely to believe that the external world was subject to a few knowable laws, and was systematically capable of productive manipulation.

The conception of the traditional society is, however, in no sense static; and it would not exclude increases in output. Acreage could be expanded; some *ad hoc* technical innovations, often highly productive innovations, could be introduced in trade, industry and agriculture; productivity could rise with, for example, the improvement of irrigation works or the discovery and diffusion of a new crop. But the central fact about the traditional society was that a ceiling existed on the level of attainable output per head. This ceiling resulted from the fact that the potentialities which flow from modern science and technology were either not available or not regularly and systematically applied.

* Taken and adapted from *The Stages of Economic Growth*, Cambridge: Cambridge University Press, 1960, pp. 4–11.

Both in the longer past and in recent times the story of traditional societies was thus a story of endless change. The area and volume of trade within them and between them fluctuated, for example, with the degree of political and social turbulence, the efficiency of central rule, the upkeep of the roads. Population — and, within limits, the level of life — rose and fell not only with the sequence of the harvests, but with the incidence of war and of plague. Varying degrees of manufacture developed; but, as in agriculture, the level of productivity was limited by the inaccessibility of modern science, its applications, and its frame of mind.

Generally speaking, these societies, because of the limitation on productivity, had to devote a very high proportion of their resources to agriculture; and flowing from the agricultural system there was an hierarchical social structure, with relatively narrow scope — but some scope — for vertical mobility. Family and clan connections played a large role in social organization. The value system of these societies was generally geared to what might be called a long-run fatalism; that is, the assumption that the range of possibilities open to one's grandchildren would be just about what it had been for one's grandparents. But this long-run fatalism by no means excluded the short-run option that, within a considerable range, it was possible and legitimate for the individual to strive to improve his lot, within his lifetime. In Chinese villages, for example, there was an endless struggle to acquire or to avoid losing land, yielding a situation where land rarely remained within the same family for a century.

Although central political rule — in one form or another — often existed in traditional societies, transcending the relatively self-sufficient regions, the centre of gravity of political power generally lay in the regions, in the hands of those who owned or controlled the land. The landowner maintained fluctuating but usually profound influence over such central political power as existed, backed by its entourage of civil servants and soldiers, imbued with attitudes and controlled by interests transcending the regions.

In terms of history then, with the phrase "traditional society" we are grouping the whole pre-Newtonian world: the dynasties in China; the civilization of the Middle East and the Mediterranean; the world of medieval Europe. And to them we add the post-Newtonian societies which, for a time, remained untouched or unmoved by man's new capability for regularly manipulating his environment to his economic advantage.

To place these infinitely various, changing societies in a single category, on the ground that they all shared a ceiling on the productivity of their economic techniques, is to say very little indeed. But we are, after all, merely clearing the way in order to get at . . . the post-traditional societies, in which each of the major characteristics of the traditional society was altered in such ways as to permit regular growth: its politics, social structure, and (to a degree) its values, as well as its economy.

The Preconditions for Take-Off

The second stage of growth embraces societies in the process of transition; that is, the period when the preconditions for take-off are developed; for it takes time to transform a traditional society in the ways necessary for it to exploit the fruits of modern science, to fend off diminishing returns, and thus to enjoy the blessings and choices opened up by the march of compound interest.

The preconditions for take-off were initially developed, in a clearly marked way, in Western Europe of the late seventeenth and early eighteenth centuries as the insights of modern science began to be translated into new production functions in both agriculture and industry, in a setting given dynamism by the lateral expansion of world markets and the international competition for them. But all that lies behind the break-up of the Middle Ages is relevant to the creation of the preconditions for take-off in Western Europe. Among the Western European states, Britain, favoured by geography, natural resources, trading possibilities, social and political structure, was the first to develop fully the preconditions for take-off.

The more general case in modern history, however, saw the stage of preconditions arise not endogenously but from some external intrusion by more advanced societies. These invasions — literal or figurative — shocked the traditional society and began or hastened its undoing; but they also set in motion ideas and sentiments which initiated the process by which a modern alternative to the traditional society was constructed out of the old culture.

The idea spreads not merely that economic progress is possible, but that economic progress is a necessary condition for some other purpose, judged to be good: be it national dignity, private profit, the general welfare, or a better life for the children. Education, for some at least, broadens and changes to suit the needs of modern economic activity. New types of enterprising men come forward — in the private economy, in government, or both — willing to mobilize savings and to take risks in pursuit of profit or modernization. Banks and other institutions for mobilizing capital appear. Investment increases, notably in transport, communications, and in raw materials in which other nations may have an economic interest. The scope of commerce, internal and external, widens. And, here and there, modern manufacturing enterprise appears, using the new methods. But all this activity proceeds at a limited pace within an economy and a society still mainly characterized by traditional low-productivity methods, by the old social structure and values, and by the regionally based political institutions that developed in conjunction with them.

In many recent cases, for example, the traditional society persisted side by side with modern economic activities, conducted for limited economic purposes by a colonial or quasi-colonial power.

Although the period of transition — between the traditional society and the take-off — saw major changes in both the economy itself and in the balance of social values, a decisive feature was often political. Politically, the building of an effective centralized national state — on the basis of coalitions touched with a new nationalism, in opposition to the traditional landed regional interests, the colonial power, or both, was a decisive aspect of the preconditions period; and it was, almost universally, a necessary condition for take-off. . . .

The Take-Off

We come now to the great watershed in the life of modern societies: the third stage in this sequence, the take-off. The take-off is the interval when the old blocks and resistances to steady growth are finally overcome. The forces making for economic progress, which yielded limited bursts and enclaves of modern activity, expand and come to dominate the society. Growth becomes its normal condition. Compound interest becomes built, as it were, into its habits and institutional structure.

In Britain and the well-endowed parts of the world populated substantially from Britain (the United States, Canada, etc.) the proximate stimulus for take-off was mainly (but not wholly) technological. In the more general case, the take-off awaited not only the build-up of social overhead capital and a surge of technological development in industry and agriculture, but also the emergence to political power of a group prepared to regard the modernization of the economy as serious, high-order political business.

During the take-off, the rate of effective investment and savings may rise from, say, 5% of the national income to 10% or more; although where heavy social overhead capital investment was required to create the technical preconditions for take-off the investment rate in the preconditions period could be higher than 5%, as, for example, in Canada before the 1890's and Argentina before 1914. In such cases capital imports usually formed a high proportion of total investment in the preconditions period and sometimes even during the take-off itself, as in Russia and Canada during their pre-1914 railway booms.

During the take-off new industries expand rapidly, yielding profits a large proportion of which are reinvested in new plant; and these new industries, in turn, stimulate, through their rapidly expanding requirement for factory workers, the services to support them, and for other manufactured goods, a further expansion in urban areas and in other modern industrial plants. The whole process of expansion in the modern sector yields an increase of income in the hands of those who not only save at high rates but place their savings at the disposal of those engaged in modern sector activities. The new class of entrepreneurs expands; and it directs the enlarging flows of investment in the private sector. The economy exploits hitherto unused natural resources and methods of production.

New techniques spread in agriculture as well as industry, as agriculture is commercialized, and increasing numbers of farmers are prepared to accept the new methods and the deep changes they bring to ways of life. The revolutionary changes in agricultural productivity are an essential condition for successful take-off; for modernization of a society increases radically its bill for agricultural products. In a decade or two both the basic structure of the economy and the social and political structure of the society are transformed in such a way that a steady rate of growth can be, thereafter, regularly sustained.

. . . [One] can approximately allocate the take-off of Britain to the two decades after 1783; France and the United States to the several decades preceding 1860; Germany, the third quarter of the nineteenth century; Japan, the fourth quarter of the nineteenth century; Russia and Canada the quarter-century or so preceding 1914; while during the 1950's India and China have, in quite different ways, launched their respective take-offs.

The Drive to Maturity

After take-off there follows a long interval of sustained if fluctuating progress, as the now regularly growing economy drives to extend modern technology over the whole front of its economic activity. Some 10–20% of the national income is steadily invested, permitting output regularly to outstrip the increase in population. The make-up of the economy changes unceasingly as technique improves, new industries accelerate, older industries level off. The economy finds its place in the international economy: goods formerly imported are produced at home; new import requirements develop, and new export commodities to match them. The society makes such terms as it will with the requirements of modern efficient production, balancing off the new against the older values and institutions, or revising the latter in such ways as to support rather than to retard the growth process.

Some sixty years after take-off begins (say, forty years after the end of take-off) what may be called maturity is generally attained. The economy, focused during the take-off around a relatively narrow complex of industry and technology, has extended its range into more refined and technologically often more complex processes; for example, there may be a shift in focus from the coal, iron, and heavy engineering industries of the railway phase to machine-tools, chemicals, and electrical equipment. This, for example, was the transition through which Germany, Britain, France, and the United States had passed by the end of the nineteenth century or shortly thereafter. But there are other sectoral patterns which have been followed in the sequence from take-off to maturity. . . .

Formally, we can define maturity as the stage in which an economy demonstrates the capacity to move beyond the original industries which powered its take-off and to absorb and to apply efficiently over a very wide range of its resources — if not the whole range — the most advanced fruits of (then) modern technology. This is the stage in which an economy demonstrates that it has the technological and entrepreneurial skills to produce not everything, but anything that it chooses to produce. It may lack (like contemporary Sweden and Switzerland, for example) the raw materials or other supply conditions required to produce a given type of output economically; but its dependence is a matter of economic choice or political priority rather than a technological or institutional necessity.

Historically, it would appear that something like sixty years was required to move a society from the beginning of take-off to maturity. Analytically the explanation for some such interval may lie in the powerful arithmetic of compound interest applied to the capital stock, combined with the broader consequences for a society's ability to absorb modern technology of three successive generations living under a regime where growth is the normal condition. But, clearly, no dogmatism is justified about the exact length of the interval from take-off to maturity.

The Age of High Mass-Consumption

We come now to the age of high mass-consumption, where, in time, the leading sectors shift towards durable consumers' goods and services: a phase from which Americans are beginning to emerge; whose not unequivocal joys Western Europe and Japan are beginning energetically to probe; and with which Soviet society is engaged in an uneasy flirtation.

As societies achieved maturity in the twentieth century two things happened: real income per head rose to a point where a large number of persons gained a command over consumption which transcended basic food, shelter, and clothing; and the structure of the working force changed in ways which increased not only the proportion of urban to total population, but also the proportion of the population working in offices or in skilled factory jobs — aware of and anxious to acquire the consumption fruits of a mature economy.

In addition to these economic changes, the society ceased to accept the further extension of modern technology as an overriding objective. It is in this post-maturity stage, for example, that, through the political process, Western societies have chosen to allocate increased resources to social welfare and security. The emergence of the welfare state is one manifestation of a society's moving beyond technical maturity; but it is also at this stage that resources tend increasingly to be directed to the production of consumers' durables and to the diffusion of services on a mass basis, if consumers' sovereignty reigns. The sewing-machine, the bicycle, and then the various electric-powered household gadgets were gradually diffused. Historically, however, the decisive element has been the cheap mass automobile with its quite revolutionary effects — social as well as economic — on the life and expectations of society.

For the United States, the turning point was, perhaps, Henry Ford's moving assembly line of 1913–14; but it was in the 1920's, and again in the post-war decade, 1946–56, that this stage of growth was pressed to, virtually, its logical conclusion. In the 1950's Western Europe and Japan appear to have fully entered this phase, accounting substantially for a momentum in their economies quite unexpected in the immediate post-war years. The Soviet Union is technically ready for this stage, and, by every sign, its citizens hunger for it; but Communist leaders face difficult political and social problems of adjustment if this stage is launched.

16..... Planning for Development*

ALBERT WATERSTON
World Bank

In an attempt to determine where, when, how, and why development planning has been successful, a small group within the World Bank has since 1958 been examining data for countries throughout the world — over 100 countries, developed and less developed, in Africa, Asia, Europe, and the Americas, including socialized as well as mixed-economy countries. Out of this great assemblage of raw material, a comprehensive comparative study was published in December 1965.[1] Those who are interested in development planning are now able to consider not only how it *might* be done but how in fact it *has* been done.

While countries about to start planning their development can learn much from the planning experience of other countries, few make use of this experience: this is the first lesson of the study. The reason, in part, is that the experience of other countries is not known; but mostly, it is because countries will not be guided by the experience of other countries, since they consider their own political, economic, and social conditions to be unique.

Yet the study reveals that most countries not only encounter the same planning problems; they make the same mistakes. They frequently confuse the mere formulation of a plan with planning, fail to take adequate account of what can be done, and hence plan for less than is realistic in some sectors and more than is realistic in others. They have their planners take on extraneous tasks which divert them from planning, set up unsuitable planning machinery, set it up in the wrong places, and so forth.

* Taken and adapted from "A Hard Look at Development Planning," in IMF-IBRD, *The Fund and Bank Review,* June 1966, pp. 85–91.

[1] Albert Waterston, *Development Planning: Lessons of Experience* (Baltimore, 1965).

116

Plans Versus Planning

Planning has undoubtedly promoted development in many countries. But postwar history reveals that there have been many more failures than successes in carrying out development plans. Indeed, among developing nations with some kind of market economy and a sizable private sector, only one or two countries seem to have been consistently successful in carrying out plans.

Except for short periods, most countries have failed to realize even modest income and output targets. What is even more disturbing, the situation seems to be worsening instead of improving. In Asia, where countries' experience with planning has been greater than that in any other region, the rates of growth in the early 1960's fell short not only of targets but even of the growth rates of the 1950's. The situation is not very different in the other continents.

While most countries with development plans have not succeeded in carrying them out, some countries without national development plans or national planning agencies have been developing rapidly. For example, Mexico between 1940 and 1955, when it had no planning agency or plan (and even until now, since in fact it has no plan to which the Government adheres), maintained an annual average rate of growth of 5–6 per cent. Israel, which had no plan before 1961 and still does not have one which the Government follows, has been able to maintain an even higher growth rate. Puerto Rico has become a showcase of development without benefit of a development plan. And among the more developed countries, Germany, without plans, has increased income and output at least as rapidly as France with plans.

It could be contended — and I do contend — that if these countries had had development plans they might have done even better. But the fact is that a country can develop with or without a plan.

A development *plan*, however, is not the same as development *planning*. Planning as a process involves the application of a rational system of choices among feasible courses of investment and other development possibilities based on a consideration of economic and social costs and benefits. These may or may not be put into writing in a "plan." Those who equate a development plan with development planning — and they are many — confuse what should be a product of the planning process with the process itself. A plan can play an important part in the planning process when it makes explicit the basis and rationale for planning policies and measures. But if a plan is prepared before the process has begun in earnest or is unable itself to generate the process, it is likely to have little significance for development.

Importance of the Political Factor

Why are so few development plans carried out? Lack of government support is the prime reason. This lack of support manifests itself in many ways, among them the failure to maintain the discipline implied in plans and the failure to adopt appropriate policies for carrying them out. . . .

Economic Incentives

Until the political leaders of a nation become committed to development, the people themselves are unlikely to show much interest. If a country's leaders make development one of their central concerns, experience shows that the people's interest can be obtained. But except on occasion — for example, during or immediately after a war or other catastrophe or upheaval — interest is not likely to be obtained through appeals to their patriotism, devotion to abstract ideals or altruism, or panegyrics about individual or group accomplishments. Direct government controls over economic activity, or threats of imprisonment or other punishment, are also generally ineffective.

The evidence teaches that the best long-run method of getting people to act in such a way as to achieve plan objectives is to make it profitable for them. Where governments have replaced administrative controls by economic incentives, the result has usually been accelerated economic activity. . . .

Separation of Plan Formulation from Implementation

Economic development is so difficult that, if political leaders are not very deeply committed to it, the plans which they approve are not carried out because no provision is made for carrying them out. Prime Minister Jawaharlal Nehru of India, who as Chairman of the Indian Planning Commission showed an uncommon grasp of planning problems, once pointedly remarked, "We in the Planning Commission and others concerned have grown more experienced and more expert in planning. But the real question is not planning, but implementing the Plan. . . . I fear we are not quite so expert at implementation as at planning. . . ." This statement is notable not only because it recognizes — correctly I think — that the problems of plan implementation are more difficult than those of plan formulation, but also because it distinguishes — wrongly I believe — "planning" from "implementation."

The word "planning" is often used, as it was by Prime Minister Nehru, to refer to the formulation of plans, but not to their implementation. The conceptual separation of "planning" from "implementation" is more than a question of semantics: it is symbolic of an attitude which is unfortunately prevalent among planners. Experience shows that nothing hampers the success of development plans more than the separation of plan formulation from provision for implementation. Planning cannot leave off where plan formulation ends and action to execute a plan begins. Every target must be accompanied by policies and measures which have been devised specifically to fulfill it; otherwise it becomes only a forecast or projection. . . .

Discounting Overambitious Plan Targets

A planner may not be able to do much about a government's administrative inefficiency and its lack of political commitment or will to develop. But if in preparing his plans he ignores these critical factors, which together constitute the main limitations on the ability of most less developed countries to realize their economic possibilities, he ends up by separating his activities and the plans he formulates from the real world that has its being outside of national planning agencies.

This is precisely what happens in many less developed countries. National development plans are based on a country's economic potentialities or its needs as determined by population growth, and are little related to the country's administrative capacity, or to the government's will, to carry them out. In these countries, plans are not so much blueprints as hortatory instruments. It can hardly be surprising, therefore, that most planning aims are never achieved. . . .

If planners are to set realistic targets in their plans, they must somehow find means to *measure* administrative inadequacy and the lack of political will to develop, so that they can "discount" the unduly optimistic targets set when plans are formulated solely on the basis of economic potentiality. This sounds difficult, but it is not impossible. For example, it is possible to quantify the cost of administrative inefficiency, in terms of money and time, on the basis of past discrepancies between original estimates and actual performance in projects and programs. By deflating the estimates by a factor based on past errors, such adjustments can go a long way toward closing the gap between promise and performance. . . .

The Projects Problem

The current artificial separation between the formulation and implementation of plans accounts for the failure of planners, concentrating as they do on aggregative planning, to recognize soon enough that the weakness in most developing countries is not the lack of an elegantly integrated comprehensive plan based on economic potentialities but the lack of well-planned individual projects that can really be carried out. . . .

Because it usually takes several years to identify and prepare a sufficiently large number of good projects needed to implement a plan, it is too late for planners to become concerned about them after a plan has been prepared or even when it is being formulated. Unless preinvestment and investment studies of projects for implementing a comprehensive plan are sufficiently advanced, it does little good to prepare such a plan. Yet all too often this is exactly what happens. . . .

Changing the Planning Mix

One reasonable conclusion to be drawn from experience is that it may be desirable to reverse the usual proportions of the planning mix. Planners have almost invariably concentrated on aggregative planning rather than on the proper preparation and execution of projects, but experience shows that countries with well-prepared projects coordinated by sound budgetary procedures and controls can dispense with comprehensive plans, at least for a time, and still maintain high rates of growth. It seems clear, therefore, that improvements in project preparation and budgetary controls, where needed, are at least as urgent as the preparation of aggregative plans.

These findings obviously have an important bearing on the sequence in which planning problems ought to be attacked. If the planning process is to be realistic, planners must not start, as they often do, with a series of theoretical abstractions of planning as it *ought* to be, and they must not try to force these ideas in an inhospitable environment where governments are unstable, not genuinely committed to development, or otherwise unready for aggregative planning. Instead, while not forgetting the long-run objectives that theory demonstrates to be desirable, they must — at least at first — attune their plans to "things as they are."

Improving Planning Organization

Since effective projects should be prepared in the agencies that will actually carry them through, the organization of programing units in these agencies should get much higher priority than it now has in many developing countries, perhaps even higher than central planning agencies. Improved budget offices also may be more important in these countries than improved central planning agencies.

Changing Technical Assistance

The type of technical assistance needed for preparing technically and economically sound projects, and executing and operating them, differs from the type of technical assistance that has been supplied for aggregative or comprehensive planning. Aggregative planning is a business for economists who need only a modest knowledge of agricultural and industrial techniques; but project preparation requires engineers, agronomists, and other technicians, including some who are capable of translating financial costs and benefits into economic costs and benefits.

Because the preparation, execution, and operation of projects involve many people in a government, it is becoming imperative that foreign technical assistance be largely made up of "demonstrators" rather than "doers." Doers can be used for a few special purposes, but only demonstrators working on the job with groups of government employees actually engaged in project preparation and execution can hope to train in a reasonable period the large numbers of workers who must become involved in project preparation, execution, and operation.

What I have written is not an attack on comprehensive planning. Ideally, planning should be undertaken "from the top down" as well as "from the bottom up." But experience reveals that in most countries planners begin with the first and rarely get around to the second. Since planning from the bottom up is essential to development, while planning from the top down is not, it seems sensible for a country to begin with the preparation of sound projects and sector programs and, with these as a foundation, to advance toward comprehensive planning as rapidly as circumstances permit.

17..... Balanced Growth Versus Unbalanced Growth*

ROBERT E. BALDWIN

University of Wisconsin

The most fundamental policy issue that policymakers must decide is whether to attempt a massive, big-push development effort or to concentrate upon raising growth rates in selective, key sectors. Many economists maintain that successful development requires a large-scale investment program involving many different lines of production. One of them says:

> There is a minimum level of resources that must be devoted to . . . a development program if it is to have any chance of success . . . Proceeding "bit-by-bit" will not add up in its effects to the sum total of the single bits. A minimum quantum of investment is a necessary condition of success.[1]

Other economists believe that a more modest, selective growth effort is the only feasible program to follow. The doctrine of large-scale, balanced growth is, in the view of one writer in this group, "an incomplete, implausible, and even potentially dangerous solution"[2] to breaking out of the low income levels of underdevelopment.

Some proponents of the "all-out" approach rest their case on the notion of "the population trap". . . . Others stress the indivisibility of capital coupled with the profit interdependencies that exist among different investment projects. The indivisibility of capital inputs leads to production conditions in which unit costs, instead of being constant at all output levels, decrease significantly as output expands until the scale of produc-

---

* Taken and adapted from *Economic Development and Growth*, New York: John Wiley & Sons, Inc., 1966, pp. 72–76.

[1] P. N. Rosenstein-Rodan, "Notes on the Theory of the 'Big Push,'" in H. S. Ellis (Ed.) *Economic Development for Latin America* (London: Macmillan and Co., 1962), p. 57.

[2] H. W. Singer, *International Development: Growth and Change* (New York: McGraw-Hill Book Co., 1964), p. 50.

tion becomes large. Cost curves in industries that make up the social overhead capital of the economy, such as power, communications, and transportation, behave in this fashion. But, so also do cost curves in many manufacturing industries. Markets in underdeveloped countries for some of these products are so small that unit costs are above effective demand at all output levels. Consequently, these items are not produced domestically. According to the "big-push" proponents, it is necessary to bring about a large increase in demand in order to establish these important industries — to say nothing of bringing unit costs down to minimum levels.

In discussing interdependence among investment projects, the "big-push" advocates are utilizing the concept of external economies. . . . They in particular stress the importance of externalities that work on the demand side. Rosenstein-Rodan's classic illustration of the shoe industry best brings out their point.

> If a hundred workers who were previously in disguised unemployment (so that the marginal productivity of their labour was equal to zero) in an underdeveloped country are put into a shoe factory, their wages will constitute additional income. If the newly employed workers spend all of their additional income on the shoes they produce, the shoe factory will find a market and will succeed. In fact, however, they will not spend all of their additional income on shoes. There is no easy solution of creating an additional market in this way. The risk of not finding a market reduces the incentive to invest, and the shoe factory investment project will probably be abandoned. Let us vary the example. Instead of putting a hundred previously unemployed workers in one shoe factory, let us put ten thousand workers in one hundred factories and farms which between them will produce the bulk of the wage-goods on which the newly employed workers will spend their wages. What is not true in the case of one single shoe factory will become true for the complementary system of one hundred factories and farms. The new producers will be each other's customers and will verify Say's Law by creating an additional market. The complementarity of demand will reduce the risk of not finding a market. Reducing such interdependent risks naturally increases the incentive to invest.[3]

The case for the "big-push," setting aside the population question for the moment, thus rests on two points. First, the existence of significant economies of scale in many productive lines means that the demand for many items must be high even for a break-even point to exist. It must be even higher to achieve the lowest production costs possible. Second, to raise the demand for any one particular line it is usually necessary to raise income levels appreciably over the entire economy. This, in turn, can only be accomplished with a massive, all-out investment program.

The critics of this approach grant that the argument is valid as far as it

[3] P. N. Rosenstein-Rodan, *op. cit.*, p. 62.

goes. But, they claim, it rests on special supply assumptions that are unlikely to be fulfilled in less developed countries. Rosenstein-Rodan, for example, assumes in the foregoing quotation that all ten thousand workers put into the hundred factories and farms were previously unemployed in a disguised sense. The same must be true for the workers who are involved in producing specialized capital goods and material inputs used by these factories and farms. Therefore, the output of the new industries is obtained without decreasing output in other sectors or bidding up wage rates. The supply of capital must also be highly elastic, either from domestic or foreign sources, in order to prevent interest rates from rising and dampening the profitability prospects of investment.

If the supplies of labor, capital, and natural resources are not perfectly elastic, then factor prices and cost curves rise at the same time as efforts to increase demand are being undertaken. Should factor supplies be completely inelastic, a "big-push" effort will raise costs more than demand and increase the unprofitability of expansion by particular firms. Actually, the supply situation in most developing countries is, of course, neither completely inelastic nor completely elastic. In the recent past many development economists thought that disguised unemployment was widespread in the heavily populated, developing countries. Consequently, they thought that the bootstrap method of growth . . . especially if supplemented with heavy foreign aid, offered a quick and easy answer to the development problem. More experience and careful empirical investigations have shattered most of these optimistic expectations. As mentioned . . . [earlier], disguised unemployment in the sense of zero marginal productivity over the entire year does not appear to be widespread in heavily populated rural areas, if it exists at all. Moreover, it is now perfectly clear that there are crucial shortages of entrepreneurs, managers, technicians, and skilled workers of all sorts, and that any massive investment program puts a tremendous strain on these resources. The more common view now is that resource inelasticity is an effective barrier in most less developed countries to a successful "big-push" investment effort.

This does not mean that the situation is hopeless. It implies that economists and policymakers alike must abandon this escapist, unreal solution and grapple with the hard realities of growth. There are particular industries and sectors in which intensive investment efforts can pay high dividends by eliminating bottlenecks and stimulating a higher investment rate in other industries. In these leading sectors investment complementarities and resource elasticity can be effectively utilized.

Pointing to the potentialities of a more selective approach to growth does not mean that we can simply forget about balance in the development process. Obviously we cannot ignore either the technical input-output relations of production or the demand patterns of consumers. As more people are brought into industry, domestic agricultural output must be expanded or farm imports increased if this industrial growth is not to be choked by raising food prices. Likewise, if farm incomes are to rise steadily, the greater demand for manufactures on the part of farmers must somehow be met and, on a more detailed commodity level, there are thousands of similar interrelationships. Any successful development program must proceed on enough fronts to meet the balances that these interrelations involve. But this still leaves a wide range of choice concerning the best activities to undertake and the degree to push different output lines.

In the "all-out" approach every industry takes a giant step forward. This includes consumption-goods industries in the manufacturing and agricultural sectors, capital-goods industries, and even social-overhead investments. Under the selective approach, giant steps are taken only in a relatively small number of productive lines at any one time. For example, large investments might be made in such projects as a multipurpose dam, an oil refinery, a steel mill, a road between two important cities, or an irrigation scheme. At the same time, public authorities must be sure that small investment steps are being taken throughout the rest of the economy's productive structure. Without this, the economy will be unable to secure, either by direct production or trade, the greater amounts of many other goods and services that consumers desire when their per capita income levels rise. In short, selectivity must still involve overall balance. Giant steps on all lines are physically impossible; giant steps in a small number of lines are physically possible but are soon likely to lead to economic imbalances. Steady across-the-board progress coupled with big steps in selective sectors seems to be the best policy. . . .

18..... The Regional Approach to Development*

WALTER KRAUSE
University of Iowa

Rationale

... [What] is there about a regional approach that serves to recommend it to some people as a means for the promotion of development? The basic answer is found in the fact that the political boundaries of countries frequently do not circumscribe the particular geographic areas which, taken as distinct entities, can offer a good environment for well-ordered economic activity. The system of national states, as it exists today, in important measure represents the outgrowth of a series of political decisions, not of decisions made in terms of economic considerations. If individual countries are then to experience economic gains, and are to do so effectively and efficiently, they are obliged — so the argument evolves — to create an environment more conducive for well-ordered economic activity. Since a wholesale re-drawing of political boundaries is not a practical suggestion, the remaining alternative which comes to mind is to de-emphasize the significance of political boundaries in their bearing upon the pace and direction of economic activity.

If it is agreed that a de-emphasis of national boundaries makes good economic sense, one could next argue that the liberalization movement should be global in scope. Seemingly, if any liberalization of this type is good, then nothing short of the maximum is ideal. There are obstacles, however, to the pursuit of such an all-out goal. Not all countries are equally ready to proceed — and understandably so, given the degree of diversity in situations and responses to be found within a complex of roughly a hundred countries, all nominally sovereign and ever concerned with their own special national well-being. The result, as envisaged

* Taken and adapted from "Current International Economic Problems," *Iowa Business Digest,* University of Iowa, Spring 1961, pp. 30–34, 36–37.

by many persons, is that effort aimed to achieve the ultimate in short order is doomed to failure as individual impediments act and interact to form an end situation which is insurmountable generally. It is more hopeful, these people argue, to proceed piecemeal — with specific action undertaken at any point where and as it is readily possible. In short, the governing philosophy is that "half a loaf is better than no loaf." Translated into an implementation framework, closer economic contact is sought — at least as a first step — *within regions* and in *particular connections*, rather than universally and indiscriminately.

Forms of Regionalism

Basically, economic action at the regional level can proceed in any one of three main veins: projects, trade, and payments. . . .

Projects

Some projects are possible, in a physical sense, only if undertaken on a regional basis, involving activity in two or more countries, or become possible on a more efficient basis, in an economic sense, if undertaken regionally rather than nationally. This situation is observable in three distinct types of cases.

First, some basic facilities can be created and managed more readily on a regional basis than separately by each country concerned. To illustrate, assume a river which crosses or borders on two or more countries. Development of hydroelectric, irrigation, and transport facilities can then probably occur to better advantage if all countries act in unison rather than independently — in which case one country might choose not to act at all, and thereby hamper even that activity contemplated by others. Specific instances in which a regional approach seems apropos include the finalization (in 1960) of the Indus Waters Treaty, involving the development and utilization by India and Pakistan of the water resources of the Indus River basin, and the possible future development along TVA-lines of the Mekong River basin in Southeast Asia (embracing no less than four countries: Thailand, Laos, Cambodia, and South Viet-Nam — and possibly also Mainland China).

Second, the areal distribution of resources frequently makes their pooling necessary, as between two or more countries, if effective utilization is to follow. To illustrate, assume a case in which one country has iron ore but no coal, while an adjacent country has coal but no iron ore. A steel mill might be possible if the iron ore and coal can be linked. Theoretically, trade makes such a linkage possible; however, a formal arrangement covering the steel mill itself may prove necessary, as a first step, in order to set in motion those market forces which can result in the actual bringing together of the resources. A conceivable case in point involves Philippine iron ore and Taiwan coal.

Third, individual national markets may prove too limited to permit an economic scale of operations on the part of given productive units. In contrast, however, the same productive units, if situated in each instance in only one country among a grouping of two or more countries, while given untrammeled access to the domestic markets of each of these countries for any output accruing, may succeed in reaching a scale of operations which can prove economic. To illustrate, assume again the previous case involving iron ore in one country and coal in another country. The normal process of trade would then, of course, make possible a linkage of these resources, eventuating in the establishment of a joint processing facility; however, it is possible that each country, when left to act unilaterally, would instead strive for a steel mill of its own, with a resultant scale of operations in each country perhaps incapable of yielding efficiency in output. Therefore, a basis arises for a formal inter-country arrangement to cover the pooling of effort in resource utilization on behalf of a single enterprise, and the subsequent disposal of this enterprise's output within a shared market.

Notwithstanding its economic plausibility as respects particular projects, the regional approach often is difficult to implement — largely because of frictions stemming from the matters of cost-sharing and location. Thus, there is a tendency for individual countries to underestimate the amount reflective of their legitimate share of the cost of a joint undertaking. Again, when an end facility has to be situated in its entirety in one country, but is destined to service a regional grouping of countries, the typical participant tends to begrudge location anywhere outside itself. It is significant, however, that such impediments ordinarily can be substantially lessened if outside financing is capable of being drawn upon — and is available, specifically, in terms of use in conformity with the basic pattern of a regional approach previously agreed upon in principle. It is in this vein that this country's foreign-aid agency . . . introduced the Asian Economic Development Fund in 1956, under terms of which $300 million was earmarked for use in support of qualifying regional-development projects arising in Asia. And, the previously cited Indus Waters Treaty, which followed a dispute in existence between India and Pakistan since partition, is backed by an Indus Basin Development Fund of almost $900 million, capitalized largely with funds derived from external sources.

Trade

Examination of flows of global trade reveals that, characteristically, only relatively little exchange occurs among underdeveloped countries situated within the same general region; instead, individual underdeveloped countries tend to trade largely with industrial countries, generally located at some distance (while, further, the larger proportion of inter-country trade occurs within the complex of developed countries). Some persons feel that underdeveloped countries within the same general region ought to do more trading with one another. If more trade occurred regionally, so it is argued, added gain as a by-product of greater specialization might accrue to the participating countries. Accordingly, a frequent suggestion is that *particular* barriers to trade between countries within the *same general region* be eliminated or lessened, in the hope that greater intra-regional trade might result. Generally a customs-union arrangement of some sort comes to be proposed, the usual term invoked in such references being that of "common market."

Why do underdeveloped countries within the same general region currently trade so little with one another? The answer is found, basically, in the type of production prevailing within a given region in which all countries are underdeveloped. As matters stand, these countries are committed to raw-materials production — in fact, most are non-diversified raw materials producers, with output concentrated in relatively few major commodities (and with high similarity in the array of commodities characteristic among the several countries within a particular geographic region). Under these circumstances, the end output of each of the countries tends to be competitive, not complementary, with that of the others within the region. The exportable portion of each country's output is obliged to find its market outlet largely in advanced industrial countries located outside the immediate region; concurrently, many commodities — especially industrial-type items — not produced within the region but desired by the individual countries must derive from sources entirely outside the region, or be done without. As one sees in practice, the individual countries of Southeast Asia, all engaged in roughly similar types of raw-materials production, are not favorably geared for large-scale trade with one another, but do find a firm basis for trade with Japan, Western Europe, and the United States, all of which have an interest in the region's raw materials and in its demands for industrial-type goods; or, to cite another case, the countries of Latin America trade only little with one another, but are heavily dependent upon the exchange of local raw materials for a variety of imports, especially of industrial-type goods, originating in Western Europe and the United States.

In short, little economic complementarity prevails within a region comprised entirely of underdeveloped countries; and, to the extent that economic complementarity does not prevail, the basis for mutually advantageous trade tends to be weak. Interestingly enough, however, this lack of economic complementarity within a region of underdevelopment stands in sharp contrast to the situation evident in regions already developed. To illustrate, most of the countries of Western Europe are heavily industrial — but despite the fact that an industrial emphasis is the general rule, the flow of trade between the countries of the region is great. The essential point is that the industrial process tends to yield a diversity in end output which conforms with the principles of economic complementarity, and which can then serve to sustain a substantial exchange of goods between countries within the same region. Thus, French luxury goods, German heavy machinery, and Italian light machinery can be expected to fit reasonably well into a regional trade framework — even while it is unreasonable to expect Honduras and Nicaragua to carry on a thriving interchange in bananas, or Burma and Thailand to carry on a thriving interchange in rice. It is perhaps not surprising, therefore, that regional market arrangements of a formal nature should be suggested within locales such as Western Europe, and should come into being with minimum transitional difficulty and over only little opposition (considering that immediate benefits of a mutual order are widely regarded as likely); indeed, it is against this background that the early histories of the European Common Market (linking Belgium, France, West Germany, Italy, Luxembourg, and the Netherlands) and of the Outer Seven trade pact (linking Austria, Denmark, Norway, Portugal, Sweden, Switzerland, and Great Britain) appear to take on special significance within the context of issues raised here.

Notwithstanding the current lack of economic complementarity between countries within regions of underdevelopment (which situation then hampers large-scale intra-regional trade), a regional-type trade arrangement may nevertheless hold plausibility in the case of these countries. Just because complementarity is not currently present does not mean that it cannot become a fact at some future date. Indeed, should the possibility exist that the presence of a regional-type trade arrangement can help to *create* greater complementarity within a given region, such an arrangement quickly acquires a special attraction. Thus, the introduction in individual countries within a region of underdevelopment of some industrial-type enterprises may have the direct effect of generating greater complementarity between these countries, which — if realized — would make greater intra-regional trade possible. But, the introduction of these new enterprises may be long delayed, or indeed prove entirely impossible, in the absence of an ability for the end output to reach an area-wide market. Accordingly, a case arises for the establishment of regional-type trade arrangements — not as a means to yield participating countries' immediate gains from an interchange of goods arising under the prevailing economic order of things, but rather as a means to promote economic development itself. Then, as economic development proceeds, individual countries come to enjoy a new and higher level of economic activity generally, and as a companion feature, find themselves engaged in a new and higher volume of intra-regional trade. Significantly, it is in this manner that the introduction of regional-type arrangements (e.g., "common market" arrangements) is especially meaningful for underdeveloped countries desirous of economic development; put simply, a common market arrangement, in making intra-regional trade *possible*, may help to bring about the introduction of some new enterprises.

Payments

Some persons regard regional currency-clearing arrangements to be of help in the promotion of regional trade. As matters stand, many underdeveloped countries continue to rely upon exchange controls (unlike Western Europe, where convertibility was restored as the problem of the dollar shortage faded in severity for the individual countries of the region during the latter 1950's). The common situation in the underdeveloped world, as a consequence of the environment of underdevelopment, is one of heavy demand and low supply-potential as respects foreign exchange, so that a rational pattern of utilization of whatever foreign exchange is available appears dependent upon governmental intervention. But if upgraded foreign-exchange usage derives from such intervention, it is true also that a free market in goods is thereby ruled out. All the while, of course, more trade seems needed, not less trade or constant trade. Accordingly, the hope is readily fostered that somehow means can be found which might allow the volume of trade to be expanded *despite* the persistence of payments obstacles. Perhaps, to cite a seemingly reasonable ambition, some trade can be fostered outside and beyond customary foreign-exchange channels. Unfortunately, an attempt to proceed in this vein on a global basis is subject to many complications, particularly as each country and region adds further variables to what is a complex undertaking even under minimal circumstances. More hopeful, many feel, is an attempt geared to more limited arrangements. Perhaps a regional currency-clearing arrangement offers a practical course for gain, even if world-wide multilateralism appears beyond immediate grasp.

The idea of a regional currency arrangement as a means to foster intra-regional trade received a great boost through initiation of the European Payments Union (EPU) in Western Europe roughly a decade ago. The countries of Western Europe at the time were much subject to the dollar shortage, one effect of which was to undermine the process of settling international accounts as related to even purely intra-regional trade. The hope was that payments impediments to trade might be lessened through resort to a currency-clearing arrangement of regional scope, and that a growing volume of intra-regional trade might thereby result, notwithstanding the persistence of payments impediments between the region and the rest of the world. Significantly, the EPU proved successful, at least to a point, in the promotion of intra-European trade — indeed, in strengthening the economic capacity of the region in its trade relations with the rest of the world. In view of the general success experienced in this instance, it was perhaps only to be expected that thought should be given to the applicability of this means in efforts to promote intra-regional trade elsewhere, including regions of underdevelopment whose past records showed a low volume of intra-regional trade activity.

An important point, however, is that a currency arrangement can be expected merely to *accommodate* a trading arrangement economically justifiable on real grounds (i.e., on grounds other than pure currency considerations). Applied to regions of underdevelopment, it is well to recall that the basic reason for a low volume of intra-regional trade is found in the characteristic feature of a current lack of economic complementarity in the production patterns of the countries concerned; and, as long as there is no firm commodity basis for intra-regional trade, the case for a special currency-clearing arrangement as a means of easing the movement intra-regionally of present goods is undermined at the very outset. Thus it is that a currency-clearing arrangement can offer hope for beneficial impact upon current trade between countries within developed regions, such as Western Europe, even while the prospect for like benefit for countries within underdeveloped regions remains gloomy; it is simply that economic complementarity is present to substantial extent in the first instance, but is essentially absent in the case of the second.

Nevertheless, even if the magnitude of intra-regional trade in underdeveloped regions appears uncertain of marked increase during the near-term future as a consequence of the introduction of currency-clearing arrangements, there is good reason to believe that longer-run economic growth — and the trade pattern dependent upon this growth — is capable of being much influenced by the presence of such arrangements. Granted that a currency arrangement tends to yield little trade impact as long as underdevelopment is characteristic, the fact still remains that considerable meaning would attach if a regional production pattern were to evolve under which economic complementarity did prevail. Of significance in this connection, it is possible that the adoption within a region as yet underdeveloped of an appropriate currency arrangement might foster the introduction there of the very enterprises which, once they were part of the scene, could assure that region of the measure of economic complementarity essential for the support of a thriving intra-regional trade. In short, a currency arrangement, even if it does not result in a rapid rise in intra-regional trade, may have major impact in terms of *speeding economic development* — with this stimulation of economic development attributable, basically, to the salutary effect of the special arrangement in terms of curbing the deterring doubts of prospective entrepreneurs as to how and where disposal of future output is to occur.

An Overall View

As one surveys the potentialities of a regional approach as a means to foster economic development, several points seem to stand out:

1. Economic development calls for greater output. Such added output requires the introduction of various new projects. Some of these projects can be handled in more economic fashion on a regional basis than if left for unilateral action by single countries.

2. Important advantages are to be had from foreign trade. Efforts to promote such trade can take many forms — but one approach, the regional one, is to cultivate closer economic links among countries situated near one another.

3. Implementation of a regional approach to trade, in the case of underdeveloped countries, is hampered by two main obstacles: non-complementarity in trade items and weaknesses in the payments mechanism.

4. When all is said and done, growth in intra-regional trade remains fundamentally dependent upon the evolution of *both* (a) an appropriate production pattern and (b) an appropriate currency mechanism — and, in this sequence, *the production pattern is basic* . . . .

Implications for the United States

What are the implications for the United States of a movement in the underdeveloped world to proceed along regional lines in grappling with pressing economic problems? A reasonable general answer seems to be that action there which serves to improve economic conditions for the countries concerned, and for the world at large, is of benefit to the United States. Specifically, improved economic conditions in underdeveloped regions stand to help this country by easing world tensions and by rendering beneficial impact upon foreign trade generally. Therefore, if a regional approach can be helpful in the promotion of economic development (as is argued here), the United States should normally feel kindly disposed toward it.

The foregoing may suffice as a general answer, but what is to be said on more particularized scores? For example, there is the question of how the United States Government might reconcile a pro-attitude toward "regional economic confederations" with its long-standing position that the proper goal is all-out multilateralism. And, there is the question of how American business should choose to react, given its particular set of interests. These two questions seem sufficiently important to merit special comment.

Multilateralism versus Regionalism

Historically, the United States Government has adhered to the policy position that multilateralism should be the goal of this and other countries. The particular position undoubtedly was grounded in this country's appraisal of its own self-interest — specifically, the need for added export markets and investment outlets. Actually, of course, this country has not always practiced what it has preached in this respect (witness, for example, repeated resort to various protectionist actions: "escape clauses" in tariff concessions, tying provisions in loan agreements, etc.). Notwithstanding such apparent deviations from avowed policy, however, considerable progress toward liberalization has been recorded by this country since, say, the days of the Great Depression.

Once the idea spread that particular problems should be attacked along regional lines (as in the realms of trade promotion and payments accommodation), the question arose as to how this country should react. Should it sanction the new approach, and at the same time forego the goal of multilateralism? Or, should it endorse the new approach, at least in instances, while clinging to the hope that specific action along regional lines might somehow prove compatible with attainment of the dominant goal of multilateralism? Following a period which clearly reflects indecision, the country began to give selective endorsement — first in Western Europe in terms of some measures inspired by the Marshall Plan, and then in a sequence of measures applicable within the underdeveloped world.

How was the United States to rationalize even limited endorsement of such regional measures? Basically, the sustaining logic was premised on three main considerations: a conviction that the presence of formidable obstacles made impractical an all-out movement to multilateralism in the here and now; a belief that some specific problems merited immediate attention, and that the regional approach held potential in their case; and a hope that current actions along regional lines would not hamper attainment of the greater goal, world-wide multilateralism, at that future time when environmental factors are more favorable. Thus, the regional approach found favor (say, in trade and payments) in terms of what it might offer during the near-term future — even as multilateralism continued as the long-run goal of foreign economic policy. Besides all this, of course, it was possible that some regional-type actions would have occurred anyway, even in the absence of this country's sanction — in which case nominal sanction, and a continuation of rapport with those who guide action, may well represent the course of wisdom.

In principle, therefore, the United States remains committed to multilateralism. But with an environment in the world today that is not conducive to all-out multilateralism, the United States feels obliged to settle for something less for now — even while it clings to the hope that *greater* multilateralism will prove to be the case over time. It is in this way that sanction and support can be given regional arrangements in the present. While regional arrangements are thus not beyond endorsement by the United States, this country is interested in assuring itself that its own economic position within an international context is not thereby specifically injured. For example, the United States commonly insists that the practices initiated under new intra-regional trade arrangements do not violate the code of conduct set forth by the General Agreement on Tariffs and Trade (GATT). In practical terms, this means that the United States tries to prevent market intervention of a type which would eventuate in particularized discrimination in international markets against American exports.

Markets and Competition

Common markets and free trade zones in essence comprise trade blocs. As these trade blocs arise, how is American business affected? And what should it choose to do about what it finds?

As intimated earlier, the fundamental purpose of a regional-type trade arrangement (and of a supporting payments arrangement) in an underdeveloped area is to promote intra-regional trade, the accomplishment of which is sought through the evolution of added economic complementarity within the particular trade region. The counterpart of greater economic unification by such a region, however, is an alteration in the status of the region vis-à-vis already developed regions. Economists in the foreign trade field commonly argue that a changing economic environment of the type cited need not prove injurious to any country; specifically, it is argued that development within regions of underdevelopment need not injure a developed economy, provided there is a willingness there to undergo adjustment (i.e., all countries can be better off as a greater volume of output and trade, albeit of changed composition, becomes characteristic).

Even if it is admitted that no advanced economy is made to suffer as long as it is willing to adjust to the new situation, the fact remains, however, that the adjustment process at issue involves *specific* firms. Some firms experience gain in the adjustment process, while others face retrenchment — quite apart from the matter of overall impact upon the total economy. Thus, individual firms are obliged to weigh their own status against the environment which is evolving.

Significantly, some firms heavily dependent upon exportation to a region undergoing economic unification may find it advantageous, as they attempt to maximize individual well-being, to contemplate a shift in production-locale to the foreign nation. To elaborate, if development within a common market area or free trade zone threatens the market of a firm based in an already developed country outside the immediate region, the firm may find that self-protection requires entry into production *within* the foreign area. It is in this way that a regional-type trade arrangement can have the effect of attracting foreign investment. Indeed, foreign investment in a magnitude perhaps never attainable through simple exhortation may prove forthcoming in response to the subtle coercive pressures of a new type of trade barrier.

C..... The Communist Bloc(s) and Ideological Rivalry*

Alongside Western Europe and the underdeveloped countries, the Communist Bloc(s) — the Soviet Union and its Eastern European satellites, Mainland China and its satellites, and a few individual countries such as Cuba and Ghana — confront the United States in its external dealings. Once a solid bloc, the current status presumably is that of "Communist Blocs": the Soviet Union and Mainland China, following loss of close rapport with one another, each heads a grouping of its own. Of course, whether we talk of a bloc or of blocs, the important fact for an outside power, like the United States, is that however great the disagreements on dogma between the Soviet Union and Mainland China, the disagreements between them and the countries of the West are greater. Unlike Communist-oriented countries, committed to a socialist-type of economic order, the countries of the West, including especially the United States, pay considerable heed, in word and deed, to a private approach to economic activity. In the realm of ideology, East is East and West is West.

Given the ideological distinction between East and West, a situation of rivalry has evolved; it is expressed in various ways. The United States, bent on a containment of expansionist tendencies attributed to "the other side," in essence "drew a line." The "cold war" struggle ensued — mutual antagonism, well backed by arms on both sides; a state of "coexistence" — not peace, but not outright war either. Within this context, the underdeveloped countries, either avowedly neutral or as yet uncommitted as to ideological preference, have become a pawn, actively wooed by both sides. The United States initiated on behalf of the underdeveloped countries a massive foreign-aid program — composed of military assistance, to prop immediately the will to resist, and of economic assistance (partly for economic development), to bolster longer-term morale and well-being. The Communist camp quickly countered with its own assistance program, the so-called "trade-and-aid offensive." Thus began an active rivalry at the political-military level, reinforced through reliance on economic means.

In addition to this somewhat spectacular headline-making type of rivalry, a second form of rivalry goes on — the quiet rivalry implicit in comparative economic performance. The Soviet Union, along with other

136

Communist-oriented countries, claims a growth rate far greater than characteristic of capitalist countries of the West. Statements by Soviet spokesmen convey, in fact, a conviction of the West's eventual "burial" under the avalanche of expanded output elsewhere. The apparent message for third countries is "Do it as we do it."

All the while, the Soviet Union and its allies envisage trade as a political, as well as economic, instrument. Foreign trade for these countries, while never truly large, is growing — and the capacity to sustain trade is growing. Relative to trade within the "trade and aid" context, the policy premise is that trade is part of the aid process. And, relative to trade in general, the procedure applied is that of "state trading." Exporting and importing are done by government — not by private traders, as is the practice for the bulk of trade in countries of the West. A relevant question, again, is — Which way is preferable? Certainly, superior bargaining strength is had when trade is between a monopolist-monopsonist, at home, and an unorganized array of private traders abroad. And, certainly, trade can then be directed more readily toward political ends (although at a possible loss of economic efficiency).

The present section includes two selections. The first, by Professors Mikesell and Behrman, examines the structure of East-West trade — the magnitude, composition, and direction of trade, and the procedural aspects of state trading: trade agreements, payments arrangements, etc. The follow-up selection focuses on the Communist "trade-and-aid offensive," concluding with an appraisal of the Communist-oriented area's future trading capacity.

19..... The Structure of East-West Trade[*]

RAYMOND F. MIKESELL
University of Oregon

JACK N. BEHRMAN
University of North Carolina

The volume and character of trade between the Sino-Soviet bloc and the Free World have been determined primarily by the national economic and political security policies of the trading partners, and to only a limited degree by free market forces. All of the foreign trade on the bloc side and most of the trade with the bloc on the Free World side is subject to government controls. Controls on the Free World side range from security restrictions on exports of certain goods to the bloc or to certain bloc members,[1] to licensing and quota controls on all trade with bloc countries.

Pre-World War II

Soviet trade relations and those of the countries under Russian domination have undergone several major shifts since World War I, reflecting basic changes in Soviet economic and political policies and objectives. During the interwar period Soviet policy emphasized internal self-sufficiency, and Russia limited her foreign trade to that necessary to achieve her basic development goals. Both imports and exports during the interwar period were well below the 1913 levels.[2]

During her first Five-Year Plan (1928–1932), Russia placed large or-

[*] Taken and adapted from *Financing Free World Trade with the Sino-Soviet Bloc,* Princeton, N.J.: Princeton University Press, 1958, pp. 3–11.

[1] The United States government prohibits all trade and financial transactions with North Korea and Mainland China.

[2] During the interwar period, Soviet exports never exceeded a half billion dollars annually as compared with $780 million in 1917, and imports never rose over $570 million as compared with $707 million in 1913. See *Foreign Commerce Yearbook,* U.S. Department of Commerce, 1939, p. 125.

ders for machine tools and other heavy industrial equipment in the United States and Germany. Technical excellence rather than reciprocal commercial advantage tended to be the predominant consideration.[3] Russia's imports of industrial raw materials were largely imported from traditional sources and not under bilateral agreements.

In contrast to the period following World War II, Russia's interwar trade was largely multilateral in character and she made relatively little effort to use her trade as a bargaining weapon for creating economic or political advantage. Russia had trade deficits in most of the years between 1925 and 1932; these were covered by gold sales, by drawing down currency reserves, and by short-term commercial credits from abroad. After 1932 Russia's imports were sharply reduced and her trade position reversed, so that she was able to repay most of her commercial indebtedness by 1935.[4] By 1938 Russia's trade was approximately balanced at about a third of a billion dollars . . . as compared with exports and imports of more than double this amount in 1930.

In contrast to the widespread bilateralism practiced by other Central and Eastern European countries, Russia negotiated but few clearing agreements. She was a partner to only three agreements in 1936 and five in 1939.[5] In 1937 only 18 per cent of Russia's imports and 9 per cent of her exports were financed through clearing agreements. In contrast, Bulgaria financed 88 per cent of her imports through clearing agreements in 1937; Czechoslovakia, 29 per cent; Germany, 53 per cent; Hungary, 60 per cent; Italy, 46 per cent; the Netherlands, 23 per cent; Rumania, 75 per cent; Sweden, 24 per cent; Switzerland, 36 per cent; Turkey, 72 per cent; and Yugoslavia, 61 per cent.

The Early Postwar Period, 1947–1951

Following World War II, the trade of Eastern Europe came under Russian control. Before the war, trade between Russia and Eastern Europe had been almost negligible, and among these countries themselves relatively small, but Russian postwar policy was directed toward increasing trade within the Soviet bloc at the expense of satellite trade with the rest of the world. By 1950 about one-third of Eastern Europe's trade was with the USSR and intra-Soviet bloc trade represented about two-thirds of the total trade of this area.

[3] A. M. Baykov, *Soviet Foreign Trade,* Princeton University Press, Princeton, N.J., 1946, pp. 73–74.

[4] Soviet indebtedness reached 1.4 billion rubles in 1931 (about a quarter of a billion dollars), mainly in the form of short- and medium-term credits for the purchase of goods. See Harry Schwartz, *Russia's Soviet Economy,* Prentice-Hall, New York, 1954, p. 589.

[5] See Margaret S. Gordon, *Barriers to World Trade,* Macmillan, New York, 1941, p. 131. In contrast, Bulgaria was a party to 13 clearing agreements in 1936; Czechoslovakia, 10; Germany, 28; Hungary, 12; Rumania, 17; Turkey, 18; and Yugoslavia, 11. (*Ibid.,* pp. 130–131).

Following World War II, trade between Western Europe and the Soviet bloc rose slowly. By 1948 Soviet bloc exports to Western Europe were only 31 per cent of the 1938 volume and imports from Western Europe were but 59 per cent of the 1938 volume. Czechoslovakian and Polish exports to Western Europe were substantially larger, relative to 1938, than was the case with the Russian exports. In fact, these countries achieved fairly substantial surpluses in their trade with Western Europe in 1948, a portion of which were received in sterling available for making purchases of raw materials in the outer sterling area.

By 1949 the Soviet bloc's trade surplus with Western Europe had disappeared. During the next three years both exports and imports (by volume) with Western Europe declined. . . . This was caused partly by the low level of cereal production in Eastern Europe and partly by a shift of Eastern European trade to the USSR. While Western Europe's trade was expanding, both within Western Europe and outside of Europe, the Soviet bloc's trade with the outside world was contracting. Between 1948 and 1952, Sino-Soviet bloc exports to the Free World declined by over $350 million and imports by more than $500 million. . . .

Soviet bloc trade with non-European countries (other than Communist China) also decreased sharply between 1948 and 1951; well over half of this trade was with the outer sterling area. The Soviet bloc countries had a substantial trade deficit with the outer sterling area and other primary commodity-producing areas, including Latin America. Trade with non-European countries (excluding Mainland China) was relatively small; imports averaged $340 million in 1950–1951 and exports $225 million for the same period. In volume terms this was less than half of the bloc's trade with these countries in 1938.[6] Soviet block exports to the United States were $113 million in 1948 but declined to $40 million in 1952; United States exports to the Soviet bloc fell from $122 million in 1948 to only $1 million in 1952.

During 1948–1952, Communist China increased its trade with Eastern Europe more than fivefold. China's trade with the Free World declined sharply, especially after China's entrance into the Korean War and the imposition of the United Nations' embargo on the export of strategic materials. China's trade with countries outside the Soviet bloc was very largely with the sterling area countries of the Far East, particularly Hong Kong, Malaya, Pakistan, India, and Ceylon.

Postwar Trade, 1953–1956

In 1948, trade between the Free World and the Sino-Soviet bloc was approximately balanced at about $2 billion each way, but the value declined thereafter to a low in 1953 of less than $1.4 billion for Free World exports and $1.6 billion for Free World imports. Since 1953, however,

[6] United Nations, *Economic Bulletin for Europe,* Geneva, November 1952, p. 37.

trade between the two areas has been rising steadily, so that in 1956 Free World exports to the Sino-Soviet bloc were $2.5 billion and imports were $2.9 billion. . . .

The bulk of this rise was accounted for by increased trade between Eastern and Western Europe. The volume of trade between Eastern and Western Europe increased by nearly 50 per cent between 1952 and 1956. . . . The proportion of East-West trade to total trade for both the Soviet and the non-Soviet countries of Europe has also risen in the past few years, but the relative importance of East-West trade in 1956 for both areas was still well below that of 1948. . . .

Trade between the Sino-Soviet bloc countries and the less developed countries of the Free World approximately doubled between 1953 and 1956. In 1956 this trade accounted for about one-fourth of total Free World Trade with the bloc. Among the less developed countries which substantially increased their trade with the bloc during the 1953–1956 period were Argentina, Brazil, Burma, Cuba, Egypt, India, Indonesia, Israel, South Africa, the Sudan, Turkey, and Uruguay.

Not only has trade between the Soviet bloc and the Free World grown since 1953, but there have also been important shifts in its relative composition. Manufactures and crude materials and fuels have gained at the expense of cereals in Eastern European exports to Western Europe. Grain, coal, and timber, which accounted for about half of Eastern European exports to Western Europe a few years ago, now make up less than one-third. Growing exports of steel and heavy manufactures reflect the emphasis on industrialization in Eastern Europe.

The growth of manufacturing exports has been even greater in Eastern Europe's trade with overseas countries. While the bulk of the Soviet bloc exports to these countries continues to take the form of petroleum, coke, crude steel, cement, and light-industry commodities such as textiles, the recent agreements provide increasing exports of machinery and heavier manufactures. In exchange, the Soviet countries are eager to buy foodstuffs and raw materials, and their bargaining power is particularly high with countries seeking to export commodities like cotton and rubber, which tend to be in surplus on Free World markets.

The negotiation of new trade and payments agreements, together with a broadening of old agreements and the granting of credits between bloc members and Free World countries, has played a part in this trade expansion. But the role of the agreements should not be overemphasized. Fundamental demand and supply factors arising from economic causes have been of major importance in bringing about the expansion of trade and a shift in its commodity composition and geographical pattern.

Among the economic factors responsible for this growth in East-West trade are (1) the increased Soviet demand for consumers' goods following the death of Stalin; (2) the growing West European demand for imports which accompanied the industrial boom beginning in late 1952;

(3) the greater availability of manufactured goods in Eastern European countries; and (4) the rising East European requirements for raw materials and foodstuffs.

A more favorable political climate since the death of Stalin has of course permitted these forces to operate more effectively. The conclusion of the Austrian Peace Treaty ending the occupation of Austria in 1955, the resumption of normal trade relations between Yugoslavia and the Soviet bloc countries in 1954, and the August 1954 reduction of the items on the list of strategic commodities embargoed by the Western European countries to the Soviet bloc also contributed to the expansion of trade between Eastern and Western Europe.

20..... Communist Trade and Aid*

WALTER KRAUSE

University of Iowa

The Economic Offensive

Committed to a political and economic ideology different from that of the West, and involved with it in a "cold war" conflict since virtually the close of World War II, the U.S.S.R. launched a much-publicized *economic offensive* during 1953. The new program (or approach), representing in toto a *trade-and-aid offensive,* was launched at this particular time because the international setting was regarded as "right," the capacity to branch out was present, and the attitude at home was favorable for action. In the years after 1953, the trade-and-aid offensive gained strength and stature. The U.S.S.R. was able and chose to devote added energies to the program. And other countries, oriented to the U.S.S.R., helped — making the economic offensive a Communist Bloc effort.

The Trade Drive

. . . [The] foreign trade of the Soviet Union during pre-World War II days was small, relative to GNP. The trade that did occur was largely with the industrial countries of the West. Trade with underdeveloped countries was limited almost entirely to occasional imports of raw materials not available within the Soviet orbit, with payment made from proceeds acquired through sales to the West.

Following World War II, the Soviet Union stepped up the tempo of its foreign-trade activity, although, even so, its foreign trade never reached a high proportion of GNP. First, within Europe, the Soviet Union sought to increase its trade with the satellite countries of Eastern Europe and, also, with the industrial countries of Western Europe. The Soviet Union

* Taken and adapted from *International Economics,* Boston: Houghton Mifflin Company, 1965, pp. 325–330, 337–340.

hoped to tie the semi-dependent satellite countries to it more closely by inducing them to trade with it rather than with the West. And the Soviet Union hoped to capitalize on the persistent balance-of-payments difficulties of the industrial countries, offering them foodstuffs and other raw materials in exchange for manufactures and semi-manufactures (much needed for the program of reconstruction).

Second, within the underdeveloped world, the Soviet Union began, in 1953, to push vigorously for greater trade. Special trade missions were empowered to negotiate bilateral trade agreements; participation in trade fairs and exhibitions was encouraged; and the country's interest in foreign trade was stressed in propaganda media. Much of the emphasis on trade with underdeveloped countries was coupled with arrangements for the provision of economic and/or military assistance — giving added meaning to the parallel between trade and aid in the country's economic offensive. In its trade drive the Soviet Union attempted, as in the case of foreign aid, to join forces with companion countries within the Communist Bloc. The Soviet effort thereby comprised only a part (albeit, the major part) of a combined Communist Bloc trade-and-aid endeavor.

1. The Trade Drive: Importance and Motivation. Contrary to the common impression within the Free World that the Communist economic offensive emphasized aid over trade, the Soviet Union's own appraisal placed the importance of trade ahead of aid. A leading Soviet economist stated: "The most important form of economic cooperation of the U.S.S.R. with other powers, including the countries which are poorly developed in regard to economic relationships, is foreign trade. . . ."[1]

Further, the Soviet Union's basic objective in trade has been political, rather than economic. As Khrushchev stated: "We value trade least for economic reasons and most for political purposes."[2] However, while political factors have been fundamental, economic factors have entered, too. Strategic imports were needed (e.g., copper and rubber); and, more generally, since the country's dedication to forced growth led to uneven growth, foreign trade offered a way to relieve both acute shortages and occasional surpluses. But even when an economic motivation has been present, the trade action invoked has been intended to yield political benefit for the country, quite apart from economic benefit.

2. The Trade Pattern. Though never a high proportion of GNP, the foreign trade of the Soviet Union rose markedly during the decade of the 1950's — by roughly 150 per cent, in value. While most of this added trade involved other Bloc countries, a growing proportion of it was with

[1] V. Alkhimov, "Cooperation between the U.S.S.R. and Economically Underdeveloped Countries," *Voprosi Ekonomiki*, No. 6, June 1957.

[2] Nikita Khrushchev, speaking in 1955, as quoted in Department of State, *The Sino-Soviet Economic Offensive in the Less Developed Countries*, Washington, May 1958, p. 6.

underdeveloped non-Bloc countries, reflecting an important shift for the Soviet Union in trade direction and composition.

Although Bloc efforts at trade promotion were widespread geographically, they had *particular* impact in a few underdeveloped non-Bloc countries. While trade between the Bloc countries and the underdeveloped countries roughly doubled during a five-year period in the mid-1950's, the growth in trade was disproportionately great in the case of Egypt, Syria, India, Burma, Indonesia, Malaya, etc. By the late 1950's, a number of underdeveloped countries, especially in the Middle East and South Asia, had become heavily oriented toward the Bloc countries, in terms of both exports and imports. In some of these countries, in fact, Bloc trade (as a proportion of total exports or imports) approached one-third of total trade.

The U.S.S.R.'s exports to underdeveloped countries, during these years, consisted chiefly of rolled steel, petroleum products, lumber, cement, cotton cloth, sugar, and wheat; imports from these countries consisted mainly of foodstuffs and raw materials — e.g., cotton, wool, rubber, nonferrous metal ores, rice, tea, and coffee. Only relatively small amounts of machinery and equipment have been supplied to underdeveloped countries. Either the Soviet Union has not had enough machinery and equipment to trade (and so has failed to live up to its propaganda claim that it stands ready to supply other countries with the means of production) or the Soviet Union has been waiting until *later* when assistance agreements call specifically for the delivery of items in this category. Nevertheless, Soviet trade, *in general,* has been important to the underdeveloped world. Particular trade items have loomed large for some countries; for example, the bulk of Afghanistan's imports of petroleum products and a large portion of India's imports of rolled steel have come from the Soviet Union, while the Soviet Union, in turn, has been a major purchaser of Egyptian cotton and Burmese rice.

In contrast with the Soviet Union, the satellite countries of Eastern Europe have engaged with underdeveloped countries in basically an exchange of manufactures (including machinery and equipment) for various raw materials (including foodstuffs). And, in contrast with both the Soviet Union and its European satellites, Mainland China has continued essentially as an economy in transition. Its trade has consisted of an exchange of some raw materials for other raw materials, although, with new manufacturing capacity, Mainland China has shown a greater tendency to export finished goods.

3. *Trade Agreements.* The Bloc's trade drive has been spearheaded by a campaign to conclude bilateral trade agreements. While common to Soviet trade prior to the launching of the economic offensive, the number of trade agreements roughly tripled during the first five years of the offensive. By 1958, some 150 of these agreements existed between Bloc

countries and underdeveloped non-Bloc countries alone and additional agreements were concluded thereafter (with both underdeveloped and developed countries), though at a slower pace.

In form, these agreements express a willingness on the part of the signatory countries to engage in trade; they establish the types of commodities to be exchanged; they set trade targets for commodities (but leave individual transactions to be worked out within the general framework); they establish procedures for the settlement of balances (generally through clearing accounts). In a sense, the agreements are "hunting licenses": they express an *intention* to trade, but are not firm contracts to do so. Though the agreements do not guarantee that trade will occur, an increase in trade is the customary result.

Trade, under the agreements, is akin to barter. While the agreements do not stipulate the exchange of one particular commodity for another, they do indicate the tradeable commodities (along with a procedure for the settlement of any uncleared balance) — so that the result tends to be a bilateral exchange of goods. An equivalence in value between a "package" of exports and a "package" of imports is sought, though individual transactions occur over time and through the monetary mechanism.

The agreements readily lend themselves to propaganda. In announcing the signing of an agreement, Bloc countries are able to call attention to themselves (in advance of any physical trading whatsoever) and, then, are able to call attention to themselves again, if and when specific trade transactions occur.

The Assistance Program

Foreign aid was the second part of the Communist Bloc's trade-and-aid offensive. Ironically, the Soviet Union, having "pulled itself up by its own bootstraps," now offered, in cooperation with other members of the Communist Bloc, to pull up other countries, as yet underdeveloped. A number of explanations have been made of the motivation of the Soviet Union and its partners in embarking on a program of foreign aid. The following factors seem to add up to a plausible explanation.

The very presence of a revolution of rising expectations in the underdeveloped world suggested an opportunity for the Soviet Union and for the Communist Bloc generally. It appeared likely that direction could be given to the aspirations of underdeveloped countries through the contact and persuasion inherent in a program of aid — a direction pleasing to the Communist Bloc. Indeed, the fact that the United States was already giving aid (and presumably was using it as a means of persuasion) gave the Communist Bloc *added* reason to initiate its own program. In fact, the Soviet Union believed that it, and its partners, could offer potent competition to the United States. The Soviet Union could draw upon its own developmental achievements in conveying its ideological and policy message to recipient countries. And communist aid could be integrated with trade to form a combined trade-*and*-aid offensive — a combination, in the case of the Communist Bloc, that would permit a sizable aid program to be carried on without proving an unduly heavy burden. . . .

As the Soviet Union and its partners launched into the foreign-aid program, they did their utmost to make it sound both altruistic and humanitarian. As one Soviet spokesman stated to an international conference attended by representatives from underdeveloped countries in Africa and Asia: "We are prepared to help you as brother helps brother, without motives. Tell us what you need and we will help you and send, according to our economic capabilities, . . . [assistance] for industry, education, and hospitals. . . . We do not ask you to join any Blocs . . . ; our only condition is that there will be no strings attached."[3] Despite such statements, the political motive has appeared important — indeed, paramount. The prospect of being able to influence the domestic and foreign policies of recipient countries has seemed to outweigh any advantages that might stem from new trade during the foreseeable future.[4]

Scope for Action

In addition to the fact that the Soviet Union and the United States, the respective lead countries in the Communist Bloc and Free World country-groupings, compete in trade and aid, they compete in an arms race, too. Given the overall rivalry, the global environment is one that lies somewhere between full-scale war and genuine peace — an environment of *coexistence*, the normal state of affairs under the cold war.

Given a cold war and coexistence, what about the future? While speculation holds hazards, some major trends are clear. . . .

Potentials of the Communist Bloc

Production in the Soviet Union (and in the Communist Bloc as a whole) is well below that of the United States. This holds true for industrial production (Table 1), and also for agricultural production (Table 2). In a very real sense, the world of the Communist Bloc, despite past progress, is still somewhat "underdeveloped."

However, the prevailing rate of economic growth in the Soviet Union (and in the Communist Bloc) is relatively high (Table 3), so that the disparity between the Communist Bloc and the United States is narrowing. In the Bloc countries, the central emphasis is on capacity for greater output (and on what the presence of such greater capacity and output will permit). To cite Khrushchev: "We declare war upon the United States in the peaceful field of trade. . . . We will win over the United States. The

---

[3] A. A. Arzumanyan, President of the Soviet Institute of International Economics, speaking at the Afro-Asian Solidarity Conference, Cairo, 1957.

[4] For an elaboration of this point, see W. Krause, *Economic Development* (Belmont, Calif.: Wadsworth Publishing Company, Inc., 1961), pp. 474–477.

TABLE 1

Population and Industrial Output, Free World and Communist Bloc, 1960

Item	Unit	Free World			Sino-Soviet Bloc			
		Total	United States	European OECD	Total	USSR	European Satellites	Communist China
Population	millions	1,970	181	329	1,029	214	99	689
Industrial Production:								
Aluminum	1,000 MT	3,630	1,829	836	915	670	165	80
Cement	mil. MT	229	54	94	87	46	23	15
Coal	mil. MT	1,118	392	488	1,127	419	269	425
Electricity	bil. KWH	1,811	841	522	475	292	115	58
Motor vehicles	1,000	15,008	7,872	6,045	749	524	199	23
Petroleum	mil. MT	889	348	14	168	148	15	5
Steel	mil. MT	238	90	107	105	65	21	18

Source: AID, *Select Economic Data for the Less Developed Countries*, Washington, March 1962.

threat to the United States is not the ICBM, but in the field of peaceful production. We are relentless in this and it will prove the superiority of our system."[5]

When the U.S.S.R. launched its Seven-Year Plan, covering 1959–1965, the country's aggregate GNP bore a ratio to that of the United States of roughly 1:2½. . . .[6] Reflecting the rapid growth contemplated, the Plan called for the attainment, by 1965, of an income level some two-thirds

[5] Nikita Khrushchev, speaking in 1957.

[6] Approximately a decade earlier, the comparable ratio was 1:4.

TABLE 2

Agricultural Performance, United States and Soviet Union, 1960

Item	Unit	United States	Soviet Union	USSR as Percentage of US
Population[1]	mil.	182	216	119
Labor force[2]	mil.	69	106	153
Farm labor force	mil.	7	48	653
Sown cropland	mil. acres	329	501	152
Tractors on farms	thous.	4,770	1,090	23
Yield per acre:				
Corn	bu.	54.5	21.7	40
Wheat	bu.	26.0	11.4	44

Source: Department of Agriculture, *Foreign Agriculture*, Washington, September 1961, p. 6.
[1] Jan. 1961.
[2] 1959.

above that prevailing in 1958. Further, this Plan was scheduled to be followed by a second Seven-Year Plan, at the end of which (in 1972) the output of the U.S.S.R. was expected to be double or triple the 1958 volume. At that time, according to a Soviet statement, the aggregate GNP of the U.S.S.R. would equal or surpass that of the United States and the aggregate GNP of the Communist Bloc would equal or surpass that of the Free World.[7] This expectation gave rise to the now classic comment by Khrushchev to the effect that "we will *bury* capitalism."

In terms of the composition of output, the Seven-Year Plan (1959–1965) called for continued, even greater, emphasis on producer goods. Output goals, 1965 over 1958, were set at an increase of some 85 to 88 per cent in heavy industry, at an increase of some 62 to 65 per cent in consumer goods, and at an increase of some 70 per cent in agriculture. It seemed significant that the greatest increase contemplated was in heavy industry, despite the paucity of consumer goods and the perennial "squeeze" in agriculture.[8] All this reflected the central theme of Soviet planning: continued economic build-up.

Thus, the Soviet Union (and the Communist Bloc in general) has been growing richer and the planning emphasis is on growing even richer. This process of enrichment has important implications within a cold-war

[7] For a summary of the contents of the projected Seven-Year Plan, and its follow-up Plan, see *The New York Times*, November 15, 1958, p. 1–L.
[8] Agriculture has been a "weak link" in the Soviet Union's production pattern for many years. Equipment shortages and other deficiencies have resulted in a relatively low level of productivity in this sector (Table 2). Nevertheless, the highest priority in planning has continued to be assigned to heavy industry, to the neglect of consumer goods and of agriculture in general.

context. First, with heightened economic capacity, it becomes possible to support a greater communist trade-and-aid effort. Second, a dramatic performance record is likely to enhance the appeal of a communist economic system, especially for underdeveloped countries desirous of development and not yet firmly committed to an ideology.

TABLE 3

Comparative Growth Rates (GNP),
Selected Countries, 1951–1960

Country	Percentage
EEC Countries (average):	5.3
Belgium	2.6
France	4.2
Italy	5.8
Luxembourg	2.9
Netherlands	5.1
West Germany	7.2
EFTA Countries (average):	3.2
Austria	6.0
Denmark	3.7
Norway	3.4
Portugal	3.6
Sweden	3.8
Switzerland	5.0
United Kingdom	2.7
Japan	8.4[1]
U.S.S.R.	6–7.0[2]
United States	2.6

Source: Data, except when specified otherwise, are from Hearings of the Joint Economic Committee (U.S. Congress) on *Foreign Economic Policy, 1962*, December 4–14, 1961, Washington, 1962, pp. 456–457.

[1] From *Review of Economics and Statistics*, February 1964, p. 34; covers 1951–58.

[2] From Hearings of the Joint Economic Committee (U.S. Congress) on *Employment, Growth, and Price Levels*, (Part 2), April 7–10, 1959, Washington, 1959, p. 251; covers 1951–59 (gross domestic product at 1955 prices).

D..... The Problem of the Balance of Payments

As the United States deals with the several differing categories of countries, problems arise and present themselves — some closely linked to particular regions, others more general in scope; some minor or transitory, others major or persistent. Among these problems, a few stand out. One of them relates to the country's balance-of-payments status.

The United States of a few years back had grown accustomed to a balance of payments that, if it did not actually show a surplus, at least oscillated with some regularity to and from a surplus position. There was a wide excess of exports over imports, a margin *sufficiently* wide to cover, more or less, whatever deficiencies arose through, say, capital (investment) flows, foreign-aid allocations, and external military outlays. Indeed, the United States began to take this for granted and to lecture other countries to — "Do as we are doing in order to enjoy the equivalent"; "Put *your* house in order"; and so forth. Yet, by the late 1950's and continuing on into the 1960's, the United States was registering balance-of-payments *deficits* — deficits so large and persistent that people both at home and abroad became concerned and then alarmed.

Why did the United States' balance-of-payments position shift from surplus to deficit? In the largest sense, the reason was rooted in a basic shift occurring at a global level. World War II, and its attendant circumstances, had thrust new international responsibilities upon the United States, and, concurrently, had knocked out Europe economically. Within a few years, however, the United States' new responsibilities were proving costly (even more costly than initially anticipated, given the onset of the "cold war"), and, again, concurrently, Europe had recovered — indeed, recovered with a vengeance in the sense that it had built anew and had become a potentially strong rival.

Viewed more narrowly, the United States' balance-of-payments position weakened at a number of points: the margin of exports over imports narrowed, ostensibly because of a relative deterioration in competitive strength; foreign outlays rose because of military commitments (outlays of a type only slightly offset by exports); American producers became more eager to acquire plant capacity inside the lucrative Common Market area; and so on. Which of these points is judged to be *the* special "villain" depends on who is making the judgment. In any case, an abundant literature on the subject now exists.

In our present section (first selection), Professor Hansen examines this balance-of-payments shift. His appraisal is that the military outlays this country has been making abroad on its own behalf have been the real — the foremost — cause of difficulty.

Yet, we know that *multiple* factors are involved. Certainly, for example, there is no denying that trade competition has intensified during recent years; even a casual look at what has occurred in automobile trade bears out this point. Addressing himself to the matter of trade competition, Professor Drucker (in our second selection) stresses that today the United States *must* give priority attention to the export-import relationship.

It is well and good to examine what has happened to the balance of payments in the past, and to attempt to ascertain why it happened. Beyond this, however, there is the question of what the country's balance-of-payments situation is likely to be in the near future. In a third selection, Walter S. Salant outlines the conclusions of a Brookings Institution study (1963) concerned with balance-of-payments projections to 1968. Pursuant to stated assumptions, the overall prediction is that, primarily because of disproportionate price rises in Western Europe (the result of pressures engendered by super-full employment), the probability is that disparities in competitive positions will be lessened and that the United States' balance-of-payments position will improve.

Interestingly, contrary predictions have been made — especially during very recent periods, as additional years of continuing deficit are being chalked up. One of the recent predictors, Robert W. Stevens ("Wishful Thinking on the Balance of Payments," *Harvard Business Review,* November–December 1966), analyzes trends in the major balance-of-payments components, and finds little basis for hoping for a change for the better.

21..... The U.S. Balance of Payments*

ALVIN H. HANSEN

Harvard University, Emeritus

Dollar Shortage

The United States is today the storm center around which international monetary problems revolve. This is nothing new, but the wind now blows in a different direction. Prior to 1950 the great world monetary problem was "dollar scarcity." The United States was always exporting too much and importing too little. Foreign countries did not earn enough dollars selling goods and services to the United States (or to other countries in command of dollars) to pay for the goods and services purchased from the United States. There was a gap in the trade balance.

A trading country that buys less goods and services than it sells may even the score by buying assets — direct investments or foreign securities and real estate. The United States did this on a big scale in the twenties. In the decade 1924–1934 the overall accounts were sufficiently balanced so that the U.S. gold stock in January, 1934, stood at around $4 billion, the same level as in 1924 (both in terms of the old price of gold), although there were violent fluctuations up and down in the intervening period.

In the succeeding decade, 1934–1944, gold inflows into the United States (in terms of the new price of gold) amounted to $14 billion. Of this vast amount about one-third represented an offset to an export surplus, and two-thirds an offset to a capital flight from Europe induced first by the threatening international situation and finally by the outbreak of war.

Thus it was that the United States held 27 per cent of the world's monetary gold stock in 1913, 44 per cent in 1924, and 60 per cent in 1944. At the 1948 peak the aggregate gold holdings amounted to about $25

* From *The Dollar and the International Monetary System* by Alvin H. Hansen, pp. 3–7, 22–26, 35–37. Copyright 1965 by McGraw-Hill, Inc. McGraw-Hill Book Company. Used by permission.

billion. The United States was accumulating "cash." It was mopping up the world's stock of gold.

In the twenties and thirties the United States was, in the eyes of the world, the *bête noire*. The American tariff, boosted still higher in the Smoot-Hawley Tariff Act, and the American Depression were the chief irritants. Books were being written about the twentieth-century Midas. Europeans were directing homilies at the United States demanding that it "put its house in order." The United States was not playing the game fair. It wanted to sell but not to buy. The task of remedying the imbalance in world trade devolved upon the United States.

The deficit countries could indeed have acted to balance up their accounts (and were in fact often forced to do so) by restricting their purchases of U.S. goods. One restriction led to another. In the final analysis, however, both economics and international "political morality" pointed the finger at the surplus country — the United States.

Dollar Glut

Since 1950 the tables have been turned. The dollar scarcity problem is gone. But so firmly was the idea planted in the minds of everyone concerned with international trade that monetary authorities continued to talk about "dollar scarcity" long after it had been metamorphosed into the "dollar glut." . . .

Beginning with 1950 the United States has been paying out more dollars to foreign countries than they pay for the goods, services, and assets which they wish to purchase from the United States. The United States has become a deficit country. Its payments exceed its receipts, and so it is losing cash — gold — or increasing its short-term liabilities.

The Western European countries, notably the Common Market countries and Switzerland, are now the surplus countries. It is they who are now absorbing more and more of the world's international reserves.

The U.S. overall deficits (or surpluses) for the period 1948 to 1962 are given in Table 1, together with U.S. gold stocks for certain years. It will be noted that foreigners did not demand full payment in gold, especially in the earlier years. They counted, as part payment, liquid dollar holdings — deposits in New York banks or U.S. Treasury bills or other short-term U.S. government securities. But official holdings *could* all be converted on demand into gold. And the Continental monetary authorities did demand gold.[1]

Why were the experts so slow about recognizing that the United States had switched over from being a surplus country to a deficit country in

---

[1] Beginning with July, 1963, gold outflows declined. Indeed the U.S. gold stocks stood in April, 1964, at a level slightly above that of July, 1963.

TABLE 1

U.S. Payments Deficits or Surpluses, 1948–1963,*
and Gold Stocks, 1948, 1956, and 1963
(in billions of dollars; gold stocks in round numbers)

Year	Deficits (−) or Surpluses (+)	Gold Stocks, Billions
1948	+$1.0	$25
1949	+ 0.2	
1950	− 3.6	
1951	− 0.3	
1952	− 1.0	
1953	− 2.2	
1954	− 1.6	
1955	− 1.1	
1956	− 0.9	22
1957	+ 0.5	
1958	− 3.5	
1959	− 3.7	
1960	− 3.9	
1961	− 2.4	
1962	− 2.2	
1963	− 3.1†	15.5

* Note should be taken of the fact that the U.S. official figures of balance of payments overstate the deficits. This is due to the fact that the United States, unlike most other countries, does not set out the short-term claims of U.S. commercial banks on foreigners against their short-term liabilities to foreigners. The statistics include the gross short-term liabilities instead of the net figures because all the short-term liabilities can readily be converted into gold since private holdings can easily be shifted over to the central banks. Still the net figures would tell a more accurate story.

Also it should be noted that our net international assets, long-term and short-term, have been growing all through the period of balance-of-payments deficits.
† The deficit was much lower in the second half of 1963 due largely to the proposed interest equalization tax. The low annual rate of $1.5 billion in the first 5 months of 1964 (which may have been temporary) was due to such factors as (1) the tax on new foreign issues, (2) higher interest rates, (3) reduced overseas government spending, and (4) an increase in U.S. exports induced by rising European incomes. The deficit in the last half of 1963 was less than one-half that of the first half of that year.

terms of international payments? The answer is very simple: There has been in fact no switch in the "trading balance."[2] The United States continues, as of yore, to export far more goods and services than it imports. The United States still has, as we shall see, a huge surplus in its trade account. In these terms we are still confronted with "dollar shortage."

Do the recent losses of gold indicate that the United States is losing out

[2] For short, I use the term "trading balance" to include goods and services, excluding military expenditures abroad from the "services" category. For "goods" alone, I use the conventional phrase "merchandise trade."

in its competitive position in world trade? What criteria should be used to judge? In what follows, we attempt to evaluate various criteria of competitiveness.

The Overall Picture

. . . [A] clean-cut measure of competitiveness is not easily available.[3] We can, however, gain some impression of the shifts in competitiveness from a quick, overall statistical survey of the changes in the U.S. balance of payments during the last dozen years.[4] With this in view I present below summary tables of the various component parts, beginning with merchandise trade and finally an overall picture of the exchange-market balance and the transfer balance.

U.S. merchandise exports soared to $16 billion in 1947 while imports fell to $6 billion. But from 1947 on, Europe rapidly recovered. For the pre-Korean period, 1947–1949, merchandise exports averaged $13.8 billion, while imports averaged $6.8 billion. Thus merchandise exports exceeded merchandise imports by $7 billion. But this reflected the low postwar productivity of European countries. The Marshall aid program and the boom after the Korean Conflict hastened their rehabilitation. The share of the United States in world trade was settling down to more normal proportions. But the value was more than maintained, merchan-

---

[3] On the difficulties of measuring competitiveness see P. R. Narvekar, "The Role of Competitiveness in Japan's Export Performance, 1954–1958," *Staff Papers*, International Monetary Fund, vol. 8, pp. 86–87, November, 1960.

[4] Mr. Thomas Balogh, Oxford University, England, points out the folly of judging the U.S. competitive position largely in terms of its payments deficits. Against the surrender of gold and low-interest-bearing liabilities incident to these deficits, he places the increases in American investments abroad — investments that, according to the Department of Commerce, earn well over 15 per cent. He cites President Kennedy's estimate of $35 billion (book value) of American investments abroad and argues that this was a gross understatement of market value. Balogh warned lest the "unwarranted inferiority complex which has beset American decision-making" may prevent that "efflorescence of American technological ingenuity and superiority through innovation which has been the basis of the vast exports of manufactures, especially capital goods." Balogh deprecated the tendency of balance-of-payments statistics to "reflect an ebbing of the American gold reserve week by week, instead of emphasizing the immense increase day by day in American wealth and productive power at home and abroad." *Materials Submitted to the Joint Economic Committee*, 88th Cong. 1st Sess., 1963, pp. 40–41.

A. R. Conan, author of *Capital Imports into Sterling Countries*, and one of the authorities invited by the Joint Committee to appraise the Brookings Report, (see the *U.S. Balance of Payments, Materials Submitted to the Joint Economic Committee*, 88th Cong. 1st Sess., 1963, p. 101), says that the recent decline in the U.S. share of world trade in manufactures "does not reflect any general decline in the competitive position of the United States but was occasioned by special factors of a transient nature. Moreover no adequate support was found for the view that the trend of U.S. export prices, at least during the past few years, has seriously impaired competitiveness."

See also Sir Donald MacDougall, *The Dollar Problem: A Reappraisal*, International Finance Section, Princeton, N.J., no. 35, November, 1960. On balance, MacDougall takes an optimistic view of the competitive position of the United States.

dise exports rising to $18.5 billion per year in 1958–1962.[5] Indeed the net
export surplus rose to $3.8 billion per year compared with $2.8 billion in
1951–1956. These data are summarized in Table 2.

TABLE 2

U.S. Merchandise Trade*
(in billions of dollars;
average per year)

Years	Merchandise Exports	Merchandise Imports	Merchandise Export Surplus
1947–1949	+$13.8	−$ 6.8	$7.0
1951–1956	+ 14.0	− 11.3	2.7
1958–1962	+ 18.5	− 14.7	3.8

* The minuses contribute to an overall deficit; the pluses to a surplus. Data from: *Survey of Current Business.*

Meanwhile services netted $1.6 billion per year in 1947–1949; $2.0
billion per year in 1951–1958; and $2.7 billion per year in 1958–1962.
Combining services and merchandise we get a net excess of exports of
goods and services of $8.6 billion in 1947–1949; $4.7 billion in 1951–1956;
and $6.4 billion in 1958–1962. These data are summarized in Table 3.

TABLE 3

The "Trading Balance": Goods and Services
(in billions of dollars;
average per year)

Years	Merchandise Export Surplus	Services Export Surplus	Net Trading Balance Surplus: Goods and Services
1947–1949	+$7.0	+$1.6	+$8.6
1951–1956	+ 2.7	+ 2.0	+ 4.7
1958–1962	+ 3.8	+ 2.7	+ 6.5

The spectacular goods and services surplus of $8.6 billion in 1947–1949
could not of course be maintained once Europe had recovered her
competitive position. But after the shakedown the United States still
retained a strong surplus position which has been substantially increased
in 1958–1962. In terms of goods and services the dollar shortage is far
from being over. This statement, to be sure, oversimplifies the complex

[5] World trade data were profoundly distorted in the year 1950 by the September,
1949, currency devaluations and by the Korean Conflict and in the year 1957 by the
Suez crisis. I have therefore excluded these years from my data. See the *U.S. Balance
of Payments of 1968*, The Brookings Institution, Appendix, Table 1.

interrelationship of all the factors involved in the overall balance-of-payments picture. Still in the tangle of casual relationships . . . it is important not to lose sight of the fact that as a world trader in goods and services, the United States has a large and growing surplus.

In addition to the goods and services balance there is the private capital account (long-term and short-term) and net private remittances. These data are summarized in Table 4.

TABLE 4

Net Private Capital Flows
(in billions of dollars;
average per year)

Years	Net Flow of Private Long-term Capital	Net Short-term Capital Outflows	Net Private Remittances*	Total
1947–1949	−$0.8	+$0.9	−$0.6	−$0.5
1951–1956	− 0.9	+ 0.3	− 0.5	− 1.1
1958–1962	− 2.2	+ 0.5	− 0.5	− 3.2

* Admittedly this item is rather difficult to classify. But since it is a relatively small and highly stable item, its inclusion here creates no disturbing problem. More disturbing is the fact that "errors and omissions" are dropped into the "short-term capital" basket.

The Basic Causes of the U. S. Deficits

. . . I have stressed the difference between the *trading* balance (including both goods and services) and the *transfer* balance and also the difference between the exchange-market balance and the government transfer balance. These distinctions are of the greatest importance. Are the U.S. deficits of the last six years due to basic shifts in trade or are they due to shifts in the transfer of funds? If the deficit were due to a drastic falling off of exports, primary attention should be directed to our export situation. The trouble might lie in our own export industries, or the trouble might be found in restrictive import policies on the part of foreign countries. If the deficit were due to a drastic increase in U.S. imports the cause might conceivably be located in inefficiency in those American industries that compete with imports. If it is a trade-oriented deficit that is one thing. But if it is a transfer-oriented deficit, that is quite a different matter. True, in the long run, the trade will respond to established transfer flows. But in the short run transfer shifts cannot be offset by corresponding trade shifts without serious disruption in international trade relations. Transfer shifts can however be met without causing dislocations by deliberately offsetting capital flows implemented by adequate institutional arrangements. But in the contemporary world economy it may require international monetary machinery to facilitate the flow of funds across international borders.

Thus the U.S. balance-of-payments deficits emerge basically from two situations, neither of which has to do with the short-run, cyclical or episodic types of imbalances for which the International Monetary Fund was set up or that central bankers contend with when they make short-term loans to tide a country over a temporary crisis. The two persistent sources of the U.S. balance-of-payments problem are (1) the U.S. program of military and economic foreign aid and (2) the New York capital market which, on top of the government aid programs, supplies capital to foreign countries. The current U.S. balance-of-payments problem is perhaps unique in all history. Yet many economists and bankers discuss the problem as though it were just the familiar short-run, cyclical, or episodic case.

What I am saying does not mean that adjustments cannot be made over time which could end the overall U.S. deficits even though the New York market continues its role as major supplier of funds abroad and the United States continues its aid programs. The progressive rise of investment income alone will automatically play an increasing role as a balancing factor. And the feedback effects will gradually show up in the trade balance and perhaps also in the capital account. If however a more equitable distribution of foreign aid cannot be achieved, and if European capital markets cannot be substantially improved, it is highly improbable that the goods and services account can fully make the needed adjustments barring policies (tariff increases, exchange control, etc.) that are injurious to a prospering and growing world trade.

Professor Zolotas, governor of the Bank of Greece, has summed up the matter admirably as follows:

> As a matter of fact, in the last two years the annual outflow of long-term capital alone accounts for more than the corresponding overall deficit in the U.S. balance of payments. The still existing restrictions on capital exports in several industrial countries, and, more significantly, the organizational and institutional shortcomings of capital markets outside the U.S., impose on her, in addition to the responsibilities of a reserve center, the task of satisfying capital requirements in the rest of the world, including the highly developed countries. This situation is incompatible with the smooth functioning of the gold exchange standard, which requires some measure of correspondence in the availability and freedom of movement of capital among major trading countries. The resulting strains from this lopsided operation of the international financial mechanism are being accentuated by the movement of short-term funds, partly in reference to interest rate differentials. Under these conditions one can hardly deny the necessity for the industrial countries of Europe to liberalize and develop their capital markets in accordance with the overall potential of their economies. This, however, is likely to be a gradually evolving process, leaving the main burden of the task at present to the United States. The resistance of the latter to the easy solution of direct capital controls should be generally appreciated.[6]

[6] *Summary Proceedings,* Annual Meeting, IMF, 1963, p. 93.

22..... International Competition and Business*

PETER F. DRUCKER

New York University

. . . [Until only recently], America's international economic position seemed impregnable. So eminent an expert as Sir Geoffrey Crowther — then retiring as editor of *The Economist* (London) — called the "dollar gap" the one unalterable and basic fact of international economics for years to come. Those few who dared warn of dangers ahead got short shrift. . . . Today, who can doubt that the "dollar crisis" has replaced the dollar gap as the central problem of the international economy?

At the root of the dollar crisis is, of course, our balance of trade. Nontrade payments have risen neither absolutely nor relatively (except for movements of short-term "swing" capital which are effects of the payments balance rather than of its causes). Clearly, the real problem is not that imports have risen unduly, but that exports have lagged behind. Let's take a look at the facts:

Imports have been going up at the rate of 5% a year since 1953 (which can be considered the first "normal" postwar year, with reconstruction largely completed and the Korean War impact largely liquidated). This has been, however, a less rapid rise than we should have expected on the basis of our own country's experience and that of all other industrial countries. Imports of industrial raw materials and supplies (which make up two thirds of our total imports) have tended to rise one-and-a-half to two times as fast as the gross national product.

By contrast, our exports have risen no faster than the GNP — showing an average gain of 3½% to 4% for the 1953–1959 period. During that same period, the economy of the rest of the Free World expanded at a 6% to 7% annual clip.

* Taken and adapted from "This Competitive World," *Harvard Business Review*, March–April 1961, pp. 131–135.

Actually, these figures underrate the falling off of exports, for, during that period, the "terms of trade" swung heavily in our favor. Two-thirds of our imports are industrial raw materials and supplies which had a downward price trend during the period. This was especially true over the later years when our trade balance so rapidly deteriorated. Two-thirds of our exports are manufactured goods which, through 1959, had a strong upward price trend. Probably we did not export more, in volume, during 1959 than in 1953 — the bulk of the increased export income deriving from higher prices. But we bought an increased volume of raw materials and supplies over what we could have bought if 1953 commodity prices had continued to prevail — or even if they had moved parallel to manufactured prices.

How has American industry reacted to this challenge? By and large, it has responded so quickly that 1960 ended up as a year in which American exports increased sharply. Obviously, a good many companies found effective ways of restoring the competitive edge to their products in foreign markets.[1]

But few American businessmen seem as yet able to understand what is really happening. They are responding with a good deal of energy to what they feel is a "temporary emergency" that requires "crash" measures.

Permanent Changes

What most American businessmen fail to realize is that there have been basic structural changes in the world economy — particularly with reference to the position held by the United States. What we must face is the fact that these are permanent changes which require new basic attitudes, new policies, and new concepts on the part of the American policy maker and, especially, on the part of the American businessman.

What are these new, but permanent, conditions that American businessmen have to understand and live with? Let me present them in a series of "theses."

1. *The world economy has become competitive again for the first time since 1913 or, at the very least, for the first time since 1929.*

This means, first, that everyone in the Free World can get anything he wants — and can pay for — in the quantity and quality he wants, from a number of different suppliers, and in a number of different countries. It means, secondly, that these suppliers are actively competing for business in every market.

This is a great achievement — one that has been the aim (the almost utopian aim) of American policy since the end of World War II. It means not only that we have been able to rebuild a shattered world economy,

[1]See Raphael Hodgson and Michael Michaelis, "Planning for Profits in World Business," *Harvard Business Review*, November–December 1960, p. 135.

but also that we have been able to infuse hope, dynamism, and economic growth into the countries of the Free World, despite the trauma and destruction of the war.

But this achievement is not an unmixed blessing. One rather disquieting implication is that there no longer will be any "orderly" prices for any major industrial supply or product in the world market. As recently as two years ago, the world-price structure was essentially based on prices set by American companies and on American costs and market conditions. Prices outside this country tended to be determined by adding a percentage to the American price. This was true in the automobile industry, for example, where the Chevrolet-Ford-Plymouth price was the "norm" against which all non-American car manufacturers priced their goods. It also was true in steel, coal, oil, aluminum, and a host of other major products.

But a decisive event suddenly brought this entire price structure of the world market crashing down. It was the collapse in 1959 of the oldest, most deeply entrenched, and most "sacred" of these prices — the Gulf Coast price base for petroleum. Today, there is only one such American-based world-market price left — that for aluminum. And there is every indication that it will not last long.

A further implication of this first thesis is that even in the domestic market major industrial products and supplies will not be priced on the basis of American conditions. What will determine the price in any major market in the world (including the American domestic market), is the marginal, incremental income of the most efficient major producer anywhere in the Free World. Here are some illustrations of how this price determinative has worked and will work in the future:

> Look at the way the American "compact" cars have been priced. Clearly, domestic producers paid just as much attention to the price of the Volkswagen as to the price of yesterday's "standard" car.

> Another indication is the inability — or the unwillingness — of the American steel industry to raise prices in spite of the sizable increase in labor costs which followed the 1959 steel strike. . . .

2. *Our ability to increase exports determines whether (and by how much) America's national income can grow; it can only grow less — and quite a bit less — than U.S. exports. The international economy, not the domestic economy, sets the limitations on U.S. growth and prosperity and is the determining area of economic performance.*

This situation is something quite new for modern America to face — though it was pretty generally accepted for the largely agricultural United States that existed before 1900. For the rest of the world, and especially for our allies in Western Europe, it is, of course, "old hat."

It is not only that 4 million to 5 million jobs depend directly on export production and export sales (perhaps 3 million jobs in manufacturing and up to 2 million jobs in distribution, transportation, banks, insurance, and other services). It is also the fact that 15 million jobs or more depend on our ability to obtain raw materials and supplies abroad on the same terms, at least, as those on which the other industrial countries obtain them. As we grow, our import demands will grow disproportionately. Hasn't this been our experience over the last ten years? And too many of us forget that there is only one way to pay for imports from abroad — with exports.

As our gold stock dwindles to the minimum reserve we need for internal uses and for the settlement of normal current balances, economic growth and a healthy and balanced economy will increasingly depend on our ability to raise exports *faster* than the national product, and at least as fast as our imports.

We can, within limits, control the impact of domestic events on the economy. But no economic or fiscal controls of ours are effective on the international economy. There we have to perform — and there our performance will determine the limits of our domestic economy. How we stand in the world markets will indicate the sickness or health of the American economy and of American business.

3. *Protective tariffs, despite the fact that many businessmen regard them as panaceas, only serve to make matters much worse.*

When I postulate this, I am not arguing for or against government support of industries hard hit by foreign competition. I am only saying that a protective tariff is highly unlikely to help such industries. In fact, it is almost certain to hurt them, as well as everybody else in our country. If there has to be support for endangered industries, direct subsidies are much cheaper, much more effective, and much less distorting.

The reason that protective tariffs can harm our economy is simply that our major export markets are precisely the countries from which those "undesirable imports" come. The major market for most of our exports simply cannot be the "underdeveloped countries," no matter how much aid we pump into them. . . .

Let's face some other facts. . . . Most probably, we escaped a serious depression in 1960 only because the developed countries (i.e., our industrial competitors) greatly stepped up their purchases from the United States. This was accomplished mainly through lowering barriers against U.S. imports. The resulting additional 1960 exports to the industrial countries abroad provided something like an *extra* half-million jobs for the American economy — over and above the one-and-a-half million jobs that exports to these countries had already provided in 1959. . . .

As this 1960 experience proves, we stand to *gain* infinitely more through a liberal low-tariff policy on the part of "competitive" countries than we stand to lose from their exports into the United States. And we stand to *lose* infinitely more — in jobs as well as in balance of payments — from a high-tariff policy on the part of these countries than we could possibly gain from a high-tariff policy on the part of the United States.

Thus, while our tariff policy can be criticized for not being in step with the realities of our present international situation, our tariffs cannot be criticized for being too low. The real criticism should center on the fact that we have not yet used our control of access to the increasingly tempting American market as the bait with which to lure other countries into lowering their barriers against American goods. . . .

For us to go protectionist would, in other words, serve only to destroy major American markets. But for us to have and use the *threat* of going protectionist — unless we are granted abroad what we grant here — would certainly create major world markets.

4. *Equally defensive — and equally dangerous — is the moving of productive facilities for the American market to another "low-wage" area.*

First, let me stress that building plants abroad is all to the good — if the purpose is to broaden the market for American goods and hence increase our income. This includes building or expanding plants to serve markets abroad which have grown to such size and absorptive capacity that they can support fully efficient operations. Indeed, in such a situation the United States manufacturer, by building a plant, creates jobs for Americans — for suppliers of machines, for architects, for designers, and so on. And, in such a case, the only critical decision to be made is whether, when the plant is built, the American economy will benefit. This is at least more probable when an American company builds the plant, as opposed to having it built by someone else who, presumably, would be less likely to create export demand for U.S. machinery and equipment. At any rate, if the market is there, the plant will be built by someone.

There is also nothing wrong with building a plant in areas where tariffs or foreign-exchange shortages make importation impossible. An underdeveloped country, in particular, can often become a customer for American products only if a local plant using local materials for the small local market (even though at prices way above the world market) saves enough foreign exchange to make possible the importation of machinery and equipment from the U.S.

What I do hold to be completely foolhardy is the building of a foreign plant to supply the American manufacturer for the home market. This is rank defeatism; furthermore, it aggravates the disease by eroding purchasing power at home.

Here is the criterion that should be applied: *Does building the plant result, ultimately, in a strengthening of America's competitive position?* If it does — by supplying a part, for instance, that makes the finished product more salable at home and abroad — then all is well. But if it does not, this decision, in fairly short order, will not even be intelligent policy for the individual company — let along for the economy. Such a move amounts to strangulation of our nation's economic power and competitive capacity.

5. *There is no way out but to restore U.S. competitive edge and product leadership — and above all to retain it in the many areas where it is still unimpaired.*

The economic developments in the world that produced the "dollar crisis" are fundamentally "good" in the sense that they are situations calling for aggressive, offensive action by American business. But if we fail to rise to the occasion, things will not be good in *any* sense.

Thus, the maintenance of American competitive strength must be a major goal of American economic policy and of the policy of any U.S. business. This is something all other countries have had to learn. . . . [We] have to learn a few lessons ourselves. One such lesson is in the area of labor relations; both management and unions will have to accept the fact that ability to remain competitive is just as important as ability to pay or the political balance of strength.

6. *It is not likely that raw material prices today are too low; it is much more likely that prices of manufactured goods are too high — by something like 25%.*

This assumption (and it is no more than that, even though it has high probability) rests on the fact that, measured by historical relationships, today's raw material prices are not too low in relation to the profitability of the most efficient producer. In such a situation any attempts to inflate the price through "price agreements" or cartels (such as the international oil cartel recently proposed by Venezuela and some of the Arabian oil countries) are totally ineffectual.

This indicates, then, that manufactured goods are far overpriced in relation to raw materials. The orthodox way to restore the balance between them is to cut manufactured goods prices without cutting raw material prices and other costs — i.e., to deflate. There is plenty of this going on today, of course. "Quoted prices" bear little relationship to actual prices in a host of industries from paper to locomotives. . . .

But there is a second way to restore a proper balance between raw material and finished goods prices. This is the Keynesian method of "reflation" whereby raw material prices (and wages) are raised while finished goods prices remain unchanged. . . .

There is still a third way, which is, in an expanding, dynamic economy, both the easiest and the best method. It involves substitution. . . .

Developing substitutions which cut the cost to the customer without disrupting the price structure or the economy offers special opportunities to American manufacturers. Here the tremendous amounts of effort and money poured into research and development during the last ten years should pay off. By judicious substitution, we might actually get substantially lower prices without any resultant lowering of returns on investments. . . .

To bring about such price lowering through substitution should be a continuing, major aim of business management. . . .

7. *Any American businessman, especially a manufacturer, should gauge the effectiveness and the efficiency of his business by its ability to compete in the world.*

Even if the businessman has no export business and does not intend to have any, the question he asks about his market, even his local one, should be this: "*What will I have to do to make my product capable of competing in the Japanese market?*" The one suggestion I can offer that applies to every case I have seen is that manufacturers concentrate their product lines.

The shibboleth of the "full product line" is, in my experience, a major cause of American inability to compete. Typically, our manufacturing businesses offer a thousand "lines." Of these, 20 or 30 account for four-fifths of all sales and for all profits while constituting only two-fifths of the costs. The remaining 900 or so account for one-fifth of all sales, make no profit (even with all the "breaks" given to them by traditional cost accounting), and eat up three-fifths of all costs. The same situation, to a lesser extent, applies to all kinds of staff activities.

To be competitive . . . companies have to concentrate on the three or four products (or activities) that account for the overwhelming bulk of all sales — and consider the others merely as "sales promotions" on which one spends only carefully budgeted amounts.

Conclusion

My purpose here has not been to discuss any form of "how to do it." Rather, it has been to get across to American executives the fact that ability to be competitive begins right here at home. Such an ability begins by looking at the market in Kokomo, Indiana, as a market in which one competes against all comers. It begins with one simple but all-important question: "What would I have to do to be able to compete in Osaka, or Dusseldorf, or Bordeaux?" If a product cannot compete in foreign markets, then foreign products can drive it out of Kokomo.

Seizing the offensive is the only strategy that can work in an expanding and competitive economy — regardless of whether it is national or international. U.S. business must take the initiative internationally — in price, in styling, in innovation and design, and in marketing. We have to accept what we all know to be elemental — that taking a defensive position can, at best, only limit losses. And we need gains.

23..... Prospects for the U. S. Balance of Payments*

WALTER S. SALANT
Brookings Institution

Economic Significance

The U.S. dollar in the markets and eyes of the world has undergone a dramatic change during the past decade. The dollar, 10 years ago, was regarded as a superstrong currency. It had been in short supply since before World War II, and some observers expected it to remain in short supply for the indefinite future, owing to basic forces which they claimed to see at work in the world.

For most of the period since 1958, however, it had been weak. This weakness has been an important factor in inhibiting the United States from pursuing domestic monetary and fiscal policies that could raise its national output, with its present manpower and other resources, by a substantial amount — an estimated $30 to $40 billion per year, according to the Council of Economic Advisers.

The change in the position of the dollar from a strong to a weak currency reflects in part the deterioration of the U.S. balance-of-payments position. But it also reflects other things — changes in the liquidity position, the state of confidence, and other factors that affect the willingness to hold dollar assets. . . .

Framework of Analysis

While there may be greater immediate interest in our conclusions, I think there is . . . value in the analytical approach we use. . . .

* Taken and adapted from "The United States Balance of Payments," *Hearings Before the Joint Economic Committee*, 88th Congress, 1st Session, Part 2, 1963, pp. 233–237, 239, 243–245. The report states that participants in its preparation, in addition to Walter S. Salant, included Alice Rivlin, Emile Despres, Lawrence Krause, William Salant, and Lorie Tarshis.

The first point is that any substantial and persistent changes in the U.S. net balance of payments will be reflected in opposite changes in the net balances of Western Europe. This generalization — and it is a broad one, to be applied with caution and qualifications — reflects the empirical observation that the rest of the world, in the aggregate and over periods of several years, does not have substantial net surpluses or net deficits. This generalization is basically a reflection of the fact that most other countries of the world have a demand for imported goods and services so intense that they cannot, or in any case, do not, accumulate reserves, and that they also do not have sufficient reserves to run deficits for any protracted period.

It is true that some of these countries run deficits which may be fairly substantial for a year or so, but they then have to curtail their imports and restore their positions, i.e., they pay off or fund the short-term debt incurred in financing the deficit or they replenish the depleted reserves. Some of these countries also may have substantial surpluses for a year or two, but the evidence is that they then tend to expand their imports and run down their reserves. This generalization is a simplification. It may not be true for every country, but it seems to be true in the aggregate.

One implication of this generalization is that one can test any proposition about whether a given change will affect the U.S. net balance significantly and over a period of several years by asking whether it will have the opposite effect on the net balance of Western Europe. If something which appears in the first instance to affect the U.S. balance of payments does not have an opposite effect on the balance of payments of Western Europe as a whole, it is advisable to look again, to see whether the change that one originally thought would affect the U.S. balance may not directly or indirectly cause some compensating change, leaving the U.S. deficit or surplus substantially unaffected.

This test leads to my second general point: Because the U.S. economy is a very large one, different types of transactions in the U.S. balance of payments are closely interrelated. Changes in some transactions tend to be offset by changes in others. For example, changes in U.S. imports are very likely to result in changes in U.S. exports — or in U.S. dividend receipts, if the imports come from countries in whose export industries we have large investments.

Similarly, increases in foreign aid are likely to feed back to changes in U.S. exports, if the aid is to countries which obtain a large portion of their imports from the United States. There are also relations between U.S. capital outflow and U.S. trade. Some of these relations are obvious, but some of them are more roundabout and less obvious. For example, an increase in U.S. business activity which increases demand for imported raw materials and raises their prices may raise the cost of production of our European competitors more than it raises ours, and thereby improve our competitive position in manufactured products.

Similarly, savings in foreign aid may give rise to compensating changes in capital movements or vice versa.

In all these cases, there is an interrelationship between the first and second points I have made. Increases in imports from non-European areas are more likely to increase U.S. exports than are increases in imports from Western Europe because non-European countries tend to spend their foreign exchange receipts, not to accumulate reserves.

These feedbacks must be taken into account in appraising efforts to reduce the U.S. deficit. For example, a million dollars of foreign-aid expenditures has much less effect upon the deficit than a million dollars of military expenditures because the military expenditures go to Europe and cause very little feedback to our receipts, whereas the foreign-aid expenditures go mostly to non-European countries and in most cases do have a substantial feedback to our receipts. It is also desirable to distinguish among non-European countries according to the portions of changes in their payments that go, directly and indirectly, to the United States and the portions that go, directly and indirectly, to Europe. U.S. payments to Latin America, for example, affect U.S. receipts to a much greater extent than do U.S. payments to Africa.

The third main point is that U.S. international transactions are in large part a reflection of relations between internal developments in the United States and elsewhere. And, as the first point implies, "elsewhere" means mainly Western Europe. The balance of payments is only the part of the iceberg that is showing. If we want to understand and project it, we must understand and project the larger part that is submerged. Ideally, we need to know all the quantitative relations between these internal factors — not only in the United States but in the rest of the world — and international transactions, including the division of other countries' international payments among the payee countries.

So much by way of background.

The Projections

The focus of our study is on the year 1968, as the Council [of Economic Advisers] requested. . . .

Assumptions

I shall not describe all the assumptions in detail. It is sufficient to say that the first projection is based on the assumption of a gross national product in 1968 of approximately $743 billion for the United States — measured in 1961 prices — or a rise of 43 per cent from the 1961 level. For Western Europe, the rise of GNP is projected at 33 per cent in the same period. As to prices, we assumed an 11 per cent rise in the implicit deflator for the U.S. gross national product between 1961 and 1968. We obtained assumptions regarding the level of foreign aid and military expenditures abroad, and assumed that exchange rates will remain at their present levels.

We were given no assumptions about price movements in Western Europe. To deduce them, we projected cost pressures and, concluding that they would increase greatly, then projected aggregate demand in relation to output to see if the cost pressures would be likely to force European prices to rise. For the initial assumptions, we assumed that any such tendencies could not or would not be effectively counteracted by Western European governments. We also had to make our own judgments about the rise in export prices of manufactured goods relative to the rise in GNP prices — for both Western Europe and the United States.

The alternative projections assume that GNP in the United States and Western Europe will grow by 10 per cent less than under the initial assumptions. We assume, however, that the GNP deflator for the United States will rise by the same amount as under the initial assumptions, and that foreign aid and military expenditures abroad would be the same as under the first assumptions. In the second projections, however, we assume that European governments will use monetary and fiscal policy more effectively to dampen the price rise.

Thus, the main differences between the two sets of assumptions are (1) that the growth in GNP is lower in the second than in the first set for both the United States and in Western Europe and (2) that resistance to price rises in Western Europe is assumed to be greater and more effective under the second set than under the first. . . .

Conclusions About 1968

On the first set of assumptions, we conclude that fundamental forces at work will make for a basic surplus of nearly $2 billion by 1968, an improvement of $3.4 billion compared to the 1961–62 average basic deficit of $1.5 billion. The improvement shows up largely in increases in net exports of goods and services, including a substantial rise in income from private investment abroad. This increase is reinforced by a decline in military expenditures and by a somewhat smaller decline in the outflow of private long-term capital. These gains are offset, but only partially, by an increase in expenditures for foreign aid. . . .

There are two major reasons for the projected improvement under the first set of assumptions. One is the improvement in the U.S. competitive position. Our assumptions imply that prices and costs in Western Europe — primarily on the Continent — will rise substantially relative to prices and costs in the United States. Reinforced by the assumed rise in Western Europe's real income, the effect will more than offset the effects of the assumed rise in our real income on imports of goods and services and the adverse effects of discrimination by the EEC against us and some of our customers.

The improvement in our competitive position arises fundamentally from differences between the United States and Western Europe in the prospective growth of the labor supply. The growth of the labor force in Western Europe is expected to decline and this decline will be reinforced by a projected cut in the average length of the workweek. In the United States, however, the existing labor force is underemployed and the growth in the labor force will accelerate. On our assumptions as to Western European policies, the tightness in Western Europe's labor market will cause a substantial increase in wages and also in labor costs per unit of output — more than double the average annual rise in the United States. Thus, we project substantial upward cost pressure in Western Europe, and sufficient aggregate demand to carry this cost pressure through to a substantial rise of prices.

In our judgment, this rise in Western Europe's GNP prices would be accompanied by a rise of export prices — a situation which did not occur during the 1950's. During most of the postwar period, investment in Western Europe was more concentrated on export goods and import-competing goods than we think it will be between now and 1968. That is why we expect the relationship between movements of export prices and of GNP prices in Western Europe in the future to be different from the relationship in the 1950's.

The second major reason for the projected improvement in the basic balance is a substantial rise in net receipts assoicated with past and current international long-term investments. This rise results from both an increase in investment income and a decline in the net outflow of long-term capital.

These influences are reinforced by an expected decline in military expenditures abroad. They are only partially offset by the adverse effects of discrimination by the European Economic Community on imports from the United States and some of its customers, and by the net effect of assumed increases in foreign aid.

Under the alternative set of assumptions, which on the whole we think more realistic, the improvement in the basic deficit compared to the revised figures for 1961 — revised since we submitted our report to the Council of Economic Advisers — is so small in relation to the possible error that it should not be regarded seriously, but it is a large improvement over 1962. It leaves the United States in basic deficit to the extent of about one-half billion dollars.

Most of the differences between the results obtained under the two sets of assumptions reflects the difference in European prices, rather than the difference in the assumed changes in real income. Under the second set of assumptions, the competitive position of the United States improves by a good deal less than under the first. . . .

Actions Needed

The United States should immediately begin to press for an agreement to strengthen international liquidity. Since the study and negotiations needed to obtain agreement on a new mechanism for international liquidity may take a long time, however, the United States will be obliged to deal with its balance-of-payments problems within the framework of the present mechanism.

Measures to Finance the Deficit

Even if the projections of this report are realized, there probably will be deficits in the U.S. balance of payments for the next several years. However, U.S. reserves are so large, compared to likely levels of the deficit, that we see no reason for concern about financing these deficits while working to improve the international monetary system. Despite the substantial reduction in U.S. monetary reserves and the large increase in liquid dollar claims of foreigners, U.S. reserves and other resources for meeting continuing deficits remain very great. The U.S. Government should make clear that it regards its reserves as existing to be used for these purposes.

The statutory requirement of a gold reserve against Federal Reserve notes and deposit liabilities long ago ceased to serve any useful purpose. It should be abolished. Its abolition would make clear that the reserves are available to the full and at all times, not merely in emergencies, to serve their only useful function.

The United States should also draw on the IMF . . . to finance some of its future deficit. Such drawings would help to promote the idea that use of the Fund's resources is not an act of last resort; more willingness of IMF members to draw on it would increase effective liquidity.

Such steps would establish that the United States is willing to use its reserves and credit facilities to support the dollar.

Measures to Improve the Balance of Payments

We do not recommend that the Government at this time take any steps to improve the balance of payments other than measures which seem desirable in themselves. Actions already taken, such as tying aid and restricting certain types of military expenditures abroad, should be regarded as temporary. Further restrictive measures of this type would be of negligible benefit, if not positively harmful. To cut aid or military expenditures for balance-of-payment reasons would be an unwise and unnecessary sacrifice of more important objectives.

As the balance-of-payments deficit declines, foreign aid expenditures should gradually be untied.

We have stressed that measures which might endanger U.S. economic growth and the restoration of high employment levels should not be adopted for balance-of-payments reasons. This means that it is inadvisable to raise interest rates in an attempt to affect international flows of capital, unless the adverse domestic effects of higher rates can be fully offset by fiscal expansion. The balance of payments and other goals will be served, however, by wage and price restraint during the course of recovery to high employment. Restraint on wage and price increases will benefit the U.S. competitive position without retarding domestic growth. The Government's efforts in this direction should be stepped up as the country moves toward full employment.

Devaluation of the dollar also should be rejected. Devaluation might actually weaken, rather than strengthen, the dollar. If other countries — especially those in the European Economic Community (EEC) — devalued their currencies in line with the dollar, the U.S. deficit would not be reduced, but the future willingness of foreigners to accumulate dollar assets would be curtailed. Even if other major currencies were not devalued, however, devaluation of the dollar should be rejected. Devaluation is appropriate only when a balance-of-payments deficit is clearly caused by a fundamental disequilibrium that is not likely to diminish in the future. Our projections suggest substantial future improvement at the current exchange rate. Devaluation, therefore, might throw the United States into substantial surplus and other countries into deficit.

The United States should bargain vigorously with the EEC for trade liberalization . . . and insist on some minimum concessions. A satisfactory agreement should preserve and enlarge foreign markets for Temperate Zone agricultural products, liberalize EEC imports of manufactured goods, especially those from Japan and underdeveloped countries, and reduce discrimination against tropical products of Latin America and other non-EEC countries. Agreement should not be sought at any price.

Measures to Improve Arrangements for International Liquidity

The U.S. Government should make a major effort to establish with other countries an adequate international liquidity mechanism. The immediate task is to formulate a plan which meets the criteria for a satisfactory system. The next task is to seek international agreement on such a plan. We propose four requirements of a satisfactory system:

1. It must provide enough liquidity at the outset to finance substantial imbalances while adjustments are taking place, and it must provide for increases in liquidity as the need for liquidity grows.
2. Additional liquidity which takes the form of credit should be available readily and promptly, and for a period long enough to permit elimination of the deficit. Substantial amounts should be obtainable automatically by deficit countries. By agreement, additional amounts should be made available to countries with particularly intractable balance-of-payments problems if appropriate measures for dealing with these problems are being taken.

3. The possibility of shifting reserves from weak to strong currencies must be prevented. These problems would be avoided if industrial countries committed themselves to hold a substantial fraction of their reserves in an international institution, with creditor countries accumulating credits in an international unit of account and debtor countries accumulating similarly denominated debits or reducing previously acquired credits.
4. For such a system to work it is probably necessary that the principal financial and industrial countries consult fully and frequently and coordinate policies that have substantial effects on international payments.

As to getting an agreement, Western European countries are not likely to be receptive to U.S. proposals which seem only to ask them to commit themselves more irrevocably and firmly to propping up the present dollar exchange standard. If the United States wishes to gain European support for an expanded international liquidity arrangement, therefore, it must consider the possibility that the dollar's role as a reserve currency would be curtailed. . . .

An Alternative International Monetary Mechanism

If it becomes clear that agreement on a satisfactory liquidity mechanism cannot be obtained, the United States must seek an alternative. The best alternative, in our view, would be a modified system of flexible exchange rates consisting of a dollar-sterling bloc and an EEC bloc, with fixed rates within each bloc and flexible rates between them. . . .

This modified flexible exchange rate system would allow the United States greater national autonomy in the use of fiscal policy, since the external consequences of such policies would be offset by movements in the exchange rate. . . .

Nevertheless, there are some true costs in adopting our second-best, two-bloc proposal. The volume of international trade and capital movements between the members of the two blocs would probably be smaller than under a system of fixed parities with adequate provision for international liquidity. . . .

Our decisive preference is for a system of fixed rates with an adequate liquidity mechanism. More important than the choice of mechanism is our major policy thesis: That the United States seek agreement on an international payments mechanism that permits adjusting national balances of payments without compromising the important goals of national and international policy.

E..... The Problem of International Liquidity

The preceding section dealt with the United States' balance of payments. As we saw, there is a problem — and problems call for solutions. In the present case, two basic courses immediately suggest themselves. Over time, the country can work on the fundamental environment — in an attempt to assure itself of competitive strength in trade, to bring its overseas commitments in line with carrying ability, and so on. But pending this alteration of the environment, the country can rely on stop-gaps aimed at diminishing (or expanding) the magnitudes of select components in the balance of payments. The United States has been pursuing both courses. Relative to the first, the need for competitive strength is being recognized — though official action takes the form of admonition rather than compulsion; and overseas commitments are being given closer scrutiny. Relative to the second (the stop-gap type of action), the country is discouraging some private foreign investment; allowing fewer take-home tourist purchases to enter duty-free; restricting private spending by overseas military personnel; tying more of foreign aid to the American market; and so on.

Despite all that has occurred to date, however, the country's balance-of-payments deficits have persisted. Indeed, what is at issue involves not only a balance-of-payments problem but also a "dollar problem."

When the United States runs a deficit, other countries (say, in Western Europe) run a surplus — a surplus they will normally hold in the form of dollar-claims. If, however, such dollar-claims continue to mount and doubt about the future worth of the dollar develops (say, because persistent balance-of-payments deficits suggest eventual devaluation), the temptation is to request gold in lieu of dollar-claims. And if the right to thus shift into gold is exercised extensively, a "dollar crisis" is invited. Indeed, the foregoing is precisely what happened in 1960–1961, and what continues as a threat to the United States. Under the pressures of the situation, gold stocks in this country now stand at their lowest level in decades — and the balance-of-payments deficits continue.

The average American is concerned about the "dollar crisis" because the associated gold drain jeopardizes, he has heard, the backing for our domestic money supply. Unfortunately, this concern is, in fact, one of the "least of our worries." Decidedly more important is what goes on outside the United States. The dollar is a "key currency" internationally, serving as a reserve medium; upon it depends the liquidity essential to the handling of much of the world's commercial and financial transactions. As frequently observed, a balance-of-payments deficit for the United States provides other countries with needed liquidity. A dilemma arises, however; international dealings depend on the dollar, but the status of the dollar depends on the United States balance of payments — which is in trouble! Conversely, if the United States were able to overcome its deficits (by restoring equilibrium to its balance of payments), other countries would be denied access to the dollars — the liquidity — they need.

To generalize the problem: use of a *national* currency as *international* reserve has the drawback that others are jeopardized when the key-currency country is in trouble. Indeed, the extent of liquidity currently may be tied to the wrong thing; seemingly it should be determined by the *need* for it, not the presence or absence of deficits (which, after all, rest on many considerations, including strictly internal policies). Many are aware of the apparent shortcoming, and have thought deeply about what might be done to improve matters.

Essentially, their thought has produced three sets of views. The first is a *laissez-faire* view: deficits have come and gone before; the present situation will resolve itself; therefore, the proper approach is to "let it alone." Of course, people (and governments) are less willing today than formerly to wait. And years of waiting without a sign of alleviation is enough to shake the confidence of even the firmest of the "let it alone" advocates.

The second and third sets of views fall into a more serious category. The second emphasizes fairly drastic reform — premised on the need for a whole new approach, including new machinery. For example, according to the "Triffin Plan," proposed by Professor Triffin of Yale, national currencies should no longer be used as international reserves; a new supranational authority should take on the responsibility of international reserves; and, in fact, this new authority should possess certain reserve-creating powers in order to *assure* the availability of needed international liquidity.

The third set of views emphasizes modification — a revamping undertaken essentially within the confines of existing institutional arrangements. Many forms of modification are, of course, possible — and many have been suggested: the International Monetary Fund should extend the scope of its lending and stand-by services; the major central banks should agree among themselves on "swapping" arrangements to prepare them to "bail out" key countries in situations that require intervention; and so on. Names associated with proposals in this category include (in the United States) E. M. Bernstein, formerly with the International Monetary Fund

(IMF), and Robert V. Roosa, one-time Under Secretary, U.S. Treasury. What has occurred to date? Basically, (a) expanded authority for the IMF; (b) a "swapping" arrangement between major countries, the so-called "Group of Ten" plus Switzerland; and (c) intervention in the exchange market, on a limited basis, by the U.S. Treasury.

The selections in the present section survey some of the basic literature relative to the above. A first selection presents excerpts — in sequence — from the "Triffin Plan" (by Professor Triffin), from the "Bernstein Proposals" (by E. M. Bernstein), and from Robert V. Roosa, speaking about U.S. Treasury actions.

In a second selection, Professor Kenen, writing after a number of tries at amelioration had been made, assesses the status of international liquidity. His appraisal is that the situation is "livable": there is enough liquidity on hand to tide us through a period of adjustment.

However, the tone of the Council of Economic Advisers' January 1967 *Report to the President,* the substance of our final selection, dashes cold water on any full-fledged optimism. They see continued unmet needs as requiring further action — and then explain *what* action.

24..... International Monetary Reform

I. The "Triffin Plan"*

ROBERT TRIFFIN

Yale University

... Our main problem is not to retrench, but to advance, not to cut our imports and our capital contribution to economic development abroad, but to restore our exports to levels sufficient to enable us to pursue in the future, on a sounder and more durable basis, policies which have abundantly proved their worth and which are indispensable both to our own internal growth and to the maintenance of our economic and political position in the world of tomorrow.

After saying what we should *not* do, let me say what I think we *should* do.

We must, first of all, strengthen, or recover, our competitiveness in world trade, by arresting creeping inflation here, while stepping up our rates of growth and productivity by appropriate investments in research and technology.

We should, secondly, continue to press more and more vigorously for the elimination of remaining discrimination on dollar goods and the further reduction of other obstacles to trade and payments by foreign countries, and particularly by prosperous Europe.

Thirdly, the liberalization of foreign obstacles to American exports should stimulate our own producers to devote more attention than they do now to prospecting foreign markets and expanding their sales abroad.

* Taken and adapted from *Gold and the Dollar Crisis,* New Haven: Yale University Press, 1960, pp. 7–13. (The cited material comprises part of a statement — The International Monetary Position and Policy of the United States — offered initially by Professor Triffin before the Joint Economic Committee, 87th Congress, October 28, 1959. The reader is referred also to, especially, Chapter 4 — A New Charter for the International Monetary Fund — of *Gold and the Dollar Crisis,* where operational aspects of the proposal are treated more extensively.)

Fourthly, we should do everything to prod European countries to assume their fair share of development financing abroad, particularly through multilateral assistance programs rather than through bilateral, tied loan, procedures.

Last, but not least, the current relaxation of world tensions may possibly enable us to reduce the terrifying and disproportionate defense burdens — internal as well as external — which probably account, more than any other single factor, for the revolutionary shift which has taken place in the international dollar balance from prewar to postwar days. This, however, is only a hope yet, and one about which I feel totally incompetent to hazard any guess or suggestion. If . . . we were to be disappointed once more, we should probably re-examine with our allies the problem of a fair allocation of our joint defense costs.

1. . . . Even the most successful readjustment of our overall balance of payments will leave in its wake two major problems, of vital concern not only to us, but to the rest of the world as well. Both have to do with the functioning of international monetary convertibility in an expanding world economy. The satisfactory functioning of such a system necessarily requires an expanding pool of world monetary reserves and international liquidity, to bridge temporary and unavoidable fluctuations in each country's external receipts and payments. Such fluctuations would, otherwise, force widespread and recurrent recourses to deflation, currency devaluation or trade and exchange restrictions.

Gold has long ceased to provide more than a fraction of the minimum requirements for the preservation of adequate reserve and liquidity levels. Most — although not all — countries, however, have shown themselves willing to accumulate a substantial portion of their monetary reserves in the form of foreign exchange — primarily sterling and dollar balances — alongside of gold itself. The trouble with this solution — known as the "gold exchange standard" — is that it is bound to undermine, more and more dangerously as time goes on, the international liquidity position of the currencies used as reserves by other countries and, by way of consequence, to impart an increasing vulnerability to the world monetary superstructure built upon these so-called "key currencies." Indeed, the additions to international liquidity made possible by the system are entirely dependent upon the willingness of the key currency countries to allow their own net reserve position to deteriorate, by letting their short term liabilities to foreigners grow persistently and indefinitely at a faster pace than their own gold assets.

I recall . . . how this led, in 1931, to the devaluation of the pound sterling, to the collapse of the international gold exchange standard, and to the consequent aggravation of the world depression.

Circumstances are undoubtedly different today. Yet two problems are inescapable.

The first is that the elimination of our overall balance of payments deficits would, by definition, put an end to the constant deterioration of our monetary reserves and deprive thereby the rest of the world of the major source by far — two-thirds to three-fourths — from which the international liquidity requirements of an expanding world economy have been met in recent years, in the face of a totally inadequate supply of monetary gold.

The second is that the huge legacy of short term foreign indebtedness already inherited by us from the past is likely to place a heavy handicap on sound policies for economic growth and stability in this country. Refugee capital has flown here in large amounts after the second world war, as it had flown to London after the first world war. Some of it may return home, as currency conditions become definitely stabilized in Europe, just as it left London in the late 1920's. Our huge gold losses of last year were due in part to such a repatriation of foreign capital at a time when interest rates had fallen here well below the rates available in Europe. They have been slowed down this year by an extremely sharp rise of interest rates in this country, prompted by our domestic concern about creeping inflation. In this case, external and internal interest rate policy criteria happily coincided, but they may diverge tomorrow. If and when we feel reassured about our internal price and cost trends we may wish to ease credit and lower interest rates in order to spur our laggard rate of economic growth in comparison not only with Russia, but with Europe as well. We may then be caught, however, exactly as the British were in the 1920's, between these legitimate and essential policy objectives and the need to retain short term funds here in order to avoid excessive gold losses.

I cannot resist quoting an incisive remark of Santayana, most aptly used by the Managing Director of the International Monetary Fund in several of his recent speeches: "Those who do not remember the past will be condemned to repeat it."

2.   Can we find a way out of the double dilemma which I have just mentioned? I think we can. The problem lies in both cases, with the absurdities associated with the use of *national* currencies as *international* reserves. It can be met, most directly and simply, by the *internationalization* of the foreign exchange component of world monetary reserves.

Let the United States, the United Kingdom, and other major countries bar the use of their national currency as monetary reserves by other countries. Give all countries, instead, the choice of keeping in the form of international, gold-convertible, deposits at the International Monetary Fund, any portion of their reserves which they do not wish to hold in the form of gold. Attach to these reserve deposits at the Fund exchange rate guarantees that would make them a far safer medium for reserve investment than any national currency holdings, always exposed to devaluation, inconvertibility, blocking, or even default by the debtor country. Let them, finally, earn interest at a rate to be determined, and varied from time to time, in the light of the Fund's earnings on its own loans and investments.

These various features, combining the earning incentive of foreign exchange holdings with the safety incentive of gold holdings, should ensure in time a large and continuing demand for Fund deposits. In order, however, to take account of initial diffidence and inertia, and to guarantee the system against the vagaries of sudden and unpredictable shifts between gold holdings and Fund deposits, all countries should undertake to hold in the form of Fund deposits a uniform and agreed proportion of their gross monetary reserves. They would be entitled, but not compelled, to convert into gold at the Fund any deposits accruing to their account in excess of this minimum requirement.

A minimum deposit ratio of 20 per cent would probably be ample to initiate the new system, and would substitute for the present, exceedingly complex and rigid, system of national quota contributions to the IMF capital. This ratio might have to be increased in time, however, in order to provide adequate lending power to the Fund, and to ensure beyond any shadow of doubt the full liquidity and convertibility of Fund deposits into gold or any currency needed for settlements. On the other hand, prudent management of the system would, in all likelihood, make it unnecessary to resort to compulsion for that purpose, as the member countries' own interest would lead them to maintain with the Fund, rather than in gold, a much larger proportion of their total reserves than the minimum percentages imposed by the Fund.

The only major objection to this proposed reform in the Funds's operations would be the same as that raised against the Keynes plan for an International Clearing Union.[1] Such a system would endow the Fund with a lending capacity which, if improperly used, might impart a strong inflationary bias to the world economy. This danger, however, can be guarded against more effectively, simply and directly by limiting the Funds's annual lending authority to the amount necessary to preserve an adequate level of international liquidity.

Various alternative criteria could be retained for this purpose. The simplest one might be to limit the Fund's net lending, over any twelve months period, to a total amount which would, together with current increases in the world stock of monetary gold, increase total world reserves by, let us say, 3 to 5 per cent a year. The exact figure could not, of course, be determined scientifically and would, in any case, depend in practice upon the compromise between divergent national viewpoints which would emerge from the negotiation of the new Fund Agreement. A reasonably conservative solution would be to retain a 3 per cent figure as definitely

---

[1] The Keynes plan, named after its initiator, the late Lord Keynes (Great Britain), was advanced prior to the Bretton Woods Conference of 1944, from which emerged the International Monetary Fund — *Editors.*

non-inflationary, and to require qualified votes (two-thirds, three-fourths, and ultimately four-fifths of the total voting power, or even unanimity) to authorize lending in excess of 3, 4 or 5 per cent a year.

The Fund's lending operations, moreover, should be no more automatic than they are at present, and this discretion should enable it to exercise a considerable influence upon members to restrain internal inflationary abuses.

A new and different category of Fund lending, however, would arise from the reform proposed here. This would consist of open-market investments in the financial markets of member countries, undertaken at the initiative of the Fund itself.

The first investments of this character would result automatically from the initial absorption by the new Fund of the outstanding national currency reserves transferred to it by members in exchange for Fund deposits. The bulk of these reserves would be in the form of bank deposits, acceptances and Treasury bills previously held by the central banks themselves in New York and London. The Fund would have no immediate need to modify the pattern of these investments, but should be empowered to do so, in a smooth and progressive manner, insofar as useful for the conduct of its own operations. This purpose would be served by giving the Fund an option — which it would not necessarily wish to use every year — of liquidating such investments at a maximum pace of, let us say, 5 per cent annually.

3. . . . I close now with a few words about the advantages, and disadvantages, which such a reform would entail for the United States itself.

Its major advantage emerges clearly, I hope, from our previous discussion. The United States would no longer have to bear the burden, and court the dangers, inseparable from the use of the dollar as a reserve currency by other countries. This would, it is true, deprive us of unrequited capital imports which have, in the past ten years, allowed us to carry a heavier burden of foreign lending and aid programs than we could have financed otherwise. We would now have to share these responsibilities — and the political influence that might accompany them — with other countries, through processes of multilateral decision-making which would, at times, be irritating and frustrating. We would, on the other hand, have consolidated in the hands of the Fund a large portion of highly volatile foreign funds, whose sudden and unpredictable outflow might otherwise unleash, at any time, an unbearable drain on our gold reserves. Most of all, we would have shed thereby the straitjacket which the need to prevent such an outflow would impose upon monetary management and interest rates in this country, whenever the success of our price stabilization efforts allows us to give primary consideration once more to the furtherance of maximum feasible rates of employment and economic growth.

A second, and closely related, consideration is that these reforms would put an end to an absurd situation under which we have been in practice — with only minor exceptions — the sole net lender in the IMF in spite of our persistent deficits and of the equally persistent and huge surpluses accumulated over the last ten years by other IMF members. We would, moreover, be able for the first time to obtain assistance ourselves from the IMF — through the more flexible procedure of IMF investments rather than loans — without triggering the dangerous psychological reactions which would now accompany a United States request for such assistance. The IMF itself would need to look for safe investment outlets for its expanded resources, particularly during the initial years of the new system, and this would fit in particularly well with our own need to buy the time necessary for effecting, in as smooth a manner as possible — in the interest of other countries as well as in our own — the readjustment of our current overall balance of payments deficits. . . .

II. The "Bernstein Proposals"*

E. M. BERNSTEIN

Private research;
formerly, IMF and U.S. Treasury

The U.S. Balance of Payments and International Liquidity[1]

The measures taken by the United States to restore its balance of payments are already having a great effect on the international money market. Once the U.S. deficit is eliminated, there will be no net addition of dollars to monetary reserves. If monetary reserves do not grow over a period of years, this would place a severe strain on the international monetary system. That is why steps must be taken soon to assure the steady growth of monetary reserves on the scale which is essential to an expanding world economy.

* Taken and adapted from "Guidelines for International Monetary Reform," *Hearings Before the Subcommittee on International Exchange and Payments of the Joint Economic Committee,* 89th Congress, 1st Session, Part 2, 1965, pp. 230–231, 245–246, 257–258, 269–270.
[1] June 18, 1965.

The need for monetary reserves has been reasonably well met by gold and foreign exchange, supplemented by reserve credit from the Fund. But the increase of reserves over the past 30 years has been due to special factors that cannot recur. These are the change in the price of gold from 1931 to 1936, the wartime accumulation of sterling balances, and the sharp rise in foreign dollar holdings as a consequence of the U.S. payments deficit since 1950. While the prolonged deficit of the United States had the beneficial effect of creating additional reserves and of redistributing reserves on a massive scale, it must be eliminated.

Since 1958, the gold reserves of all countries excluding the United States increased by nearly $11 billion. In the same period, the U.S. gold reserves decreased by $7.4 billion. From 1958 to 1964, the foreign exchange reserves of these countries increased by about $6.5 billion, while U.S. reserve liabilities increased by about the same amount. These reserves have gone to the surplus countries of continental Europe. At present, it can be said that aggregate reserves are adequate although not excessive. Once the U.S. balance of payments is restored, the growth of reserves will be sharply curtailed. Some other means must be found for providing a steady but not excessive growth of monetary reserves.

It has been suggested that the Fund be changed into an institution that would create monetary reserves through loans and investments. The creation of reserves by the Fund would be wholly at variance with the principles on which it was established. The Fund agreement states that its transactions are limited to providing currencies it holds to members in exchange for their own currencies or gold. The obligation of members of the Fund to provide it with resources for reserve credit is limited to their quota subscriptions, although the Fund may propose to a member that it lend its currency to the Fund. In any case, it would not be desirable to amend the Fund agreement to permit it to create reserves.

The best way of assuring an adequate growth of monetary reserves is by establishing a composite gold standard based on gold and Reserve Units consisting of the currencies of the Group of Ten and Switzerland. Each participant would be required to match its holdings of gold with Reserve Units in the ratio of $2 in gold to 1 reserve unit and to convert balances of its currency held by other participants in this ratio. The Fund should be a party to an agreement to establish a composite gold standard and it should be allotted 25 per cent of the Reserve Units created. This would be a recognition of the Fund as the central international monetary institution and it would enable the Fund to perform more effectively its function as the principal source of reserve credit.

Changes in the International Monetary System[2]

The present international monetary system is based on the provisions of the International Monetary Fund requiring its members to define their

[2] October 27, 1964.

currencies in terms of gold and to maintain their foreign exchange value within 1 per cent of parity. In order to maintain fixed parities, countries must have reserves to meet their payments deficits. At present the monetary reserves of all countries amount to over $40 billion in gold and $25 billion in foreign exchange. In addition, members of the Fund have access to reserve credit from that institution; and the large industrial countries have agreements with each other for currency swaps.

Although the present system has worked well, it is not a satisfactory method of providing reserves. From 1958 to 1963, a major part of the increase in the reserves of other countries came from the U.S. payments deficit. Some European countries feel that the financing of the U.S. deficit through the accumulation of dollar reserves tends to encourage inflation and to transmit it to other countries. In fact, the United States has been free of price and cost inflation in recent years. Despite the deficit, it has made a large net contribution to the resources of the rest of the world through its $6.5 billion surplus on current account.

The magnitude of the U.S. payments deficit has been greatly exaggerated. Even properly defined, the deficit is not always a satisfactory measure of the U.S. payments position. One striking feature of the U.S. deficit from mid-1963 to mid-1964 is that very little of it was settled by a decrease of U.S. reserve assets or by an increase in reserve liabilities to foreign official institutions. The recent change in the U.S. balance of payments is indicative of an impending decline in the growth of monetary reserves. It will be necessary to find some other method of supplementing gold, dollars and other foreign exchange in order to assure adequate monetary reserves.

One feature of the present international monetary system is that all reserves are linked to gold as the ultimate reserve asset. The prospective growth of gold reserves is too small to enable it to function satisfactorily as the ultimate reserve asset. A larger part of the financing of international settlements will have to be in some other reserve asset used jointly with gold. This could be done by establishing a composite gold standard of gold and Reserve Units consisting of the currencies of the large industrial countries. The participating countries could undertake to hold Reserve Units in an agreed ratio to gold — say, $2 of gold to $1 of Reserve Units — and to convert their currencies for each other in this ratio.

The composite gold standard is intended to deal with a problem that is peculiar to the large industrial countries. Nevertheless, it may be desirable to give the Fund a more positive role in the creation of Reserve Units by assigning to it 20 per cent of the total. The Fund could sell the Reserve Units for the currencies of the participating countries. This would strengthen the Fund's liquidity and enable it to provide reserve credit on a larger scale and with greater assurance to its other members. In this way all countries could share in the benefits of the composite gold standard.

Two Reports on International Liquidity[3]

The reports on international liquidity recently issued by the 10 large industrial countries and by the International Monetary Fund are the most important official statements on the international monetary system since Bretton Woods. The present international monetary system has worked well, although the Group of Ten is particularly concerned to see that a proper blend of economic policies is used by countries to secure a faster adjustment of payments imbalance while achieving essential internal objectives. The Group of Ten has suggested that the Organization for Economic Co-operation and Development undertake such a study. To improve international cooperation on liquidity problems the Group of Ten has decided that bilateral short-term credit facilities be kept under surveillance and review and the Bank for International Settlements will be asked to compile statistical data bearing on the means used to finance surpluses or deficits.

The two reports agree that there is at present adequate international liquidity. The real problem is regarding the growth of monetary reserves in the future. The Fund estimates that in the past 10 years reserve assets, such as gold, foreign exchange, and the gold tranche of members of the Fund, have increased at an average annual rate of 2.8 per cent. If account is taken of Fund quotas and other reserve credit facilities, the growth of international liquidity in all forms averaged 3.3 per cent a year. The growth of reserves in the future is unlikely to match the needs of the world economy. Although gold reserves may increase at 2 or 2½ per cent a year, the growth of foreign exchange reserves may be at a slower rate as the U.S. balance of payments is further strengthened.

The Fund occupies a central position in the supply of international liquidity. In 1959 quotas were increased by 50 per cent. Since then, there has been a large expansion of trade and payments. An increase of 25 per cent in quotas would match the increase in the trade of most countries. A larger increase could be justified for some countries as a means of strengthening the liquidity of the Fund or as a reflection of their larger role in the world economy. The Fund should liberalize its policy by giving countries assured access to the first credit tranche of the quota. The Fund should also extend compensatory credits up to a normal maximum of 50 per cent of the quota and place such credits completely outside the framework of the gold and credit tranches.

The Group of Ten states that "gold will continue to be the ultimate international reserve asset." Gold will not be able to perform this function if the supply of monetary gold is too small. The burden on gold can be reduced by supplementing it with a new type of reserve asset such as the Reserve Unit which would be composed of the currencies of the Group of Ten and Switzerland. The large industrial countries would hold such

[3] August 19, 1964.

Reserve Units in an agreed ratio to their gold reserves. This would raise by one-third the amount of monetary reserves that could serve as the ultimate international reserve asset. The Group of Ten has appointed a Study Group to assemble material for evaluation of this and other proposals for creating reserve assets. The two reports provide the basis for a practical program for meeting international liquidity needs through evolution of the present international monetary system.

The Underdeveloped Countries and Monetary Reserves[4]

The underdeveloped countries have the same interest as other countries in improving the present reserve system. The basic reserve problem of the underdeveloped countries is that their reserves are too small to meet ordinary fluctuation in their balance of payments. The underdeveloped countries hold about $12.3 billion of reserves (17 per cent of the total outside the Communist bloc), but about one-fourth of these reserves are held by six oil-producing countries. These countries cannot afford to invest real resources in reserves. For this reason, their needs will have to be met out of a common reserve to which they have access when they have balance-of-payments difficulties.

The underdeveloped countries have made great use of the IMF. Since 1947, they have drawn $2.9 billion in various currencies and at present nearly half of the $2.6 billion of net drawings on the Fund still outstanding are those of underdeveloped countries. On the whole, the underdeveloped countries have fared well in the general readjustment of quotas in 1959 and the readjustment that will take place this year. The interest of the underdeveloped countries is to have IMF policies on drawings made more liberal and to have its liquidity strengthened by acquiring more of the currencies of the surplus countries of Europe.

The present system of providing monetary reserves is not satisfactory for the long-run needs of the world economy. Professor Triffin has proposed that the IMF be converted into a world central bank with the power to create reserves through loans and open market operations. There could be no consensus on how much reserves should be created by a world central bank, it would be impossible to secure a steady increase in reserves through loans, and open market operations would place an even greater burden on the reserve centers than they bear now. Mr. Stamp's suggestion that the world central bank could create reserves by buying bonds of the IDA would add nothing to the flexibility of the Triffin proposal, it would be unacceptable to the industrial countries, and it would reduce the present flow of aid for development.

The proposal for a composite gold standard in which the industrial countries would convert their currencies two-thirds in gold and one-third in Reserve Units would provide for an orderly growth of reserves, dimin-

[4] March 24, 1965.

ish dependence on dollars and sterling in the growth of reserves, and maintain gold settlements at an acceptable level. The Reserve Units would consist of the currencies of the participating countries (80 per cent) and claims on the International Monetary Fund (20 per cent). The International Monetary Fund would be able to sell the Reserve Units it acquires for the currencies of surplus countries, thus strengthening its liquidity.

This is an evolution of the present reserve system. Gold and foreign exchange would continue to be used as reserves, although the pressure on gold reserves would be reduced through joint use with Reserve Units. The International Monetary Fund would be strengthened and would be in a position to liberalize its drawing policies, particularly on compensatory credits. This is the best way of meeting the reserve needs of the underdeveloped as well as the industrial countries.

III. Payments Deficits and Treasury Action*

ROBERT V. ROOSA
Formerly, Under Secretary, U.S. Treasury

Over the past 14 months the United States has, for the first time since the later 1930's, entered into foreign exchange transactions for monetary purposes, as distinct from the more or less routine handling of foreign exchange to meet the Government's operating needs abroad. The Treasury began limited operations in March 1961, acting through the Federal Reserve Bank of New York as its fiscal agent. In February of this year the Federal Reserve System announced its decision to enter the exchange markets for its own account.

To date, U.S. action in the foreign exchange markets has been largely exploratory in character, designed to probe and possibly to limit tempo-

* Taken and adapted from "Factors Affecting the United States Balance of Payments" (The Beginning of a New Policy), *Hearings Before the Subcommittee on International Exchange and Payments of the Joint Economic Committee*, 87th Congress, 2nd Session, 1962, pp. 327–332.

rary disturbances in the exchange markets. All operations have been carried out in close consultation with, and usually jointly with, the financial authorities of the other countries involved.

These activities in the foreign exchange markets have sometimes been referred to as the financial component in the outer perimeter defenses of the dollar. This is probably a good characterization, since of course the inner defenses depend upon the productivity, production, and competitiveness of the American economy. But in what we have been doing, both basically and peripherally, to defend the dollar, we have also been defending, in concert with others, the whole system of convertibility at stable exchange rates that has been so painstakingly reconstructed since the end of World War II. And the effective functioning of that system is, in turn, essential for diversified growth and integration among the free, capitalist economies of the world.

In addition to the short-run objectives of our foreign exchange operations, . . . there are longer-run implications and potentialities of an approach in which a key currency country becomes an active participant in the international exchange markets. As we go along we are also, therefore, trying to think through some of these possible implications for the long run — can such participation aid in assuring the stability of the international financial mechanism? Can it, if properly executed, reinforce the fundamental work of the International Monetary Fund? Does it afford a helpful means toward providing sufficient international liquidity for the continued growth of the world economy? Does it strengthen the role of gold as the base of our international reserve arrangements?

These are the kinds of questions that central bankers, and commercial bankers and treasuries can usefully ponder together, in our joint efforts to find the combination of private and governmental monetary facilities that a flourishing capitalism needs. While I cannot presume to suggest any of the answers, it may be of some help as background for others who can, if I discuss two themes that seem to run through our American experience of these recent months. First, what has thus far been the nature of our foreign exchange operations within the framework of the system of convertibility based on fixed exchange rates? Second, what possibilities seem at this early stage to be suggested, concerning the accumulation by a key currency country of balances in the convertible currencies of other leading countries?

Other countries have long accepted direct intervention in the exchange markets as a customary way of life. At the least, they must be buyers or sellers as exchange quotations reach the acceptable limits of variation around their own fixed exchange rates. The United States, on the other hand, was and still is, the only country that maintains complete interconvertibility between gold and its own currency at a fixed price, and until recently, was content to leave all operations concerning the exchange relations between the dollar and other currencies to the officials of those other countries. The recent decision to participate in the international markets in cooperation with other financial authorities reflects, as do many other governmental and private actions, a growing awareness within the United States of the dual nature of our own balance-of-payments problem.

We must not only respect and fulfill the balance-of-payments disciplines to which other countries have been accustomed for so long; but we must do this while also keeping our own currency and gold equally and alternatively available as reserves for all other countries. We must gain and keep the initiative for influencing the factors that affect our balance of payments, but we must do so in the impeccable manner that assures and retains bankers' confidence. This means that, both as trader and as banker, the United States has to keep its markets open and free. We have, therefore, a major stake, which the Western World shares with us, in resolving our balance-of-payments problem within the framework of a free international economy, with stable exchange rates and an immutable gold price of $35 an ounce.

Let me make it absolutely clear again that there is no thought that foreign exchange operations can provide the solution to the U.S. balance-of-payments deficit. More fundamental correctives are necessary for this end, and I know that you are all familiar with the many-sided program of American business, finance, and Government . . . toward a restoration of equilibrium, and surplus, in the American balance of payments.

Our foreign-exchange operations have so far been mainly designed to help in providing a breathing space during which these basic programs could have a chance to become effective. In our judgment, they have been most helpful in deterring unwarranted speculation and unwanted capital flows, and in reducing the drain on our gold stock, which stands as the bulwark of the whole international currency system.

. . .

A solution of the balance-of-payments deficit is fundamental if we are to ward off a steady attrition of the U.S. gold stock. But, the problem goes even beyond this. The United States is a ready seller of gold on demand, but other countries are not necessarily sellers to us when they have exchange deficits, partly indeed because their own gold reserve is cushioned — in many cases substantially — by dollar reserves.

It is consequently a matter of first priority for us to develop methods that will minimize our gold losses whenever our balance of payments swings into deficit — by no means avoid them, but certainly avoid conditions that exaggerate them. Under present procedures, we cannot be sure that gold will return to us when we move into surplus — and we must and will have surpluses from time to time.

This kind of consideration leads directly into my second main theme — the potential uses of foreign exchange holdings by a key currency country. As I had mentioned earlier, our exchange operations to date have been largely dictated by clear, current opportunities and needs. We have acted in response to market developments and have not sought to become permanent and regular participants in the market for any currency. Our spot exchange holdings — which, on the latest published figures were about $150 million, built up partly from borrowing and partly from purchases in the easier markets that have prevailed for some currencies so far this year — have mainly been required to back up our forward sales. But looking ahead to the future, there may well be good reason for more or less continuous holdings by the United States of some moderate amounts of the convertible exchange of various leading countries.

While it is premature to see clearly where we may be heading so far as the currency holdings of the United States are concerned, it may well turn out that some contribution toward resolving a part of our problem may be found in building up — in time of surplus — holdings of other currencies that are not thought of as reserve currencies in the same way that the dollar and the pound sterling are viewed. Should we do that, either with open holdings or through hedged forward positions, our exchange holdings might be able subsequently to handle a considerable part of the normal swings in payment patterns, leaving the gold reserves available to cover more fundamental and lasting adjustments. There would be no commitment to hold any particular currency, of course, and the relative size of any such holdings would presumably be comparatively small. Nor would there be any lessening of the needed balance-of-payments disciplines upon us or upon others. For changes in our combined reserves of gold and foreign exchange, taken together with changes in our short-term liabilities to foreigners, would then become as significant to the determination of our policies as changes in gold alone have been over recent years.

If such a system were bolstered by suitable international arrangements to insure a steady and orderly distribution of newly mined gold into monetary reserves, much of the pressure — both psychological and real — that arises from the accident of shifts in reserves among other central banks would be lifted from the U.S. gold stock. With such a system we might perhaps be able to view in better perspective our gold loss of the past 5 years as a basic and healthy redistribution of available world gold reserves, a redistribution that has added to the strength of the international financial community.

What I am suggesting is that we need to build further the outer defenses around the liquidity of the International Monetary Fund, which will be substantially augmented by the standby agreement on which progress toward ratification is going ahead with gratifying dispatch. We need to provide a means of further economizing on gold reserves, while insuring that the liquidity needs of our expanding world economy will be met in a manner consistent with the sovereignty of individual countries and with heavy reliance on the discipline provided by the balance of payments.

The net effect, if this line of development should be followed, would be to multilateralize a part of the role performed now by the two key currencies, within a framework that would place great stress on still further cooperation among monetary authorities of the type that has been so successfully developed over the past year or so. It is clear that the attributes of a key currency involve many things — its use in international trade, its relationship to gold as the ultimate reserve, the existence of broad and deep capital and money markets. In all these respects the dollar is now unique, although we hope to see further progress in the freeing up of European money and capital markets. But what makes a currency good basically is the way the country manages its economy. Where there are a number of strong countries — as there are today — a plausible case would seem to exist for some sharing of the burden placed on the key currency.

It may be, too, that a system such as I have outlined would be a sensible way to provide for any large increase in long-run liquidity requirements. Long before there can be any agreement on any of this, however, there are many knotty problems that will have to be resolved by our own policymakers and through international consultations — through the Basle Group, through the Organization for Economic Cooperation and Development, and through the International Monetary Fund. But explorations along these lines are far preferable, it seems to me, to the often proposed types of action (involving still more difficult decisions and negotiations) that basically involve an oath of allegiance by all governments and central banks to a synthetic currency device, created by an extranational authority bearing neither the responsibilities nor the disciplines of sovereignty.

On the other hand, a system where countries maintain some mutual holdings of foreign exchange has the extreme advantage of using existing institutions and practices. Within such a system the patterns of reference are known to all; no one will be asked to do things that fall outside the realm of his experience. A system erected on established currencies and mores, would surely have a firmer foundation than one based on artificial devices. At the least, I suggest, there is food for thought in such a possibility. . . .

25..... The Status of International Liquidity*

PETER B. KENEN

Columbia University

The international monetary system is in better health today than for many years. The stock of reserve assets is adequate for now and for the next decade. The central banks have shown great skill and vigor in their efforts to defend the monetary system. The recent growth in European reserves has been achieved at the expense of the United States, but this country can still purchase all the time it needs to solve its payments problem if only it is willing to pay out reserves and to use the time it buys for a good adjustment. The less developed countries have inadequate reserves, but their payments problems cannot be resolved by a simple increase in liquidity, for they will spend any cash they can earn or borrow.

Yet there is a lingering concern about the future. Few critics still take aim at the margin, arguing the need for more reserves. But many still complain that the structure of reserves is unsatisfactory, arguing the need for consolidation to protect the quality of the reserve media. And too few people have examined the implications of the new arrangements connecting central banks.

The problems of the margin and of asset structure cannot, of course, be segregated. Concern about prospective growth first drew our attention to the structure of reserves. Critics argued that such growth could impair the quality of the dollar as a reserve currency.[1] Then the critics' own proposals met with similar objections. Triffin's plan for reform of the

---

* Taken and adapted from "International Liquidity: The Next Steps," *American Economic Review*, May 1963, pp. 130–135, 138.
[1] Robert Triffin, *Gold and the Dollar Crisis*, . . . pp. 64–69, and my own "International Liquidity and the Balance of Payments of a Reserve-currency Country," *Quarterly Journal of Economics*, August 1960, pp. 572–586.

IMF, for example, could expose the Fund to a dangerous gold drain as it went about incurring liabilities.[2]

But recent history calls direct attention to the structure of reserves. There has been a quiet drift toward gold, with several central banks increasing their gold holdings or running down their dollar assets as they lost reserves. And though gold production has grown steadily since 1957, the annual accretion to official holdings has been falling off. Recent changes in the monetary system likewise stress consolidation rather than expansion. They seek to discourage or offset massive flows of private money that could drain reserves from New York and London, impairing the confidence of other central banks. They also seek to supplement national reserves and the lending powers of the IMF. These changes are described with great candor in two recent articles,[3] but a brief summary may be helpful here.

To forestall speculation and related cash flows, the U.S. Treasury and Federal Reserve System have begun to intervene in the foreign exchange markets. In adroit maneuvers against speculation, they have forced the forward mark and Swiss franc toward their interest parities. The United States, United Kingdom, and European governments have also forged a common policy toward the London gold market, which apparently includes a set of ground rules governing central bank transactions and provision for joint intervention to contain the price of gold.

This new activity has been financed by intricate credit arrangements. In some cases, the United States has made outright purchases of foreign currency or borrowed by issuing special obligations denominated in a foreign currency. More often, it has drawn on new stand-by credits set up in its favor by foreign central banks. Under these arrangements, each central bank agrees to swap its currency for dollars. The two countries then agree to liquidate their balances at a fixed exchange rate and a fixed date three to six months later. Some of the foreign currencies drawn under these arrangements have apparently been used in spot operations; some were set aside to meet the deferred obligations incurred by the United States in its intervention on the forward markets.

The details of these "swap" transactions vary from instance to instance. So do the operations in each foreign currency. The American authorities have tried to mesh their interventions with the money-market tactics of the other central banks. Because there is a shortage of money-market assets in most European countries, commercial banks hold foreign currencies, especially dollars, as secondary cash reserves, and central banks

[2] *Hearings: International Payments Imbalances and Need for Strengthening International Financial Arrangements*, Joint Economic Committee, U.S. Congress, 1960, pp. 193–196.

[3] Charles A. Coombs, "Treasury and Federal Reserve Foreign Exchange Operations," *Federal Reserve Bulletin*, September 1962; Robert V. Roosa, "Assuring the Free World's Liquidity," Federal Reserve Bank of Philadelphia, *Business Review*, September 1962. . . .

must operate in the foreign exchange markets to carry out domestic monetary policies.[4] They cannot control bank reserves using the familiar tools; they have instead to influence Eurodollar flows. Paradoxically, the development of the Eurodollar market may delay the formal monetary integration of Western Europe — the creation of a common currency for the European Economic Community. The many kinds of Eurodollar credit substitute for more familiar money-market instruments, and the Eurodollar market gives the EEC and adjacent countries a unified money market. We may have to wait some years for a European reserve currency to join the dollar and the pound.

The United Kingdom has also used central bank credits to strengthen its reserve position. After the revaluation of the deutsche mark and guilder in the spring of 1961, there was a massive run on sterling. But other central banks supplied the equivalent of $900 million in short-term credit to supplement Britain's own reserves. A few months later, the United Kingdom turned to the IMF and purchased $1.5 billion worth of foreign currencies. It used part of this record drawing to repay its debts under the so-called "Basle arrangements." In effect, Britain used the IMF to consolidate its short-term obligations and supply an indirect but uniform exchange guarantee.

In order that the IMF may continue serving this important function, ten major countries have agreed to place $6 billion worth of convertible currencies at the disposal of the Fund should it need this money to finance a major drawing. . . . This agreement is embodied in a protocol, the General Arrangements to Borrow, which provides that the Managing Director of the IMF shall propose a call on these currencies if a participating country applies for a drawing on the Fund to "forestall or cope with an impairment of the international monetary system" and if IMF resources are inadequate to finance the drawing. A call must then be approved by a complex qualified majority of the ten participants, and any member may opt out of its obligations by giving notice that its "present and prospective balance of payments and reserve position" cannot honor further calls.[5] Money borrowed by the Fund under the General Arrangements will be repaid within three to five years, when the drawing on the Fund is itself repaid, but may be paid back earlier if any of the lending countries encounters a payments problem of its own.

These credit arrangements are an intriguing mixture of reserve transfer and reserve creation. All of them involve the creation of new reserve media. A swap transaction between the United States and Germany adds dollars to German reserves and deutsche mark to U.S. reserves. It is not a transfer of outstanding reserve assets from one country to another. Nor is it reserve growth in the ordinary sense. The reserves created by the

---

[4] Oscar L. Altman, "Foreign Markets for Dollars, Sterling, and Other Currencies," IMF *Staff Papers*, December 1961, pp. 339–342.

[5] IMF, *International Financial News Survey*, January 12, 1962.

swaps will be extinguished as soon as they are used. When the United States uses its deutsche mark in the foreign exchange market, its balance at the Bundesbank is eradicated rather than transferred to a third country.[6] Furthermore, the cash assets created by the swaps and by special loans to the IMF are matched by liabilities and slated for repayment within a brief time; they do not bring a lasting increase in owned reserves.

But the architects of these new arrangements envisage further innovations that could enlarge owned reserves. When the United States moves over into payments surplus, it can accumulate European currencies instead of forcing other countries to run off dollar assets or to sell us gold. New reserves may also be created by more swap transactions, but larger and without express provision for repayment. Presumably, these balances could be used in any way — transferred to another country or converted into a third currency.

Underlying all these innovations is the fact and expectation of close co-operation among the key central banks. Such co-operation is essential to orderly official intervention in the foreign exchange markets and to an alignment of fundamental policies affecting trade and payments within the industrial community. But it may not be the proper basis for an international monetary standard. Reserve-asset structure can only pose a problem if some central bank decides to hold less of one reserve asset and more of another, or because a central bank does not want to hold its new reserves in the form they take when they are created. A monetary standard based on "close co-operation" rather than binding commitments and arrangements is built on a bad premise: It relies on acquiescence to cope with a crisis that can only be brought on if one central bank has declined to co-operate. Despite the talk and evidence of close co-operation, moreover, the reservoir of good will could easily run dry. . . .

Finally, *ad hoc* acquiescence in collective measures may have a high price. The Under Secretary of the Treasury, Robert Roosa, has opposed exchange rate guarantees because, he says, "one country after another will interpose conditions on its readiness to accept a guarantee — conditions that will at the least interpose their judgments more specifically into the determination of our military, aid, or investment activities abroad." "And where would we find ourselves," he goes on to ask, "when the demands of one of our guaranteed creditors conflicted with those of another?"[7] If Mr. Roosa is convinced that we would have to pay for the privilege of giving a guarantee, how much more costly might it be to purchase close co-operation without giving any guarantee? And what would be our price for co-operation once the United States had begun to hold large amounts of foreign currency? One might reply that every country would then have a club with which to beat the other into close

---

[6] The same thing will happen to dollar balances held by a foreign government, but in only one of several likely cases — if the balances are used to buy up foreign currency from Americans.

[7] Roosa, *op. cit.*, p. 6.

co-operation. But this apparent parity would soon vanish if one country ran a payments deficit and lost reserves — and that would surely be the time when other countries would be nervous about holding the first country's currency.

All of this is not to say that the central banks are fair weather friends. I merely argue that we should obtain binding assurances and more automaticity when the weather is its fairest so that every country can count on help when the sky begins to cloud. I shall not . . . present another "plan" for reform of the monetary system. It would be quite wrong to backtrack now, searching for perfection, when the recent innovations offer a foundation on which to build a very strong monetary system.

In my view, these recent innovations start a major change in financial practice. They begin to substitute governmental credits for a further growth in national reserves. Carried further, these arrangements can provide liquidity without doing damage to the reserve position of any center country of the IMF. They point to a system of overdraft financing rather than the more familiar methods of deposit growth. I shall therefore urge some minor changes that will make the credit network a more perfect substitute for growth in owned reserves — changes aimed at automatic access to existing credits and at steady growth in overdraft facilities.[8]

As a first step toward a stronger system, I would favor the rapid completion of the stand-by network. Every major central bank should undertake to lend $150 million or $200 million to the United States and a like amount to the United Kingdom, obtaining a reciprocal commitment from each of those two countries. One might even want asymmetry in each overdraft agreement, with the United States committed to lend more than it is allowed to borrow. Many countries use the dollar when they intervene in the foreign exchange markets. Granted larger dollar credits, they would not need to draw on one another. In brief, bilateral asymmetry would give rise to over-all symmetry; each other country could draw dollars to defend its currency, and the United States could draw every other money.

These stand-by arrangements should be permanent, with provision for immediate drawings and for repayment in six months at the exchange rate that prevailed when the drawing first took place. A country should be able to use its stand-by credits whenever its currency falls beneath its parity with that of its partner. It should not be allowed to use borrowed funds for purchasing a third currency. With these restrictions and, perhaps, an end to cross-crediting, no country could do damage to its partners, nor influence its partners' economic policies.

There is, of course, one danger in a credit network connecting the

---

[8] I do not claim any originality for these proposals or for the way in which I have combined them. Readers who have followed the burgeoning literature will recognize bits of Triffin, Angell, Bernstein, Zolotas, and others. All remaining faults are, of course, those of the gold exchange standard.

United States with every other country. The United States might find itself financing a French deficit with some other country, say Germany or Britain. At present, by contrast, such a deficit is financed by a transfer of existing dollar balances, not with newly drawn dollars. But if American financing went on very long, the dollar would tend to a discount on the foreign exchange market and the United States could draw marks or pounds to correct the situation.

Next, I would favor two important changes in the General Arrangements to Borrow, making those arrangements fully automatic and allowing them to grow. Under the existing agreement, two or three potential lenders can prevent Fund borrowing merely by casting negative votes. Furthermore, each country is the final judge of its own ability to lend. I would consequently urge that the IMF be empowered to invoke the General Arrangements at its own discretion . . . and that every country be compelled to participate unless the Fund's holdings of that country's currency are above the usual three-fourths of quota.

The General Arrangements also fix each participant's commitment. As time goes on and trade and payments grow, these commitments may prove far too small. They may even be too small to cope with the next crisis. The IMF cannot draw the whole $6 billion because that sum includes the currency of the deficit country. Each country's obligation should therefore be tied to its own reserves. Its commitment should be equal to, say, half its gross reserves less an exemption fixed in advance. . . .

Some critics of the present monetary system would like to give the IMF a much larger role. They would dispense with stand-by credits and rely directly on drawings from the Fund. They would give guarantees through the IMF by having it take dollars in exchange for new deposits. But bilateral arrangements have a place in any system; they can be invoked quickly and quietly, giving faster aid than a drawing on the Fund. They can then be paid off by a drawing on the Fund when calm is again restored. As I see it, moreover, expansion of the IMF comes at a later stage. When it comes time to enlarge national reserves, the necessary growth should be secured by a further change in the General Arrangements to Borrow. The Fund's obligations should be made transferrable (or exchanged for deposits at the IMF). The IMF could then create reserves when countries came to it for aid, and the attendant growth in total reserve assets would be a response to manifest needs. At that point, too, the IMF would become quite Triffinesque. But most of the sensible proposals lead in this direction. They differ more in rates of change than in their objectives. And while all roads may lead through Yale, after some meandering, we do not have to travel them at a breakneck speed.

26..... International Liquidity: A CEA View*

COUNCIL OF ECONOMIC ADVISERS

The avoidance or appropriate correction of large-scale payments imbalances is of key importance in facilitating sound world economic growth and relatively unfettered international trade and payments. But better adjustment alone is not sufficient to attain these objectives.

In the long run, most countries seek some steady increase in their international reserves. With growing world transactions, this has meant that they have sought to have surpluses rather than deficits in their balances of payments. Obviously, however, all countries cannot attain such a goal simultaneously. At present, only the flow of new gold into monetary reserves can permit a steady accumulation of reserve assets by some countries without corresponding deficits for others.

This flow of new gold has, for many years, been inadequate. For much of the postwar period, dollars supplied through U.S. deficits served as the major supplement to gold in new reserve creation. . . . [However], the dollar can no longer be expected to perform this task in the same way; nor can it be assumed that adequate new reserves will accrue in the form of automatic drawing rights at the IMF, as the byproduct of the Fund's normal lending operations. To satisfy desires for rising official monetary reserves over the longer run and to eliminate dependence of the world economy on the vagaries of gold production, deliberate generation of new reserve assets is needed on a cooperative international basis.

In 1966, significant progress was made toward setting up a mechanism for such deliberate reserve creation. Representatives of the major industrial countries known as the Group of Ten agreed that it is prudent to begin the preparation of a contingency plan now. They also agreed that deliberate reserve creation should be tailored to global needs rather than the financing of individual balance of payments deficits; that decisions on the amount of reserves to be created should be made for some years

* From *Economic Report of the President*, January 1967, pp. 195–197.

ahead; and that reserve assets should be distributed to all members of the Fund, on the basis of IMF quotas or comparable objective standards. While the negotiations in the Group of Ten, and parallel deliberations by the Executive Directors of the Fund, did not result in complete accord on the precise form and use of new reserve assets, the exploration of technical details produced substantial agreement regarding the nature of alternative "building blocks" that might be incorporated in the final contingency plan.

A major accomplishment in 1966 was the initiation of a second stage of international monetary negotiations late in the year, involving joint discussions of the Executive Directors of the Fund and the Deputies of the Finance Ministers and Central Bank Governors of the Group of Ten. It is hoped that these meetings, which have already shown great promise, will by the time of the next Annual Meeting of the Fund lead to a wide consensus on the key remaining points at issue.

Differences of view on two of these points already seem to be narrowing. There now appears to be a widespread feeling that the needs of the international monetary system can best be served if deliberate reserve creation is effected through the development of an entirely new reserve unit, distributed to all Fund members. At the same time, there is increasing recognition that satisfactory procedures can be developed to make the new reserve asset generally acceptable without linking its use to specified payments of gold.

Probably the most important outstanding issue is the precise manner in which decisions on reserve creation are to be made. There is good reason to expect, however, that this question can be resolved in a way that takes account of the legitimate needs and interests of all the countries represented in the negotiations.

While the progress made in the negotiations thus gives ground for considerable satisfaction, it is also true that the need for developing a contingency plan for deliberate reserve creation has become more urgent.

One reason is that it can no longer be assumed that U.S. deficits will automatically increase world reserves. These deficits, which for much of the postwar period were the main element in new reserve creation, have since the end of 1964 made no net contribution to the rise in world reserves. . . .

Second, the flow of gold into monetary channels has been sharply reduced recently. . . . In 1965, only $240 million of new gold entered into monetary stocks. This contrasts with an annual average of about $600 million in the decade ended in 1964.

Third, it is significant that the modest increase in over-all world reserves that did occur in the recent past reflected very special circumstances. During the 21-month period from the end of 1964 through September 1966, world reserves increased by about $1.8 billion. But the largest part of this increase was a byproduct of the difficulties experienced by the

British pound, which caused the U.K. authorities to draw $1.4 billion from the IMF; a large portion of this drawing, in turn, increased reserve claims on the Fund by other countries. Not only can transactions of this kind no longer be counted upon to add to world reserves as the British situation improves, but repayment of Britain's debt could actually lead to a contraction of reserves.

These considerations suggest that the time when deliberately created reserves are needed may be closer at hand than is often realized. In any event, continued uncertainty regarding the nature of a contingency plan and the timing of its adoption can be a growing source of uneasiness in international financial markets and interfere with the smooth working of the adjustment process. Clear agreement on a contingency plan, on the other hand, would be a major factor in strengthening confidence in the world monetary system and in reducing gold hoarding and would help lessen the tendency of countries to pursue unattainable balance of payments aims.

The essential tasks . . . [ahead] thus are to improve the process of payments adjustment through increased international cooperation and to move decisively toward establishing a mechanism for deliberate reserve creation. The two tasks are intimately interwoven; success in both is necessary to provide a sound climate for world economic growth and relative freedom in trade and capital transactions, as well as to assure an adequate flow of long-term capital from the developed to the less developed countries.

F..... The Problem of Commodity Status

Many problems attach to commodity trade. Nowhere is this fact more apparent, however, than in the realm of raw-materials commodities (primary products). There, particular supply-and-demand circumstances assure a built-in problem of first magnitude.

Raw-materials commodities (foodstuffs, fibers, minerals) entering international trade face a demand that is inelastic and relatively inflexible to growth. This is true with rare exception (petroleum being a possible exception). The "inelastic" aspect means that an attempt, at any given time, to augment proceeds is likely to prove self-defeating (i.e., volume does not respond enough to price concessions to increase total proceeds). The "inflexible" aspect means that total proceeds, over time, tend to lag because the particular commodities give claim to only a declining proportion of rising income in the purchasing countries (chiefly, the advanced countries). Further, an attempt by any one country to win gains for itself at the expense of others similarly situated is likely to fail as, all-around, self-interest prompts retaliation. And, as if all this were not enough, some of the advanced (industrial) countries in which the raw materials seek their outlet are producers also of identical products (as in the case of wheat, cotton, corn, etc.), or are developing synthetics that can serve as substitutes (as in the case of rubber and textile fibers).

In short, countries closely tied to the production and export of raw materials occupy a special status; the similarity they share in production and export is matched by their common fate in the markets of, chiefly, the advanced countries, on which they depend. This common fate involves lagging export proceeds and a reinforcement of the relative poverty that is an earmark of underdevelopment — matters discussed earlier (in Part Two-B). But it includes, also, an *instability* of proceeds. Variable output and marketing in the face of a relatively fixed demand (i.e., a demand that is relatively inflexible to growth, at least in the short-term sense) can only — given the circumstance of inelasticity in demand — mean price (and proceeds) instability.

The problem, then, centers on a proceeds level that, quite aside from its deficiency in magnitude over time, is deficient in terms of short-term stability. Certainly, given this set of affairs, producers are disadvantaged (income-wise), as are consumers (via uncertain access to import goods) — and, certainly, as are whole countries, such as the underdeveloped countries, whose programs of development must necessarily take into account the supply of foreign exchange available.

A great many people have concerned themselves with this matter. Some have focused particularly on longer-range income aspects — a usual assessment then being that raw materials do not make for high income (except in special cases, such as petroleum), and that, therefore, emphasis needs to be on structural change: the acquisition of more industry. Others have focused more particularly on how greater proceeds stability might be achieved in raw-materials trade; in fact, this group includes some who, while seeing no solution short of industrialization, nevertheless stress export-proceeds stability in raw materials on the grounds that such returns provide the necessary "lever" by means of which new industry can be acquired.

How can greater stability in the export proceeds of raw materials be achieved? One suggested approach is "compensatory financing" — a financial arrangement under which reserves built up during good periods are paid out, subsidy fashion, during slack periods. This approach is, to date, only talked about at the international level. However, a second approach — "international commodity agreements" — is well established and in considerable use. Under international commodity agreements, a number of countries, usually both producer and consumer countries, agree on conditions of volume and price to apply to a particular internationally-traded commodity. International commodity agreements currently cover such major commodities as wheat and coffee.

The present section includes two selections about international commodity agreements. The first, by Professor Mikesell, surveys international commodity agreements from the standpoint of their forms and procedures, and goes on to relate them to the developmental aspiration of underdeveloped countries. The second, by Professor Brandt, offers critical commentary; international commodity agreements, he suggests, probably do more harm than good.

27 ..... Stabilization of International Commodity Markets*

RAYMOND F. MIKESELL

University of Oregon

Individual Commodity Agreements

By and large, individual commodity agreements are of three types: (1) those based on limiting market supply by means of export quotas in order to maintain price at or near the desired level; (2) those employing multilateral long-term contracts; and (3) those which rely upon an international buffer stock to maintain prices within a given range by means of purchases and sales from the buffer stock. Where the basic purpose is the elimination of sharp and reversible fluctuations in world-market prices of storable commodities, the buffer-stock arrangement has important advantages, particularly if the manager of the stock is permitted to operate freely on the basis of his informed judgment regarding longer range demand and supply conditions and if he is provided with sufficient resources in the form of both foreign exchange and commodities to offset the reversible fluctuations peculiar to the demand and supply patterns of the individual commodity. A wise manager will, of course, take into account the effects of this year's prices upon supply, and perhaps demand, in succeeding years. However good his judgments, they may be thwarted by national programs which provide for subsidies to producers to compensate for reduced international prices. In addition, the existence of large national stocks, such as exist today in the case of coffee, would pose a continual threat to the operations of the buffer-stock manager unless there was an agreement with respect to the maximum rate of

---

* Taken and adapted from "International Commodity Stabilization Schemes and the Export Problems of Developing Countries," *American Economic Review*, May 1963, pp. 78–82, 90–91.

liquidation of these stocks. In the absence of such national programs or of large national stocks, there is theoretically no reason why a competent buffer-stock manager could not achieve the objectives of a true commodity stabilization program for individual commodities and the result, so far as the proper allocation of resources is concerned, could be more beneficial than that which would occur without a stabilization operation. Unfortunately, these ideal conditions have rarely, if ever, been achieved. Moreover, many commodities cannot be stored except for short periods.

The best example of the multilateral long-term contract arrangement is provided by the series of International Wheat Agreements. Under this type of agreement, each consuming country undertakes to purchase agreed quantities at prices no less than a stipulated minimum while producers agree to supply certain amounts at prices no higher than a stipulated maximum. Even if virtually all producers and consumers are members of the agreements, there will almost inevitably be a free market price outside of the maximum and minimum range. Producers will tend to sell their extraquota output at the free market price, and if this price is well below the minimum contract purchase price, it will tend to undermine the contract price and also create a two-price system in the consuming countries. This may also occur under a straight export-quota system if some producing and consuming countries are not members of the agreement. On the other hand if the individual producers are required to sell extraquota output at low free market prices, this might tend to discourage production.

Much more common has been the export-quota approach under which prices to producers are divorced from realities of the world market, with governments either absorbing the extraquota production or limiting output through national price or direct production controls. Theoretically, it is possible to achieve the same results in terms of world-price stabilization through the export-quota method as might be achieved under a buffer-stock arrangement. Thus, excessive stocks accumulated by governments in years of heavy supply or low world demand would be followed by a liquidation of these stocks in other years. But, administratively and politically, a true stabilization operation by this means is almost impossible to achieve, since the determination of national quotas must be made through international negotiations as opposed to stabilization operations undertaken in the world market in accordance with the informed judgment of an independent buffer-stock manager. Under the export-quota system, each participating country has two somewhat conflicting objectives when entering into negotiations: to keep the world's total supply as small as possible and to maximize its own share of that limited supply. Moreover, if the country is an important world supplier and has built up a large stock as a consequence of export curtailment, this enhances its bargaining power for obtaining a larger export quota for itself. For example, in . . . negotiations on the International Coffee

Agreement, Brazil has argued that because it has accumulated stocks in excess of annual world consumption, this fact should be taken into account in the determination of Brazil's export quota.

A true stabilization program . . . can only operate successfully if the long-run equilibrium price which the scheme seeks to approximate is permitted to have an unobstructed impact on output in individual countries. Otherwise stocks will be accumulated in certain countries and these will constitute a continual threat to the market. Alternatively, of course, the agreement can provide for production controls to be imposed by individual members which are consistent with the export quotas established. Indeed, such controls are provided for in the International Coffee Agreement of 1962 (see Articles 48–50). But it must be recognized that the introduction of production controls constitutes a departure from the traditional principles of stabilization operations, and the objective of the scheme becomes one of establishing "fair" or "equitable" prices rather than limiting fluctuations above and below a long-run equilibrium price. Thus, for example, in the 1962 International Coffee Agreement, there is a curious kind of contradiction in the statement of objectives of the Agreement which reads: "To achieve a reasonable balance between supply and demand on a basis which will assure adequate supplies of coffee to consumers and markets for coffee to producers at equitable prices, and which will bring about long-term equilibrium between production and consumption."

What I have been saying in effect is that commodity agreements operated in accordance with true stabilization principles are probably not politically feasible. If the schemes really aimed at establishing a long-run equilibrium price, substantial changes in the relative shares of the export markets of individual countries, as a consequence of differing costs and supply conditions in producing countries, might well take place. Politically, countries are motivated by a desire to maintain or increase their share of the world market, and this has certainly been reflected in the negotiations among Latin-American and African producers for a coffee agreement. It should also be said that in the case of commodities like coffee with long gestation periods, long-run equilibrium prices are at best difficult to determine, and arrangements to maintain them might require an accumulation of large stocks over relatively long periods of time during which both the supply and demand conditions under which the equilibrium price was originally calculated might well have changed to a considerable degree.

Implications for Development

The implications of various international stabilization or price-fixing schemes for economic development depend in considerable measure on the national programs accompanying the international arrangements.

For example, if under an international export-quota system domestic output is maintained and above-quota surpluses purchased and accumulated by the government, there is an investment in stocks of commodities which is not only unproductive but which in later years may have to be destroyed or dumped at prices far below the purchase price. In addition to involving an unproductive governmental investment, such a policy would continue to promote, or at least not discourage, investment in the primary-product industry and delay the movement of resources out of the industry.

What would be highly desirable for an individual producer country is a modernization of its primary-product industry, which will enable output to be maintained or expanded at a lower cost. This might be desirable even under an international scheme which seeks to limit exports to the world market. Ideally, what is required then is increased productivity achieved through modernization and the elimination of high-cost producers, while at the same time keeping output from rising so fast as to depress world prices. But simply letting prices to domestic producers fall will not necessarily achieve either of these objectives in the short run. Increased investment for modernization may be discouraged by low prices and, in many countries, for various institutional reasons plus the existence of plentiful low-wage labor, investment for increased productivity in primary production has not been encouraged by high prices either. On the other hand, low prices alone may not greatly affect output or the transfer of resources in the short run. What may be needed, therefore, is a government program designed to take marginal land (or other resources) out of production of the commodity in question while at the same time encouraging investment for higher productivity in the remaining area. This also means that productive employment will need to be found for the displaced resources, including labor.

It is very doubtful whether any international export-quota scheme can maintain world prices above long-run equilibrium levels for any substantial period of time. What schemes like the International Coffee Agreement might be able to do is provide time for countries to adjust output and costs to the long-run realities of world-market conditions. By and large, however, such adjustments, if they are to be made at all, must be done on a national basis, possibly with assistance from external financing and technical assistance agencies. In the absence of an adjustment program, it can well be argued that the very existence of international commodity stabilization schemes will remove the urgency for making the necessary adjustments and that it would be better simply to let market forces run their course. On the other hand, sharp decreases in export proceeds may hinder the process of long-run adjustment.

Although I tend to be skeptical regarding the possibility of successful individual commodity stabilization schemes in modifying price fluctuations, it is not my intention to take a position against them. Perhaps it is worth experimenting more with them, particularly where an effort is made to include both consumer and producer countries in the agreements and where countries are encouraged to intensify their efforts to increase productivity and to diversify their economies, and are discouraged from relying on such schemes to maintain or increase their foreign exchange earnings from the export of two or three primary commodities in the face of uncertain or possibly adverse long-run demand and supply conditions.

Even under the most ideal administration of buffer-stock or quota schemes, there are many commodities that simply do not lend themselves well to operations of this type. This is true, for example, in the case of commodities which compete closely with synthetics or with other natural commodities which are close substitutes and in the case of commodities such as cotton, sugar, and wheat, which are produced by highly industrial countries for their own use and for export, and where price and output policies are largely determined by domestic political forces. This does not mean, of course, that commodity study groups with power to make recommendations to governments on export and import policies with respect to commodities such as cotton, wool, wheat, sugar, and rubber cannot be of value in achieving more orderly world markets for these commodities, but I seriously doubt the feasibility of international stabilization agreements with respect to more than a few international commodities such as perhaps coffee and cocoa. Certainly any idea that the whole problem of stabilizing the export proceeds of the vast majority of less developed countries by means of a series of international commodity agreements is highly unrealistic. . . .

. . .

There is certainly no doubt that instability of export earnings can have an adverse effect upon the level of investment and upon planning for economic development. However, I am of the opinion that short-term fluctuations in export earnings can and should be dealt with as a balance-of-payments problem by the International Monetary Fund. I would say further that the Monetary Fund might consider a revision of its regulations which would provide for more liberal drawings on the part of members, both for meeting temporary shortfalls in export proceeds arising from changes in international commodity market conditions and even for sharp declines in export proceeds which appear to call for more permanent adjustments in a country's balance-of-payments structure. However, I am convinced that the most serious problem arising out of international commodity trade which faces most less developed countries is not that of reversible fluctuations, but rather long-run declining or stagnating export proceeds, or a slow rate of growth in export proceeds relative to the country's foreign exchange requirements for imports and debt service necessary for sustained growth. These are structural problems which concern the volume and direction of investment in developing countries, and they cannot be dealt with simply by compensating for all or a portion of the shortfalls in export proceeds in accordance with some automatic formula. Rather than providing income transfers under . . . compensation schemes, . . . I would far rather see the same or larger funds made available by international development financing institutions expressly for the purpose of broadening the export base and in other ways of improving the export capacity of low-income countries.

Projections of the world demand for primary products from the low-income countries over the next couple of decades indicate low rates of growth in export proceeds relative to their foreign exchange requirements, especially for countries whose principal exports consist of tropical foods, beverages, and fibers.[1] Yet, far too little attention is being paid to this problem, either in the national economic plans of the individual countries or by the various development assistance organizations.[2] In fact, one of the dangers of concentrating on schemes for dealing with shortfalls in over-all export proceeds or for maintaining the prices of individual commodities such as coffee and cocoa is that the longer run problem of changing the entire export base of the developing countries will not receive adequate attention. Most developing countries cannot continue to grow without broadening their export base to include not only additional primary products but also an increasing volume of manufactures. This is, of course, not simply a problem of the direction of investment and development policies, but also involves world-trade policies.[3] . . .

[1] Raymond F. Mikesell and Robert L. Allen, *Economic Policies Toward Less Developed Countries,* Subcommittee on Foreign Economic Policy of the Joint Economic Committee, Congress of the U.S. (Nov., 1961).

[2] Raymond F. Mikesell, "The Capacity to Service Foreign Investment," *U.S. Private and Government Investment Abroad,* Ed. by Raymond F. Mikesell (Univ. of Oregon Press, 1962).

[3] Raymond F. Mikesell and Robert L. Allen, *Economic Policies Toward Less Developed Countries,* Subcommittee on Foreign Economic Policy of the Joint Economic Committee, Congress of the U.S. (Nov., 1961); *Trends in International Trade,* A Report by a Panel of Experts (GATT, Geneva, 1958).

28..... International Commodity Agreements: A Critical View*

KARL BRANDT

Stanford University

. . . What can be done to improve the trade position of the nonindustrial countries?

The most frequently suggested remedy for improving the . . . situation is the so-called "stabilization" of prices of primary products through international commodity agreements. This would result in the establishment of the same sort of intervention in the world agricultural market that has been used since World War I in domestic markets, namely compulsory commodity cartels which fix prices, operate stockpiles, and buy or sell.

Such price fixing would create a structural change in the entire global market economy for the commodity in question. Hence, while it might mitigate the violence of short-term price fluctuations, it inevitably causes profound and serious dislocations for production, processing, stockholding and consumption. This is not a theoretical speculation, but a matter of historical record. The "stabilization" of cotton prices in the U.S. has not only frozen production in high price locations, but it has spurred and accelerated cotton production in other countries. And 60 years of efforts to stabilize coffee prices have led to such extreme methods as destroying within a period of 12 years a quantity equivalent to three years' total world coffee consumption. This did not appreciably help Brazil or Colombia, but instead spurred competitive production in other parts of the world, primarily in Africa.

None of the primary commodities have such a safe and unassailable monopoly position that a cartel-manipulated pegged price could avoid a

* Reprinted from *Challenge, The Magazine of Economic Affairs,* a publication of Challenge Communications, Inc., February 1963, pp. 35–36.

consumer response of partial substitution and reduced demand or prevent producers of competitive commodities from taking advantage of the artificially created price edge for their products.

It has been demonstrated in recent years that even a commodity like steel faces tough and effective competition from organic materials like lumber, and inorganic compounds and commodities like concrete, aluminum, magnesium and formica. The same is true of all agricultural commodities, irrespective of whether they are food, animal feed or industrial raw materials. Whenever substitution is feasible, cartel-manipulated high prices usually result in a net gain for the substitute commodity.

What, then, is the potential effect of . . . adjusting raw materials prices through international commodity agreements? Such agreements necessitate diplomatic machinery, institutional arrangements and the adoption of elaborate administrative procedures for each individual commodity. All producing and exporting countries, and preferably all importing countries, have to be persuaded to participate. If the time-consuming preliminaries do not founder on the noncooperation or the hostility of some countries with a strong comparative advantage, then efforts can be made to "stabilize" prices by reducing export quotas and, consequently, production quotas. But reduced exports at somewhat higher prices may yield no actual improvement in the balance of trade.

The worst feature of this sort of planned economic intervention is the confinement of measures to prices, trade and production of one single commodity, which distorts the relation to prices of all other goods and services. Within an environment of dynamic change, such static and isolated single commodity measures create more maladjustments within a few years than improvements. One of these maladjustments is the higher real estate values accruing to efficient producers. In a short while these values become higher costs in the fixed cost structure. This is one reason why the U.S. government finds it politically impossible to extricate itself from the price-support program.

There are some commodities for which price fixing by international agreement would be disastrous: natural rubber, for example, with its sharp competition from a whole range of synthetic materials; or such fibers as jute, Manila hemp, silk or wool, for which substitute materials are competing effectively. If, on the other hand, international cartels just go through monopoly motions to perform what the market would do anyway, their work would be a costly waste.

This leads to the conclusion that international commodity agreements, at best, do not offer more than a temporary sedative that may give the political sensation of relief. Any attempt to ameliorate the problems of the raw materials-exporting nations requires a different approach.

It must be recognized that agricultural protection in highly industrialized countries creates export surpluses which seriously impede the necessary exchange of goods, services and capital with underdeveloped countries. The same applies to the unwillingness of industrial countries to accept an increasing amount of semimanufactured and consumer goods from the underdeveloped countries without duties, excise taxes, import quotas and other restraints. The opening of borders to such imports would increase the purchasing power of underdeveloped countries which, in turn, would be used for imports of industrial producer goods.

The correction of the . . . situation could, of course, also proceed via a moratorium on price increases for industrial goods. Indeed, there is a fair prospect that more competition among industrial exporting countries and the loss of markets in overseas areas could do exactly that. However, keeping price inflation in industrial countries in check is largely a question of relieving the cost-price squeeze in industries which have a reduced profit margin. Here a thorough revision of corporate income taxes in several leading industrial countries would be extremely helpful.

The main assistance government can give to industrial expansion without inflation begins with appropriate policies which serve to strengthen the currency and keep it hard, i.e., freely convertible. Recurrent anxiety about the strength of the world's leading currency is certainly no help in the trade difficulties between developed and underdeveloped nations. Strengthening the currency requires the creation of a business climate in which the expansion of exports can proceed without rising costs. Since wages make up the lion's share of costs in industry, and since competition is the only force that can effectively stimulate the private actions that increase productivity, free competition must be the rule for all the parties involved — union, farmers and cooperatives, as well as business enterprises.

This leads to one major issue of Western strategy concerning the underdeveloped parts of the world. These countries need a heavy capital import for many years to come to enable them to develop faster than their population increases. But the imported capital must lay the groundwork for its amortization. . . .

PART THREE ....

INTERNATIONAL ECONOMIC POLICY

OF THE UNITED STATES

In Part Two, we identified the major global areas that confront the United States abroad and surveyed each in terms of its special interest to the United States. We examined, also, some problems of special concern to the United States in the course of its external dealings. Now, in Part Three, we focus on the foreign policy posture the United States has adopted for itself.

The central objective of United States foreign policy can be stated simply: the protection and advancement of the national interest. The same objective holds for foreign *economic* policy — which comprises one part of overall foreign policy. The three guidelines for foreign economic policy are as follows. First, the United States desires to promote its own economic strength. To this end, it is interested in large and growing markets abroad, capable of underwriting this country's growing export capacity; in an assured supply of raw-materials imports, needed for consumption and also by industry; in more trade, all-around, so as to heighten the potential benefits of specialization; and in the presence abroad of an investment climate able to provide, to mutual advantage, an outlet for some of this country's capital, especially private capital.

Second, the United States desires to promote the economic strength of other "Free World" countries. To this end, the hope is for prosperity (with peace) everywhere within the "Free World" — and for, with special reference to the underdeveloped countries, the realization of an accelerated rate of development.

Third, the United States desires a high degree of unity within the "Free World." To this end, it seeks to eliminate disputes among other "Free World" countries and to lessen tensions generally, so as to prevent any weakening of the "Free World" front.

As is evident, the United States' approach to foreign economic policy reflects a mixture of economic and political-military considerations. The

213

country wants prosperity and growing economic well-being, as well as political-military security, for itself — all goals toward which it sees its foreign economic policy as contributing. These considerations, leavened with humanitarian goals, provide the basis for policy formulation.

In translating the foregoing ingredients into a formal policy framework, the United States has at its disposal the possibility of action in three realms. First and foremost, in the realm of foreign trade, the United States is committed — as it has been for many years — to the goal of multilateralism. Thus, it supports a program of its own for the lowering of existing tariff barriers (proceeding along lines of reciprocity in concessions); it discourages governmentally-imposed barriers to trade by others (through continuing endorsement of GATT principles); and it opposes private barriers to trade (as in the case of cartel activity).

Second, in the realm of foreign investment, this country has sought ways to eliminate or lessen deterrents to the movement abroad of American private capital. And, though recent balance-of-payments deficits caused it to reappraise its policy, it reversed itself only in respect to investment destined for other developed countries. Its interest in measures to promote capital flows to underdeveloped countries has continued.

Third, in the realm of foreign aid, this country's avowed policy — for some years now — has been to provide assistance abroad, economic and/or military, whenever and wherever such asssistance would be used in mutually beneficial ways. It has provided commodity assistance of multi-billion magnitude, along with technical assistance in generous quantity.

Thus, the implementation of American foreign economic policy proceeds in terms of "a basic triad": trade, investment, and aid — which, in Part Three, we will examine in that sequence.

A..... Commercial Policy

The ideal of multilateralism serves as a cornerstone of United States commercial policy. Philosophically, multilateralism is closely allied to the law of comparative advantage. The law of comparative advantage, as we have seen, holds that countries need to specialize and trade in order to maximize efficiency and income. This, pursued to its ultimate, requires not a mere bilateral exchange of output, but a trading context within the *totality* of which output may flow in all directions and yet be settled for with receipts from any quarter — the essence of multilateralism.

Actually, the United States has espoused multilateralism for a long time; official policy statements have appeared in abundance over the years. Moreover, the United States has acted in tangible ways to "pull" the world nearer to the multilateralist ideal. During the early post-World War II era, having assumed the role of "Free World" leader, this country took the initiative in laying the groundwork for the Havana Conference (1948), at which a proposed International Trade Organization (ITO) was up for consideration. The ITO was to manage an international "code of conduct" that, in essence, would give the sanction of "law" to components of a multilateralist philosophy. As fate would have it, however, the ITO never came into being; sentiment in underdeveloped countries was opposed to the ITO on the grounds that it would merely underwrite the status quo, and even the Congress in this country failed to ratify the charter, ostensibly on the grounds that compliance would impinge on national sovereignty.

Though the ITO never came into being, a portion of what was at issue did get activated. This was the General Agreement on Tariffs and Trade (GATT), which (a) sets forth certain standards on commercial policy (especially relative to tariffs, quotas, and subsidies) and (b) provides machinery for periodic tariff-reduction bargaining on a mass-country basis. The United States and some 60 other countries have become adherents of GATT — though this country adheres by strength of Executive order, not Congressional approval. Over the years, numerous sessions have been called to implement multilateralized tariff-cutting, the most recent of which involved the so-called "Kennedy Round" of tariff-concession negotiations.

Thus, the United States has "'favored" a multilateralist approach, along

215

with, necessarily, its most important single policy expression — "freer trade." Vigorous talk has been matched, in practice, with some trade liberalization — though accomplishments in this direction can hardly be described as having resulted from all-out or consistent action. The United States has not appeared to want truly "free trade," and has, in fact, even gotten "in trouble" with GATT from time to time.

Viewing American tariff policy in broad perspective, we note a long period of overall increase in tariff levels (as the country was pushing toward economic maturity and, hence, presumably needed to deter competitive imports), followed by a policy shift to lower tariffs (initiated once a certain economic build-up had been reached, after which the premium was on external outlets for domestic output). The official turning point came in 1934 with adoption of the Reciprocal Trade Agreements Program, under which this country sought to reduce its tariffs *in exchange for* equivalent concessions by other countries.

True, this country's tariffs were lowered over the years following 1934 — from an average duty rate of 52.8% in 1930–1933 to one of 12.3% in 1962. Throughout, many domestic producers chose to criticize the program — and, as a concession to those producers who could not endure resultant competition (or did not want to?), various "escape" provisions came to be included in the covering legislation — provisions which were criticized, usually indirectly, abroad. Europe was prone to allege that the presence of escape provisions meant uncertainties detrimental to investment-and-production planning in anticipation of export to the American market. Underdeveloped countries were prone to criticize the quid-pro-quo aspect of tariff bargaining; high duties, they claimed, made good sense in their case (because the new industries they were trying to build up needed, or deserved, protection), even though lower duties made sense for the United States, an established producer.

In 1962 (under the Kennedy administration), the United States moved to new legislation: the Trade Expansion Act. Two important features were introduced. First, tariff bargaining, henceforth, could go on with blocs of countries, not only with individual countries. This adaptation was regarded as necessary in the light of the new European Common Market, a competitive threat of first magnitude. Second, provisions were included to cover "assisted readjustment": the resort to escape-clause provisions whenever competition threatened could be replaced by help to firms, industries, and workers in need of weathering a period of adjustment.

Thus, movement toward "freer trade" has long been, and continues to be, an official United States policy. But "freer trade" has not been an across-the-board goal. For example, strategic (and other) considerations have dictated a policy of close control over trade with countries of the Communist Bloc(s). And while the United States has officially intervened to *restrict* East-West trade, it has stepped in, also, to *foster* particular other categories of trade. For example, cartel-like action by American firms for purposes of export promotion has been exempted from antitrust prohibitions (under terms of the Webb-Pomerene Act). Somewhat similarly, too, the country has moved to a type of "state trading" activity to promote massive disposals abroad of domestic agricultural surpluses (under the P.L. 480 program).

The selections in our present section deal with United States commercial policy. The first selection, in two parts, expounds the multilateralist philosophy. Professor Kenen explains how and why GATT came into existence. His explanation is followed by excerpts from GATT "policy principles."

The second selection, again in two parts, goes into the Trade Expansion Act of 1962. After excerpts from the new legislation, we turn to Professor Brainard, who examines the rationale behind the legislation and gives his appraisal of its major provisions.

A third selection covers aspects of the United States treatment of East-West trade: excerpts from the Export Control Act; an indication of the volume and composition of East-West trade; and a sample of argumentation being heard at official level apropos possible liberalization of prevailing trade controls.

The final selection, by President Brewster of Yale, presents material relative to antitrust exemption for certain American export activity.

29..... The Multilateralist Goal and GATT

I. The Movement to GATT*

PETER B. KENEN

Columbia University

The American Initiative

The Second World War damaged world trade even more than the Great Depression. Most of the belligerents imposed strict *exchange controls* to prevent their citizens from spending foreign currencies; they sought to reserve their precious foreign earnings for purchasing war materiel and food. Many countries carried their controls into the post-war period in order to save scarce foreign currency for their reconstruction programs.

Very early in the war, however, experts began drawing plans to liberalize trade and payments in the post-war period. Even before the shooting stopped, the Allied governments established two new financial institutions — the International Monetary Fund (IMF) and the International Bank for Reconstruction and Development (IBRD) — to revive and sustain the payments system and encourage flows of long-term capital. They also planned to promote a fast recovery of world trade by relaxing the complex controls that had slowed recovery in the 1930's and strangled trade during the war.

The experts found serious flaws in the [United States'] Trade Agreements Program. During the pre-war negotiations, many governments had withheld tariff concessions from the United States to save some of their limited bargaining power for negotiations with other countries. The wartime planners consequently urged a *multilateral* agreement rather than a new set of country-by-country bargains. Each government might then weigh all it had won — the concessions it had obtained directly in

* From Peter B. Kenen, *International Economics,* © 1964, pp. 40–41. Reprinted by permission of Prentice-Hall, Inc., Englewood Cliffs, New Jersey.

return for its own and those it had obtained indirectly through the *most-favored-nation* clause. The American experts likewise worried about the import quotas, payments agreements, and other trade controls that had been used abroad in lieu of tariffs. Quotas frustrate the price mechanism by barring imports no matter how cheap. Tariffs handicap the foreigner but do not freeze trade patterns or prevent price changes from affecting resource allocation. Furthermore, quotas were sometimes used abroad to nullify negotiated tariff cuts; some countries had imposed import quotas after they had cut their duties. The United States consequently sought a comprehensive agreement on commercial policy, not just a new tariff treaty.

The new U.S. trade policy found its first expression in wartime agreements between the United States and Great Britain — in the Atlantic Charter and Lend-Lease Agreement. The new policy was then embodied in a charter for an International Trade Organization (ITO) to be affiliated with the United Nations. But the ITO never came into being. Its charter was too long and complicated, and was perforated by exceptions and qualifications. It antagonized opponents of international cooperation, who charged that the ITO would meddle with domestic economic policies. It antagonized the advocates of cooperation, who complained that the exceptions and qualifications had swamped the principles, and that no one would be bound to obey the rules.

In 1947, however, the major governments were able to agree on interim rules for trade policy and began a series of conferences to reduce tariffs and dismantle other barriers. This interim arrangement has survived and is known as the General Agreement on Tariffs and Trade (GATT). The GATT is a simple document compared to the ITO charter; it does not seek to deal with every issue or to anticipate every contingency. The heart of the GATT is a *most-favored-nation* clause which provides that every tariff bargain made at GATT meetings shall be extended to all member countries. This is how the system works: At each GATT conference, national negotiators meet in pairs to swap tariff cuts in which they have special interest. Thus, American and British representatives may sit down to exchange concessions on cars and woolens, even as British and French representatives are bargaining on pharmaceuticals and wines, and the Americans and French are bargaining on office machinery and perfumes. When all the separate bargains are complete, they are listed in a single schedule and applied to every member country. This combination of bilateral and multilateral negotiations seems cumbersome, but has had great advantages. Each government negotiates with the others that will gain most from its proposed concessions, thereby securing the largest foreign concessions in return for its own. At the same time, every government can keep track of the benefits it will obtain from all other countries and appraise its global bargaining position as the negotiations proceed.

The GATT commercial code outlaws discriminatory tariffs and prohibits the use of import quotas except by countries suffering from balance-of-payments problems or by those imposing similar quotas on domestic production — on farm products, for example. It allows the less-developed countries to protect their infant industries, but subjects them to regular GATT review. The GATT provides machinery to resolve disputes arising from trade policy. During the last few years, for example, it has been disentangling the problems raised by the creation of the European Economic Community, or Common Market. The formation of the Common Market poses a host of problems for outsiders, including the United States, and GATT members have asked the European countries to adjust their policies to minimize damage and dislocation.

II. GATT Principles*

Article I: Objectives

1. The contracting parties recognize that their relations in the field of trade and economic endeavour should be conducted with a view to raising standards of living, ensuring full employment and a large and steadily growing volume of real income and effective demand, developing the full use of the resources of the world and expanding the production and exchange of goods, and promoting the progressive development of the economies of all the contracting parties.

2. The contracting parties desire to contribute to these objectives through this Agreement by entering into reciprocal and mutually advantageous arrangements directed to the substantial reduction of tariffs and other barriers to trade and to the elimination of discriminatory treatment in international commerce.

Article II: General Most-Favoured-Nation Treatment

1. With respect to customs duties and charges of any kind imposed on or in connection with importation or exportation or imposed on the international transfer of payments for imports or exports, and with respect to

---

* From GATT, *Basic Instruments and Selected Documents,* Vol. 1 (revised), Geneva, April 1955, p. 7.

the method of levying such duties and charges, and with respect to all rules and formalities in connection with importation and exportation, and with respect to the application of internal taxes to exported goods, . . . any advantage, favour, privilege or immunity granted by any contracting party to any product originating in or destined for any other country shall be accorded immediately and unconditionally to the like product originating in or destined for the territories of all other contracting parties. . . .

30 ..... The Trade Expansion Act of 1962

I. Legislative Statement of Purpose*

It is the purpose of this Act, by lowering trade barriers through trade agreements affording mutual benefits, to stimulate the economic growth of the United States, maintain and enlarge foreign markets for the products of United States industry and agriculture, and make available to the people of the United States a greater variety of goods at lower prices; to strengthen economic and political relations with the European Economic Community and foreign countries through the development of an open and nondiscriminatory trading system in the free world; to assist in the sound economic progress of countries in the earlier stages of economic development; and to counter economic penetration by international communism. In addition, it is the purpose of this Act to provide appropriate assistance to enterprises, workers, and farmers of the United States in adjusting to new conditions which may result from increased trade with the European Economic Community and foreign countries.

* From "Trade Expansion Act of 1962," *Hearings Before the Committee on Ways and Means,* House of Representatives, 87th Congress, 2nd Session, on H.R. 9900, Part 1, March 1962, p. 13. The paragraph shown is the opening statement of Title I, Trade Expansion Act of 1962.

II. The Trade Expansion Act: An Appraisal*

HARRY G. BRAINARD

Michigan State University

On October 11, 1962, President Kennedy signed into law the Trade Expansion Act of 1962, which was hailed as a landmark in the foreign trade policy of this country. Whether or not this act ranks as a milestone in the history of the United States international commercial policy depends upon the answers to three major questions. If the evidence is in the affirmative, then the act is a significant break with the past; if not, then much of the publicity given this law as it passed through the legislative process was mere window dressing.

What are the questions to be raised and answered? First, does the Trade Expansion Act represent a new approach in philosophical terms to our tariff policy? In other words, is this nation now going to embark upon a distinctly new and different approach to the protection of American products from competition abroad? A second fundamental consideration relates to the objectives to be achieved. Are the provisions of the new law designed to meet objectives which are new and different from those sought by the Reciprocal Trade Agreements program initiated in 1934? And finally, even without reference to the two questions just posed, does the act provide new devices or techniques for implementing our commercial policies with other nations? The philosophy and the objectives may be basically the same as have existed for about three decades, but it may be that new and better tools of administration are provided by the Trade Expansion Act.

Foreign Trade Policy

The answer to the first question, namely, the basic philosophy of the Trade Expansion Act of 1962 in comparison with the Reciprocal Trade

---

* Taken and adapted from "The Trade Expansion Act — 1962," *Business Topics,* (East Lansing, Mich.: Bureau of Business and Economic Research, Graduate School of Business Administration, Michigan State University), Winter 1963, pp. 7–19.

Agreements program, is neither yes nor no. It is, rather, that in certain important ways the new law represents a change in thinking on the part of the government; in other respects there is no change in the general approach to the foreign trade policy of this country. In order to give substance to this observation it is necessary to take a look at the tariff history of the United States during the past 30 years.

Hawley-Smoot Act

Congress in 1930 passed the Hawley-Smoot Act which established the highest tariff rates in the history of the nation. This action was taken in the sincere belief that it would contribute to a solution of the economic depression gripping the country. It was thought that the best way to save jobs for American labor and to provide orders for business was to drastically limit competition from foreign industry and agriculture. Imports of many commodities shared the market with domestic goods and hence added to the depressed economic conditions. Economic isolation contributed to domestic activity and was, therefore, not only good but desirable. This was a philosophy of economic self-containment.

Under the guidance of Secretary of State Cordell Hull, the Roosevelt administration promoted a foreign trade program which differed sharply from that embodied in the Hawley-Smoot Act. The new approach could not be characterized as "free-trade" in the literal sense, but it was based on a belief that a policy of economic isolation could not contribute to the creation of greater business activity. Reducing imports by the imposition of restrictive tariff rates would clearly leave a larger share of the home market to domestic producers. At the same time, however, markets for American products abroad could be expected to decline. Trade, it was argued, is a two-way street and a nation can export only if it also imports. The foreign trade policy of the Roosevelt administration was, therefore, to expand exports and in this way to raise the level of economic activity.

Reciprocal Trade Agreements Act

The Reciprocal Trade Agreements Act of 1934 implemented the basic philosophy of the Roosevelt administration and represented a milestone in United States tariff history. Henceforth tariff rates on selected commodities were to be reduced through bilateral negotiations with other nations in order to expand trade. This was a bold new program and a direct break with the philosophy of the Hoover administration expressed in the highly restrictive Hawley-Smoot Act of 1930. It is to be emphasized, however, that this was not a free trade program; instead it was a means to promote freer trade. This distinction is important because it puts into proper focus the nature of the policy inaugurated by Secretary Hull.

From 1934 to 1962 the Reciprocal Trade Agreements Act was renewed on 11 different occasions and typically for a period of three years. There were no significant changes in the legislation until 1948, although certain administrative procedures had been introduced to meet congressional criticism. For example, while World War II was still going on, the Reciprocal Trade Agreements program was attacked with ever increasing intensity on the grounds that American producers were being injured or might be by tariff concessions granted to other nations. It was argued that a policy of reducing tariffs was acceptable so long as there was no injury to American industry and agriculture. Such a contention was, of course, without meaning for the simple reason that a tariff which was not sufficiently high to limit imports was not protective and hence of little use to those for whom it was intended. In practice the advocates of the no-injury concept did not push their argument this far, but were content to seek relief if a tariff concession threatened to cause a significant loss of market to the industry concerned. It was in response to this argument that an escape clause was included in the 1943 trade agreement with Mexico.

Peril-point and Escape Clauses. When the reciprocal Trade Agreements Act was under consideration for renewal in 1948 the proponents of the no-injury philosophy of tariff negotiations were successful in including in the act of that year a peril-point provision and an escape clause. The law required a review by the Tariff Commission of each list of commodities proposed for tariff negotiation for the purpose of establishing the maximum concession that could be granted without inflicting injury on the industry concerned. A concession beyond this point could be negotiated but had to be justified in a report to the Congress. The escape clause established a procedure by which a tariff reduction already granted could be withdrawn on the Tariff Commission's finding an injury. If such action was not taken by the President an explanation had to be submitted to the Congress. Even though the no-injury provisions were withdrawn the following year, the protectionist philosophy had been accepted briefly as the prevailing sentiment of the Congress. It was again expressed in 1951 when peril-point and escape clauses were written into the law, where they have remained ever since.

A Shift in Attitude. The no-injury philosophy of the Trade Expansion Act of 1962 represents a sharp break with the past. The peril-point clause was dropped. In its place is a provision requiring the Tariff Commission to study carefully the probable economic effects of modifications of duties or other import restrictions on industries producing commodities appearing on the tariff bargaining list. The law does not require the determination of minimum duties essential to the protection of the industries concerned — the basic characteristic of the peril-point provision. An escape clause was retained but the newly enacted law recognizes that tariff concessions may be expected to cause a hardship on industries, firms, and workers. With few exceptions, the remedy provided is not to be found in an upward adjustment of rates but rather in helping those concerned to meet the new competition. In other words, it is assumed that in the administration of the Trade Expansion Act industries, firms, and workers can expect to be injured by tariff concessions. This is a reversal of the philosophy of tariff negotiations which has prevailed since 1948. . . .

Objectives of the Act

An appraisal of the Trade Expansion Act of 1962 must include a study of objectives to be attained by the legislation. . . .

Specific Ends

The language of the Trade Expansion Act of 1962 is clear and unequivocal in stating the purposes to be attained. There are two main objectives. The first is to achieve certain specific ends by lowering trade barriers through tariff negotiations. The resulting agreements will afford mutual benefits to such basic interests as the general welfare, foreign policy, and national security. In more precise terms these specific ends are:

To benefit the economy of the United States;
To strengthen economic and political relations between the United States and the other countries of the free world and in particular with the European Economic Community;
To assist the economies of countries in the earlier stages of economic development;
To counter penetration by international Communism.

New Methods

The second purpose of the act deals with new methods of meeting cases of actual or potential hardship arising out of trade negotiations. These adjustment provisions are in keeping with the new philosophy that the reduction of trade barriers can be expected to cause injury to industries, firms, and workers as foreign competition is intensified. In other words, a second purpose of the act is to expand the trade of the United States even though various segments of the business world may be subjected to loss of markets, profits, and even jobs. This objective is based on a rejection of the no-injury philosophy which had prevailed for more than a decade.

When the objectives of the Trade Expansion Act of 1962 are put alongside those of the Reciprocal Trade Agreements Act of 1934 as amended, it becomes clear that the new law represents a significant departure from the past. In the first place, the bargaining provisions are viewed as a tool to combat foreign trade barriers and thereby to expand the nation's exports. Secondly, it is proposed to expand commerce in specific areas as a consequence of trade negotiations. These are the Common Market and the nations that are developing economically, particularly those in South America. Finally, it is believed that an expansion of our foreign commerce will contribute substantially to overcoming balance of payments deficits experienced in recent years.

Expansion of Foreign Trade

A final area of investigation concerns the procedures by which the expansionist philosophy of the act is to be implemented. As with other aspects of the legislation, one finds here that improvements have been made on the former tariff negotiating procedures and new methods have been created.

Broadening of the Bargaining Unit

A feature of the Trade Expansion Act of 1962, which is new, although implicit in the 1958 Reciprocal Trade Agreements Act, relates to a broadening of the bargaining unit. Specifically, the new law recognizes the European Economic Community as an economic entity for trade negotiations as distinguished from its member nations (The Netherlands, Belgium, Luxembourg, West Germany, France, and Italy). The significance of this new arrangement cannot be fully appreciated until one understands earlier procedures. When the Reciprocal Trade Agreements program was first established, trade negotiations were conducted on a bilateral basis. Thus the United States government entered into separate bargaining sessions on a nation-by-nation basis and worked out a trade agreement containing tariff reductions on commodities of most importance to the country concerned. The lower rates thus negotiated were then extended to all other nations with which the United States maintained friendly trading relations. This was done in conformance with the most-favored-nation policy long accepted by our government. During the first 13 years of the program, 1934–1947, 29 reciprocal trade agreements were negotiated on a purely bilateral basis.

Beginning in 1947 the trade agreement negotiating process was modernized when the United States and 22 other nations met in Geneva, Switzerland, as a group to bargain collectively. There were altogether 123 sets of negotiations covering roughly 50,000 items. The end product of the conference was the adoption by the participating nations of the General Agreement on Tariffs and Trade (GATT). Since that first bargaining session four additional negotiating conferences have been held. The most recent was in late 1961. These conferences do not replace the conclusion of bilateral agreements as such but they greatly accelerate the process of negotiation. Only for individual nations that are not members of the GATT are bilateral sessions held.

What the new law does is to carry the trade negotiating process one step further by providing that tariff bargaining will henceforth be conducted between the United States and the European Economic Community instead of its member nations individually. This is a logical procedure because there will be coming into existence over a period of years a single uniform external tariff schedule applicable to all nations trading with Common Market countries. Hence it makes sense to deal with the European Economic Community as an entity in itself, and as the Common Market expands to include more nations, so will the importance of bargaining with it become more all-inclusive.

A Special Representative

As a corollary to the broadening of the bargaining unit Congress wrote into the Trade Expansion Act a section providing for the creation of a Special Representative for Trade Negotiations. The establishment of a new agency to conduct trade negotiations is also a natural extension of the former Reciprocal Trade Agreements program. It is designed to provide a more efficient administration of this country's foreign trade policy in an international climate different from that of the past few years. . . .

Greater Bargaining Authority

The heart of the Reciprocal Trade Agreements program has been the authority Congress has granted to the President to negotiate trade concessions and to enter into foreign trade agreements. This authority is continued in the Trade Expansion Act for five years, that is, to June 30, 1967 which, incidentally, is longer than any previous period. The ability to negotiate trade agreements has meaning, however, only to the extent that concessions can be granted and it is in this respect that the present act is of particular importance. The basic authority to modify import duties remains essentially unchanged from the Trade Agreements Act of 1958. Tariff rates may be reduced by 50 per cent of those prevailing at a specified base period which in the new legislation is July 1, 1962. In addition, rates may be increased over the July 1, 1934 level (Hawley-Smoot Act rates) and additional import restrictions may be imposed.

It is in the authority to grant concessions beyond those indicated above when negotiating with the European Economic Community that the new law gains special significance. In the first place, the President is permitted to reduce *by more than 50 per cent* or eliminate entirely duties on categories of articles instead of item by item when it can be established that the United States and Common Market countries together accounted for 80 per cent or more of the free world trade in these groups of commodities in a representative base period. Secondly, similar duty reductions can be granted on certain agricultural goods when a determination is made that such reductions will tend to assure the maintenance or expansion of United States exports of similar articles. A final special negotiating authority is dependent upon similar action by the European Economic Community. Specifically, duties on tropical agricultural and forestry products may be reduced by more than 50 per cent if it can be shown (1) that similar commodities are not produced in significant amounts domestically, and (2) that Common Market countries have agreed to give these products access to their market on equally favorable terms.

The law also permits the President to reduce duties in excess of 50 per cent on those commodities subject to a rate of 5 per cent or less on July 1, 1962. This authority is designed to facilitate administration of the law, since there is little likelihood that a duty of this magnitude would have economic significance.

Limitation on Use of Authority

In accordance with previous legislation, the new trade law places certain restrictions on the bargaining power of the President. These limitations are in all major respects the same as those of the Reciprocal Trade Agreements Act of 1958. . . .

A New Approach to Injury Cases

Earlier in this article it was suggested that in writing the Trade Expansion Act of 1962 Congress departed from its philosophy of "no injury" and accepted the idea that American industries might indeed suffer hardship as a consequence of tariff reductions. In accordance with this concept the new law contains special provisions in addition to the traditional escape clause for dealing with injury cases. This approach to hardship situations is a complete break with earlier legislation and, therefore, merits special attention.

Industry Adjustment. A petition for tariff adjustment may be filed with the Tariff Commission by a trade association, a firm, a trade union, or by an entire industry. When such action has been taken the Commission is then required to conduct an extensive investigation of the claim to determine if increased imports have caused or threaten to cause the injury alleged. When the Commission has completed its investigation, which must be done within six months, a report is made to the President and also to the public. In case of an affirmative finding, several types of action can be taken by the government. If it appears that an entire industry is adversely affected by a tariff concession, two kinds of relief are available. Under the terms of the escape clause carried over from the 1958 Act, the President may proclaim an increase in, or the imposition of a duty on, the article in question to the degree necessary to prevent serious injury to the industry. The word "may" is used advisedly since the Chief Executive is not required to take such action. In this instance he must report to Congress, which by a majority vote can override his decision and thereby compel action by the President.

Another kind of action that can be taken in industry hardship cases appears for the first time in the Trade Expansion Act. As an alternative to the escape-clause procedure, the government is authorized to negotiate international agreements with foreign countries designed to permit the orderly marketing of certain commodities exported to this country. Where this action is taken, tariff concessions are not affected but imports are limited by mutual agreement. For several years such arrangements have been in existence, having been negotiated under laws not directly concerned with trade policy. The most notable of these agreements is the one with Japan which limits the flow of a wide range of textile products to this country. In the future these agreements can be negotiated formally and directly between governments under this law which deals specifically with our foreign trade policy. It is to be emphasized that industry relief will be given as a last resort and only after it is certain that the various adjustment measures designed to assist firms and their workers to meet the new conditions are inappropriate.

Company Adjustment. An increase in imports arising out of reduced trade barriers may not affect an entire industry but rather be felt by certain firms only. It is quite possible for a high-cost domestic producer to be forced out of the market while other more efficient firms are able to meet foreign competition. To provide relief for adversely affected firms and their workers, Congress has written into the present law special adjustment provisions for individual companies and employees. The relief made possible by the act is not intended to shield the firms or workers from foreign competition; instead, it is designed to enable them to shift to the production of other kinds of commodities and employment. Since this kind of relief is new in tariff legislation and constitutes a rejection of the no-injury philosophy, a closer look at the adjustment procedure is warranted.

Once a company is certified by the Tariff Commission as eligible for relief, it may apply to the Secretary of Commerce who can provide assistance by one of three methods, singly or in combination. Assistance may take the form of technical aid which will be provided by a governmental agency or in unusual cases by outside firms or individuals. Appropriate technical assistance may include market and other economic research, managerial advice and counseling, training, and help in research and product development. A second kind of aid may take the form of financial help including guarantees of loans, agreements for deferred participation in loans, or outright loans. The extent of financial assistance is limited to the amount that will contribute to the firm's economic adjustment. Finally, a firm may be granted tax relief. Where this is done, a company is permitted a five-year loss carry-back as compared with a three-year period for taxpayers in general. This concession is allowed only on the condition that the company's losses were occasioned by increased imports resulting from a trade agreement concession.

The granting of assistance by any of the above methods is conditioned upon the acceptance by the government of a definite proposal of the firm applying for relief. A proposal will be approved if it can be expected (1) to contribute to the firm's economic adjustment, (2) to give adequate consideration to the interests of its workers, and (3) to require the company to make all reasonable efforts to use its own resources in the adjustment process. The requirement that a firm's proposal will meet such standards is intended to insure a systematic approach to the problems of economic adjustment, to increase the likelihood that the adjustment will be successful, and finally to restrict governmental aid to those firms prepared to help themselves to the maximum extent possible.

Assistance to Workers. Just as firms may be eligible for assistance due to injury caused by tariff concessions granted in a trade agreement, so also may workers in industries thus affected be given aid. If the Tariff Commission finds an injury, workers may apply to the Secretary of Labor for assistance. Eligible workers who meet minimum qualifications may receive unemployment compensation up to 65 per cent of their average weekly wage instead of the current national average of about 35 per cent. Moreover, payments may be extended beyond the normal 39 weeks to a full year. Older workers and those taking training may qualify for an even longer period of payments. This is the trade readjustment program and its cost is borne entirely by the federal government.

Of more importance are two other kinds of assistance. The first of these is the aid that can be given to train a worker for a different kind of employment. Governmental agencies can make available to these workers testing, counseling, training, and placement services to the greatest extent possible. Where the appropriate kind of training program is not available in his own community, the worker may be given financial aid to defray transportation costs and living expenses while away from home. For the worker who is totally separated from his job, who cannot find suitable employment locally, and who obtains a satisfactory position elsewhere, a relocation allowance may be granted. This allowance includes the reasonable and necessary expenses incurred by the worker in transporting his family and household effects to a new community. In addition, the worker is entitled to a lump sum payment equal to two and one-half times the average weekly manufacturing wage.

The training and relocation allowances are of special significance, since they are designed to do for labor what technical, financial, and tax relief programs do for injured firms, namely, to promote a shift of resources to more efficient uses. Worker training and relocation programs will reduce the number of persons eligible for trade adjustment allowances and thereby lessen the cost of this kind of assistance. But of more importance is the fact that through these programs workers can be removed from an over-supplied market and their talents directed to those areas where they are needed. . . .

Conclusions

In order to reach general conclusions concerning the Trade Expansion Act of 1962 it will help to suggest certain features which may limit its effectiveness and to indicate its strong aspects. The act retains in essentially the same language several restrictive provisions of the Reciprocal Trade Agreements Act of 1958. These are the escape clause, national security, and Communist area provisions. The use of the escape clause is actually made easier in the present law than in its predecessors in two ways. It now requires but a simple majority of both houses of Congress to override a negative decision by the President where formerly a two-thirds vote was needed.

Secondly, the profit criterion has been changed so that now one evidence of injury is the ability of an industry to demonstrate that it cannot operate at "a level of reasonable profit." Formerly, the profit criterion could not be used if the industry had any profits at all. By this change, injury due to increased imports resulting from a trade agreement concession can be more easily established.

The section in the law prohibiting the extension of tariff concessions to Communist-dominated nations cannot be criticized in strong terms. The fact that the Senate bill excluded Poland and Yugoslavia from this provision raises some doubt, however, about the action finally taken. It may well be that the use of tariff concessions would have made economic penetration possible in these two countries. In the long run, therefore, this limitation may prove to have been unwise, but there is no sure way to know.

A part of the new act which would appear to be a forward step may in the end turn out to be an empty gesture. Reference is made here to the authority granted to the President to reduce to zero duties on commodities exchanged between the European Economic Community and the United States, provided 80 per cent or more of such trade is between these two areas. Under the present definition of the Common Market (The Netherlands, Belgium, Luxembourg, West Germany, France, and Italy), the only commodity that can qualify is certain types of aircraft. The administration based its argument for the authority on the concept of a Common Market that would include the United Kingdom. If and when Great Britain becomes a member, a broader definition will have to be adopted by Congress to make the above bargaining authority meaningful. As of now, it is an authority without substance.

The insistence of Congress upon direct representation in trade negotiations must be considered as a weakness. This is so because it is a direct extension of Congressional power into the area of administration and hence is in contravention of the separation of powers inherent in our system of constitutional government. It may not be a significant intrusion but the fact that it exists at all is to be deplored. If the Congress lacks faith in the administrative ability of the executive branch, then it should require detailed reports and perhaps consultation, but to take part directly in tariff bargaining would seem to be undesirable.

Among the many virtues of the Trade Expansion Act three are deserving of special comment. The acceptance of the European Economic Community as an entity for bargaining purposes is important because it is a recognition of the trend throughout the world towards economic regionalism. Where a trading area with a common external tariff exists it makes sense to deal with it as a unit. Other trading areas are coming into existence, the most notable being the common market established by the nations of Central America.

The Interagency Trade Organization, as a replacement for the Interdepartmental Committee, will serve to strengthen considerably the administration of the act. The new organization is a creation of Congress with clearly specified duties and with responsibilities going well beyond tariff bargaining to include problems of injury adjustment. The administrative machinery is further strengthened by the establishment of the office of Special Representative for Trade Negotiations. This is an important change in administration because it centralizes in one person responsibility for carrying out the bargaining provisions of the law. . . . It is because of these major improvements in the administrative machinery that one wonders why Congress has insisted upon direct participation in the negotiating process.

The strongest feature of the Trade Expansion Act is its rejection of the no-injury concept of tariff bargaining. By assuming that an expansion of trade will cause hardship to industries, firms, and workers, and by providing intelligent adjustment procedures, Congress in passing this act clearly set our foreign trade policy on a new and forward-looking course. In this sense the new law constitutes a milestone in the international commercial policy of the United States and gives this nation added stature as a leader in world affairs.

31..... Treatment of East-West Trade

I. The Export Control Act of 1949*

The Export Control Act of 1949, as amended, provides the President with the authority to prohibit or curtail exports from the United States, its territories, and possessions; and authorizes him to delegate this authority to such departments, agencies, and officials of the Government as he deems appropriate. The export control authority, which has been delegated to the Secretary of Commerce, is administered by the Office of Export Control of the Bureau of International Commerce.

The Act authorizes controls over exports for three purposes — "national security," "foreign policy," and "short supply." National security controls, and short supply controls as required, are always coordinated to reflect U.S. foreign policy and international responsibilities. In addition, the 1965 amendment to the Act included a policy statement that the United States opposes restrictive trade practices or boycotts by foreign countries against other countries friendly to the United States, and required exporters to report to the Secretary of Commerce any requests they receive for information or for action that would interfere with normal trade relations such as restrictive trade practices and boycotts.

National security controls are instituted to provide control of exports from the standpoint of their significance to the security of the United States. They include an embargo to Communist China, North Korea, the Communist-controlled area of Vietnam, and Cuba, as well as broad controls over exports to the U.S.S.R. and other Eastern European areas. Controls to free world countries apply to a highly selected list of commodities and technical data to prevent their unauthorized diversion or reexport to the foregoing countries, thus frustrating U.S. controls over shipments to them.

Short supply controls, as directed by the policy of the Act, are used only when it becomes necessary to protect the domestic economy from the

* Description contained in *Export Control*, 76th Quarterly Report by the Secretary of Commerce, 1966, pp. 1–2.

excessive drain of scarce materials and to reduce the inflationary impact of abnormal foreign demand.

With two exceptions, all commercial exports from the United States, its territories, and possessions are prohibited unless the Department of Commerce has either issued a "validated license" or established a "general license" permitting such shipments. These two exceptions are: exports from the United States *to* its territories and possessions, and most[1] exports to Canada for internal consumption.

A validated license is a formal document issued to an exporter by the Department. It authorizes the export of commodities within the specific limitations of the document. It is based upon a signed application submitted by the exporter.

A general license is a broad authorization issued by the Department of Commerce which permits certain exportations under specified conditions. Neither the filing of an application by the exporter nor the issuance of a license document is required in connection with any general license. The authority to export in such an instance is given in the Comprehensive Export Schedule, published by the Department of Commerce, which specifies the conditions under which each general license may be used.

[1] Other than certain technical data.

II. Trade Volume With the Soviet Bloc*

DEPARTMENT OF COMMERCE

Under current circumstances East-West trade is . . . marginal. Free World trade with the bloc in 1962 did not exceed 5% of total trade. U.S. trade with the bloc is still less than 2% of the total U.S. trade. Expanded trade in peaceful goods could take place without any major impact upon either the West or the East.

In 1963 Free World exports to the European Soviet bloc reached approximately 4.5 billion dollars. Free World imports from the bloc during the same period reached nearly 4.6 billion dollars. Three-fifths of this trade has been with the industrialized nations of the West. In terms of

* From Department of Commerce, *East-West Trade*, June 1965, p. 2.

Western total trade, however, trade with the bloc represented a mere 4 to 5% of their total trade. On the basis of 1963 statistics, the Federal Republic of Germany exports to the European Soviet bloc were $653 million; the United Kingdom, $374 million; Italy, $270 million; France, $226 million; and Japan, $179 million. On the other hand, U.S. exports to the European Soviet bloc during 1964 totaled $341 million, compared with $167 million in 1963; and $194 million in 1960. These 1964 exports constituted less than 2% of total U.S. exports of $25.6 billion.

During 1964 the principal Eastern European recipients of U.S. exports were Poland ($137.5 million); the USSR ($148.6 million); Hungary ($13.7 million); Czechoslovakia ($11.3 million); and East Germany ($20.2 million). In terms of commodities, wheat was the largest single export in 1964, with shipments totalling $179.5 million. Other principal commodity exports were unmanufactured cotton, $25.5 million; inedible tallow, $17.5 million, and rice, $10.4 million.

U.S. imports from the Eastern European countries during 1964 totalled $98.6 million, of which $54.2 million were from Poland. The principal items imported were meat and meat preparations, valued at $27.3 million; undressed fur skins, $11.5 million; iron and steel, $7.4 million; glass and glassware, $5.5 million, and chrome ore, $5.4 million.

U.S. imports from the European Soviet bloc countries during 1965 totalled $137.5 million, or less than 1 per cent of total U.S. imports. U.S. exports to those countries during 1965 totalled $139.5 million, or less than 1 per cent of total U.S. exports.

III. Arguments for Liberalization*

DEPARTMENT OF STATE

. . . [A 1966 proposal, the East-West Trade Relations Act,] would give the President authority to use trade with Eastern European countries and the Soviet Union as a flexible tool in the conduct of relations with these countries. As a companion to existing provisions of law which use the negative power of trade denial — the Export Control Act, the Battle Act,

* From Department of State, *East-West Trade Relations Act of 1966*, August 1966, pp. 7–8.

and restrictive provisions of other laws — the East-West Trade Relations Act would equip the President to use the positive aspects of trade to serve our national objectives.

The major substantive provision would be authority to extend most-favored-nation (MFN) tariff treatment to certain individual Communist countries when this is determined to be in the national interest. The authority could be exercised only in a commercial agreement with a particular country in which such MFN treatment would be granted in return for equivalent benefits to the United States. MFN treatment for the products of any country would stay in effect only as long as the commercial agreement with that country would be in effect.

The purpose of these commercial agreements would be both to facilitate individual business transactions and to afford the United States Government an opportunity to deal with individual Communist countries on a variety of matters in the context of periodic trade negotiations. Agreements made pursuant to the act would set the framework for trade, but the trade itself — both exports and imports — would depend on decisions of individual firms.

Principal Features

Purposes

The stated purposes of the proposed act were to use trade with Communist countries as a means of advancing the national interests of the United States, to provide a framework for U.S. firms to conduct business with Communist state trading agencies, and to expand markets for U.S. products in those countries by giving their products an opportunity to compete in U.S. markets on a non-discriminatory basis.

MFN trade treatment. The act would give the President authority to use most-favored-nation treatment as a bargaining instrument in negotiating commercial agreements with individual Communist countries. The authority to conclude agreements could be exercised only upon a determination by the President that an agreement with a particular country would promote the purposes of the act, would be in the national interest, and would result in benefits to the United States equivalent to those provided by the agreement to the other country.

Exchange of benefits. Commercial agreements under the act would be made only on the basis of exchange of benefits. . . . Among the possible benefits are arrangements for protection of industrial property, settlement of commercial disputes, promotion of trade and tourism, trade fairs, trade missions, entry and travel of commercial representatives, most-favored-nation treatment for United States products, other arrangements to secure market access and assure fair treatment for United States products, improvement of consular relations, and settlement of claims.

32..... Antitrust Exemption
for Export Activity*

KINGMAN BREWSTER, JR.

Yale University

The [United States'] principal policy development concerning export restraints . . . [is] their carefully guarded exemption in the Webb-Pomerene Export Trade Act of 1918.[1] . . .

. . . After a lengthy investigation, the Federal Trade Commission [had] concluded that American exporters were at a disadvantage in foreign markets because of the possible illegality of export combinations under the Sherman Act.[2] One disadvantage was the inability to pool costs in order to meet the competition of foreign selling combines. This was felt to be a special disadvantage to small American firms who might not be able to export alone but could afford it in combination with competitors. The second handicap noted was that American export competitors could be played off against each each other by cartelized foreign buyers. The Webb Act was a deliberate effort to allow American exporters to band together to pit their combined power to countervail the foreign buying cartels.

Although the reasons for the Webb Act were peculiarly persuasive in the case of small businesses, the act was drafted in terms of all export businesses, big as well as small. But having made the act general in its availability to exporters, Congress proceeded to hedge it with provisos in order to prevent exempt associations from being used to restrain domestic competition or to put independent export competitors at a disadvantage. As a further safeguard, any association seeking the benefits of exemption had to file its articles of agreement with the Federal Trade

---

* From *Antitrust and American Business Abroad* by Kingman Brewster, Jr., pp. 24–25, 102–104, 111, 113. Copyright 1958 by McGraw-Hill, Inc. McGraw-Hill Book Company. Used by permission.

[1] 40 Stat. 516–518 (1918), 15 U.S.C. §§61–65 (1952).

[2] FTC, *Report on Cooperation in American Export Trade*, pt. I. at 372–75 (1916).

Commission and submit to the Commission's investigatory jurisdiction. ... It ... [should be noted] that the Webb privilege apparently does not extend to foreign investment activities[3] nor does the Federal Trade Commission feel that the Webb Act's immunity extends to an agreement with foreign competitors of the American exporters.[4] Only a small fraction of United States exports have ever been covered by Webb associations. Some of the firms which resorted to Webb arrangements initially have since disbanded their associations, and the number of associations in active existence at any one time has never exceeded fifty-seven.

Reasons for Export Cooperation Among Americans

Collective bargaining with foreign buyers or foreign governments is one objective which has prompted the formation of agreements among or joint action by exporters. It is the desire of American exporters to avoid being played off one against the other by a big foreign buyer or by a foreign government.

Of course this may simply be the desire to obtain higher prices than each could charge if he were competing with the others. However, it may involve collective action to force access to a foreign market for a greater aggregate volume than would be achieved if each negotiated on his own. This basis for joint action seems most crucially illustrated in the case of the industry which operates under quotas negotiated with foreign governments at relatively frequent intervals. These quotas may be directly reflected in foreign governmental limitations on the volume of American products which may be imported into the foreign market, or indirectly in the currency and exchange restrictions which may block repatriation of the earnings of Americans. This may be attributable either to foreign economic necessity (i.e., dollar shortage) or may reflect a protectionist desire to favor local producers; a foreign government may use a local association of powerful importers to effect a quasi-governmental rationing of imports. If foreign sales involve import or currency permits of one type or another, this use of collective bargaining may be highly desirable. It can be demonstrated in some situations that the total volume of foreign business achieved by exporters is greater because the industry as a unit can bargain on a "give us more or we won't play at all" basis. Further, it can be argued that collective bargaining for quotas allows the weaker firms to ride in on the bargaining power of the stronger. Finally, some would say that, at least where the foreign market is rationed by quota, the suballocation among the American exporters by the industry is more equitable than if accomplished by leaving each firm to curry individual favor with the foreign political authorities.

---

[3] United States v. Minnesota Mining & Mfg. Co., 92 F. Supp. 947 (D. Mass. 1950).
[4] United States v. United States Alkali Export Ass'n, Inc., 86 F. Supp. 59 (S.D.N.Y. 1949).

Where the only purpose of joint action is to obtain jointly a larger foreign import quota than could be obtained severally, the joint functions might not go beyond bargaining for that quota and allocating it among members. After that point, product and price decisions might be made by the individual exporters.

Economies of joint selling may well seem desirable or even necessary for some small firms in order to undertake the considerable investment and negotiation overhead required for direct foreign selling. The urge here is merely the foreign commerce counterpart of those joint selling agencies at home which seek the advantages of partial merger of distribution functions, not necessarily in order to affect prices but to save costs. This may not be feasible if product differentiation and the distinctive good will of different companies are involved. But small producers of interchangeable commodities or materials have on occasion adopted a common trade name for export, and have sold jointly in order to be able to compete effectively with rivals who were large enough to engage in direct selling on their own.

Pooling the risks of promoting new products in a relatively thin foreign market may be a special example of the economy of jointness which may prompt export agreements or joint foreign sales arrangements. . . .

Restraint on competition may be the principal business objective of export cooperation. Higher earnings may be sought by fixing export prices, limiting export volume, or allocating products or foreign territories. These objectives will be realizable, of course, only to the extent that the cooperating group has a large enough share of the export market affected so that jointly they can determine or substantially affect prices. . . .

Kinds of Activities Inside . . . the Exemption

Loose agreements concerning members' prices, export volume, or territories of sale appear to be within the Webb Act's haven. . . .

Collective action to gain access to foreign markets by joint bargaining with foreign governments for import quotas or with foreign monopoly buyers for purchase contracts is apparently an acceptable activity within the Webb exemption. Likewise, the suballocation of such quotas or contracts among members is a legitimate activity of an association. . . .

B..... Foreign Investment

The second major component of the basic "triad" of United States foreign economic policy is investment. Relative to it, the United States is today the world's leading creditor country, a position it assumed during the World War I era and has built on steadily ever since. Occurring partly on private account and partly on government account, the country's investment holdings abroad currently approach the $100 billion mark — the net figure being about half that amount (i.e., this country's investment abroad, less foreign-held investment in the United States). The total continues to rise, with the incremental additions tending to rise at an accelerated pace (in the absence of hampering restrictions).

The United States has long adhered to a policy of encouraging investment abroad by private Americans — indeed, this policy is quite consistent with the multilateralist bent of the country's thinking. Official action to this end has, in fact, been extensive and varied — including not only clear-cut policy statements but concrete measures as well. The government has engaged in gathering and providing information on investment opportunities abroad. It has negotiated treaties to clarify the rights of investors. It has initiated the Investment Guaranty Program under which investors can insure against loss due to inconvertibility, expropriation, and war damage. It has provided preferential tax treatment on foreign-earned income — as in the case of Western Hemisphere Trade Corporations which are eligible for a special 14 percentage point tax break. It has initiated a program of "tax sparing" arrangements with other countries. It has made certain loan funds available (Exim Bank funds, aid-agency funds, "Cooley Amendment" funds from the P.L. 480 program, etc.). It has backed up the American investor's position abroad through diplomatic means.

Thus, the historic pattern has been a continuing dedication to the promotion of a flow of private investment from this country to foreign countries. However, during very recent years this dedication has wavered. As balance-of-payments deficits appeared and persisted, Washington began to hesitate, even to backtrack, on its all-out endorsement — and to date Washington has taken three major steps toward retrenchment.

First, the Investment Guaranty Program, applicable to direct investment, was placed on a more selective basis, beginning in 1960. Thereafter, *new* American investment in other developed countries was held ineligible for insurance coverage, even as efforts to extend the guaranty provisions to additional underdeveloped countries continued.

Second, following sharp increases in offerings of new issues of foreign securities in the American market, an Interest Equalization Tax was imposed, in 1963, on purchases from foreigners of securities of issuers in developed countries other than Canada. The IET was supposed to remove the special attraction of higher rates of interest on the foreign securities (i.e., rates of interest higher than characterisic on comparable American securities) — a subsidiary fact being that, at the time, this country deemed itself under pressure to pursue an "easy money" policy (yielding low interest rates) for reasons of fuller employment at home.

Third, given continued balance-of-payments difficulty, a further program was introduced in 1965: a program of voluntary restraint on foreign investment by American corporations and banks. The restraint was to apply, broadly speaking, to capital outflows to developed countries, not to underdeveloped countries. Relative to the "bank" portion of the program, the Federal Reserve requested that banks, during a given year, limit their increase in claims on foreigners to a percentage of claims outstanding at the beginning of that year — 5% in 1965; 4% in 1966. Relative to the "non-financial business" portion of the program, the Department of Commerce requested corporations to make a maximum effort to expand their net payments balances and to repatriate liquid funds; to limit their average annual direct investment outflows (including reinvested earnings, but net of corporate borrowing abroad) to specified developed and oil-exporting countries to a percentage of an earlier year — 135% of 1962–1964 being the allowable percentage for 1965–1966; and, in financing undertakings abroad, to draw upon foreign sources of financing, rather than American sources, to the maximum extent possible.

Thus, in the present day, the official United States position on foreign investment is one of "endorsement, albeit with major qualifications." All the while, the matter of foreign investment is important for the American economy and for American business. Foreign investment has many implications for the economy at large: it leads to exports; it helps to create needed sources of supply; and so forth. Relative to business, restrictions on foreign investment raise many questions. How can American firms compete if they cannot acquire needed plant capacity? Or, *if* they can compete now from a United States base, can they compete later without having gotten a foreign base? Questions of this type abound, and continue to be raised and debated.

Three readings on foreign investment follow. In a first selection, Professor Mikesell presents the international investment "balance sheet" of the United States and proceeds, then, to examine the interest of this country in foreign investment.

A second selection, by Professor Vernon, is concerned with the American investor abroad. What does he do there? How is he viewed there? While much of Vernon's presentation is cast in a Latin American context, the basic conclusions appear to have fairly broad applicability. Certainly they provide useful guidelines for an appraisal of the merit of foreign investment, a pertinent consideration when official measures of restriction exist and may be added to.

A final selection, by Professor Behrman, treats the United States' program of voluntary restraint on foreign investment. In his opinion, the program is ill-advised; barriers in the path of investment in developed countries have effects, he argues, that tend to cancel out their initially-intended balance-of-payments benefits.

33..... United States Investment Abroad*

RAYMOND F. MIKESELL

University of Oregon

The International Investment Balance Sheet of the United States

At the end of 1919, the United States had investments abroad totalling about $7 billion, while foreigners had assets in investments in the United States totalling about $4 billion. Of the foreign investments in the United States, liquid dollar assets in 1919 amounted to an estimated $800 million, while the remainder was largely in the form of private long-term investments . . . [see Table 1]. By 1930, U.S. investments abroad had grown to $17.2 billion (excluding World War I debts), and foreign assets in the United States had risen to $8.4 billion, so that the United States was a net creditor of $8.8 billion. Liquid dollar assets had risen from $800 million in 1919 to $2,700 million in 1930, indicating the importance of the United States as an international financial center. By 1939, however, the value of U.S. investments abroad had declined to $11.4 billion, largely as a consequence of the reduction in value of foreign dollar bonds and reduced holdings of short-term assets abroad. Foreign assets in the United States rose by $1.2 billion during the 1930–1939 period, about half of which represented increased holdings of liquid dollar assets. By 1946, the value of U.S. investments abroad had risen to $18.7 billion, while foreign assets in the United States had risen to $15.9 billion. Thus, in 1946 the *net creditor* position of the United States was slightly below that of 1919, while over half of the foreign assets held in the United States constituted liquid dollar assets, i.e, deposits in U.S. banks and other private short-term liabilities and U.S. government bonds. Thus, as may be seen from

* Taken and adapted from Raymond F. Mikesell (ed.), *U.S. Private and Government Investment Abroad,* Eugene, Ore.: University of Oregon Books, 1962, pp. 72–73, 585–588.

TABLE 1

International Investment Position of the United States:
1919, 1930, 1939, 1946 and 1959
(millions of dollars)

	1919	1930	1939	1946	1959
U.S. investments abroad, total	7,000	17,200	11,400	13,693	64,779
Private investments	7,000	17,200	11,400	13,525	44,775
Long-term	6,500	15,200	10,800	12,263	41,152
Direct	3,900	8,000	7,000	7,227	29,735
Other[1]	2,600	7,200	3,800	5,036	11,417
Short-term	500	2,000	600	1,262	3,623
U.S. Government credits and claims[2]	. . .	. . .	(x)	5,168	20,004
Foreign assets and investments in the United States, total[3]	4,000	8,400	9,600	15,880	40,658
Long-term investments	3,200	5,700	6,300	6,985	16,652
Direct	900	1,400	2,000	2,503	5,220
Other	2,300	4,300	4,300	4,482	11,432
Short-term assets and U.S. Government obligations[3]	800	2,700	3,300	8,895	24,006

Source: *Survey of Current Business,* various issues.
x Less than $50,000,000.
[1] Consists primarily of securities payable in foreign currencies, but includes some dollar obligations, including participation in loans made by the International Bank for Reconstruction and Development.
[2] Excludes World War I loans; the amounts outstanding at the end of 1919 were $10.0 billion, at the end of 1930 $11.5 billion, at the end of 1939 $11.4 billion. Data for 1930 and 1939 include funded interest.
[3] Includes U.S. currency not distributed by areas, as follows: 1946, $633 million; 1947, $704 million; 1948, $746 million; 1949, $812 million; 1950, $772 million; 1951, $817 million; 1952, $848 million; 1953, $839 million; 1954, $838 million; 1955, $841 million; 1956, $849 million.

. . . [Table 1], since 1919 the United States has become increasingly a debtor on short-term account and a creditor on long-term account. During the postwar period, U.S. investments abroad have risen at a somewhat faster rate than foreign investments in the United States, so that by 1959 U.S. investments abroad totalled $64.8 billion as against foreign investments in the United States of $40.7 billion. However, over $24 billion of the foreign investments in the United States took the form of liquid dollar assets, while the vast bulk of U.S. investments abroad were in the form of long-term loans and direct investments. These changes in the U.S. international investment position are in part a reflection of the U.S. balance of payments which has been in deficit in most years since 1949. (It was also in deficit during the 1943–45 period when a large portion of our exports were financed by lend-lease, while most of our imports were paid for in dollars.) The balance of payments deficit since 1949 has resulted in part in an outflow of gold from the United States and in larger measure in increased liquid dollar holdings of foreigners. Although the U.S. deficit can be accounted for by a number of factors, including long-term investments, U.S. government grants, and large military expenditures abroad, the deterioration in our international reserve position has been more than compensated for by the rise in income-earning investments abroad, both on government and private account.

These developments in the U.S. international balance sheet are reflected in the rising level of income on private and government investments abroad relative to the income payments on foreign investments in the United States. Thus, in 1959 income payments transferred to the United States from U.S. private and government investments abroad totalled $3,048 million as against out-payments arising from foreign investments of the United States of $830 million. In addition, of course, reinvested earnings of U.S. subsidiaries abroad totalled over a billion dollars in 1959. . . .

U.S. Foreign Investment and the National Interest

. . . It is clear that no simple answer can be given to the question of whether or not foreign private or public investment is in the national interest or whether such investment should be promoted or actively discouraged by governmental action. Assuming that the promotion of economic growth and social progress in the less-developed areas is important to U.S. foreign policy, the flow of U.S. capital, skills, and enterprise to these areas must be regarded as desirable. There remain, however, important questions of how much and what kinds of capital are necessary or are most effective in achieving U.S. objectives in the less-developed areas and the relative costs in relation to the yields of making available various types of private and public capital. For example, will the subsidization, through tax measures or otherwise, of direct private investment yield greater returns in terms of promoting development abroad than an equivalent amount of public loans for the same purpose? Such decisions are not always easy to make because of the difficulties of estimating costs and yields; moreover, as we have seen, capital is not homogenous and private and public capital are not substitutes for one another for most fields of investment in developing countries.

Perhaps more difficult, however, are questions pertaining to the relationship of private capital outflow, both direct and portfolio, to foreign countries where no special foreign policy interest is to be served. . . . Professor Paul B. Simpson has shown that foreign investment as an alternative to employing capital in domestic investment is likely to reduce total output in the capital exporting countries except where foreign investment goes into the development of foreign natural resources. This adverse effect on domestic output is more likely to be true where the foreign investment is directed to industries similar to those of the capital exporting nation. The fact that the tax laws of the United States and of most other capital exporting countries permit investors to offset foreign taxes against domestic income liabilities provides from the national point of view, a kind of subsidy to capital exports (even though the investor may pay the same rate of tax at home and abroad). The additional income generated abroad is taxed frequently up to 50 per cent or better by the host government, while income generated from the same investment in the capital exporting country would yield revenue to the domestic government.

Any implications for public policy which might be derived from such an analysis must be tempered by several considerations. First, for direct investment particularly, the flow of capital, skills, and enterprise between countries cannot, in a modern world economy, be separated from trade. To take an extreme case, the prohibition of the flow of U.S. direct private investment to the industrialized countries of the world would impede international trade in commodities, techniques, and ideas and we would therefore sacrifice a portion of the gains from international trade. Much of our portfolio capital movements are related to direct investment and trade in one way or the other, and an attempt to embargo the outflow of portfolio capital from the United States would have serious repercussions on the operation of the world economy. Moreover, the introduction of capital controls by the United States would affect capital inflow as well as outflow and it would be difficult to determine in advance whether the results would be a net gain or net loss of capital resources.

Another basic consideration in any decision to interfere with capital movements is how we regard our role in the world economy. Given reasonably free trade and capital movements, it is quite difficult to predict the feedback effects on the capital exporting country of promoting growth in another part of the world. There is an interrelationship between economic developments in various sectors of the world economy, and prosperity and welfare have proved to be highly contagious within the international economy. Moreover, do not our long-run political, social, and humanitarian interests lie in the general increase in world output and social betterment? Even though it may be shown that a change in the allocation of resources based on free movements of capital, skills, and ideas may retard somewhat the *relative* growth of more prosperous nations in favor of a more rapid growth of poorer nations, is this in the long run an undesirable result? We certainly have accepted this principle within the United States as demonstrated by our acceptance of the progressive income tax and of the distribution of social expenditures in accordance with relative needs. If we really believe in the concepts of world unity and the achievement of common social goals, must we not be willing to sacrifice some of our potential rate of growth for high rates of growth in other countries? And as a final point, our recent balance of payments difficulties and the rapid postwar change in our relative economic position raise questions about the future of the United States as the major source of the world's capital. In the longer run, may not the re-establishment of an international economy in which capital, skills, and ideas are free to move in response to basic economic forces be as much to our own advantage as to that of other countries?

Most countries that have imposed controls on capital exports have done so on balance-of-payments grounds. Although such controls are not being seriously considered by the United States as a means of dealing with its current balance-of-payments deficit, we have seen how the existence of this deficit has influenced certain U.S. policies affecting capital exports. There are undoubtedly emergency situations, particularly in countries with slender reserves, that warrant the imposition of capital or other types of balance-of-payments controls. However, as a means of dealing with the present U.S. balance-of-payments problem, capital controls, or for that matter any interference with international transactions in goods, services, or capital, should be rejected. This is not to say that every capital export by a U.S. resident is desirable from the viewpoint of the national interest, any more than every internal transaction may be said to promote the general welfare. Selecting desirable transactions from the undesirable and policing international capital transactions would entail enormous policy and administrative problems. Moreover, the institution of capital controls by the United States would deal a severe blow to the re-emergence of the international economy and to the role of the United States as an international financial center. Finally, the way to deal with deficits (or surpluses) in a country's international balance of payments, which is a product of millions of interrelated transactions, is not to control specific transactions any more than controlling specific prices is the proper way of dealing with fluctuations in the price level in a free economy.

One final word regarding the relationship between capital exports and the balance of payments is perhaps in order. . . . [It has been] noted that the United States has for a number of years been accumulating dollar liabilities, largely in the form of foreign bank deposits and foreign holdings of U.S. government securities on the one hand, and increasing our long-term investments abroad on the other. In brief, we have been borrowing on relatively short-term while lending or investing on long-term. Yet in the usual analysis of our balance of payments, emphasis is placed on our continual deficit which is defined as a loss of gold plus the accumulation of liquid dollar assets by foreigners. While this analysis is appropriate for some purposes, it does tend to obscure the significance of the accumulation of valuable income-earning assets abroad, the receipts from which are continually strengthening our balance-of-payments position. Thus, between 1950 and 1960 U.S. balance-of-payments receipts on private and governmental foreign investments increased from less than $1.6 billion to over $3.2 billion. So long as we can avoid excessive gold drains and maintain confidence in the dollar, it is not, in my opinion, highly undesirable that the United States continue to expand its investments abroad while adding to the world's liquidity by modest increases in dollar liabilities. In this way the *real* burden of our capital exports and grant assistance to the less-developed areas is reduced, and indeed shared by those nations which, for one reason or another, prefer to increase their international liquidity. In time, our balance of payments will shift, and it is unrealistic to project current developments to 1975 or to the year 2000. The important thing is to devise means by which confidence in the dollar is not impaired and which will avoid the necessity of the United States having to impose artificial restrictions on international transactions or reduce her foreign military and economic assistance commitments. It is for this reason that I favor serious consideration of imaginative proposals for dealing with the problems of international liquidity, such as those suggested by Professor Robert Triffin and others.[1]

---

[1] See, for example, Robert Triffin, *Gold and the Dollar Crisis* (New Haven, 1960). For another interesting proposal see James E. Meade, "The Future of International Trade and Payments," *The Three Banks Review*, June 1961 (Edinburgh), pp. 15–38.

34..... The American Investor Abroad*

RAYMOND VERNON

Harvard University

"To the North American millionaires converted into government, Latin America appeared an easy prey, a 'big business.' The inhabitants of this part of the world came to be looked upon as international *braceros*. The multiple-faceted exploitation was carried out with intelligence, with shrewdness, with the precision of clockwork, with 'scientific' coldness, with harshness and with great arrogance. From the South the river of millions began to flow Northward and every year it increased.

"The United States became great while progress in Latin America was brought to a halt. And when anything or anyone tried to interfere with the bankers or the companies, use was made of the Marines. . . ." — From Juan José Arévalo, *The Shark and the Sardines*.[1]

To most Americans who know something of the operations of United States business overseas (especially those who are involved in such business firsthand) the vitality and persistence of caricatures of rapacious U.S. millionaires are frustrating and baffling. Once upon a time, as every American businessman knows, there *was* a United Fruit Company which was entangled deep in the politics of the banana republics. And once upon a time, as all our history books tell us, the Marines *did* land at Vera Cruz. But that was long ago, as the memories of U.S. business run.

Today, wherever U.S. business exists abroad, it generally tends to set the national standards for probity in taxation, decency in labor relations, dedication to growth and development, and discreetness in its involvement with domestic political issues.

Why, then, does the outmoded image so bitterly portrayed in *The Shark and the Sardines* persist in Latin America, Africa, and Asia? And

* Taken and adapted from "Saints and Sinners in Foreign Investment," *Harvard Business Review*, May–June 1963, pp. 146–161.
[1] New York, Lyle Stuart, 1961, p. 10.

why does the incubus invade even such countries as Canada, Australia, and France?

One obstacle in the search for an answer is the fact that many Americans think they have already found it. In their discussions about the future direction of the Alliance for Progress, for instance, many U.S. businessmen seem to take it for granted that those Latin Americans who are against *foreign* private investment are usually against *domestic* private investment as well — that they are, in short, cold to the whole concept of a private enterprise system.

This is not a wholly baseless view. In some countries, it is clear, a good deal of the opposition to foreign private enterprise does represent a special case of opposition to private enterprise in general. But much of the opposition is of quite another kind. Some of it reflects an aversion to foreigners — governmental *or* private. Some of it represents the response of economists and other technicians to the real or assumed economic consequences of foreign private investment on the local economy. And some of it is the response of local businessmen, not of socialists or government technicians, to the competition of their foreign-financed rivals in the local market.

The first need in defense is battlefield intelligence. To respond in some effective way to the hostility that so often confronts U.S. private investors abroad, we need to understand why this hostility exists. In this article, I want to explore some of the economic roots of anti-U.S. feeling and to suggest some steps which might serve to reduce the distrust on both sides.

History's Echo

One reason for hostility lies in history — or at least in history as it is now perceived by teachers and writers in underdeveloped countries. Among intellectuals, for example, it tends to be taken for granted that the European and U.S. investors in Latin America during the nineteenth century made a giant killing at the expense of the Latin nations. Some investors did, of course. But the more sober compilations of foreign investment (such as that produced by J. Fred Rippy in his book, *British Investments in Latin America, 1822–1949*)[2] suggest that the nineteenth century experience yielded fairly dismal returns for foreign investors as a whole in Latin America.

During that century, large issues of bonds were raised in the rich countries of Europe — partly to build rail lines and improve ports in the poorer countries; partly to finance the export of rail cars, steel, and machinery; and partly to support the local officials who made these transactions possible. Any flow of foreign capital such as this eventually entails a transfer problem. But the transfer problem of the nineteenth century was often solved in Latin America by bankruptcy and default.

[2] Minneapolis, University of Minnesota Press, 1959.

The nineteenth century history of Mexico, for instance, is studded with ten-cents-on-the-dollar settlements of defaulted debt.

The nineteenth century saw another type of foreign investment as well: investments by Europeans and Americans in the mining of raw materials and the cultivation of agricultural products for export. In sharp contrast to the unglamorous business of bond buying, these pursuits generated some great fortunes for foreigners. It was these operations that tended to create the early image of foreign investment in Latin America, Africa, and Asia.

The basic psychological stance of most of these investors was that of minimum involvement in the local economy. What the foreign mining ventures and plantation companies of Chile, Peru, Mexico, and Central America needed more than anything else from their host countries were physical security, a supply of labor, and transportation to the sea. If it was possible to satisfy these needs inside an enclave, this was the ideal solution; if involvement with the national economy was unavoidable, the objective was to hold the involvement to a minimum.

Of course, as the years went on, the existence of the mining and plantation companies had various subtle side effects on the economies in which they operated. For example, in some countries, such as Mexico and Chile, the companies attracted immigrants with skills and generated an indigenous group of middle managers. In practically all countries, operations of this sort helped provide the basis for establishing or expanding a rail system and a power grid.

After World War I, as many foreign mining and plantation companies began to realize that the security of their enclaves depended partly on the contentment of the inhabitants, cases began to appear in which the housing, schools, hospitals, and utilities of the foreign companies were the best to be had in the host countries. Companies like ARAMCO in Saudi Arabia, Firestone in Liberia, W. R. Grace in Peru, and history-haunted United Fruit in Central America, became exemplary guests in the areas in which they operated. But they were guests whose principal attachment was to the raw materials of the host country, not to the country itself. In countries on which history had imposed a sense of inferiority, the enclaves out of which such foreigners operated were a constant symbol of the second-class character of their country's sovereignty.

Of course, much of this is ancient history. Its relevance today is still great, but it is chiefly the relevance that memories have, not the relevance of current events. The figures in Exhibit 1 reflect the fact that since 1929, while *total* U.S. foreign direct investment has quadrupled, U.S. foreign direct investment in the old plantation type of agriculture has actually declined. Mining investment has lagged; and much of the increase that has occurred has been in Canada, a comparatively low-pressure area. Petroleum investment, to be sure, has broken out all over — in Canada, in the Middle East, in Africa, in parts of Latin America. But the terms of modern-day concessions are dramatically different from those of 10 or 15 years ago. The international oil companies can hardly be pictured as the powerful swashbucklers they once could claim to be.

Most important of all, however, is the fact that recently a new type of direct investment has been growing in spectacular fashion, a type which automatically has the effect of involving the foreign investor intimately in the fortunes and vicissitudes of the host country. Here I refer to investment in foreign plants for the manufacture and sale of products to local foreign markets.

Anatomy of Hostility

At first glance, foreign investment in local plants would seem to be responsive to all the aspirations of the Latin American or his counterpart in other less developed areas. Such investment brings foreign capital and technology into that sector of the economy which is thought to be most in need of development — the industrial sector. Its identification with the host country seems complete; its growth depends on the growth of the internal markets of the country. Yet hostility toward U.S. investment in areas like Latin America seems not to abate but to mount over the years; indeed, today it exists not only among the intellectuals but also among a large proportion of government economists and other technicians. So the reaction is presumably based on more than the current memories of early investment history. What, then, are the other elements behind it?

Raw Deal in Raw Materials

Some of the roots of the hostility could probably be better analyzed and understood by a social psychiatrist than by an economist. The best we can do here is to appraise those reactions that take the form of economic arguments.

Despite the recent changes in the nature of foreign investment, U.S. foreign direct investments in agriculture and mining in the underdeveloped areas still approximate those in manufacturing. (This comparison does not include the very special category of petroleum investment, which of course is large enough to upset the balance.) As long as these proportion exist, the technicians in the developing countries will continue to link their distaste for foreign direct investment with their more general dislike for specialization in raw materials exports.

The reasons for that dislike now fill many shelves of the libraries on economic development. It is evident, for instance, that the technicians assume —

> . . . that raw material prices, over the long pull, tend to decline in relation to the prices of manufactured goods, thereby penalizing any country that lives by exporting raw materials and importing manufactured products;

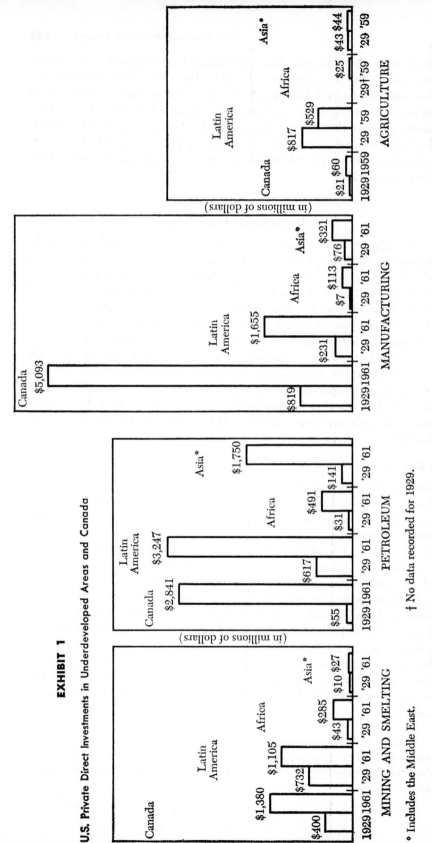

EXHIBIT 1

U.S. Private Direct Investments in Underdeveloped Areas and Canada

(in millions of dollars)

AGRICULTURE

Canada: 1929 $21, 1959 $60
Latin America: 1929 $817, '59 $529
Africa: '29 †, '59 $25
Asia*: '29 †, '59 $43 $44

MANUFACTURING

Canada: 1929 $819, 1961 $5,093
Latin America: '29 $231, '61 $1,655
Africa: '29 $7, '61 $113
Asia*: '29 $76, '61 $321

PETROLEUM

Canada: 1929 $55, 1961 $2,841
Latin America: '29 $617, '61 $3,247
Africa: '29 $31, '61 $491
Asia*: '29 $141, '61 $1,750

MINING AND SMELTING

Canada: 1929 $400, 1961 $1,380
Latin America: '29 $732, '61 $1,105
Africa: '29 $43, '61 $285
Asia*: '29 $10, '61 $27

* Includes the Middle East.   † No data recorded for 1929.

Source: Samuel Pizer and Frederick Cutler, *U. S. Business Investments in Foreign Countries* (Washington, D. C., U. S. Department of Commerce, 1960), p. 93; and *Survey of Current Business* (Washington, D. C., U. S. Department of Commerce, August 1962), pp. 22–23.

Capital Transactions by U.S.-Owned Enterprises in Underdeveloped Countries,

Key

Capital Inflow

Remittances of Subsidiaries and
Profits of Branches

Middle East

(in millions of dollars)

$510
$72
$701
— $72
$760
$108

1957   1960   1961

Latin America

(in millions of dollars)

$1,086
$912
$641
$95
$711
$141

1957   1960   1961

Africa*

(in millions of dollars)

$24 $29
$99
— $50
$124
— $62

1957   1960   1961

Asia†

(in millions of dollars)

$56
— $1
$99
$39
$118
— $13

1957   1960   1961

* Not Including Union of South Africa.
† Not Including Australia, Japan, or New Zealand.
Source: *Survey of Current Business* (Washington, D. C., U. S. Department of Commerce, August 1959, pp. 30–31; August 1961, pp. 22–23; and August 1962, pp. 22–23.)

. . . that raw material extractive industries tend to impart scarcely any of the benefits of development to the areas outside the enclaves in which they operate;

. . . even worse, that the enclaves tend to draw in and preempt those few people of education or initiative that exist in the early stages of a developing society, so depriving the rest of the developing country of their scarce services.

The evidence on all these points, as usual, is equivocal. For some periods, for some products, in some countries, the case of the technicians seems fairly sound. On any careful reading of the facts, for instance, Mexico seems to have benefited surprisingly little from the operations of the foreign oil companies in the period from 1910 to 1938; but one would hardly draw the same conclusion for oil company operations in present-day Libya, Argentina, Venezuela, or Kuwait. One may doubt just how much the Belgian Congo benefited from six or seven decades of foreign diamond mining; but it would be hard to denigrate the investments of the foreign rubber planters of Malaya or the bauxite miners of Dutch Guiana.

Whatever the technicians in underdeveloped areas may think of foreign investment in the raw material extractive industries, the U.S. businessman unfamiliar with this particular battleground might suppose that they would welcome — or that they *ought* to welcome — foreign investment in manufacturing enterprises. And once more the U.S. businessman's view of the universe would be at variance with the realities of the underdeveloped areas. Let us explore some of the areas in which the thinking of U.S. businessmen is most likely to seem naive.

Balance of Payments

The first and most prominent conflict in views is over the balance-of-payment effects generated by private direct capital from abroad. It comes as a rude shock to many U.S. businessmen to discover that many of the economists in the developing countries think of such foreign investments as a drain — not as a support — to their country's balance-of-payment position. The technicians point out (correctly, as Exhibit 2 indicates) that for most areas and for most types of direct investment the added capital sent in by foreigners each year is less than the drain of dividends and royalties remitted in that year in connection with the existing investments already in the country. Latin American economists speak of foreign investment, therefore, as "decapitalizing" their countries; and many insist that such investment is harmful on balance-of-payment grounds.

The argument may be good propaganda, but it is bad economics. The balance-of payment effects of even the simplest kind of investment are exceedingly complex. They include not only the original capital inflow and the later dividend outflow, but also the direct and indirect impact of the investment on the imports and exports of the country. For instance:

Import-replacing industries presumably save some foreign exchange (although, of course, the amount of foreign exchange they save will be reduced in measure as imported materials are used).

Export-producing industries presumably add to the country's foreign exchange earnings (although, once again, there may be offsets in the form of increased imports).

All industries, whether engaged in import-replacement or in exports, have further effects on the pattern of imports and exports through their impact on income and prices.

Once effects such as these are totaled up, the net balance-of-payment impact can go either way. In the case of Mexico, for instance, I am persuaded that foreign direct investment probably makes a major contribution to the country's balance-of-payment position. But there is no reason a priori why this need be so for all countries; in other economies and in other periods, the opposite might be the case.

Nevertheless, the response of the U.S. businessman to the onslaught of his critics is sometimes as incomplete and untenable as the attack. The standard form of reply is that the "true" contribution of foreign investors to the host country consists of much more than the capital they ship into the economy. There is also a heavy plow-back of the earnings generated in the country, as well as a willingness to assume local debt in order to increase industrial investment.

The spokesman who makes such a reply takes it for granted, of course, that the local credits and the local capital goods that foreign-owned enterprises have mobilized would otherwise lie fallow or be less effectively used. He sees these companies as the catalyst, drawing together the idle resources of an underdeveloped country into an operating and producing whole; and sometimes he is right in describing the role. In countries where local industrial credit sources are scarce and where local capital goods are in short supply, however, the reply is calculated to have the same effect as waving a red flag in the *plaza de toros* on a Sunday afternoon. For in such countries the response is taken to mean that scarce local resources, which might otherwise be used productively by nationals of the country ready, willing, and able to use them, are being bid away by foreigners through their superior bargaining power.

Export Anxieties

Technicians in the underdeveloped areas profess also to have worries about the export policies of foreign-owned manufacturing facilities. Today the underdeveloped countries are high-cost producers for most manufactured products. But this situation need not exist forever; indeed it is already changing for some products, as the scale of operations in some of the underdeveloped countries grows. The gnawing question, however, is whether foreign-owned subsidiaries in the local market — plants producing radios, refrigerators, food preparations, and the like

— will be willing at some stage to export any of these products back into the large established markets of the industrial countries.

Certainly, the backflow has not amounted to anything so far. Though exact figures are not available, exports of U.S.-owned manufacturing subsidiaries in underdeveloped areas seem to have been less than $250 million in 1957. In observing the paltriness of the flow of exports, the technicians allude darkly to patent and trademark licensing agreements, to dealer distribution policies, and to other factors that might make such exports embarrassing, even downright impossible, from the viewpoint of the parent company. And, of course, the technicians could be right.

Thus, there are genuine questions accompanying these foreign investments, questions that justify the concern both of the investing nation and of the host country. Nevertheless, the economists of the developing countries sometimes push their allegations about the behavior of the foreign-owned subsidiary a bit too far, especially when they characterize the activities of such subsidiaries in the field of import replacement.

It is perfectly clear that many foreign-owned plants in less developed areas were originally designed to make as little contribution as possible to the import-replacement process of the host countries. Many of these investments were originally created under duress. For example:

> Having previously established a profitable export market in some underdeveloped area, companies in the United States suddenly discovered their markets threatened by import restrictions. In response, some of these companies reluctantly created the most limited manufacturing facility consistent with maintaining the local market. The automotive manufacturers set up local assembly plants to put together knocked-down automobile units. The pharmaceutical houses set up modest little local assembly lines to mix and package the imported bulk ingredients. In such cases, the local plants were really no more than departments of the parent plant in the United States or Europe, putting the last touches on an already fabricated product.

Over the past few years this situation has changed very rapidly, at least in Latin America. Under pressure from the host countries, foreign-owned plants have been forced to turn to local sources for a growing proportion of their supplies. There have been problems of quality and of delivery times, inevitable when dealing with inexperienced suppliers; but apparently they have not been insurmountable. Despite these changes, many economists in the underdeveloped areas still glibly refer to foreign-owned facilities as assembly or packaging plants. The illusion persists even though the data point strikingly to the opposite conclusion.

In Latin America, for instance, the local manufacturing plants of U.S. companies now buy most of their materials from the local economy and import very little directly from their U.S. parents — or indeed from any other foreign source. The speed with which integration has been taking place is illustrated by the fact that in 1955 a very large sample of U.S.-owned manufacturing plants in Latin America reported buying only about 56% of their materials, supplies, and equipment from the local economy. But by 1957 local purchases of materials and services, as reported by U.S.-owned firms operating in the area, had increased to 82%.

Yanqui vs. Domestic Monopoly

In time, perhaps, technicians, economists, and intellectuals of the less developed countries might be reassured on many of these points. But another type of concern would probably persist — a concern based on the problem of internal monopolies. The internal markets of most under-developed countries, generally speaking, are small and limited. The policy of import protection commonly insulates these markets from foreign competition. So the chances are very high that just a few producing companies will dominate the local market.

To be sure, the Latin American intellectual is not easily aroused over the existence of business monopolies. Though the Mexican constitution prohibits monopolies outright and other Latin American constitutions have similar strictures, the realities of Latin business life are such that genuine price competition in the domestic marketing of manufactured products is a rarity. The question in the minds of most Latin American intellectuals, therefore, is not whether to tolerate monopoly. Rather the question is: Who is to control the monopolies that will inevitably exist? Better a national, according to the near-universal assumption, than a foreigner. Better on several grounds — first, because the monopoly profits will stay inside the national family; second, because the application of official price controls, if they seem necessary, will generate a purely domestic row, not an international squabble.

Like most of the long list of complaints with which the foreign investor is confronted, this complaint rests partly on solid ground, partly on sand. Observation suggests that the U.S. manufacturer who is in a monopoly position in a small protected market can generally be expected to set his monopoly price somewhat lower than that of a local businessman similarly placed. Perhaps this difference occurs because the U.S. producer's markup target is influenced by the norms set in the more competitive markets to which he is accustomed; or perhaps it is because of his assumption, unfamiliar among local entrepreneurs, that aggregate demand is really quite sensitive to price differences and will be much larger at lower prices. Still, one can understand and even sympathize a little with the reluctance of Latin American intellectuals to allow local monopolies to fall into foreign hands.

How Ugly the American?

There may be one last reason for the poorly suppressed hostility of many of the leaders in the less developed countries toward foreign investment; perhaps it is the most important reason of all. This is the conditioning generated by contacts between the local representatives of the foreign companies and representatives of the host country.

The principal officials and intellectual leaders of many large underdeveloped countries are an elite, drawn by one imperfect means or another out of tens of millions of people. And to an increasing extent, they are a sophisticated elite, educated abroad in the better schools or propelled to the top by sheer native ability.

The chief representatives of the foreign firms whom these leaders confront from day to day are still foreigners for the most part; the practice of using foreign top managers, according to various surveys of the subject, is still dominant in the underdeveloped areas. These foreign managers, if my own observation of U.S. companies overseas is at all representative, are usually well trained and competent — typical of the middle ranks that make up large-firm management. However, except in a few rare and impressive cases, they are not — and they cannot be expected to be — the cultural, intellectual, and social match of the national elite they confront. Yet in any encounter with the local leaders, the foreign manager appears in a sense as the representative of a more powerful and more advanced culture, indispensable to the well-being of the host country. Human frailties being what they are, *amour propre* being man's most precious treasure, one can easily picture the cumulative impact of these encounters on the local elite. Perhaps this is the issue, after all, which plays the largest role in the adverse reactions of the leaders of the underdeveloped countries.

Et Tu, Entrepreneur?

It comes as no news to the U.S. businessman that in most underdeveloped countries he must live with the latent or active hostility of the publicists, the teachers, and the government officials. What the U.S. businessman may not be prepared for is the fact that he had better not count on a sympathetic point of view from the entrepreneurs of Bombay, Medellín, São Paulo, or Manila. Indeed, he would do well to be prepared for a certain undercurrent of restraint, perhaps even of hostility, from local entrepreneurs.

Such hostility is not inevitable. As long as a country is not yet heavily committed to a process of industrialization, its leading local businessmen are usually in lines of activity which are complementary to, not competitive with, the foreign investor in the country. They service foreign-owned mines, oil fields, and plantations with local materials and transport, they run the local banks and utilities, and so on. In these pursuits, they may have their differences from time to time with foreign enterprises in their country; but the differences cannot obscure the fact that, in such settings, the long-run interests of foreign and local businessmen are not in basic conflict.

A deliberate policy of industrialization, however, tends to change all this. Import restrictions are applied in order to preserve the local market for those who have plants inside the country. Tax exemptions, special industrial credits, and various other inducements are offered. Once these restraints and inducements are applied, new entrepreneurs generally step forward. Some, as we have observed, are foreign; however, many of these are home-grown and home-financed.

Practically every large underdeveloped country that has followed the import restriction route has managed to stimulate the growth of an indigenous entrepreneurial middle class, with deep commitments to the growing industrial sector of the new country. Bear in mind the circumstances under which these groups have blossomed. Like some of the earlier U.S. industrialists, they have owed their first spurt of growth partly to the new policy of national protection; their paths have been eased by tax credits; their markets have been widened by government buying. In many cases, they have been nurtured by cultures which had drawn little or nothing from the philosophies of Adam Smith and Thomas Jefferson. This is hardly fertile soil for any U.S. business group interested in fostering such principles as the open competitive society and minimum interference from government.

Unfair Competition

The lack of empathy between many entrepreneurs in the less developed countries and their foreign counterparts is heightened by various factors. One of these is the feeling of the local entrepreneurs that foreign-owned enterprises are unfair competitors. There are many reasons for this feeling:

In the first place, foreign producers often enter a local economy on the basis of a strong trade name or trademark position, built up on prior imports.

On the top of this, the foreign-owned producer usually has much easier access to international credit (or so it seems to the hard-pressed local competitors). While the local producer pays the 12% to 20% interest rate that is characteristic for short-term money in much of Latin America and Asia, the foreign owner of a local company can usually extend credits to its subsidiary at very much lower interest rates.

Insult is added to injury when credit is rationed in local markets; and the injury is multiplied several times over in the eyes of local competitors when the credit rationing is done as an anti-inflationary measure, on the urging of the wealthy creditor countries or the International Monetary Fund. For then, while the local company is cut off from its source of funds by outside pressures, the foreign-owned subsidiary may still use its international sources to draw down any needed credits. In the end, the foreign subsidiary is seen as a competitive juggernaut, unfairly crushing the frail local opposition in its path.

Obviously, local producers are not at a hopeless disadvantage in the face of these difficulties; if the difficulties were overwhelming, they could hardly survive. They have managed to overcome some of their competitive handicaps by various means: by generating ample internal sources of capital out of profits; by entering into foreign licensing arrangements; bv hiring foreign technicians, and later by training domestic ones; by establishing their own local brand names through advertising; and, finally, in some cases, by enlisting their government's help in curbing the foreign-owned subsidiary.

Mexico, in particular, has carried to a new high the processs of subtle and pervasive government intervention in behalf of locally owned firms. It would be unwise to assume that more countries will not move as far as Mexico, once they feel able. And as they do, the U.S. entrepreneur investing in such countries will find it even more difficult to make common ideological cause with his local competitor.

Basis for Action

Despite all these difficulties, there *is* a basis for a mutually profitable movement of foreign direct investment out of the more advanced countries into the less developed nations. It is a basis created not by a common ideology, but by compatible interests. For the foreign investor, the interest is what it should be — an interest in profit.

In some lines of manufacturing in the less developed countries, profit opportunities considerably exceed those available in the United States. The official figures, it is true, are not very exciting in this regard. U.S. direct investment in Latin American manufacturing facilities, for instance usually shows an annual net income of only 12% or 13% of book net worth, as reported to the U.S. Department of Commerce. My own judgment is, however, that the real return is probably a good deal higher when all the effects of interfirm pricing, royalty payments, administrative charges, and the like are included. In any case, the individual opportunities for investment can be much more profitable than the global average.

On the side of the host country, the motivation for inviting foreign direct investment is just as obvious. In many industries at various stages of development the desirability of admitting foreign direct investors is clear almost beyond question, in view of the technology, skill, and capital they have to offer.

What the foreign investor needs in such cases is security of tenure (defined in the broadest possible way, to include not only freedom from nationalization but also freedom from discrimination and harassment). On the other hand, what the governments of many underdeveloped countries need is some indication that one day, if they wish, they will be able to bring the enterprise back into the fold of national ownership.

A great deal of thought has been given to the use of the joint enterprise as a partial answer to problems such as these. The use of the joint enterprise, however, has its decided limits. A number of surveys indicate that most U.S. investors still prefer wholly owned foreign subsidiaries and still operate largely on that basis. At the same time, local businessmen generally prefer to run their own show without interference from the foreigners. When marriages take place, therefore, they are often of the shotgun variety; desperation and compulsion of one sort or another are frequently involved.

Nonetheless, where the joint enterprise route can be arranged, it may be the best of all available solutions. Where it cannot, however, there still should be some basis for investment by foreign entrepreneurs in underdeveloped areas, mutually profitable to both the investor and the country.

Mutual Guarantees

Perhaps a line of solution could be developed if foreign investors were prepared, at the outset, to acknowledge that their sojourn in the country might well be of limited duration and to make their calculations on that basis. This recognition could take the form of an offer on some fixed future dates to sell portions of the equity in their enterprises to nationals of the country concerned, in accordance with a schedule agreed on in advance and at prices to be determined by some agreeable formula or procedure. There are many difficulties with any such approach, of course, not the least of them being that of finding private buyers and of establishing a market price for the shares. In some less developed countries, the beginnings of a local market in equities suggest the possibility of an eventual solution to both these problems.

A provision of this sort might meet some of the psychological and political needs of the host countries. This might be so even if the calls were never actually exercised in any significant quantity. But one could hardly expect the arrangement to encourage foreign private direct investment in underdeveloped countries unless it were coupled with some added rights and guarantees for the foreign investor. The obvious guarantee would be "national treatment," that is, freedom from harassment or from discrimination based on the foreign ownership of the enterprise.

Such treatment is now guaranteed to U.S. investors in many countries under various bilateral treaties, such as the United States treaties of friendship and establishment. In reality, however, the treatment still remains a distant ideal.

Perhaps ideal and reality could be brought a step closer if the national treatment guarantee were backed up by an indemnity fund and an impartial international court to which investors could have direct access. This is an approach which might well justify the sponsorship of the Alliance for Progress, as one tangible step in support of the future position of private investors in the Western hemisphere.

35.....Regulation of the Investment Process*

JACK N. BEHRMAN

University of North Carolina

After years of urging U.S. business to contribute through investment to the recovery of Europe and to the economic development of emerging nations, the Government is now requesting curtailment of overseas investment. . . . At the same time it does not want the curtailment to affect adversely the economies of Canada, Japan, or the United Kingdom; even more, it wants an increase in the outflow of funds to the developing countries.

The present attitudes and programs are set against a background of increased antipathy toward overseas operations reflected in the Revenue Act of 1962 and an announced policy of removing some developing countries from the "less developed" categories. The background includes also assertions by top officials that the recent constraints were "necessitated" by the "alarming" outflow of private capital into foreign securities in 1963 and the "abnormal" level of overall private capital outflow in late 1964, topping off fifteen years of deficits. . . . This background suggests that a potential investor cannot know what the Government's posture on overseas operations in advanced countries *will be,* whether a given country may be classified as one not to be "adversely" affected by restraints or dropped out of the LDC class, or whether some new "abnormality" might lead to still further Government constraints.

I submit that this posture is one which weakens rather than strengthens the U.S. economy. Further, it is a result of not identifying the problem correctly, thus leading to "solutions" which waste resources. . . .

There are three main reasons why we should reverse our stand: first, our tactics of constraint are inequitable and damaging to our long-run

---

* Taken and adapted from "Foreign Private Investment and the Government's Efforts to Reduce the Payments Deficit," *The Journal of Finance,* May 1966, pp. 283–296.

interests internationally and vis-à-vis business and economic policy; second, our strategy is inappropriate since it is harmful even when effective; and third, we have now the ability to negotiate from strength rather than weakness.

Constraint Tactics

The tactics of constraint on investment are inequitable in that they have focused on one facet of the international accounts to bear the brunt of restriction. The rationale has been said to be the "excessive and abnormal" increase in capital outflows.[1] But there have also been substantial increases in the travel and tourist account and even larger ones in the import account. Since the really "abnormal" expenditures in the U.S. balance of payments are those of the Government for military purposes, it is certainly irrational to pin on the capital account the "responsibility" for the deficit even on short-term. (For example, what next after capital outflows are again "normal" and the deficit remains?) Yet for policy reasons considered more important than the payment's deficit, the Government has explicitly excluded reductions in imports and has failed to move strongly on the travel account, refused to provide a really effective stimulus to exports (such as a tax incentive), and considers various domestic measures worse than the deficit in international payments.

Conversely, private investment has made positive contributions to the strength of the free world. . . .

Sacrifice of the contributions made by such capital outflows should be made only after a careful offsetting against gains elsewhere and a careful comparison with other potential restrictions. To let these decisions be made by business, the Government set voluntary controls, with business having the choice as to tactic, but then the Government limited the area of discretion. . . .

The creation of inequities should be supported by strong reasons, demonstrating offsetting benefits. I have looked in vain in official statements for such reasons — that is, those indicating why the capital account should be forced to bear the brunt of constraint. (Neither tied aid nor "economy" in military expenditures are serious *burdens* on the U.S. economy.) The nearest thing to an explanation I found is the repeated statement that the constraints "must" of necessity be maintained until "basic improvements" in the balance of payments have been achieved — but I fail also to find a clarification of what these improvements are or from whence they are to come. . . .

I can only conclude that the constraints on capital movements were imposed because they were "easier" or "less offensive to other countries" in

[1] Former Under Secretary of Treasury Roosa spoke on October 1, 1965 of "The strength which the United States balance-of-payments position would have been showing for some time if the added capital outflows of recent years had not occurred." (*International Financial News Survey*, No. 39, Oct. 1, 1965, p. 367.)

some sense in seeking a satisfactory level of disequilibrium. It seems also that the greater willingness to sacrifice overseas business resulted in part from a basic lack of understanding of the benefits of the somewhat inevitable expansion of U.S. business overseas — or maybe from an outright lack of sympathy with overseas operations stemming from criticism arising in 1962, criticism from labor quarters, complaints from foreign governments, and a long-standing skepticism of the contributions of private foreign investment.[2] I doubt that there was a careful assessment of the damages to our long-run international position from capital constraints. . . .

The first damage to our position stems from the misunderstanding of the potential pay-out and contribution of foreign direct investment. While there is undoubtedly a short-run contribution to the payments position from a *reduction* in capital outflow, it is quite short-run; for within less than 3 years the outflow is repaid through the international accounts largely because of the strong impetus investment gives to U.S. exports.[3] Foreign investment makes a net positive contribution within 3 years to the "basic improvement" that is said to be the bellwether of removal of the constraints, and all returns after that (above any small outflow of funds for expansion) are net additions. Constraint itself, therefore, delays the improvement needed to remove the constraint. Other contributions lie in the additional jobs at home resultant from accompanying exports and ability to meet future competition better — to say nothing of strengthening investment levels abroad and meeting demands for liquidity. In addition, the income effects strengthen economies abroad and raise U.S. exports.

The second damage relates to the loss of opportunity when an investment is cancelled. While some benefit may result from forcing companies to look more carefully at projected investment, if a "good thing" is bypassed the opportunity may well disappear — not simply be postponed; or, if postponed, the competitive position of the company may be damaged beyond recovery, thereby reducing the pay-out over the longer-run. And, if the investment was economically sound, the net contribution to the strength of the free world is lost or delayed.

Collaterally, if the investor decides to go ahead, despite the drain on payments, he may make others dissatisfied with the voluntary controls, reducing their effectiveness, or may lead a bandwagon revolt against them, bringing on direct controls. The threat of direct controls (which avowedly no one wants) is, of course, a strong sanction in the program. . . .

[2] Even among economists there is disagreement as to the value of capital outflows to the exporting economy. There is not time or space available to engage in this discussion; suffice it to note that the *asserted* objective of the U.S. Government is to permit a free, non-discriminatory choice of investment opportunities over the world for U.S. enterprises and that a decision to constrain capital outflow as "uneconomic" should not be justified solely on balance of payments grounds, but on domestic reasons as well. . . .

[3] See my article in . . . the *Columbia Journal of World Business,* on "Foreign Investment Muddle," Fall 1965, pp. 51–60.

But avoiding direct control even by means of *voluntary* controls . . . leads to a third damage — to the concept that market processes should decide economic matters and to the free movement of goods, capital, and ideas. Rather than decisions based on market factors, hortatory statements from government officials, with varying emphases by different agencies, require action under indefinite sanctions. These pronouncements change business decisions. . . .

The problem in using such voluntary measures are exemplified in the repeated assertions that companies were not asked to cease making foreign investments but merely to "cancel or postpone marginal investments in developed countries," with the company left to decide what is marginal. Now the policy is to serve *national* ends, and what is marginal to one company may not be marginal in comparison to a projected investment by another company when viewed either from its impact on U.S. balance of payments or its effect on other national objectives of the U.S. (to say nothing of the recipient country, which may end up with the less desirable project). . . .

Still another damage of the program is that it expands and solidifies the process of partial and *ad hoc* devaluations of the dollar, of which the interest equalization tax was the beginning. The fact that the company must borrow abroad at higher interest rates or seek to make foreign sales rather than domestic ones means clearly that the foreign currency is to be sought even at a premium — i.e., a devaluation of the dollar. The recent restraint is also a partial exchange control — prohibiting use of dollars beyond certain amounts for capital outflows. Rather than strengthening the dollar, its role as a key currency is weakened by such measures. . . .

The use of voluntary controls, with the apparent feeling that it is necessary to emit veiled threats against noncompliance, constitutes still another damage — this time to the improved rapport between business and government. . . . Whatever the *intent* of Government officials, the interpretation has been drawn by some companies that they had best stay out of foreign investment completely. . . .

The last damage relates to the posture of U.S. companies toward investment in the LDCs. Although Government officials have taken pains to explain that they want expansion of outflows to the LDCs rather than restriction, the attitude of many companies is that a dollar of investment is best put in advanced countries; if they must restrain, they will also cut LDC investments. For some integrated companies, investment in processing and marketing facilities in Europe is necessary to justify further investment in materials production in LDCs. There is evidence that some projects are simply not being picked up in the LDCs because of the general posture of the Government. . . .

Finally, it should be questioned whether the constraints are producing the results which were claimed for them during the early part of the year [1965]. The overall data on capital outflows suggests that direct investment during 1965 slackened after the voluntary program but still continued their rise.[4] . . .

. . . Let me turn [now] to what I consider were the errors of strategy which later seemed to necessitate the above tactics.

Errors of Strategy

The major error of strategy was that the Kennedy Administration (and the Johnson Administration after it) took a defensive position on the balance of payments by asserting that it was a crisis of the first order and required extraordinary measures. . . . By 1961, the U.S. had sustained 10 years of deficits (only 1957 showing a surplus as a result of the oil crisis). . . . The Administration became a "town crier" of the danger of the deficit and the weakness of the U.S. economy internationally and accepted the responsibility for achieving a satisfactory equilibrium.

There were two alternative postures which might have been taken: one was to admit that the dollar was no longer to perform the functions of a key currency (for example, by drawing extensively on the IMF) and to move so as to turn over reserve functions to the IMF; this would have reduced pressure on it and taken steps toward internationalizing liquid reserves (such was the intent of the Triffin plan . . .). The other was to maintain the key currency standing of the dollar, demonstrating that the dollar was stronger than gold, and accepting the pressures which are imposed on such a position. This meant at all events not to undercut its status by crying weakness. . . .

A key currency should have several characteristics: ready acceptability, stability of value, and availability in adequate amounts. Acceptability is a function of commercial and financial custom, which certainly favored the dollar; it also is a function of stability and availability. Stability of value relates, *inter alia,* to solvency of the country and fundamental soundness of the dollar but importantly also to what foreign holders think is the stability of the currency. No one charged the existence of a fundamental disequilibrium (in the IMF sense) and a few advocated a devaluation; and, in fact, the basic asset-liability position of the U.S. has long been quite sound. The only question was that concerning availability; criticism here was the reverse of the 1950's — directed at there being "too much" not "too little" dollar liquidity.

Two aspects of the liquidity issue should be stressed: First, the problem was essentially a bilateral one — between the U.S. and each surplus country. There was no feeling that there was too much *world-wide* liquidity; on the contrary, the questioning was whether there was enough for

---

[4] There seems to be a general practice of the prescription . . . that "business must cooperate with the President's balance-of-payments program," but "business must find ways to continue to expand its investments abroad." One way, of course, is to rely more heavily on foreign financing. . . .

the world as a whole, which was partly a function of the strength of the dollar and its acceptability as a reserve currency. If worldwide illiquidity was the problem, as a key currency, dollars should have been placed *more* in supply. But this obvious solution was not acceptable — because of the few surplus countries which already held enough dollars, in their view, thus threatening the dollar's position. On these counts then, the problem was essentially bilateral with a few countries. Secondly, it is obvious that the surplus countries *should* have held even more dollars — just as the U.S. permitted Europe to run deficits, in the 1940's and 1950's, for which it picked up the tab under various programs. At the extreme, the surplus European countries could have extended "aid" to the U.S. Government or at least accelerated payments on debt to the U.S. Government or even the World Bank, reducing their liquid holdings.

Instead, we accepted the very culpability which we did not press wholly on the debtors during the Marshall Plan. In fact, it would have been appropriate to quote to the Europeans their admonitions to us as the creditor in that period. . . .

The crisis stance assumed by the U.S. and its willingness to accept responsibility for the deficit gave our critics overseas the initiative and the stronger bargaining position. All they had to do was to complain about dollar plethora, withhold credits, and threaten conversion of dollars to gold to put pressure on the U.S. to take uneconomic measures. . . . Instead, we should have repeatedly proclaimed the strength of the dollar.[5]

In the name of "balance-of-payments crisis," several programs were undertaken which were economically harmful. . . .

Negotiating from Strength

Let's define first what the problem is and is not. It is not the weakness of the U.S. economy or an inability to produce. This was the problem of the European economies when they were charged with "living beyond their means." But the U.S. is not faced with an inability to export accompanied by high import demand; rather, it has sustained a substantial export surplus, which it raised in 1964 despite a decline in Europe's rate of growth, though the surplus has dropped off this year [1965] despite an increase in exports. The fundamental trade strength of the U.S. would give rise to cries of dollar shortage once again if other aspects of its international payments were reversed.

[5] In his analysis of "Balance of Payments Deficits and the International Market for Liquidity" (Princeton International Finance Section Essays in International Finance, No. 46, May 1965, p. 25), Charles Kindelberger concludes that ". . . the dollar is strong today, not weak in an objective sense, and it is important that subjective appraisals discard the terrifying definitions we have allowed to creep into the discussion, and recognize this fact. Objective circumstances of strength can be turned into chaos by subjective judgments. The need is far more for central-banker and money-market education than it is for voluntary restrictions, higher rates of interest, or new interferences through tax or exchange policy."

Nor is the problem one of surplus credit funds seeking outlets overseas. Rather, the domestic opportunities remain high, but the rates in the U.S. remain lower than in Europe, attracting borrowers. There is, therefore, a demand in Europe for funds that can be met most readily from the United States. If a pushing of U.S. credit were the problem, and the results were unwanted in Europe, all that would be needed would be restrictions in Europe on capital outflow — such as Germany has employed. Rather, there is a difference in liquidity preferences and therefore in capital demands between Europe and the U.S., which the outflow of long-term U.S. funds fulfills. The reverse inflow of short-term European funds, however, is counted as an addition to our deficit and liabilities.

The problem stems essentially from the assumption by the United States of the defense of the free world — most importantly in Europe and in Asia. The expense of supporting NATO, the Viet-Nam war, and troops and naval vessels elsewhere causes a continued outflow of funds, ending up in European coffers. These are really the "abnormal" and "excessive" outflows in the balance — at least they should be so considered both in economic and political terms, unless we should assume that the U.S. will be normally and habitually committed in foreign wars and defense efforts during the rest of the 20th Century.

Either view of the defense expenditures requires agreement from our European allies as to the nature and handling of the problem. If our commitments are to be continued into the long run, no short-term expediencies such as have been taken will meet the problems which will arise. And we need a much more fundamental understanding of how the burden is to be shared — if the French are dissatisfied with NATO, no "basic improvement" in the U.S. payments deficit will avoid eventual confrontation on the issue. But, if these expenditures are to be assumed "abnormal" and terminable in the foreseeable future, it would still be desirable to obtain an agreement from our allies as to how the temporary increase of dollar funds is to be accommodated.

Seen in this light, the problem reduces to the political question of how far and in what way the French, Germans, and Dutch are willing to support U.S. expenditures abroad.[6] It is not an economic question, for there

---

[6] The difficulties and strains which underlie the present situation were seen some 22 years ago by Lord Keynes in writing on problems of the gold-exchange standard: "There might be a number of bilateral arrangements, having the effect of providing international overdrafts, as . . . for example, an agreement by the Federal Reserve Board to accumulate a large sterling balance at the Bank of England, accompanied by a great number of similar bilateral arrangements between these and all the other banks in the world. The objection to arrangements of this kind, in addition to their complexity, is that they are likely to be influenced by political considerations; that they put individual countries in a position of particular obligation toward others; and that the distribution of the assistance between different countries may not correspond to need and to the real requirements which are extremely difficult to foresee." (Quoted by Albert E. Cooper, "The Adequacy of Monetary Reserves," in Management Bulletin #68, *The Balance of Payments Problem*, American Management Assoc., New York, 1965, p. 9.)

are ways of treating economic-based deficits that are generally agreeable to all advanced countries. (Note those taken by the U.K., but which would be inappropriate for the U.S.) . . .

The problem should be publicly stated as a political one — not economic — in origin and in solution. It is really not a question of financial rectitude, nor of the need for a gold standard, or even of additional international liquidity.[7] It is an unwillingness of surplus countries to support (not through long-term loans, but through holding dollars on short-term and with interest) the purposes for which the U.S. is making the abnormal foreign expenditures. There should be no doubt about the ability of the U.S. to convert the dollar holdings into gold or goods.

But it seems necessary now to prove this ability. By doing so, the U.S. would regain a lost position of strength in negotiations on international problems — a strength which it has dissipated in pleading for restraint on conversion of dollars into gold. . . .

---

[7] Alvin Hansen summed up the dilemma facing world bankers at the Tokyo meeting (1964) of the IMF: "In terms of ideology the central bankers were still calling for an end to U.S. payments deficits. But as a practical matter nobody really wanted this to happen. A balance contrived by means of U.S. restrictive policies would seriously injure world trade. A balance achieved by somehow making the United States sufficiently competitive in terms of traded goods and services to offset the gigantic imbalance created by U.S. military expenditures and untied foreign aid would constitute a hard blow to Western Europe. A balance achieved by completely closing New York to European borrowers or the institution of vigorous controls designed to stop American direct investments abroad would not be in the interest of the world community. Moreover, as well recognized at Tokyo, no practical alternative to U.S. payments deficits as a source of needed additional reserves is visible over the horizon or indeed likely to become visible in the foreseeable future." (*The Dollar and the International Monetary System*, N.Y., McGraw-Hill, 1965, pp. 209–210.)

C ..... Development Aid

Standing alongside trade and investment, aid — foreign aid — comprises the third big area of concern under American foreign economic policy. What is the nature of this aid? Why is it provided? Is the effort justified? These are matters to which we now turn.

What should be classed as "aid" is always debatable. If we take popular interpretations as our guide, the United States effort encompasses a number of programs: activity under A.I.D. (an agency that bore other labels earlier); contributions to multilateral agencies (the United Nations and certain affiliates); shipments of P.L. 480 agricultural commodities; loans through Exim Bank; activity under the Peace Corps; and so on. Among these, the largest — in fact, larger in dollar terms than all the others combined — is the A.I.D. program. It, in turn, dispenses both economic assistance and military assistance. And only some of this economic assistance is directly for purposes of economic development.

Actually, the multiplicity of aid outlets reflects the fact that the United States, at various times and under various circumstances, has had various ends in mind: export promotion, relief abroad, political suasion abroad, balance-of-payments support abroad, and the promotion of economic development. Reliance on multiple outlets offers the advantage of having the "right" channel for whatever purpose.

In the case of the A.I.D. program, the most important component of the foreign-aid complex, the basic rationale, as we noted in an earlier context, is political-military in nature. Dating in its present form from the onset of the Korean Conflict, the program bears the imprint of having been set up to thwart Communist encroachment. In this effort, military assistance has a role, and so does economic assistance. But only some of the economic assistance is necessarily for economic development. And even it is provided on the premise that a developed country is more resistant to appeals of the left than an underdeveloped one. In short, economic development becomes only a sub-goal of a political-military goal.

A common criticism leveled at the A.I.D. program is that it fails to achieve sufficient economic development. The thought is that the United States has a *direct* and clear-cut stake in seeing more development in the world. Indeed, the argument is sometimes heard that the underdeveloped countries comprise the world's "number one" problem — that what happens among them will determine the nature of the world order in decades to come.

Certainly the United States, the richest country and leader of the "Free World," has a great deal to gain from a healthy environment in the present-day underdeveloped countries. To derive the maximum from its already enviable position, this country needs peace in the world — and peace is related to a situation of general economic well-being. Moreover, what can be said, on this score, of the country as a whole can be said, also, of the components of its economy — businesses and individuals.

With this country's aid linked to developmental progress abroad, great importance attaches to what this country does. There are, of course, many "aid issues." And special complexities abound. For example, how can we balance the need for greater aid and the balance-of-payments troubles of the foremost supplier-country? How can we integrate private-sector potential with official aid to maximize overall impact?

In the selections that follow, the first, by Professor Meier, offers an assessment of development status at the present juncture; his verdict is one of doubt about the adequacy of effort and performance. This is followed by a selection evaluating foreign aid as an instrument of developmental promotion. And, in a third selection (by Lincoln Gordon), the matter of foreign private investment as an ingredient in aid and development is examined.

36..... The Status of Economic
Development*

GERALD M. MEIER

Stanford University

Now that we have passed the midpoint of "The United Nations Development Decade," this should be an appropriate time to appraise the
progress toward the goals of development and review the problems encountered. Half a decade counts for little, of course, in the long sweep of
development; but when viewed against the perspective of the two postwar decades, the last five years do raise some fundamental questions
about the progress, formulation, and implementation of development
planning.

I. *The Progress of Economic Development*

The aim of the current decade is "To attain in each underdeveloped
country a substantial increase in the rate of growth, with each country
setting its own target, taking as the objective a minimum annual rate of
growth in aggregate national income of five per cent at the end of the
decade." What has been the record in attaining this objective?

It would appear that for the countries of Asia, Africa, and Latin America taken together, economic development has proceeded in the last
twenty years at an estimated rate close to four per cent per annum. This
has meant a doubling in the total income of the underdeveloped areas of
the world — certainly a major accomplishment compared with the long
preceding period of relative stagnation. Nonetheless, a number of factors
make the progress much less impressive.

When we relate the aggregate growth of four per cent to population
growth, which has in recent years been about two to two-and-one-half

* Reprinted from the Winter 1966 issue of the Stanford Graduate School of Business
Bulletin, pp. 21–26. Copyright 1966 by the Leland Stanford Junior University Board
of Trustees.

per cent in the underdeveloped world, we come down to a rate of income growth per capita of only one-and-one-half to two per cent on the average. Generally a rate of increase in per capita income of two-and-one-half to three per cent would be considered more nearly adequate, so that per capita income doubles within the life span of a generation. A few developing countries have approached this rate, but there still remains the distressingly hard core of underdevelopment in many countries which have fallen below this rate; and in some countries, it is even doubtful whether the prewar level of per capita national output has yet been regained. More distressingly, there is some indication that the aggregate rate of growth has been slowing down for many poor countries in the first half of this decade as compared with the 1950's. This poses the important question whether the development process is now running up against increasingly severe or even intractable problems.

The record of achievement is also tempered by the heavy reliance on foreign assistance. The inflow of foreign capital has accounted for approximately one-fourth of the investment resources of the underdeveloped world. If it had not been for external assistance, the ratio of net saving to domestic product would actually have fallen in many countries. And in some countries, no increase in per capita income would have been realized if there had not been a capital inflow.

We must also recognize that the course of development has been highly uneven and has perpetuated or accentuated a number of inequalities. Even within those countries that have good overall records, there has been relatively little progress in removing the inequality of income between the agricultural (rural) and the industrial (urban) population, and the inequality of income and wealth between the very poor ninety-five per cent and the very rich five per cent of the population.

Manufacturing industry still accounts for less than one-fifth of the output of the underdeveloped nations, and its employment-creating capacity remains insufficient to prevent growing unemployment and underemployment. At the same time, agricultural output has in general increased only a little faster than population. In a number of countries, agricultural output per head is even lower than it was ten or fifteen years ago. This weak performance of the agricultural sector has been pervasive and is one of the most difficult of developmental problems.

As distressing as the lag in the agricultural sector, unrelated to it, has been the lag in the export sector. Over the last two decades, world trade has expanded at a higher rate than ever before, but most of this expansion has been in trade between the advanced countries and in exports from the advanced countries to the less developed countries, while the export earnings of the underdeveloped countries have risen only slowly.

The ratio of exports from underdeveloped countries to total world exports — less than twenty-five per cent for the years 1960–63 — is now lower than at any time since the war. In contrast with the slow growth of exports, development programs have induced a sharp rise in import requirements for most of the less developed countries.

The unevenness of development also appears in the more rapid expansion of the public sector relative to the private sector. Since development plans have concentrated on public investment, and foreign aid has also been directed mainly to the public sector, private investment has lagged behind public investment. It may be argued that development planning has tended to give too much attention to the public sector and too little to the private sector: it can be contended that there has been an excessive diversion of scarce resources from directly productive investment in the private sector to public works and social overhead.

Finally, the new centers of growth within the developing countries have tended to be geographically concentrated, resulting in growing regional inequalities within many countries. The problem of "enclaves" remains as acute as it was for the historical development based on foreign capital.

From the foregoing, we may conclude that notable as has been their accomplishment in doubling total income during the past two decades, poor countries still generally confront the overriding problems of how an increase in aggregate income is at the same time to carry along with it a higher rate of increase in income per head, less dependence on foreign assistance, and a removal of inequalities.

II. *The Implementation of Development Plans*

Turning now to the methods by which the goals of development have been sought, what can we single out as outstanding features?

The widespread conviction has clearly been that government must be the primary agent in producing economic modernization, and that development efforts must be coordinated within a national development plan.

If we were to review current development plans and appraise their formulation, we would have to conclude that most of the developing countries have arrived at the point of approximating the elements of a well-formulated plan in a creditable fashion. And yet, we are left with two disconcerting questions that detract from this accomplishment.

First, what really is the merit of achieving consistency and coordination in a development plan? This is, of course, a necessary characteristic of a well-formulated program, but it is equally essential to recognize that the mere attainment of consistency and the mere act of coordination do not guarantee in any way the quality of merit of the particular decisions that are being taken: there is no magic about a program that transforms the quality of decisions beyond the virtue that coordination lends.

Regardless of improvements in the formulation of planning models, the policy-maker still cannot escape from the rendering of value judgments, and political decisions are still required. Logically prior to the attainment of consistency and coordination is the fundamental question of *what* is to be planned: what decisions are to be centralized and what is left for decision-making by firms and households? Nor does the attainment of consistency and coordination within a particular development program remove the ambiguity that is inherent in the establishment of objectives and the selection of policy instruments. A conflict among multiple objectives is frequently encountered in development programming, and it is then necessary to decide which objective should receive precedence in planning. Thus, instead of a single development program, there are in reality any number of alternative programs according to the values given to diverse objectives and to various policy instruments. The attributes of consistency and coordination cannot disguise the fact that the ultimate decision is political.

Our second question refers not to the quality of the decisions being coordinated, but rather to the capacity to implement these decisions. Has the ability to implement a development plan grown *pari passu* with the ability to formulate a plan? The record of development planning reveals that problems of implementation now need to receive more attention than problems of formulation. The major difference between policy-making in an advanced country and a newly developing country is not so much at the level of understanding economic policy, but at the level of executing policies effectively. Why is it that a development plan may meet all the tests of a good plan on paper, only to fail in practice?

Miscalculations and unforeseen changes alone do not account for the wide divergence between what has been planned and actually realized. We must look to deeper reasons.

One such reason is that there is no analytical model of development that can be readily translated into a development program. It is difficult to think of another area of economic policy in which the distance between theory and policy tends to be as great as it is for developmental problems. All the theories of development are simply ways of looking systematically at the general development process. They relate to the "economics *about* development" — the way an economist looks at the development process in the abstract and from the outside, but they do not immediately constitute the "economics *for* development" — the pragmatic way that the local practitioner must use economics in the daily administration of a development program within a particular environment. Only too often, however, a development theory has been misread as if it revealed a recipe for successful development, and access to the teachings of modern economics has been thought to have some new magical quality. In spite of the shortcomings of such a naïve approach — to which the past two decades give ample testimony — the mystique still persists. And instead of utilizing more operational concepts and empirical constructs, development economists are still prone to resort to "empty stages of growth" or empty phrases such as "a big push" or "balanced growth."

If the literary economist has allowed slogans to substitute for analysis, the mathematical economist has moved on to a much loftier view of development — but without the caution and restraint which should come from a realistic awareness of the especially acute limitation of mathematical programming in an underdeveloped economy. Whether it be due to the operation of an international "demonstration effect" among governments or the dominant influence of intellectuals on planning commissions, there has been in many developing countries an overly keen receptivity for the most refined model, the newest technique, the latest element of expertise. When the ultra-sophisticated technique has been allowed to shape the development plan, its implementation has become unduly difficult. In many cases, the solutions to immediate and crucial needs have been ignored through the over-reaching for more complex techniques of analysis and highly formalized models. In this connection, we may question whether much of the effort devoted to the use of econometric models and linear programming in framing a development program is not premature.

Attraction to the highest style analysis has also weakened the planning effort by divorcing the economic analysis from the contributions of other social sciences. The more advanced and more rigorous is the economic analysis, the less is it capable of incorporating non-economic elements. But the less developed is the country, the more does the efficacy of planning depend on non-economic factors. . . .

It has sometimes been thought that linear programming models of development provide a set of "decision rules" that can serve as specific guides to action for the policy-maker. This may be true for some types of business and military operations, but it cannot do so for a process that is as complex and qualitative in character as the modernization of an economy and the transformation of a society. Such a broadly humane undertaking cannot be viewed as a mechanical process, and its diagnosis cannot be reduced to a matter of pure technics. A good deal of the disparity between the theory and practice of planning can only too often be traced to an excessive reliance on the pure mathematics of an "optimum" or a "maximum" that has distilled the life out of the development process and left the development plan without operational significance. In order to institutionalize and sustain developmental forces, we cannot adopt the approach that "a maximum is a maximum regardless of the maximizing agent." Given the present circumstances in most of the developing countries, the cause of development might be better advanced by a sound application of some basic elementary principles of economics instead of by borrowing and imitating at too high a level.

Other reasons why development plans may be big on paper but small in result have received more attention and need be only summarized here. The implementation of development planning has been clearly handicapped by the lack of requisite data and the imperfect character of such statistics as are available. . . .

Another shortcoming involves the failure to arrive at a proper ordering or sequence in policy-making. In its formulation, a development plan must provide a comprehensive view of the economy and recognize its interrelationships. But when it comes to implementation, a simultaneous solution of the plan is not possible. In the operational realm, planning cannot be comprehensive but is necessarily only partial and phased over time. It is then essential to arrive at some effective chronological order of decision-making. . . .

Finally, implementation of a plan has been difficult because of the familiar deficiencies in political and administrative requirements. . . .

In many cases, political interests have also run counter to the economic rationale of the development plan: the political party in power has too often been concerned with only the immediate or very short run of time, has been willing to settle for "showcase" projects, has succumbed to sectional interests, or has tried to prevent a loss in social status or political power for certain groups in the society at the expense of effective implementation of the plan.

Deficiencies in administrative and managerial procedures have been especially severe impediments to planning in practice. To the extent that the organization of public administration in many poor countries has been limited to the "law and order" kind of administration, it has not had the competence for the administration of economic controls, which is a sensitive art that cannot be practiced in a routine fashion, or subjected to indecision and delay. Nor can economic enterprises be operated as if they were administrative departments. In many countries, a neglect of administrative and management considerations has allowed the development plan to envisage a public investment sector larger than is capable of effective administration and to rely on the imposition of controls that are beyond the implementing capacity of existing public administrative services.

In sum: the over-reaching for the highest level of theory in preparing a development plan, the under-supplying of the plan with needed data, the under-emphasizing of the pattern of sequential decision-making, and the over-taxing of administrative competence and managerial capacity have all combined to thwart the practical implementation of the plan.

III. *In Lieu of Prognosis*

Whether the Development Decade becomes a decade of disappointment remains in balance. The outcome will depend on effective solutions to the following major policy issues that now confront developing countries.

At this juncture in the Decade, a primary problem is whether or not to expand the role of the private sector. For reasons akin to those outlined above, a greater number of development economists now subscribe to the conclusion that the comprehensive heavy-type of central planning, based on an elaborate and complex development plan, is premature for most countries. Many believe that in conformity with their present needs and capabilities, the majority of poor countries should retrench to a lighter type of planning that would rely more on decentralized decisions operating through the market mechanism, and that governmental policy should shift in emphasis toward the devising of policies that might make private action more effective. There is now wider receptivity to the view that if an on-going momentum is to be built into the development process, it is necessary to have multiple centers of initiative based upon a greater diffusion of individual opportunities and individual activities.

In many poor countries, in which there are under-utilized natural resources but only small internal markets, it can be persuasively argued that the basic problem is one of creating a favorable social and economic environment which will lead to expansion of private activity, more effective use of the under-utilized resources, and capitalization on the existing opportunities for international trade (as is being done in the Philippines, Thailand, Malaya, and some Latin American countries).

If the private sector is to be enlarged, how is this now to be accomplished? Instead of allowing any economic resource to be left unemployed, governmental policies must try to mobilize through positive economic incentives and inducements the latent skills and capital in the private sector. Fundamentally, the stimulation of private activity depends on the establishment of markets and encouragement of market institutions. Economic and social overhead capital can help to establish the physical conditions for a market to exist and can support the interdependence of markets. The government also has a crucial role in building institutions such as a banking system, a money and capital market, agricultural cooperatives, labor organizations, rural credit institutions, training institutes, etc. It must also be recognized that many of the policy measures that can affect individual action by altering the economic environment are not of the usual monetary or fiscal type of policy, but rather those involving the legal and institutional framework, such as land tenure legislation, commercial law, property rights, etc.

Market Itself Can Be Used

Once market imperfections are removed and the structure of markets is improved, the market mechanism can itself be used as an instrument of development. Instead of relying on comprehensive and detailed economic controls, governmental policies can work through the market and provide price and income stimuli for an expansion in private output, an increase in exports, and a widening of domestic markets.

A more immediate way to stimulate private activity is through tax concessions and subsidies. Subsidy and tax schemes may be especially significant in inducing firms to value inputs according to their social opportunity costs, or to exploit external economies, or to introduce new techniques of production.

More can also be done by way of providing public foreign capital to the private sector through development corporations and banks. Foreign investment laws may also be devised to encourage a greater inflow of direct foreign investment, while channeling the investment in accordance with development objectives. Although the traditional opportunities in public utilities, mining, and plantations are foreclosed, there is a new potential for private foreign investment in import-replacing activities and the expanding industrial sector. In this connection, joint international ventures may facilitate a desirable partnership between domestic and foreign enterprises or even between the government and foreign enterprise. Various contractual arrangements for the transfer of technical and managerial skills (management contracts, technical services agreements, engineering and construction agreements) may additionally be useful in securing the equivalent of the "technical assistance" component of direct foreign investment.

Finally, and presently of considerable importance, it would be possible to induce more effective private activity by removing the distortions in internal price relations which result from physical planning and the use of numerous specific controls. A more realistic price structure could lead to both greater total investment and the avoidance of detailed investment planning. To this end, there may be merit in the adoption of flexible exchange rates to avoid currency overvaluation, the removal of price controls on foodstuffs, and the liberalization of foreign trade controls with the substitution of domestic subsidy and tax schemes.

A second set of major policy problems pertains to the inadequate growth rate of the agricultural sector. There is evidence that the development process is now severely hampered in many countries by deficient production of foodstuffs and raw materials and by the failure of productivity to rise in agriculture. The growth base for other sectors must be expanded by increasing the marketable surplus and investable surplus from the agricultural sector. To do this, more attention must be given to devising a tax system that will exploit the saving potential in the rural sector without restraining agricultural output, to the adoption of new techniques of production, and to assistance for small farmers beyond the large schemes such as irrigation, flood control, and land clearance as in the past.

The foreign exchange bottleneck gives rise to a third set of policy problems. A recent United Nations study estimates that, on the assumption of a five per cent a year growth rate in underdeveloped areas and a continuation of current trends and policies, the international payments gap on current account of the underdeveloped areas would be some $20 billion by 1970 — an increase of $15 billion during the Development Decade. Even if the net flow of long-term capital and official donations from developed countries continues to rise at recent rates, the payments gap by 1970 would still be as much as $11 billion.

To the extent that the payments gap is not met, the import requirements of the development program cannot be fulfilled, and the development rate must be curtailed. Avoidance of this requires policies to expand exports, improve the terms of trade, and increase the inflow of capital and aid. Given the limited prospects for a sufficiently large increase in the flow of capital, there will have to be more concerted efforts to increase export earnings.

Directly related to the foreign exchange shortage is the fourth major policy problem — the serious external debt servicing problem. At a time when exports are growing only slowly and foreign economic assistance is leveling off, the ratio of debt service to exports is rising rapidly, and for a number of countries service payments amount to more than twenty per cent of export earnings. Between 1956 and 1962, amortization and interest payments of developing countries in respect of public and publicly-guaranteed debt increased about two-and-a-half times to an amount of almost $3 billion. Moreover, several of the major international debtors have concentrated their debt structure in short and medium-term maturities. As a result, over the next five years, a large proportion of their foreign exchange earnings will be absorbed by debt service.

For their effective solution, the foreign exchange and debt service problems should really be treated as part of the wider problem of reform of international economic institutions. In this connection, current discussions of international monetary reform, the future of the European Common Market and the outcome of the Kennedy round of trade negotiations will have decisive importance.

A final set of policy problems relates to the requirements of social development. These are now among the most critical of all development problems. For it has become increasingly apparent that an improvement in the quality of human life cannot be simply awaited as an objective of development, but is necessarily an instrument of development. Developmental policies must ultimately merge into a common strategy that combines an increase in the quantity of economic factors with an improvement in their quality. The basic thesis of the Development Decade can truly be expressed by saying that "The problem of the underdeveloped countries is not just growth, but development. Development is growth *plus* change; change, in turn, is social and cultural as well as economic, and qualitative as well as quantitative."

37..... Foreign Aid: Appraisal and Proposal*

WALTER KRAUSE

University of Iowa

Aside from some fringe assaults on underdevelopment, the United States did not officially get into the business of "aid for development" until 1951. In that year, with Communism ostensibly "contained" in the advanced world of Western Europe (in large part because of a successful Marshall Plan) and left to search for fertile ground in the ever-vulnerable underdeveloped world (where armed outbursts promptly ensued, as in the Far East, or appeared imminent), this country chose to shift emphasis in its foreign-aid program from Western Europe to the underdeveloped world, marking a parallel shift from *reconstruction* to *development*. While the Mutual Security Program (the successor of the European Recovery Program), under terms of which aid funds were subsequently channeled, rested on a fundamental political-military rationale (i.e., a roadblock in the path of Communist advancement), development was nevertheless an integral objective. Specifically, the economic portion of the program was regarded, at least in part, as a direct stimulant for development, the achievement of which in turn was desired — first and above all — because of its supposed effect in making the recipient areas more resistant to appeals or onslaughts of the left.

With 1951, therefore, this country had embarked on an aid program aimed at the promotion of development in underprivileged countries — even though development as an avowed objective was, for all intents and purposes, "dragged in through the back door" in the MSP rationale. In the immediately succeeding years, the aid program was extended to include many underdeveloped countries — . . . in Asia, Africa, and Latin America. To these countries went varying amounts of economic aid under

* Taken and adapted from "Current Issues in Foreign Aid," *Nebraska Journal of Economics and Business,* Spring 1963, pp. 15–16, and *International Economics,* Boston: Houghton Mifflin Company, 1965, pp. 565–569; new materials added.

various guises: technical assistance; commodity assistance; aid for basic development, for agriculture, and for industry; etc.

Looked at [some] ten years later . . . , what could be said as to the American success in the promotion of development? . . .

Appraisal

After a decade of operations, the program could be adjudged a success in terms of halting the spread of Communism. In terms of the promotion of development, however, the program appeared to measure up less well. While individual projects could be pointed to with justified pride, the aid program had effected no marked increase in per-capita income. As stated by this writer:[1]

> . . . with rare exception, the overall rate of growth in underdeveloped countries within the orbit of this country's aid program had not increased to a truly marked extent. True, a few countries unquestionably did experience good growth acceleration during this period (e.g., Israel and Mexico), but invariably in these cases one or another other factor has appeared more directly responsible than this country's formal foreign aid; as an offset, however, there were other countries that had barely held their own, or that may actually have experienced retrogression at the per-capita level. As a minimum, it seems safe to conclude that *if* the underdeveloped world had gotten better off, it was *not much* better off — and, most assuredly, it was *still quite badly off.*

Why did developmental progress lag? Two factors seem central to an explanation. First, the aid program was conducted under a dual mandate: halt Communism *and* promote development. When a choice between the two was necessary, the usual choice was: halt Communism. In the words of this writer:[2]

> . . . the pattern of priority and allocation that evolved in response to the essentially dual mandate inherent in the MSP legislation (i.e., halt Communism *and* promote development) in due course bared a sensitivity to, and preoccupation with, the immediate and symptomatic unmatched as respects the long-range and deep-seated. In the end, the record the MSP built up was relatively bright in halting Communist advances in the here and now, but far from glamorous in terms of progress in development. Yet, all the while the MSP rationale pictured development as a goal — indeed, as a goal upon whose attainment rested heavily the *continuing* success, even acceptance, of this country in its global dealings.

---

[1] W. Krause, "Current Issues in Foreign Aid," *Nebraska Journal of Economics and Business,* Spring 1963, p. 16.
[2] *Ibid.,* pp. 16–17.

Second, there was a tendency to allocate available funds widely and, hence, thinly among the aid-receiving countries. Again, in the words of this writer:[3]

> . . . [a] basic reason why developmental achievements were not greater derived . . . from the fact that resources available to the program, never particularly great, were placed *among* countries in accordance with an essentially indiscriminate across-the-board approach. With aid applied broadly, but thinly, the situation became one of "token aid for all, but no big developmental impact anywhere." Given added resources, this approach might have been appropriate; however, greater resources were not forthcoming, even though requested periodically.

Thus, the aid program — given economic development as a goal — was vulnerable on two scores: (1) the manner of allocation *among* countries and (2) the manner of application *within* countries. On the first score, something was done: there was a move to channel more of total economic assistance to fewer countries, even though these countries were not always the ones having well-above-average developmental potential. Significantly, though, the *idea* of "aid concentration" was established as an operating principle. On the second score, however, no parallel change marked the procedure of aid-allocation within countries. The time-worn problem of how to resolve the competing demands posed by pressures-of-the-moment and longer-range developmental needs continued (a fact borne out by experience with the important Alliance for Progress program).

Recommendation

Given this state of affairs midway in the "Decade of Development," the pertinent consideration is what should be done *next*. On the assumption that the United States needs to be closely and clearly identified with a solid record of developmental-accomplishment in at least some substantial portion of the underdeveloped world, high importance necessarily attaches to this country's *capacity to assure* the sought-after development. In this context, two matters merit special attention. First, there is the matter of the type of organizational structure within the American government that can serve best in spearheading this country's drive for development. Second, there is the matter of the type of orientation within this country's assistance effort that can serve best in yielding development.

Organization

The distinguishing organizational pattern in foreign assistance is one of fragmentation and overlap. Alongside the core foreign-aid program

[3] *Ibid.*, p. 17.

stand the Export-Import Bank, the multilateral agencies financially endorsed by this country, the PL 480 program (within the Department of Agriculture), and the Peace Corps. Given this scattering of the foreign-assistance function, some confusion as to the basic goals of particular operations is inevitable. For instance, confusion is rampant when each of several agencies enjoying public financial support claims to be a "lender of last resort" or cultivates a posture of "preferential access" to potential business. Clearly, these circumstances invite inter-agency rivalry *or* a general abdication of responsibility. And confusion is rampant when various organizational units cite diverse goals — say, one or a combination of the following: promotion of development, short-term deterrence of political disintegration, and promotion of American exports. Clearly, under these circumstances, it becomes difficult to know even how much in the way of resources is being devoted to development rather than to some other end.

A hopeful alternative to the foregoing pattern is a greater degree of organizational unification: the creation of a *"single* aid agency" with sole responsibility for the handling of all of this country's foreign economic-assistance activities. A first advantage of this approach might be the upgrading of "development" within this country's own frame of reference. Ideally, a Department of Development could be created within the American governmental structure to embrace all activities relating to foreign economic assistance. If a Department of Development were to stand alongside the Department of State and the Department of Defense, certain benefits might be expected: the higher status accorded the aid function could result in stronger public endorsement, helpful for success-ful operation; and the elevation of the idea of development to this higher status, along with the associated implication of deep and continuing concern about development, could help this country in scoring important propaganda gains abroad and in sparking greater enthusiasm there for self-help effort. In the event that an upgrading of this decisive bent were to prove impossible, a lesser goal might be the unification of aid activities within an autonomous "development agency" — similar to the position once occupied by the ECA (in contrast to the "semi-autonomous" status within the Department of State held by the "successor agencies," a status under which the orientation toward the underdeveloped countries and toward the global situation are lumped together).

Beyond upgrading development, the unification process might lessen overlap and rivalry, thereby increasing effectiveness. The placing of all foreign economic-assistance activities within one organization, all subject to one overall set of ground rules, would stand to eliminate or to lessen the likelihood of inaction or tardy action as agencies defer to one another or of competitive action as two or more agencies vie for the same oppor-tunities. Hopefully, situations might be ended in which each of several agencies purports to be a "lender of last resort" or in which bureaucratic rivalries ensue as two or more agencies assert first claim to action. And, hopefully, some of the conflicts arising in terms of "loans *versus* grants," "easy *versus* hard loan terms," and bilateral *versus* multilateral action," so common over the years, might be resolved more readily and more rationally.[4]

Orientation

The "right" type of organizational structure must exist if aid is to be channeled effectively, and the orientation of this aid must be "right" if it is to have the desired impact.

Assuming that this country prizes a record of development in a substantial number of aid-receiving countries, the prevailing foreign economic-assistance effort has stood vulnerable to criticism. The developmental achievements of this country's core foreign-aid program, after a decade of operations, were somewhat lacking in luster. As a consequence, a move was made to concentrate more of the available aid in a few countries in the hope of assuring distinct achievement in at least these countries. But the new approach to the *areal* placement of "developmental assistance," if in the right direction, represented only a halfway reform. There remained still the matter of the *orientation* of assistance placed *within a given area.*

If development is desired, there must be a willingness to allocate on behalf of the types of activities from which development can derive. In practice, of course, the demands posed by the pressures-of-the-moment tend to run counter to the investment requirements for longer-range development. Further, many pressures-of-the-moment simply cannot be ignored. However, aid-administrators still have an element of choice in the sense that they can take an attitude of reluctance toward the urgent but non-developmental type of outlay and thereby save more of available

---

[4] Elaborating upon the alleged merits of lessened overlap and rivalry as a consequence of a unification of economic-assistance activities, this writer earlier stated: "[In addition to economic aid under the core foreign-aid program,] . . . all Ex-Im Bank activities other than the 'export credit' function would be included, thereby bringing under integrated control the traditional proclivity of the Bank to claim 'first chance' on loan business. [Further,] . . . Public Law 480 activities (involving disposals of surplus agricultural products) would be transferred to the new organization from the Department of Agriculture. The logic here is that agricultural surpluses provided as foreign aid should be handled by a foreign-aid agency, not by the Department of Agriculture — which Department might, after all, be overzealous in view of burgeoning surpluses, even to the extent of complicating matters for the Department of State and the development-oriented aid operation (as has, in fact, been charged on occasion in the past). Also, this country's activities relative to multilateral agencies in the aid field would be brought under the new organization, thereby at least centralizing decision-making power as to when a multilateral channel is to be preferred over a bilateral channel, or vice versa. And, Peace Corps would be included, thereby lessening the chance, or need, for inter-agency rivalry on its account, either directly or indirectly. In short, the main aim is to 'get on with the job that needs doing' — and in the attack, a unified approach seems to have some obvious advantages over one that is scattered." See *Ibid.*, pp. 24–25.

assistance to apply to pro-development effort. It is this matter of resolving the multitudes of "marginal" decisions that is of extreme importance in tipping the balance of aid more in favor of development. . . .

Beyond the foregoing points of concern (namely, organization and orientation), two additional matters merit attention. The first relates to assistance for American private enterprise as a means of enticing it to go abroad; the second to the foreign-aid agency's stance toward regional-type developmental programs and projects abroad.

Private Enterprise

Admittedly, the foreign-aid agency has shown an interest over the years in encouraging private Americans to undertake direct investment in underdeveloped countries being supplied with economic assistance. Official statements of a pro nature have been legion, and, somewhat more tangibly, positive programs have been introduced as an intended spur to action: the Investment Guaranty Program, the "capture" and channelization of "Cooley Amendment" funds arising under the Public Law 480 program, etc. Significantly, not even gnawing balance-of-payments troubles during recent years sufficed to trigger a wavering in basic policy. The country (and the aid agency) have consistently favored the idea of a flow of private direct investment by Americans to the underdeveloped countries encompassed by aid-program operations.

A casual glance at prevailing data, however, reveals that the magnitude of American private direct investment moving to underdeveloped countries is not forging ahead in truly dramatic fashion; in fact, actual retrogression is the case recently as respects particular regions — regions where earlier levels of capital inflow, even so, had never been more than moderate. On the assumption that this country is correct in desiring an augmented flow of private direct investment from it to the particular countries, a pertinent question arises: Is something more possible under the foreign-aid program, something not currently being done, that could help to induce Americans to sustain a greater flow of private direct investment to the underdeveloped countries?

In response to just such a question, various proposals have been advanced in the past. A number of them have shared a central idea — that at least a sizable portion of aid dollars be earmarked for use as loans, on a matched-money basis, to Americans undertaking investment in underdeveloped countries in approved lines of enterprise.[5] But no proposal in this vein was ever activated; always quick criticism emerged on the score that aid should go to foreigners, not to Americans!

The fact remains, however, that private direct investment may respond to special inducement (were such supplied via aid dollars, *or* perhaps otherwise); and that, furthermore, a flow of private direct investment may

[5] See, for example, R. F. Mikesell, *Promoting United States Private Investment Abroad*, National Planning Association, October 1957, pp. 65–77, esp. pp. 66–67.

supplement aid dollars, or even substitute, partially, for them. To this end, the search for an acceptable form (or forms) of additional inducement legitimately continues. One possible approach, potentially usable to strengthen other available means, relates to an aid-agency effort to offer a "technical assistance" type of advisory service for Americans interested in the prospect of entry into direct investment abroad. More is needed than general information about investment opportunities in Country X and the investment climate there — all now available through the Department of Commerce and elsewhere. What seems needed, above all else (at this juncture), is a small staff of highly versatile "investment expediters" whose foremost function would be that of helping would-be investors to "piece together" the financial components of particular prospective investments. How many would-be foreign investors within this country know what funds, in what currency form, and on what terms *are* available from the multiple sources currently on hand? A given venture may, in fact, be eligible for some financial support from all of the following sources (or from some combination among them): Exim Bank (dollars) and Cooley Amendment funds (local currencies) from the United States Government; IBRD, IFC, and IDA funds (i.e., funds from international agencies); private and public financial institutions within the host country; funds from private financial institutions within the United States (and possibly other advanced countries); etc. Why, with the numerous and varied sources that are on hand, should investment planning proceed on the assumption of capital availability from only one, two, or possibly three of these sources? Perhaps with knowledge about just one more likely capital source, plus access to know-how as to how to integrate all into a workable investment composite, the balance behind a decision might be advantageously tipped from one of rejection or postponement to one of action. Indeed, the fact that no great direct outlay attaches to such an approach seems all the more reason to suggest that serious consideration be given it.[6]

Regional Assistance

The present era is one reflecting considerable sentiment for regional economic integration. The integration movement, far advanced in Europe, now extends also to underdeveloped regions. For these under-

---

[6] Possible contrary arguments include the historic reluctance on the part of government to advise on private investment matters (something distinct from a general exhortation on behalf of private investment). Admittedly such activity could be construed as being "in competition" with private investment consultants, as well as on grounds of throwing the government open to subsequent criticism in the event of "bad" advice.

It should be noted, too, that the approach outlined relates to "aid for the *American* private investor," as distinct from "aid for *foreign* private-sector investment." The second entails further considerations — including, for example, a charge, frequently heard, that this country's foreign aid, as seen from the standpoint of the recipient country, is essentially "public sector" aid, not "private sector" aid.

developed regions, measures for closer economic integration represent a foremost pro-developmental device.

Viewed in a formal sense, the foreign-aid agency has been "on the side of" multi-country cooperation in underdeveloped regions for some years. In 1956, it sponsored the Asian Economic Development Fund, offering a fixed sum as special support for regional-type development projects. And, more recently, it has shown at least limited interest in the regional-development activities of Latin America, chiefly as applicable to Central America.

Yet, looking beyond the formal aspects of the record, the foreign-aid agency does not now stand as a forceful leader of the regional integration movement. Its on-going associations with regional-type developmental activities appear only token, at best. Why, we may ask, is the involvement so slight? Especially we may ask such in the light of the seeming harmony between (a) the aid agency's interest in development and (b) the pro-developmental rationale underlying regional economic integration.

An important part of the answer appears to derive from the aid agency's particular organizational structure. Proceeding in the wake of a basic political-military rationale (i.e., halt Communism — with economic development viewed as one form of implementation), the agency is geared to deal primarily along *bilateral* lines, on a country-by-country basis. Such runs counter in fundamental respects to a rational system of aid allocation on regional terms. In fact, a regional approach, pursued vigorously, stands to blur to near indistinction any close single-country relationship (and, with it, all that such can entail).

The time may have come, however, for the United States to lessen its dedication to initial operating procedures, in the interests thereby of assuming a more positive role toward matters at or near the core of current developmental stimuli. Especially this seems true relative to Latin America where, given the local sentiment, a choice of non-involvement in regional economic integration is tantamount, in essence, to abdication(or near-abdication) from responsibility for development. Given such circumstances, the plea here is for a *greater willingess* by the foreign-aid agency to throw its support (and resources) behind regional-type developmental efforts.

38..... Private Enterprise and International Development*

LINCOLN GORDON

Harvard University

How can economic development best be accelerated in the poorer countries of the world? What is the most desirable role for private enterprise to play in this process? Behind questions like these lies an even more basic problem: What is the most effective relationship between government and business?

So far, the problem seems to inspire, not considered answers, but doctrinaire attitudes:

> At one extreme (leaving aside the communist-dominated countries) there is the South Asian concept of a "socialist pattern of society" in which governments are to be democratically controlled but the state is to own and operate all "basic" industries and services, and private business is tolerated in other sectors as a necessary evil for administrative convenience.

> At the other extreme is a doctrine opposed to any and all forms of government operation or intervention in developing economies, beyond providing a currency, enforcing law and order, supplying education, and perhaps building roads.

Neither doctrine bears much relation to the facts. The South Asian concept notwithstanding, private business in India is playing an increasingly important and respected role in economic development. As for the opposing doctrine, it calls for a degree of *laissez faire* which is practiced in no economically advanced country today, and was scarcely followed even in early nineteenth century England and never in the United States. Thus, it is not at all likely to be accepted in poorer countries now bent on forced-pace development.

---

* Taken and adapted from "Private Enterprise & International Development," *Harvard Business Review*, July–August 1960, pp. 134–138.

Yet the battle of words continues, often without regard to the availability of developmental resources, the social structure and conditions that determine the status, ambitions, and attitudes of businessmen and of government officials in various cultures, the financial institutions, or the many other factors which condition the developmental process in the real world.

Enterprise and Entrepreneurship

On one issue there is at the present time no dispute, i.e., the unique role of enterprise and entrepreneurship in generating economic progress. The reworking of Western economic history and the comparative study of developmental problems in various regions of the world have converged on this point.

No longer do we hold to the mechanistic analytical framework of classical economics, with its image of atomic land, labor, and capital particles held together by the magnetic forces of pure economic rationality. In its place today we take a more realistic view which gives a central place to leadership by entrepreneurs in finding new ways to combine the factors of production for greater output. The entrepreneurs are not simply innovators in the sense of inventors; they are men with the will to act, to assume risks, and to bring about change through the organization of human effort.

This stress on the role of entrepreneurship must obviously not be carried to the point of excluding everything else. Entrepreneurs do not suddenly appear on the scene, like men from Mars or like Spanish conquistadors in Peru. Resources, capital, labor, and technology must be available to them. Equally important, there must be conditions favorable to enterprise — a framework of law and order over a sufficiently wide market area, a network of transportation and communications, and political and social attitudes which find change welcome or at least acceptable.

Based on our own historical background, and on the English agricultural, commercial, and industrial revolutions behind that, we are often inclined to regard an industrial middle class, imbued with the Protestant ethic and operating within a liberal political framework which minimizes the role of government, as the most likely source of dynamic entrepreneurship. But it is not the only possible source. As Frederick Harbison and Charles A. Myers point out in their recent study of *Management in the Industrial World*,[1] and as W.W. Rostow emphasizes in his lectures on *The Stages of Economic Growth*,[2] this form of leadership may also come from feudal family dynasties (as in Japan), from revolutionary intellectuals (as in Soviet Russia), from colonial administrators (as in much of Africa), or from military nationalists (as in parts of the Middle East, Asia, and Latin America recently).

[1] New York, McGraw-Hill Book Company, Inc., 1959.
[2] New York, Cambridge University Press, 1960. . . .

Once industrial enterprise is established, the managerial requirements for its efficient operation have much in common, whether the ownership is formally private, governmental, or mixed. And the relations between private operating enterprises and government economic policies — even if the latter are expressed mainly through the budget, monetary management, and foreign commercial and financial regulations — are considerably more complex than any simple *laissez-faire* concept would suggest.

The Russian and Chinese examples are making it evident that private enterprise is not the only possible instrumentality for achieving economic growth. Most Americans are convinced — I believe rightly — that private enterprise is a superior instrumentality for combining economic growth with the value of individual freedom, social mobility, and human development. But this is not a self-evident proposition in the underdeveloped world, where almost any means of securing a "great leap forward" seems worth its price. Mere preaching on our part will not prove the point; neither will it help us to adopt so broad a definition of private enterprise that it embraces every form of organization that leads to economic growth. . . .

We should rather seek to examine more closely the distinguishing characteristics of private enterprise and the conditions under which it can demonstrate its claim to superiority — not merely in our own highly developed and relatively affluent society, but in places and under conditions posing far greater obstacles to rapid development than we had to overcome in the eighteenth and nineteenth centuries.

Distinguishing Features

From the viewpoint of usefulness as an instrument of development, there are two essential features that characterize private enterprise and differentiate it from governmental operations:

1. Effective decentralization of authority for economic decisions;

2. Measurement of success or failure by profitability in a market.

Primary reliance on private enterprise to manage a country's economic life may provide other advantages, such as a wide choice of career opportunities for promising young men, or a reinforcement of constitutional limitations on excessive centralization of political power. It may also entail disadvantages through the waste of capital it causes in false starts and through its proneness to cyclical fluctuations unless some governmental countervailing measures are applied. But so far as economic development is concerned, decentralization and the test of the market seem to me to be the essentials.

Governmental organization can also provide for considerable dispersion of authority, through federalism, strong local institutions, and the creation of autonomous public corporations for specialized functions. But private enterprise carries dispersion so much further that it represents a major difference of kind, not only of degree.

Some will argue that this is a disadvantage — that rapid development requires investment and expansion according to plan, and the more centralized the control system for implementation of the plan the better. But the weight of experience is against this view — including the experience of large corporations in industrialized countries, and even the Soviet experience itself. Whatever the merits of planning the broad lines of development, when it comes to effective administration there is no substitute for a widely held conviction among thousands of managers that they are running shows of their own and making their own decisions within broad areas of discretion.

The market test of profit or loss as the criterion of success or failure is closely related to decentralization of authority for decision making. Profit and loss provide both a system of incentives to action and a standard for measuring the contribution of the enterprise to the economy. We all know that the market test is far from perfect. Social costs or gains are not always fully reflected in private costs or returns, and various degrees of monopoly power often blunt the effectiveness of market pressures. Where capital markets are weak or nonexistent, the most promising opportunities may not find financing and the available funds may go to distinctly inferior uses, including luxury consumption, land speculation, or investment in the safer markets of Europe or the United States.

But even with all these defects, the market remains a remarkably efficient mechanism. Public policy designed to strengthen the market, to bring social and private costs into conformity, or otherwise to correct market biases, is often more successful than policy designed to replace the market. And it is a simple fact that the "divine right to fail," which is a hallmark of private enterprise, is very hard to apply to governmental operations, however uneconomic they may be.

Public-Private Enterprise

While private enterprise has its distinguishing features, we must also recognize that there is a considerable intermixture of public and private elements in the actual functioning of both private enterprise and government. . . .

We are so used to the legal fiction that large business organizations providing important goods and services can have the same rights and freedoms as individuals — including the freedom to use their property irresponsibly — that we sometimes forget that it is almost pure fiction. This has always been recognized with public utility services, which the law has for centuries described as "affected with a public interest," but it is true today with the whole spectrum of private enterprises of any significant size.

The public impact — and this does not mean merely the public relations impact — of important corporate decisions is one of the major considerations in business action. What Berle and Means first pointed out almost 30 years ago — that large corporations are social creatures with important obligations to the society which creates them — is a fact which, within a democratic political framework at least, cannot be disregarded by corporate managers.[3] To do so is at their peril. This is even more true of large foreign corporations operating in underdeveloped countries than it is at home. But in much of the world irresponsible private enterprise is all too common, and the achievement of a sense of responsibility is one of the badly needed elements of economic growth.

The other side of this coin is that governments in most places and at most times are by no means devoted to the unalloyed service of the public interest. . . .

Moreover, the use of political power to further private interests need not involve a transcendental theory of world history; it has always been a rich field for sophisticated buccaneers. The Latin American record provides many examples. So does the record of city government in our own country — not always in the distant past. Apart from outright corruption, it is in the nature of democratic governments to respond to specialized pressures, and the political market for forging these forces into some expression of the common interest may be at least as imperfect as the economic market.

The fact is that most thinking about government-business relationships is cursed by overly simple stereotypes. It is wrong to identify private action uniformly with efficiency, productivity, and progress, and government with waste, corruption, and stagnation. It is equally wrong to identify private action uniformly with selfish irresponsibility, and government with service to the public interest.

Government and Business

. . . Much of the traditional debate on the line between public and private sectors has focused on the basic services — transportation, communications, and power. In most of the world these are owned and operated by the government. Though the record of many government operations may be abysmally poor, there *are* shining exceptions here and there, and in these fields poorly managed private enterprises are not unknown — even in the advanced countries. In any event, the public utility services are bound to be subject to close public regulation. They are largely natural monopolies. The essential requirement is the selection of competent managers, private or public, and a set of conditions and incentives which favor maximum efficiency.

In the industrial field, on the other hand, the presumption in favor of private enterprise seems to me far more compelling because it offers the

[3] Adolph A. Berle, Jr., and Gardiner C. Means, *The Modern Corporation and Private Property* (New York, The Macmillan Company, 1933).

two basic advantages mentioned earlier — decentralized authority and the test of the market. The need for flexibility, adaptability, and innovation is much greater in providing a wide variety of goods — many perhaps not yet invented — than with highly standardized services such as transportation, telephones, or electricity.

The case for widely dispersed decision making is especially strong in countries whose inadequate official apparatus is already overburdened by other basic duties which only governments can perform. But even in the industrial field there are noteworthy cases of enterprises begun under public auspices and later sold to private interests, of partial governmental participation through development corporation financing, and the like.

Apart from governmental participation and ownership, there are of course many other public devices to promote private industrial expansion — tax and subsidy arrangements, the application of foreign exchange controls and commercial protection, financial aid on a strict loan basis, and the provision of industrial estates. And there are other types of governmental intervention — such as price control and many forms of labor and social security regulation — which generally appear to the entrepreneur more as obstacles than as inducements. . . .

One important aspect . . . concerns the nature and the limits of effective developmental planning in predominantly private enterprise economies. It is evident that everything cannot be planned in detail if private enterprise is to exist in any meaningful sense. But it is also evident that a government bent on rapid development cannot totally refrain from planning.

At the minimum there should be consistency and balance among the elements of public investment in those fields for which government has direct responsibility, and a coherent relationship between public investments and the other governmental policies — monetary, budgetary, foreign exchange, and so forth, which influence the working of market forces in the private sector. How far beyond this minimum there can be effective developmental planning or programing remains to be examined.

Foreign Enterprise

The role of foreign private investment, especially direct investment, as one of the great engines of economic growth, has been amply documented in recent years. It can play an especially important part in helping to develop a strong domestic private sector — in fostering local entrepreneurship, local skills, and a local sense of participation in a growing economic system. This can be done to some extent by extractive industries producing for foreign markets and by public utility companies. But it is especially relevant to businesses producing goods and services for local consumption. Here the stimuli of example, technique, training, and direct partnership can have the greatest multiplier effect in promoting rapid economic modernization.

This aspect of foreign private enterprise has a direct bearing on the hotly disputed issue among American investors concerning the relative merits of exclusive control and joint ventures in their foreign operations. Both sides are defended passionately, usually depending on the experience of particular companies. Joint ventures are, of course, like marriages; their success depends on the selection of the partner and the attitudes brought by both parties to the partnership. By and large, however, the proponents of the joint venture seem in most cases to have the better part of the argument. There are clearly short-term costs and difficulties, as well as some obvious advantages, involved in working with local partners, but over the long term the advantage appears to be with the joint venture, not only as a means of promoting economic development but also as a safeguard for corporate survival in the country concerned.

In connection with our official aid programs, finally, private enterprise can also play a major constructive role. A series of measures to enhance this role were set forth . . . in the report to the State Department by Ralph I. Straus on *Expanding Private Investment for Free World Economic Growth*. In the preparation of that report, lengthy consideration was given to the use of the outright management contract as an aid instrument — in effect having a company act as the government's agent in exploring, designing, building, and operating an overseas industrial venture. . . . For project construction and in countries with extreme political uncertainty, this seems to me a valid device for operation over a limited period of years. *But we should beware of pushing the element of publicness in private enterprise to the point where there is no privateness left!*

If conditions make it impossible to attract any risk capital, it is certainly sound to take advantage of the personal and organizational competence of private business to get a particular governmental job done. But it is even better to maintain the pressures and incentives of the market system by requiring the private participant to assume a significant share of the risk, and to provide for the progressive conversion of the investment to a predominantly and ultimately purely private basis. In this way, the forces of the market can be allied with our own efforts at developmental aid planning — an objective no less appropriate for us than for the developmental planning of the poorer nations.

Conclusion

There is every reason to believe that where given a chance private enterprise, both local and foreign, can demonstrate its value in the poorer nations. It can win increasing respect as a major contributor to the more rapid economic development which is so desperately desired in most of the world. But the relations between government and business are almost certain to differ from the patterns in the more advanced industrial countries. Doctrinaire preconceptions on either side are likely to engender doctrinaire responses on the other. The common cause of successful development will best be served if both governments and businesses can be persuaded to concentrate on practical and effective ways of meeting specific needs in specific situations.

PART FOUR ....

UNITED STATES BUSINESS IN THE
INTERNATIONAL ECONOMY

In Part Two, we examined overall aspects of the American economy's relationship to the international economy. Then, in Part Three, we examined American foreign economic policy, noting the intent, officially, to influence the relationship between this country's economy and the international economy. Now, in Part Four, we turn to business — to the "private sector" aspects of American involvement in the international economy.

International economics, as traditionally treated, emphasizes the role of government in matters affecting the international economy. But, as we observed in Part One, business, too, is involved in matters of the international economy. Of course, the relative weights of government and business, whether gauged by extent of participation or by extent of decision-making authority, vary among countries (e.g., the United States as compared with, say, the U.S.S.R.) and within a given country over time (as, say, in the United States). While such qualifying remarks are worth noting, the central fact remains that business is on hand, and it plays a role — an important role in a country like the United States, where it clearly has a voice in the shaping of overall policy.

More recently, a newer, separately-identified body of "international" subject matter has begun to take shape: international business. Its formal presence, alongside traditional international economics, has gone far to drive home the point that, after all, *decision-making* relative to the international economy takes place at *two* basic levels — at the level of business, as well as of government.

The literature of international business is growing, along with interest in the subject. This should come as no surprise. First, the world is filled with opportunity (an opportunity, incidentally, that often coincides directly with existing need) — trade outlets grow as income levels rise, and as expectations for higher levels of living rise even faster; investment

299

outlets are added as the servicing of growing markets suggests the wisdom of closer proximity in production, and as developing regions themselves seek further access to needed capital.

Second, with special reference to American business, the environment of the United States *favors* a growing involvement abroad. The American economy is relatively "mature"; certainly, in contrast, most foreign areas appear as "virgin territory" to the aspiring trader, producer, or lender. The sheer disparity between the American economy, capital-rich and highly competitive at the domestic enterprise level, and many a foreign area, capital-poor and scarcely "tapped" thus far, is difficult to overlook when appraising potential. Not unimportant, official policy in this country endorses involvement abroad — pretty much across-the-board until recently, and then, as we noted in our introduction to Part Three-B, restricted only selectively for balance-of-payments reasons. Government's endorsement stems essentially from the benefit it presumably can derive from serving the American interest abroad and from supporting American prosperity at home.

If we suggest, as we do here, that this country's private-sector contributions abroad are important, and can become even more important, we should not be oblivious of the attendant problems, both abroad and at home. Some foreign environments, however great their need, are not necessarily receptive to outside "help." Nor is American enterprise invariably prepared to respond, quickly and effectively, to every opportunity or need.

In Part Four, accordingly, our concern is with United States private business as it relates to the international economy. We explore the nature of international business — its form, its motivation, its general role. We explore, also, the "climate" abroad that confronts international business. Finally, we explore certain select problems associated with international business.

A ..... The Nature of International Business

What is "international business"? Basically, it embraces the portion of profit-motivated private-sector economic activity that is international in scope. While the foregoing constitutes a general description, it may need a few qualifications. Not all business at the international level is private; state trading is practiced even by the United States (e.g., in P.L. 480 operations and in the stockpiling of strategic minerals from abroad). Nor is all business at the international level necessarily profit-motivated; this country's P.L. 480 program, for example, is not. While a strict definition thus reduces simply to "business at the international level," the better definition, for working purposes, incorporates the words "private" and "profit."

Traditionally, business at the international level has pertained, for much the greater part, to the movement of goods. More recently, attention has swung far more toward production abroad in lieu of the movement of goods. The foregoing, to apply standard labels, marked a shift from "foreign trade" to "foreign investment" — from business viewed primarily as a marketing matter to business viewed as a transposition of capital and management.

The selections in the present section deal with the nature of international business. Professor Kolde, in our first selection, lends perspective by examining international business in an *overall* global context. Professors Farmer and Richman, in the second selection, focus on the forms that international business takes — and also on its motivation.

A third selection, by Professor Vernon, treats the question of foreign trade *or* foreign investment. His analysis proceeds in terms of tying the firm's self-interest to a "product cycle": at some point (i.e., under certain circumstances) it "pays" to move production abroad, and, in fact, at a subsequent point it may "pay" to begin shipping goods back into the home country.

39..... Business in an International Context*

ENDEL J. KOLDE

University of Washington

Since World War II, international business relations of the United States have undergone far-reaching changes in scope, composition, and structure.

Foreign trade that used to comprise the bulk of transboundary business has shrunk to a minor fraction; total exports are now less than a third of the estimated overseas sales of United States companies.

International intermediaries — export and import merchants, commission houses, and trading companies — have been submerged by new arrangements and are on the verge of disappearing from the institutional structure of United States business.

Multinational corporate ventures have risen to remold not only the channels of international trade but also the internal organization, as well as the external relations, of the corporation itself.

The spans of corporate incentives and impediments have shifted, widened, and diversified as more and greater impacts from foreign environments compound domestic norms for managerial behavior and action.

And the changes continue.

. . . [The purpose here] is to identify the main sources — the apparent prime movers — of this process of change and thereby to move a step closer to a conceptual scheme for the emergent multinational business system. . . .

Environmental Systems. The primary distinction between international and domestic business lies in the environmental framework and the

* Reprinted from "Business Enterprise in a Global Context," *California Management Review*, Vol. VIII, No. 4 Summer 1966, pp. 31–35, 37–43, 45–48. Copyright 1966 by The Regents of the University of California.

organizational and behavioral responses that flow from it. As a company transcends a national setting, its environmental framework changes progressively in countless respects. New ground rules as defined by law, custom, and culture; new values; new contradictions, interactions, and balances among external forces; and new opportunities as well as uncertainties arise. The wider the company's international scope, the greater become the environmental diversities and multiversities surrounding it. To make rational choices among the alternatives available to it in different countries, the company must be able to identify, understand, and anticipate the negative and positive forces of the international diversity.

From a global perspective, the international business environment consists of three major divisions:

The Industrial West, with a few sprouts scattered elsewhere;

The Subindustrial South;

The Communist East.

. . . The industrial countries cluster around the North Atlantic with North America and western Europe as the two principal areas. Japan, Australia, New Zealand, and South Africa complete the industrially developed sector of the free world. All these are predominantly capitalist countries with market-oriented economies. Private property, free enterprise, and open competition form the trigonal foundation of their economic philosophy. Politically, they are guided by the principles of representative government, democratic processes, and the rule of law. In historic heritage, they all belong to the Western culture, with Japan the sole exception.

The Communist realm occupies most of the large Euro-Asian land mass and forms geographically a cohesive whole, its only detached outpost being Cuba. Primarily production-oriented, the Communist system substitutes state monopoly for private ownership and enterprise. All productive resources belong to the state. . . . The market mechanism is replaced by compulsive national planning. . . . Politically, these countries are ruled by autocratic, one-party dictatorships. . . . Culturally, the Communist world is almost evenly divided between the Occidental and the Oriental. . . .

The subindustrial or underdeveloped sector of the global economy covers vast expanses of Africa, Central and South America, Oceania, and southern Asia. Unlike the other two, the underdeveloped world has no basic doctrine or economic philosophy of its own. . . . Politically, the underdeveloped world consists mostly of pseudodemocracies and outright personal dictatorships. . . . Culturally and ethnically, these countries represent the widest possible range. However, the indigenous people far outnumber the Europeans. The cultural heterogeneity, which in the past was repressed by the disproportionate influence of the European elements, is now forging to the foreground and inviting anxious curiosity throughout the world.

. . . [The] three business systems are vastly different in size: nearly half of mankind lives in the Subindustrial South, one-third in the Communist East, and only a little over a fifth in the Industrial West. If time dimension is added to the current profile by considering the natural growth rates, the population disparities among the three divisions are certain to grow rather than diminish in the future.

Lest a misimpression is created, it should be emphasized that the three sections of the global economy, or environmental systems as they have been called here, are by no means homogenous and harmonious. To the contrary, each is full of internal differences, tensions, and even contradictions. But their internal diversities are overshadowed by the sharp contrasts among them. As the environmental systems themselves, so also the enterprises within them exhibit sharp contrasts in character and behavior.

This is not the time or place to try to identify and catalog the specific contrasts. Suffice to say that be it legal status, ownership, organization, objectives, strategies, policies, practices, social responsibilities, or intracompany relations, they can develop and function only in the context of the environmental system under which the enterprise exists. What is more important, the specific change in response to the changes in incentives and impediments which the system can offer or impose. Our focus is on the dynamic aspects of the global environment to uncover the sources and forces for change to which managements must be sensitive to succeed.

The Industrial West

International business relations in the industrial world are being transformed by a sweeping movement toward a closer integration of the different industrial economies. With a gradual shift from a bilateral to a multilateral trading system, spearheaded by GATT[1] and accelerated by the rise of supranational economic unions, arbitrary trade barriers —visible and invisible — have declined sharply, and the convertibility of currencies, at least for external purposes, has become a reassuring reality.

However, the process goes far beyond the classical concept of trade liberalization. Its primary agents, the European Economic Community and the multinational corporation, are transforming the fundamental economic structure of the Industrial West. Since one is operating on the governmental and the other on the managerial plane, they are best discussed separately.

The Common Market

International economic integration emanates from the western European continent where it took the form of the Schuman Plan in the early 1950's, . . . subsequently expanded into the European Economic Community, popularly known as the Common Market.

[1] General Agreement on Tariffs and Trade, signed in 1948, and since then the main force for tariff and trade negotiations.

The objectives and methods of the EEC are set forth in great detail and clarity in its constitution — the Treaty of Rome — which went in effect in 1958 and has in the short time since emerged, not only as a document of global consequence, but also as the blueprint for progress, prosperity, and industrial power.

What is the treaty about? Its basic dictate is to liberate business enterprise from all international hurdles and impediments and to harmonize national policies of the member countries so as to minimize economic differences among them. This freedom is not limited to trade alone. . . . In addition to a free flow of goods and services, the Rome plan provides also for a complete freedom of movement for capital, labor, and entrepreneurship, thus extending its influence to all aspects of economic endeavor.

The treaty is not a utopian scheme. It boldly deals with the problems which the exposure to competition will inevitably bring to industries and companies whose sheltered existence behind import tariffs and other protective barriers is now coming to an end. Many of these companies have found renewed vigor and vitality in the impending peril and have adjusted magnificently; others, however, have been unable to go it on their own. For the latter, the plan provides adjustment assistance to facilitate a gradual and orderly reallocation of the resources and manpower employed in the less efficient and noncompetitive sectors. By doing so, the Rome Treaty goes beyond all earlier international conventions, which at best grant to a foreign enterprise (goods or investments) the so-called *most favored nations treatment,* i.e., the rights and privileges which are accorded to foreign enterprise from the most favored country, but never what a domestic company enjoys.

Once in full force, the Rome Treaty will replace the most favored nations principle with the *national treatment principle,* under which discrimination against foreign products, investments, and companies is completely eliminated and all business transactions and institutions accorded equal treatment under similar conditions.

. . . That this precedent has already had a profound effect on international economic relations is clearly reflected in our own Trade Expansion Act of 1962, which is in part a reaction to, and in part an imitation of, the Rome Treaty. . . .

The Multinational Corporation

The second fundamental change in international business has been the shift from foreign trade to multinational operations. While this may sound like a play on words, it has nothing to do with semantics; in fact we have, so far, failed to find a word to properly describe the new phenomenon. Clearly, the word "operations" is a clumsy and ill-suited term to describe it.

To measure the magnitude of the structural changes and their managerial consequences which the rise of the multinational corporation has engendered, a starting line or base is necessary. A description of the traditional or "normal" institutional model for foreign trade would provide such a base.

"Normal" Foreign Trade Institutions. The traditional way of doing business abroad used to be through exporting or importing, i.e., selling goods and services produced by the business firms in one country to the residents of another. Thus, international business dealings consisted primarily of the movement of goods across national boundaries and the resultant monetary transactions in the opposite direction.

These flows were channeled through business firms who specialized in serving as intermediaries between the business systems of different countries: export-import merchants, commission houses, export brokers, combination managers, etc. . . .

Since the war [World War II], however, a new scheme has emerged and a massive shift from the old to the new set in motion.

International Headquarters Company. In the new scheme, the international intermediary is replaced by company-controlled but operationally and often legally separate organizations, usually in the form of a Foreign Operations or International Operations Subsidiary Company. . . . By this structural change, the management of international business is upgraded in the process: it is no longer an obscure department, subordinated to domestic sales and overshadowed by other aspects of the company business, but a much better defined and relatively autonomous entity in the corporate structure.

But that is not all. The subsidiary does not stop in the narrow confines of the independent export intermediary but goes far beyond them. In addition to exporting or importing, it tends to establish its own facilities in foreign areas for the purposes of production, distribution, and service. These foreign-based affiliates — branches, subsidiaries, joint ventures, and licensees — create many new problems which management must handle in an international setting. . . .

The World Company. Most multinational concerns are patterned after the international headquarters model. But the process of change has not ended here. A new and still different multinational structure appears to be in the making. . . . While, in the previous model . . . , the domestic and international affairs of the multinational concern were separated and most of the corporate staff of the parent company retained their inward-looking domestic orientation, the new model integrates American and international operations into a cohesive whole. The dualistic structure which the international headquarters company created is thus eliminated and the entire top echelon of the company reoriented to its multinational responsibilities.

The large corporations are currently moving in this direction. But how widespread an adoption this integrative pattern will enjoy remains to be seen. To a significant degree, the conditions which business enterprise will encounter in foreign countries, especially in the so-called underdeveloped world, will determine the future course of this trend. . . .

Viewed from a broader perspective, the growth of multinational companies brings with it political and social developments, which, in the main, have long been desired. From among them might be capsuled these:

Stronger and more permanent bonds among different countries.

More efficient utilization of natural resources, manpower, and capital.

Built-in deterrent to international conflict in the form of industrial interties which cannot be broken as easily as the flow of trade.

A surmounting pressure to rethink and redesign U.S. international economic policies and attitudes toward foreign affairs.

The Underdeveloped South

The most significant characteristic of the underdeveloped world is poverty — poverty in the absolute sense of the word, i.e., inability to secure the physical necessities for sustaining one's life. . . .

The urge to industrialize, to grow in economic strength and political stature, is the force which unites the underdeveloped world and propels it to mobilize its energies. . . .

The fact that the governments of the underdeveloped countries are irrevocably committed to industrialization at all costs does not mean that they possess the capacity to bring it about or that they go about it intelligently. But they are not standing still; they are not only hoping, but acting. Discontent to wait until what, in the West, is considered "normal economic progress" runs its course, they are determined to force the pace and to shorten this process. This, they believe, can be accomplished by artificial insemination and spawning of industrial development on a crash program basis by government initiative and action. . . .

Regrettably, the business community of the Industrial West has not possessed either the vision or the flexibility effectively to cope with the new environment in the underdeveloped areas. Instead of anticipating the course of the change and adapting to it, private enterprise too often has tried to resist or ignore the new forces and has discredited itself in the eyes of the indigenous public as the rearguard of colonialist power. . . .

What seems to be needed is . . . a deeper appreciation of the realities of the underdeveloped societies and new criteria for management action. To come straight to the point: profit motive, either with or without the accessories of what, in this country, are called "social responsibilities," is not sufficient to guide management action in the environment of the backward countries. A new and far more embracive economic calculus has to be substituted for the traditional cost-revenue accountancy to measure the other dimensions which, in these new countries, have become equally decisive for the birthright and prosperity of a business enterprise. . . .

The Communist East

. . . That a market potentiality exists behind both the iron and the bamboo curtains is a fact that only dogmatists and some professional bureaucrats fail to grasp. The question on this point is not really an economic one at all but political — not, "can we or can't we?" but, "should we or shouldn't we?" As such, it will be answered when the political questions are answered. . . .

[A further] reason for discussing the Soviet bloc is its influence upon the business environment in the other two system — the underdeveloped areas and the industrial world itself. A study of the international affairs of the postwar world with a view to causal relationships will reveal that the story for the last twenty years has been written in terms of a triangular dialectic which consists of Communist actions, Western counter-actions, and neutralist reactions to the two. *The prime mover in this global process has been the Communist camp; its initiative, ideas, and maneuvers represent a dynamic force which cannot be equalled.* . . .

Summary

The global business scene is in a greater state of flux than in any previous period. Both integrative and disintegrative forces are at work. In the free world, there is a tri-level process of fusion — through multinational corporate structures, through supranational economic unions . . . , and through multilateral trade liberalization. The intermeshing of companies, industries, and economies of different countries which these movements produce open new opportunities for growth and productiveness of business.

In the colonial realm, the old order has suffered a near-complete disintegration, giving rise to scores of new nations which, as fragments of old empires, must redefine their role in the light of the new realities. In search for new definitions, they have started to shift toward a position of solidarity and a consensus of community among themselves and to acquire an attitude of political detachment and economic independence from the Industrial West. However, nationalism and racism, which in the West have rapidly declined, are on an upswing in the backward areas and will remain a source of tension and instability for a long time to come.

Heavy population pressures, coupled with an intense yearning for higher standards of living, exert irresistible pressures for an accelerated industrialization. Radical actions, including expropriations and direct state interference and competition, are, therefore, a serious hazard to private enterprise. To survive and to prosper in these areas, it is necessary for business to synchronize company strategies and policies with the national goals and aspirations of the country involved and to be sensitive to governmental concerns about public revenues, the balance of payments, social overhead, and infrastructure as a whole.

From the Communist orbit emanate both political aggression and economic imperialism. The competitive weapons which the Soviet states possess set a private company at a disadvantage, not only because of the national power and prestige that the Soviets can command, but also because of their capacity to absorb losses on one industry to gain on another.

Through its example and propaganda, the bloc presents a frontal attack to the free enterprise system as such. The spreading of socialization, state enterprise, and compulsive planning are evidence of the seriousness of this challenge.

40..... International Business: Form and Motivation*

RICHARD N. FARMER
Indiana University

BARRY M. RICHMAN
University of California

I. The Form of Business

Any business activity which can be performed within one country can be performed internationally if the firm chooses to work in more than one country. However, various forms of enterprise do have different management and organization characteristics, and it is useful to categorize the more common forms of international business which now take place. Of particular importance in such categorization is whether or not management within the foreign country is performed largely by foreigners or by local citizens. Management of productive activity carries with it significant economic and political power, and much of the praise and objections to international activities revolve around this point. . . .

International Business Activities
Without Foreign Management

These enterprises may be categorized as follows:

1. *Import.* Here, a local buyer, who may be an independent businessman or a government body, merely buys from the foreign firm. Foreign goods enter, but . . . relatively little managerial content is imported along with the goods. . . .

2. *Export.* Here a local firm sends goods abroad. As in the first case, managerial functions are not exported along with the goods.

* Taken and adapted from *International Business: An Operational Theory*, Homewood, Ill.: Richard D. Irwin, Inc., 1966, pp. 19–24, 27–32.

3. *Portfolio Investment.* An investor may buy stocks in foreign corporations or bonds issued by public or private agencies of a foreign country. If the owners of such assets merely hold them passively for income purposes, management does not shift to them.

It is common today to find foreigners buying American securities of all sorts in this manner. Americans also invest in foreign firms, particularly in the more advanced countries of Western Europe, in a similar manner. Historically this type of foreign investment has been quite important . . . [though of relatively lesser importance since the 1930's]. . . .

4. *Licensing.* A firm may license a foreign company to utilize its trademarks, patents, processes, or other knowledge which may have proprietary value. The licensee pays a royalty for the privilege of such use. In such cases, the licensor may take very little part in the foreign operations beyond merely policing to make sure that the licensing agreements are being observed. In others, considerable interplay of managerial talent, including particularly technical talent, may be observed; but the typical role of the licensor is advisory and consultative, not direct and managerial.

5. *Contracting.* It is common in the modern world for a country or an enterprise to contract large and small projects out to foreign firms. Such companies as Bechtel in the United States and Wimpy in England derive much of their revenue from such large projects, including dams, pipelines, roads, communication systems, factory complexes. . . .

This sort of activity is a halfway house between taking management abroad and remaining at home. During the life of the construction project, the contractor is in charge. . . . But when the construction is completed, the firms leave and the project is typically turned over to local personnel for management. . . .

6. *Turnkey Projects.* These projects could possibly be considered a subset in the contracting category. Here, a foreign firm may design and construct a factory or other system, carrying the project through its initial operations. At that point, the project is turned over to local personnel for continued operations. It is useful to examine turnkey factory projects separately, however, since contracting generally involves a project which results in service production (as highway service, water power, electrical supply, flood control, etc.), while this class of international business can be considered to involve only products of an industrial sort. . . .

International Business Activities
Direct Foreign Management

Some types of international business activities require that the owners of the enterprise also provide managerial effort within the foreign country. If an enterprise is owned by foreigners, they have the right (in Western countries) to manage the firm as they see fit. Ownership and control go hand in hand, since asset owners have the right to determine how their assets should be manipulated, subject to local law. . . .

Local managers may be local citizens or foreigners, but in either case, the owner is exercising direct management control. . . . In effect, a firm has exported management (for better or for worse) to other countries. The major kinds of activities involving exported management are as follows:

1. *Sole Direct Foreign Investment.* A firm may completely own and operate a business in a foreign country. As noted earlier, all of the managers may be local citizens, but ultimate management control is provided by the owners. In such cases, local management must be carried on in the local environment, including existing legal-political, educational, sociological, and economic situations which may be unique within a given environment. . . .

2. *Joint Ventures.* These are activities of any type which are performed by at least two firms from different countries in some type of partnership arrangement. The local firm may hold majority control, or the foreign firm might be the dominant partner. In some countries, such as Mexico, local law requires that majority control be held by citizens. . . .

3. *International Services.* A major modern example of services which cross national frontiers is the international air transport industry. Here firms from various countries operate aircraft between countries, and are subject to the laws and regulations of at least two nations. Like the more traditional maritime activities, airplanes as well as the firms which operate them must be domiciled in some single country. . . .

II. *The Motivation for Business*

It is typically true that doing business locally is much simpler than performing international business functions. The local firm only has to worry about its own country's laws, economics, labor problems, financial constraints, and so on, while an international firm faces all of these complexities at home and in the host country, and in addition must struggle with complex international problems arising out of the present nationalistic organization of the world. One would expect that, unless compelling pressures arose at home, most firms would choose to remain local in orientation, confining their international business activities to import and export and possibly to the relatively simple patterns such as licensing of patents and processes.

One major reason for considering international business activities might be that opportunities at home are getting thin. Profit rates in the sector the firm is in may be declining, even though the firm is still quite profitable. Incremental investments are likely to yield lower returns than the company finds acceptable. Moreover, a mature firm organized around a cadre of professional managers may find that it has developed a surplus of competent men in both the technical and the managerial sense. Junior men, seeing paths of advancement blocked by competent senior men, may be getting restless. Most professionally managed firms have a built-in development dynamic of their own; and, if local market rates of growth tend to slow down, management actively begins to seek new alternatives for the kinds of talent the firm possesses.

The firm may also, in the routine course of its domestic business, do considerable exporting to various countries and, as a matter of course, have developed a good deal of information about their economies. . . .

The points made above fit modern, professionally managed industrial firms in the more advanced countries. Few companies of this type exist in the less developed countries, and those that do rarely lack for large opportunities at home. A less-developed country almost by definition has more to do industrially than has been done, and almost any competent management finds that it has its hands full trying to take advantage of local possibilities. . . .

The large, professionally managed firms are also much more likely to accumulate cash surpluses or to be able to obtain more funds from money markets. Financial constraints, folklore to the contrary, tend to be much less compelling in modern industry than manpower problems, particularly supplies of high-skill management and technical talent.

In such large, professionally managed firms, some factor eventually sends the company overseas in a direct way. It may be that a major export market is being cut off by exchange controls and the only way to maintain it is to build a plant inside the country. It may be that for purely economic reasons connected with good management local assembly operations are started. Transport costs on low-volume, high-weight components may be so much lower than transport costs on finished products that local assembly is a logical step. It simply may be that the president of the firm takes a vacation in a likely market, finds his products not present, and determines to do something about it in the near future. . . .

Most firms in the Western world are very reluctant to lose markets to competitors; and, if a major competitor moves overseas, it is likely that the firm also will begin similar operations. There are cases where American firms, instead of pondering seriously all of the critical factors involved in going abroad, have simply observed where their major competitors went, then promptly entered the same countries and markets. Perhaps the theory here is that the competition has done all of the preliminary work, or perhaps it is a reflection of the intense competitive pressures which large firms feel from their major rivals. But in many cases, if one firm decides to make a major commitment in an important industrial country, its competitors will not be far behind. Their managements feel that they cannot lag in any area which may turn out to be extremely important in the future.

The firm most likely to engage in international business requiring management to go with the investment is the company whose home country is highly developed and has a relatively slow rate of growth that tends to inhibit unrestricted expansion. This set of conditions defines the United States and to a lesser extent Western Europe, and, in fact, most international activities involving exported management are from these countries. As a result, the flow outward from these countries is to less-developed economies. . . .

41 ..... Foreign Trade or Foreign Investment*

RAYMOND VERNON

Harvard University

Anyone who has sought to understand the shifts in international trade and international investment over the past twenty years has chafed from time to time under an acute sense of the inadequacy of the available analytical tools. . . .

The present paper deals with one promising line of generalization and synthesis . . . somewhat neglected by the main stream of trade theory. It puts less emphasis upon comparative cost doctrine and more upon the timing of innovation, the effects of scale economies, and the roles of ignorance and uncertainty in influencing trade patterns. . . .

Location of New Products

We begin with the assumption that the enterprises in any one of the advanced countries of the world are not distinguishably different from those in any other advanced country, in terms of their access to scientific knowledge and their capacity to comprehend scientific principles.[1] . . .

It is a mistake to assume, however, that equal access to scientific principles in all the advanced countries means equal probability of the application of these principes in the generation of new products. There is ordinarily a large gap between the knowledge of a scientific principle and the embodiment of the principle in a marketable product. An entre-

* Reprinted by permission of the publishers from Raymond Vernon, "International Investment and International Trade in the Product Cycle," *Quarterly Journal of Economics* (May 1966), Cambridge, Mass.: Harvard University Press, Copyright 1966, by the President and Fellows of Harvard College, pp. 190–204.

[1] Some of the account that follows will be found in greatly truncated form in my "The Trade Expansion Act in Perspective," in *Emerging Concepts in Marketing*, Proceedings of the American Marketing Association, December 1962, pp. 348–389. . . .

preneur usually has to intervene to accept the risks involved in testing whether the gap can be bridged.

If all entrepreneurs, wherever located, could be presumed to be equally conscious of and equally responsive to all entrepreneurial opportunities, whenever they arose, the classical view of the dominant role of price in resource allocation might be highly relevant. There is good reason to believe, however, that the entrepreneur's consciousness of and responsiveness to opportunity are a function of ease of communication; and, further, that ease of communication is a function of geographical proximity.[2] Accordingly, we abandon the powerful simplifying notion that knowledge is a universal free good, and introduce it as an independent variable in the decision to trade or to invest.

The fact that the search for knowledge is an inseparable part of the decision-making process and that relative ease of access to knowledge can profoundly affect the outcome are now reasonably well established. . . . One implication of that fact is that producers in any market are more likely to be aware of the possibility of introducing new products in that market than producers located elsewhere would be.

The United States market offers certain unique kinds of opportunities to those who are in a position to be aware of them.

First, the United States market consists of consumers with an average income which is higher (except for a few anomalies like Kuwait) than that in any other national market. . . .

Second, the United States market is characterized by high unit labor costs and relatively unrationed capital compared with practically all other markets. This is a fact which conditions the demand for both consumer goods and industrial products. . . .

Assume, then, that entrepreneurs in the United States are first aware of opportunities to satisfy new wants associated with high income levels or high unit labor costs. Assume further that the evidence of an unfilled need and the hope of some kind of monopoly windfall for the early starter both are sufficiently strong to justify the initial investment that is usually involved in converting an abstract idea into a marketable product. Here we have a reason for expecting a consistently higher rate of expenditure on product development to be undertaken by United States producers than by producers in other countries, at least in lines which promise to substitute capital for labor or which promise to satisfy high-income wants. . . .

Our hypothesis asserts that United States producers are likely to be the first to spy an opportunity for high-income or labor-saving new products.[3] But it goes on to assert that the first producing facilities for such

[2] Note C. P. Kindleberger's reference to the "horizon" of the decision-maker, and the view that he can only be rational within that horizon; see his *Foreign Trade and The National Economy* (New Haven: Yale University Press, 1962), p. 15 *passim.*

[3] There is a kind of first-cousin relationship between this simple motion and the "entrained want" concept defined by H. G. Barnett in *Innovation: The Basis of Cul-*

products will be located in the United States. This is not a self-evident proposition. Under the calculus of least cost, production need not automatically take place at a location close to the market, unless the product can be produced and delivered from that location at lowest cost. Besides, now that most major United States companies control facilities situated in one or more locations outside of the United States, the possibility of considering a non-United States location is even more plausible than it might once have been.

Of course, if prospective producers were to make their locational choices on the basis of least-cost considerations, the United States would not always be ruled out. The costs of international transport and United States import duties, for instance, might be so high as to argue for such a location. My guess is, however, that the early producers of a new product intended for the United States market are attracted to a United States location by forces which are far stronger than relative factor-cost and transport considerations. For the reasoning on this point, one has to take a long detour away from comparative cost analysis into areas which fall under the rubrics of communication and external economies.

By now, a considerable amount of empirical work has been done on the factors affecting the location of industry.[4] Many of these studies try to explain observed locational patterns in conventional cost-minimizing terms, by implicit or explicit reference to labor cost and transportation cost. But some explicitly introduce problems of communication and external economies as powerful locational forces. . . . At the risk of oversimplifying, I shall try to summarize what these studies suggested.[5]

In the early stages of introduction of a new product, producers were usually confronted with a number of critical, albeit transitory, conditions. For one thing, the product itself may be quite unstandardized for a time; its inputs, its processing, and its final specifications may cover a wide range. . . . The unstandardized nature of the design at this early stage carries with it a number of locational implications.

First, producers at this stage are particularly concerned with the degree of freedom they have in changing their inputs. . . .

Second, the price elasticity of demand for the output of individual firms is comparatively low. . . .

tural Change (New York: McGraw-Hill, 1953), p. 148. Albert O. Hirschman, *The Strategy of Economic Development* (New Haven: Yale University Press, 1958), p. 68, also finds the concept helpful in his effort to explain certain aspects of economic development.

[4] For a summary of such work, together with a useful bibliography, see John Meyer, "Regional Economics: A Survey," in the *American Economic Review*, LIII (Mar. 1963), 19–54.

[5] The points that follow are dealt with at length in the following publications: Raymond Vernon, *Metropolis, 1985* (Cambridge: Harvard University Press, 1960), pp. 38–85; Max Hall (ed.), *Made in New York* (Cambridge: Harvard University Press, 1959), pp. 3–18, 19 *passim;* Robert M. Lichtenberg, *One-Tenth of a Nation* (Cambridge: Harvard University Press, 1960), pp. 31–70.

Third, the need for swift and effective communication on the part of the producer with customers, suppliers, and even competitors is especially high at this stage. This is a corollary of the fact that a considerable amount of uncertainty remains regarding the ultimate dimensions of the market, the efforts of rivals to preempt that market, the specifications of the inputs needed for production, and the specifications of the products likely to be most successful in the effort.

All of these considerations tend to argue for a location in which communication between the market and the executives directly concerned with the new product is swift and easy, and in which a wide variety of potential types of input that might be needed by the production unit are easily come by. In brief, the producer who sees a market for some new product in the United States may be led to select a United States location for production on the basis of national locational considerations which extend well beyond simple factor cost analysis plus transport considerations.

The Maturing Product

As the demand for a product expands, a certain degree of standardization usually takes place. This is not to say that efforts at product differentiation come to an end. On the contrary; such efforts may even intensify, as competitors try to avoid the full brunt of price competition. . . . Nevertheless, although the subcategories may multiply and the efforts at product differentiation increase, a growing acceptance of certain general standards seems to be typical.

Once again, the change has locational implications. First of all, the need for flexibility declines. A commitment to some set of product standards opens up technical possibilities for achieving economies of scale through mass output, and encourages long-term commitments to some given process and some fixed set of facilities. Second, concern about production cost begins to take the place of concern about product characteristics. Even if increased price competition is not yet present, the reduction of the uncertainties surrounding the operation enhances the usefulness of cost projections and increases the attention devoted to cost.

The empirical studies . . . [referred to] earlier suggest that, at this stage in an industry's development, there is likely to be considerable shift in the location of production facilities at least as far as internal United States locations are concerned. The empirical materials on international locational shifts simply have not yet been analyzed sufficiently to tell us very much. A little speculation, however, indicates some hypotheses worth testing.

Picture an industry engaged in the manufacture of the high-income or labor-saving products that are the focus of our discussion. Assume that the industry has begun to settle down in the United States to some degree of large-scale production. Although the first mass market may be located in the United States, some demand for the product begins almost at once to appear elsewhere. . . .

If the product has a high-income elasticity of demand or if it is a satisfactory substitute for high-cost labor, the demand in time will begin to grow quite rapidly in relatively advanced countries such as those of Western Europe. Once the market expands in such an advanced country, entrepreneurs will begin to ask themselves whether the time has come to take the risk of setting up a local producing facility.[6]

How long does it take to reach this stage? An adequate answer must surely be a complex one. Producers located in the United States, weighing the wisdom of setting up a new production facility in the importing country, will feel obliged to balance a number of complex considerations. As long as the marginal production cost plus the transport cost of the goods exported from the United States is lower than the average cost of prospective production in the market of import, United States producers will presumably prefer to avoid an investment. But that calculation depends on the producer's ability to project the cost of production in a market in which factor costs and the appropriate technology differ from those at home. . . .

We arrive, then, at the stage at which United States producers have come around to the establishment of production units in the advanced countries. Now a new group of forces are set in train. In an idealized form, Figure 1 on page 320 suggests what may be anticipated next.

As far as individual United States producers are concerned, the local markets thenceforth will be filled from local production units set up abroad. Once these facilities are in operation, however, more ambitious possibilities for their use may be suggested. When comparing a United States producing facility and a facility in another advanced country, the obvious production-cost differences between the rival producing areas are usually differences due to scale and differences due to labor costs.[7] If the producer is an international firm with producing locations in several countries, its costs of financing capital at the different locations may not be sufficiently different to matter very much. If economies of scale are being fully exploited, the principal differences between any two locations

---

[6] M. V. Posner, "International Trade and Technical Change," *Oxford Economic Papers*, Vol. 13 (Oct. 1961), p. 323, *et seq.* presents a stimulating model purporting to explain such familiar trade phenomena as the exchange of machine tools between the United Kingdom and Germany. In the process he offers some particularly helpful notions concerning the size of the "imitation lag" in the responses of competing nations.

[7] Note the interesting finding of Mordecai Kreinin in his "The Leontief Scarce-Factor Paradox," *The American Economic Review*, LV (Mar. 1965), 131–139. Kreinin finds that the higher cost of labor in the United States is not explained by a higher rate of labor productivity in this country.

FIGURE 1

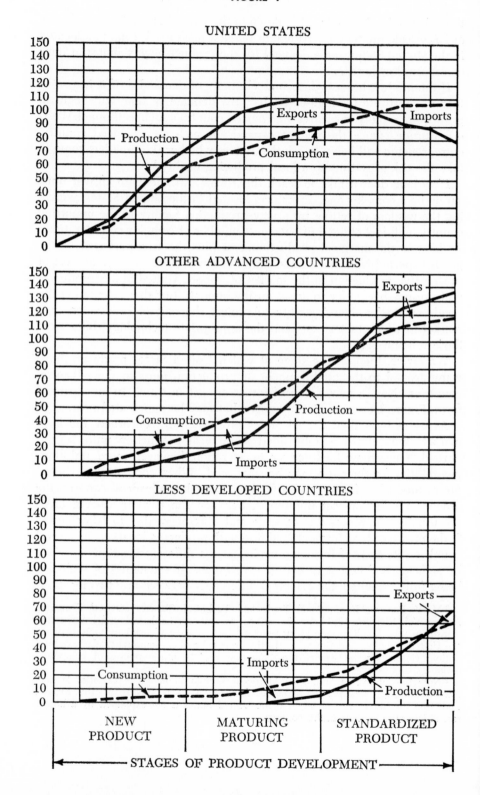

UNITED STATES

OTHER ADVANCED COUNTRIES

LESS DEVELOPED COUNTRIES

NEW PRODUCT

MATURING PRODUCT

STANDARDIZED PRODUCT

STAGES OF PRODUCT DEVELOPMENT

are likely to be labor costs. Accordingly, it may prove wise for the international firm to begin servicing third-country markets from the new location. And if labor cost differences are large enough to offset transport costs, then exports back to the United States may become a possibility as well.

Any hypothesis based on the assumption that the United States entrepreneur will react rationally when offered the possibility of a lower-cost location abroad is, of course, somewhat suspect. The decision-making sequence that is used in connection with international investments, according to various empirical studies, is not a model of the rational process.[8] But there is one theme that emerges again and again in such studies. Any threat to the established position of an enterprise is a powerful galvanizing force to action; in fact, if I interpret the empirical work correctly, threat in general is a more reliable stimulus to action than opportunity is likely to be.

In the international investment field, threats appear in various forms once a large-scale export business in manufactured products has developed. Local entrepreneurs located in the countries which are the targets of these exports grow restive at the opportunities they are missing. Local governments concerned with generating employment or promoting growth or balancing their trade accounts begin thinking of ways and means to replace the imports. An international investment by the exporter, therefore, becomes a prudent means of forestalling the loss of a market. In this case, the yield on the investment is seen largly as the avoidance of a loss of income to the system.

The notion that a threat to the status quo is a powerful galvanizing force for international investment also seems to explain what happens after the initial investment. Once such an investment is made by a United States producer, other major producers in the United States sometimes see it as a threat to the status quo. They see themselves as losing position relative to the investing company, with vague intimations of further losses to come. Their "share of the market" is imperiled, viewing "share of the market" in global terms. At the same time, their ability to estimate the production-cost structure of their competitors, operating far away in an unfamiliar foreign area, is impaired; this is a particularly unsettling state because it conjures up the possibility of a return flow of products to the United States and a new source of price competition, based on cost differences of unknown magnitude. The uncertainty can be reduced by emulating the pathfinding investor and by investing in the same area; this may not be an optimizing investment pattern and it may be costly, but it is least disturbing to the status quo. . . .

[8] Yair Aharoni [in *The Foreign Investment Decision Process,* to be published by the Division of Research of the Harvard Business School, 1966] provides an excellent summary and exhaustive bibliography of the evidence on this point.

The Standardized Product

Figure 1 . . . carries a panel which suggests that, at an advanced stage in the standardization of some products, the less-developed countries may offer competitive advantages as a production location.

This is a bold projection, which seems on first blush to be wholly at variance with the Heckscher-Ohlin theorem. According to that theorem, one presumably out to anticipate that the exports of the less-developed countries would tend to be relatively labor-intensive products.

One of the difficulties with the theorem, however, is that it leaves marketing considerations out of account. One reason for the omission is evident. As long as knowledge is regarded as a free good, instantaneously available, and as long as individual producers are regarded as atomistic contributors to the total supply, marketing problems cannot be expected to find much of a place in economic theory. In projecting the patterns of export from less-developed areas, however, we cannot afford to disregard the fact that information comes at a cost; and that entrepreneurs are not readily disposed to pay the price of investigating overseas markets of unknown dimensions and unknown promise. Neither are they eager to venture into situations which they know will demand a constant flow of reliable marketing information from remote sources.

If we can assume that highly standardized products tend to have a well-articulated, easily accessible international market and to sell largely on the basis of price (an assumption inherent in the definition), then it follows that such products will not pose the problem of market information quite so acutely for the less-developed countries. This establishes a necessary if not a sufficient condition for investment in such industries.

Of course, foreign investors seeking an optimum location for a captive facility may not have to concern themselves too much with questions of market information; presumably, they are thoroughly familiar with the marketing end of the business and are looking for a low-cost captive source of supply. In that case, the low cost of labor may be the initial attraction drawing the investor to less-developed areas. But other limitations in such areas, according to our hypothesis, will bias such captive operations toward the production of standardized items. The reasons in this case turn on the part played in the production process by external economies. Manufacturing processes which receive significant inputs from the local economy, such as skilled labor, repairmen, reliable power, spare parts, industrial materials processed according to exacting specification, and so on, are less appropriate to the less-developed areas than those that do not have such requirements. Unhappily, most industrial processes require one or another ingredient of this difficult sort. My guess is, however, that the industries which produce a standardized product are in the best position to avoid the problems, by producing on a vertically-integrated self-sustaining basis.

In speculating about future industrial exports from the less-developed areas, therefore, we are led to think of products with a fairly clear-cut set of economic characteristics.[9] Their production function is such as to require significant inputs of labor; otherwise there is no reason to expect a lower production cost in less-developed countries. At the same time, they are products with a high price elasticity of demand for the output of individual firms; otherwise, there is no strong incentive to take the risks of pioneering with production in a new area. In addition, products whose production process did not rely heavily upon external economies would be more obvious candidates than those which required a more elaborate industrial environment. The implications of remoteness also would be critical; products which could be precisely described by standardized specifications and which could be produced for inventory without fear of obsolescence would be more relevant than those which had less precise specifications and which could not easily be ordered from remote locations. Moreover, high-value items capable of absorbing significant freight costs would be more likely to appear than bulky items low in value by weight. Standardized textile products are, of course, the illustration par excellence of the sort of product that meets the criteria. But other products come to mind such as crude steel, simple fertilizers, newsprint, and so on. . . .

[9] The concepts sketched out here are presented in more detail in my "Problems and Prospects in the Export of Manufactured Products from the Less-Developed Countries," U.N. Conference on Trade and Development, Dec. 16, 1963 (mimeo.).

B..... The "Climate" Abroad

The "climate" that confronts United States business abroad, viewed from the standpoint of either marketer or investor-producer, varies widely. Variation rooted in attitude is coupled with variation in economic, political, and social conditions: some countries put out a "welcome mat," while others shun foreign contact; some countries are strong and sophisticated (e.g., countries of Western Europe), while others are weak and underdeveloped (e.g., many countries in Latin America, Asia, and Africa). Clearly, the American firm that contemplates doing business abroad is well-advised not to proceed in terms of some vaguely-understood norm. There simply is no meaningful norm. It is the *particular* environment that counts.

In another way, however, it is both possible and meaningful to generalize. Foreign markets often prove highly lucrative for exporters, many of whom choose to view this business as an "add on" to their domestically-oriented business. Certainly, in comparison, would-be investor-producers face a much harder decision preparatory to possible entry abroad; they stand to be committed by their decision in a way that does not apply to exporters. Yet, compelling attractions do prevail abroad that are bound to catch the eye of many an American investor-producer; for example, data on hand reveal a profit return on foreign effort somewhat in excess of that usual on comparable investment within this country.

True, American business has many things to think about as it considers whether or not to "go international." But, equally true, foreign countries have many things to think about in deciding how to react to possible entry by an outside firm. After all, not every contact at the international level is necessarily "good."

A number of factors tend to arouse concern in foreign countries as they view activity by outside investor-producer firms. Many residents feel that the cost to their countries — in a price sense, or in a balance-of-payments sense, or in terms of belittling treatment — is "too high" for what they get out of it. And others feel that foreign firms, sometimes strongly backed by their home governments, interfere domestically in ways that thwart legitimate national objectives. The ideal relationship, of course, is one of *mutual* benefit — one that the host country, as well as the foreign firm, can construe as advantageous.

324

The present section begins with a selection by Professors Davis and Blomstrom, describing the economic, political, and social environments that confront American firms in widely diverse locales abroad. This is followed by a selection by Professor Wells on attitudes toward foreign investors.

42 ..... The Environment Confronting Business*

KEITH DAVIS
Arizona State University

ROBERT L. BLOMSTROM
Michigan State University

The people of the world are organized into communities and nations, each in its own way according to its resources and cultural heritage. There are similarities among nations, but there are also significant differences which define the boundaries of business practice in each nation. Some nations have a customer-oriented economy, while others have a centrally planned economy, and there are various shades of practice in between. Some are economically developed, but others are just now developing. Some are a political dictatorship; others are more democratic. Some are socially advanced, while others have minimum literacy and social development. And in each case the managerial conditions of work are different because of different expectations from participants. Let us examine these social, political, economic, and managerial conditions as they affect business. We shall discuss these conditions in terms of a United States business entering other countries; however, it will be evident that a business from any nation which enters another nation will find most of the same conditions either to a greater or a lesser degree.

Social Conditions

One obvious characteristic of less-developed nations is the scarcity of human resources. There are major shortages of managerial personnel, scientists, and technicians, and these deficiencies limit business's ability

* From *Business and its Environment* by Keith Davis and Robert L. Blomstrom, pp. 284–290. Copyright 1966 by McGraw-Hill, Inc. McGraw Hill Book Company. Used by permission.

to employ local labor productively. Needed skills are temporarily imported, while vast training programs prepare native workers. . . .
Shortages of trained people and community-supported facilities cause large social overhead costs when a business moves into a developing area. . . .

Political Conditions

. . . Many nations have strong nationalistic drives. The people want their nation and their economic system for themselves without interference by foreign nationals. . . .
When a foreign company does enter another nation, it has a wide variety of licenses, foreign exchange rules, and sanctions applied by government. These are complicated by the fact that the government itself is sometimes unstable, inconsistent, and bureaucratic. . . .
The general conclusion is that in nearly all countries outside the United States, the government is more involved in business than is the case in this country. Businessmen in these nations have to be actively interested in government affairs in order to operate successfully. Sometimes they must give political considerations priority over economic and technical values when they make decisions. . . .

Economic Conditions

A common economic condition in many parts of the world is inflation.
. . . Typical "good management" through long-range planning . . . [becomes] very difficult, and even regular operations become unsettled. . . .
[Additionally,] inflation in an underdeveloped country causes capital to flee the country for one with a more stable currency. This condition increases the capital shortage and further limits business growth. . . .

Managerial Conditions

. . . Not only must an international business live up to different standards in each country, but it also must be prepared to meet these standards with more perfection than native businesses in each country are expected to do. As an interloper from afar, its public visibility is greater than that of local businesses. Nationalism, love of one's own people, and desire to protect native business make local citizens more sensitive to the effects of an international business. They know that its whole loyalty — or even its primary loyalty — is not to their economy and their people. They are quick to condemn its indiscretions and hesitant and faint in their praise of its benefits. . . .
Insight into all these nuances of social conduct is difficult for even the best-qualified manager. He needs to be broad in his thinking and have

high sensitivity to political and social trends. If he comes from outside the host country, he cannot by himself sense all the fine points that should bear on his decisions; therefore, he depends on the counsel of native associates who are loyal and communicative. If they understand that above-average behavior is required because the business is an international one, they can be quite helpful in counseling toward responsible decisions. . . .

43..... Attitudes Toward Foreign Investors*

DONALD A. WELLS

Southern Illinois University

Direct private foreign investment has been the target of severe criticism in virtually all of the poorer developing countries during the postwar period, and has been identified with colonialism and "Yankee" or Western imperialism. Moreover, notwithstanding its obvious contribution to the successful development of the more opulent capital importing countries such as Australia and Canada, it has also come under increasing attack from both official and unofficial sources in these countries. We are not concerned . . . [here] with chauvinistic expressions of extreme nationalism nor with arguments which reflect purely political biases against all foreign activity or a preference for government ownership and socialization over private enterprise. Rather, we are concerned with the economic arguments with respect to direct foreign investments, which are capable of rational analysis and deserve serious consideration by the economist.

Many of the attitudes put forward by the poorer underdeveloped countries and the relatively rich capital importing countries such as Canada are similar, but certain important distinctions may be noted. First, the attitudes expressed in the more opulent capital importing countries are less concerned with the association of direct foreign investment with colonialism and are less likely to condemn direct foreign investment as an alternative to loans by public institutions. For countries like Australia and Canada, colonialism is no longer an issue. Moreover, in these countries there is a wider appreciation of the benefits of direct private investment, and their concern is much less with direct private investment as such than with certain practices of the foreign investors. On the other

* Taken and adapted from "Economic Analysis of Attitudes of Host Countries Toward Direct Private Investment," in Raymond F. Mikesell (ed.), *U.S. Private and Government Investment Abroad,* Eugene, Ore.: University of Oregon Books, 1962, pp. 483–487.

hand, these countries where development is progressing rapidly and where domestic savings and investment are sufficient to sustain economic growth without further capital imports from abroad, are more likely to raise questions with respect to the costs versus benefits of additional foreign capital in any form than are the poorer countries. Although the latter desperately need foreign capital as a condition for their growth, they often prefer loan capital, particularly from public international lending institutions, over direct investment, and they employ strict controls over direct capital imports. . . .

Types of Concerns Expressed By Capital Importing Countries

The Cost of Servicing Capital Imports versus Real Benefits Derived

As mentioned above, the poorer capital importing countries rarely question the net benefits from loan capital, particularly on terms provided by international public lending institutions. What causes concern is the desirability of admitting foreign private enterprises which earn exceptionally high returns, perhaps of the order of 20 to 30 per cent or more per year, on their investments. That such a rate of return may be quite in line with that earned by similar domestically-owned enterprises, or may constitute a substantially lower *real* rate of return because of a high rate of inflation, is usually not taken into account. Frequently the return to the foreign private investor is compared with the rate of interest on capital borrowed from foreign public lending institutions, such as the Export-Import Bank or the World Bank, and on this basis, direct private investment is regarded as a relatively "expensive" means of obtaining capital. This attitude is based on an assumption that the impact on domestic output is the same regardless of whether or not the foreign capital is accompanied by foreign enterprise and skills.

Occasionally, the argument is put forward in the more developed capital importing countries that the real cost resulting from the servicing of the capital may be greater than the addition to the social product. As a general proposition, however, it is unlikely that foreign capital could earn more than its marginal value product. . . .

The Balance of Payments Impact of Servicing Direct Foreign Investment or Borrowed Capital

Probably the most popular criticisms of foreign investment, or at least of certain types of foreign investment, relate to the impact on the balance of payments. There is, first, the concern over whether or not the balance of payments will adjust to the additional drain resulting from the service payments on foreign capital and, second, the concern over the increased vulnerability of the economy resulting from an increasing proportion of foreign exchange receipts being committed to capital service. The first concern relates to foreign investments in industries which produce goods for sale wholly or mainly in the domestic market and which do not represent a substitute for imports. Even if the products do represent a substitute for imports, the increased demand for the products as a consequence of their production inside a tariff or quota wall may result in a foreign exchange drain, provided the commodities have a large foreign exchange content in the form of raw materials and intermediate products plus, of course, the foreign exchange payments represented by the transfer of dividends by the foreign enterprise.

Concern over the increased vulnerability of the economy to shifts in foreign demand have been expressed with respect to investments in the export industries as well as in those producing for the domestic market. Thus we find that in some countries foreign investment is criticized because too much of it flows into industries producing for the domestic market, while in other cases it is criticized because too much of it flows into the export industries. . . .

The Interference with National Objectives

The concern over whether the activities of foreign enterprises are, or may be, interfering with the realization of national economic objectives is frequently associated with emotional or irrational expressions of nationalistic feeling, so that it is often difficult to discover the basic argument which is capable of rational analysis. Although they may have had greater relevance in the past, vaguely expressed fears of political and economic domination by foreign enterprises have less significance today if we assume that governments are both strong enough and intelligent enough to provide proper over-all direction of the nation's economy. . . .

. . .

A full discussion of the arguments outlined in the . . . paragraphs above would involve us deeply in the theory of economic development. For the most part, they are not arguments against direct foreign investment as such, but rather they seek to show either that some types of direct foreign investment may not be socially desirable or that foreign investment by itself does not provide a balanced pattern of investment for the economy as a whole. Few would deny that countries cannot rely wholly on foreign investment for determining the pattern and directions of their growth. Moreover, it is generally recognized that developing countries require certain supplements to domestic and foreign private enterprise and the adoption of policies which, though not necessarily restrictive, will have the effect of guiding investment activities into the most desirable channels. We shall therefore confine our economic analysis to the arguments dealing with: (a) the benefits of direct foreign investment versus the costs of servicing the investments; and (b) the balance of payments arguments. However, before considering these arguments we shall in the following paragraphs discuss specific examples of some of the attitudes and arguments with respect to direct private investment which have emanated from the capital importing countries. . . .

C ..... The Financial Ingredient

Of the many problems that confront business in its organization and operation, perhaps the one talked about most is financing. Books on "corporate finance" detail the intricacies of how to piece together a corporate financial structure so as to use various sources of financing and yet achieve, or retain, strength in management. In addition to this, a few further factors merit mention when the corporation operates in an international context.

American firms operating internationally are potentially eligible for funds simply because they are "international." Among these funds are some made available by the United States government. For example, the Exim Bank offers both (a) export credits (loans on goods of American origin that enter export channels, chiefly industrial goods), and (b) regular investment loans (to enable purchase in the American market of goods needed in connection with investment abroad). Again, A.I.D. has limited loan funds available for use, in combination with other funds, in new investment abroad. (Details on criteria of eligibility and other information appear in an A.I.D. publication: *Aids to Business, 1966.*) Further, "Cooley Amendment" funds, arising from the P.L. 480 program, are earmarked for loans to United States businesses abroad; these funds exist in terms of a considerable range of national currencies and are of substantial magnitude (up to 25% of all P.L. 480, Title I, proceeds being channeled to this use). Other potential sources include certain international agencies: the World Bank, the International Finance Corporation, the International Development Association, and the Inter-American Development Bank.

The present section includes two selections on aspects of financing. The first, by Professor Robock, focuses on "overseas financing" — by which is meant the drawing upon "foreign country" loan funds by American companies situated abroad. Long a potential source of investment capital, overseas financing currently receives considerable attention, largely because of curbs imposed on new capital outflows from this country with the adoption, in 1965, of the "voluntary restraint" program (see introduction to Part Three B). Overseas financing represents, today, a source of financing for American companies abroad that is capable of lessening dependence on capital flows from the United States.

The second selection, by Professor Nehrt, concerns the financing of trade in capital goods. Capital goods are very important in foreign trade: they relate to the machinery ingredient of new investment in production capacity abroad, whether initiated by an American investor or by, say, indigenous enterprise in the foreign country. A complaint frequently heard in this country (chiefly from members of the capital-goods industry, but also from would-be foreign investors who represent prospective buyers of the capital-goods industry's output) is that "better credit terms" are offered by foreign suppliers located in Western Europe and Japan. Professor Nehrt examines, on a comparative basis, how capital goods are dealt with in this respect.

44 ..... Financing International Enterprise*

STEFAN H. ROBOCK

Indiana University

A Conceptual Framework for Multi-National Financial Planning

... The conceptual framework needed for financial decision-making by the multi-national enterprise is still in an early stage of formulation. Nevertheless, some of the principal differences between a global approach to business financing and the traditional domestic patterns used in the United States can be outlined as they apply to international business in general. . . . These differences and many other unique dimensions of international business arise out of foreign dissimilarities in financial attitudes, financial institutions, legal systems, governmental policies and other environmental variables.

The most obvious but most overlooked feature of international business financing is that overseas as well as U.S. sources of funds should be considered on a continuing basis. In a global approach, this principle remains valid even if the American company is generating substantial surplus funds in its U.S. operations. Such funds invariably have alternative uses and an opportunity cost.

A second principle is that financial requirements should be separated as to local currency and dollar needs. This is particularly important for operations in foreign areas with soft currencies.

Third, total financial requirements for a given size of project should be considered variable. The total investment indicated by a model based on using U.S. financial sources may not be appropriate for other areas. Unique tax advantages in specific foreign areas may favor leasing as a substitute for long-term capital. Working capital needs may be reduced because of the practice of foreign banks to permit overdrafts.

* Taken and adapted from "Overseas Financing for U.S. International Business," *The Journal of Finance,* May 1966, pp. 299–302.

335

A fourth feature of the global approach is that the composition of total financial requirements should vary with different foreign practices and financing opportunities. The "mix" of long-term versus short-term borrowing, of debt versus equity, and of local versus foreign currency should vary for different countries. For example, in some countries long-term financial needs may be most advantageously met by short-term loans from commercial banks which are traditionally "rolled over" or renewed for long periods.

Finally, the cost elements included in the decision model and the criteria against which financial proposals are judged will vary from U.S. practice and from country to country.

To summarize, the conceptual framework for financial decision-making by the multi-national firm must be extended to deal with a large number and significantly different sources of funds, with several kinds of currency needs, with both a total financial requirement and a composition of a given total that will vary for different countries, and with new risk and cost elements in the decision model that are unique for international business operations.

New Elements in Financial Decision-Making

Some of the principal new elements that enter into multi-national financing are exchange risks, differential inflation rates, taxes across national boundaries, effective versus nominal rates of interest, fringe benefits, joint ventures, special inducements, and the future benefits of developing foreign capital markets.

Exchange Risks

Exchange risks permeate all dimensions of financial management in international business and create opportunities for profits as well as losses. As an aside, the foreign exchange forecasting staff of a large multi-national firm claims to have made more profit for the company in some years than have the production and sales staffs. Exchange risks are particularly important in planning for new foreign investment. . . .

Differential Inflation Rates

Rates of domestic inflation vary greatly among countries. Local borrowing within countries with relatively high rates of inflation, even at substantially higher rates of interest than available in the United States, can result in significant financial benefits. This applies to working capital as well as long-term debt.

Taxes Across National Boundaries

Certain tax considerations are always included in financial decisions. But international business injects a new tax element into the picture — that of taxes incurred in moving funds across national boundaries. For example, in some countries interest payments on local borrowing are deductible for tax purposes whereas interest payments on foreign borrowing are not. . . .

Effective Versus Nominal Rates of Interest

A simple comparison of nominal rates of interest in U.S. versus foreign money rates of interest in U.S. versus foreign money markets is often misleading. For example, commercial banks in many foreign countries make short-term credit available on an overdraft basis, often with interest calculated daily on the overdraft. In the United States, short-term borrowing will normally require the company to keep a minimum balance in its non-interest paying current account. Thus, a rate of 5 per cent in the United States with minimum balance requirement of 20 per cent of the loan will be the equivalent of a 6.2 per cent interest rate in the United Kingdom on an overdraft basis. . . .

Fringe Benefits

. . . Experienced international business executives are convinced that the listing of securities in local markets and borrowing from local banks and other financial institutions can provide significant benefits to the multi-national firms. This practice, generally described as "good business," involves access to various business services, good will and improved public relations.

Joint Ventures

Joint ventures with indigenous private interests or even with local governments in foreign countries can reduce the financial demand on the multi-national firm and open up new alternatives for overseas financing.

Special Inducements

Special inducements offered by many foreign countries to firms for establishing certain types of industries or for locating in specified development areas can greatly influence the source and cost of overseas financing. In Western Europe, for example, a number of firms have secured multi-million dollar financing at remarkable low rates of interest by locating in geographical areas receiving special development attention. In many cases, the companies would have normally chosen such locations for their operations. The availability of special financial inducements in the underdeveloped areas is even more impressive.

Developing Local Capital Markets

Presently higher costs of financing may be offset in some cases by prospective future benefits from contributing to the expansion and increased efficiency of local capital markets. Furthermore, such contributions toward improving local capital markets through use can stimulate the overall rate of economic growth in a country and provide increased expansion opportunities for the multi-national firm. . . .

45..... Financing Capital-Goods Trade*

LEE C. NEHRT

Indiana University

Capital equipment is a significant factor in trade of both industrialized and underdeveloped countries. For the former, its importance is in exports . . . [— ranging recently] from 20 per cent in Italy to over 40 per cent in the United Kingdom. For the underdeveloped countries, on the other hand, capital equipment is vital to the import trade. In their desire to industrialize as rapidly as possible, these countries utilize . . . controls to assure that . . . sparse foreign exchange earnings are available for the importance of capital equipment.

However, . . . most of the world trade in capital equipment flows between the industrialized countries. As their economies expand, the demand for additional capital equipment far exceeds the demands of the underdeveloped countries. At the same time, each of the industrialized countries has a comparative advantage in certain types of capital equipment; none are self-sufficient. . . .

Most of the purchasers of capital equipment in the industrialized countries are able to pay for these imports with terms of less than six months. Some of the equipment, particularly in the case of U.S. exports, goes to Canadian and West European subsidiaries of U.S. companies, and if credit is extended it may only be a bookkeeping transaction. Other capital equipment importers will pay cash for the entire amount at the time of delivery, because they are sufficiently liquid — having budgeted for that particular capital expansion, or, because they can arrange for a line of credit at their own bank and avoid asking for credit from the exporter. Also, some of these buyers in the industrialized countries will only ask for short-term credit (less than six months), giving them time to arrange for credit with their bank, or time to obtain the necessary funds from the local money or capital market. Hence, a relatively small portion

* Taken and adapted from *Financing Capital Equipment Exports*, Scranton: International Textbook Company, 1966, pp. 1–5.

of the trade in capital equipment between industrialized countries gives rise to transactions where the exporter must extend credit on terms longer than ninety days or six months. The situation in the underdeveloped countries, however, is much different. There are, to be sure, some subsidiaries whose parent companies are located in an industrialized country and whose finances would permit them to pay cash. There are also a few local firms which have no need for extended credits. But, most of the companies are in dire need of the longest possible terms of payment for capital equipment imports. And more importantly, the governments of the developing countries normally follow policies of forbidding the use of foreign exchange for cash payments for capital equipment imports. Either foreign exchange regulations or administrative discretion pushes the importer into demanding the longest possible terms, so as to shift the effect on foreign exchange reserves to a future date.

Consequently, in exporting capital equipment to the underdeveloped countries, the burden falls upon the manufacturer to provide this credit. The area of competition tends, consequently, to move away from quality and price, and toward the area of credit terms. Within a given industrialized country, the firm with a stronger capital structure or better access to outside capital sources can offer better credit terms than the smaller manufacturer who cannot, himself, carry all or part of the credit of these relatively large transactions. Between countries, as for example, when a British manufacturer is competing with a French one for the sale of equipment to Argentina, and both are in need of help in financing the credit which the Argentine importer is demanding, the country whose banking community is more cooperative is likely to gain the export.

This raises the problem of a competitive war, between the industrialized countries, to provide capital equipment exporters with the best possible financing facilities. Here, the governments of the countries become directly involved. . . . [The] commercial banks in most of them are unable to provide the necessary financing. Consequently the governments, through their central banks or some other specialized institutions, provide a rediscounting facility to relieve the pressure from the commercial banks, making them more willing to extend the credit. However, the risk of loss when extending this credit to importers in underdeveloped countries is often so great that neither the exporter nor his bank would be willing to do so. Consequently, the most important involvement of the governments is in insuring the credit. For, once the credit has been insured, there is less difficulty in finding a financial institution to discount it, particularly when there is a governmental institution standing by to rediscount it.

. . .

As indicated . . . , a large percentage of capital equipment exports to industrialized countries are paid for in cash or on short-term credit.

In addition, a considerable amount of capital equipment is exported as part of a large project, where the entire project is paid for on long-term credit, over ten, fifteen, or twenty years, particularly in the under-developed countries. This leaves a middle area of "medium-term" financing.

. . .

In the United States, the United Kingdom, and a number of other countries, medium-term export credit is defined to include the period of six months to five years. . . .

Capital goods are particularly appropriate to the use of medium-term credit: the industrial buyer uses them to earn a profit and they pay for themselves over a period of years, in the medium-term range.

. . .

The importance of capital equipment in the exports of many of the industrialized countries, and the importance of medium-term credit for financing these exports to underdeveloped countries, has led, as noted . . . , to a competition between the governments to provide better and better credit and insurance facilities to capital goods exporters. The governments recognized that this type of credit war was not desirable. Consequently, representatives from the various countries meet periodically, through an organization known as the "Berne Union," to discuss export credit terms and to agree on voluntary limits. . . .

There [also] are other areas of competition besides the length of credit term available to the exporters. Among the most important are the following: credit-insurance premiums, which vary from country to country; the cost and availability of the credit itself, which are improved through special, governmental facilities; one government will refuse to insure more credit to a given underdeveloped country because of the level of its current foreign debt payments (because it is "loaned-up") while another government will follow a contrary policy; the speed with which the pertinent government agencies can give tentative and final approvals to requests for insurance or financing, which affects the speed and flexibility with which an exporter can bid on and negotiate a contract; the down payment required from the purchaser by the time of delivery, which will vary from less than 10 per cent to over 30 per cent; and, the amount of uninsured credit the exporter is asked to hold for his own account, or finance outside the lower cost export credit system, which varies from zero to 25 per cent. All of the above areas are those in which governments can and do affect the competitive position of their capital equipment exporters. . . .

D..... Investment and Operations: The Economic Impact

Attitudes — favorable and unfavorable — toward private foreign investment do exist, both in the host country and in the capital-supplier country. Many problems are posed by such investment, both when it is undertaken and later. But, fully as important as either of these sets of considerations is the matter of the *economic impact* of the investment. Is it "good" — or "bad"? The present section is devoted to an examination of this question.

Professor Behrman provides a framework for an overall pro-and-con analysis. As is evident in his presentation, there are many measures of potential merit (or liability) — ranging from the training of personnel (in host countries) to a weighing by means of cost-benefit, to effects on the balance of payments, and so on.

Professor Kreinin, next, focuses specifically on the matter of employment impact on the capital-supplier country. Does investment in foreign production capacity decrease, or increase, employment at home?

Professor Bell examines balance-of-payments impact on the United States by virtue of capital (and related) transactions. Recent governmental counter-action serves as evidence of an official conclusion of balance-of-payments impact having been adverse. Professor Bell's analysis of the country's record supports this conclusion, at least in degree.

Finally, Professors Davis and Blomstrom point to a special benefit of private direct investment abroad. Particularly in underdeveloped countries, the presence of foreign companies can serve as a catalytic agent in prompting and upgrading indigenous enterprise. The authors cite cases of on-the-scene involvement along these lines on the part of American companies.

46..... The Economic Impact

of Private Direct

Investment*

JACK N. BEHRMAN

University of North Carolina

. . . [The following seeks to analyze] the effects of U.S. direct foreign investment on the economies of the host countries and upon the U.S. . . .

Effects on the Host Country

The discussion of the effects of direct investment on the host country is organized according to the following topics: (1) additions to the real resources of the economy; (2) the impact on output, market structures, and prices; (3) the shifts in resource use and factor rewards; (4) the potential rise in GNP and real income; and (5) changes in international trade and payments.

Additions to Real Resources

The additions to real resources are three: personnel, techniques, and capital.

Personnel. The underprivileged nations are characterized by a lack of adequately trained managerial and technical personnel.[1] Although many are trying to remedy this through educational efforts, there is an immediate need for such individuals. Direct private foreign investment helps

---

* Taken and adapted from "Economic Effects of Private Direct Investment," in Raymond F. Mikesell (ed.), *U.S. Private and Government Investment Abroad*, Eugene, Ore.: University of Oregon Books, 1962, pp. 137–164.

[1] Evidence of the nature and extent of this lack is provided in Harbison and Myers, *Management in the Industrial World* (New York, 1959), chapters on India, Egypt, and Chile. See also John Fayerweather, *The Executive Overseas* (Syracuse, 1959).

to meet this need through either the actual transfer of officials or the training of local personnel by visits of U.S. officials and technicians abroad or by trips of foreign personnel to the parent company.

The value of personnel transfers is not only in the addition to the existing stock of managers and technicians, but in reorienting domestic personnel toward their roles in enterprise and production. . . .

Techniques and Research Developments. When a firm transfers personnel or capital abroad, techniques of various sorts are made available for increasing productivity in the foreign country. Foreign firms not only benefit from the knowledge of well established processes and techniques, but also from the research continuously carried on by U.S. enterprises. Research is the keystone of growth providing both the new products and the new techniques which raise industrial productivity. The advantage of a tie with an American company (or any technically advanced company) is that the results of research are obtained without large financial outlays.[2] . . .

Capital. The addition to the productive capital resources of the recipient country is not measured simply by the outflow of capital from the investing country. Not only are profits reinvested, but there is a substantial mobilization of domestic capital as well. The transfer of personnel and new techniques from the parent firm also enhance the productivity of local capital. . . .

Production, Market Structures, and Prices

One effect of the addition of real resources is to alter types of products made and their costs in various industries. The market structure in the industry affected may also change; and, as a consequence of these changes, prices are likely to alter.

Production. Production will undoubtedly increase with the addition of a new plant or company in an industry of the host country, with the expansion of a line of products in an established company, the addition of totally new products, or through a reduction of costs and a consequent increase in sales of existing items. Different production results occur, however, according to which of these is the stimulus to greater production. . . .

Market Structure. The structure of the market in which the products are sold may be altered in the direction of either greater competition or

---

[2] See J. H. Dunning, *American Investment in British Manufacturing Industry* (London, 1958), p. 167. Dunning estimates, for example, that of the $1,600 million which American industry spent on private (i.e., nongovernmental) research in 1955, 25 to 30 per cent was made directly available to British companies; this $400 to $500 million was more than twice the estimated sum spent by the whole of British industry on private research. . . .

greater concentration. Sellers of close substitutes would, in either event, suffer greater competition. . . .

Prices. The effect on prices of a cost-reducing or a product-introducing foreign investment or licensing operation cannot be determined in advance unless something is known of the market structure into which the product enters. The monopoly privilege extended by patent or trademark coverage may permit maintenance or increase of the price as a result of improved quality (or market differentiation). Output may still be expanded with a shift in the demand resulting from changed preferences, induced by advertising and better sales techniques.

There may also be a direct effect on price arising from the type of remittance made for the transferred resources. Different forms of payment for a license, technical aid, or capital may have different effects on pricing. For example, a royalty based on output would tend to be included as a given percentage of costs for all levels of output, and one based on net sales would be deducted from price at various levels (thus affecting marginal revenue). Both of these methods alter the optimum point of production and change the price of the product as compared to a method of payment which did not alter the optimum level. At the other extreme, a return in the form of a share of net profits, as under an equity interest, may not have any effect on optimum output or price. . . .

In sum, it may be stated that the transfer of real resources is likely to cause an increase in production and employment; it tends to cause an improvement in the quality of the commodities produced in the industry and by its suppliers;[3] it is likely to disrupt existing market conditions, but in different ways, depending on the extension of exclusive rights and on the previous market conditions; and it will probably reduce market prices. The distinct benefits to the consumer include the following:

1. He obtains a better adapted product, and market demands are given closer attention by the U.S. firm.
2. He obtains better servicing of the product.
3. He obtains new and different products, which although available as imports, might not be known to him for lack of informative advertising.
4. He obtains the products at a lower price — as a result of a removal of transport costs which would otherwise raise the price from between 10 to 30 per cent, a removal of tariff duties averaging between 10 and 20 per cent, and in some cases a reduction of production costs under those in the United States.[4]

[3] See Rottenberg (Simon Rottenberg, "How United States Business Firms Promote Technological Progress," in the National Planning Association's series on *Technical Cooperation in Latin America,* Aug. 1957), pp. 47–56 and 60–75.
[4] Dunning estimated that "in probably *nine cases out of ten* the British consumer is able to buy his product at a lower price than if it were imported." *Op cit.,* p. 233.

Resource Shifts and Factor Payments

In the less-developed countries, a substantial proportion of the labor supply as well as other productive factors are either unemployed or underemployed. On the other hand, in Western Europe the U.S. investor finds labor and other productive factors more or less fully employed. Resource shifts resulting from foreign investment have different impacts on factor prices and upon domestic industry depending upon these and other structural conditions.

Resource Shifts. As capital and technology move into a given industry in the host country, there is additional demand for labor, materials, and land, as well as for domestic capital funds. There is a flow of previously unemployed resources into the enterprise; or, there is a shift from less well-paid endeavors to the new enterprise, with unemployed resources moving into positions which were vacated.

Assuming less than full employment, it is conceivable that there is merely an increased demand for a variety of domestic factors and that the shifts cause no great hardship on any industry.

On the other hand, if there is relatively full employment *or* if the new enterprise adopts cost-reducing methods of production and sells in competition with domestic producers of the same or similar commodities, it is probable that marginal producers in the industry will be forced out of business. This will release resources which can be taken up by the new firm without inflationary pressure.

If the international transfer of resources involves an introduction of a new product, the shift in domestic resources is from other industries or unemployed areas into the new undertaking. Again, it is conceivable that no producer is adversely affected. But, the consequent rise in costs of factors may force some existing enterprises out of business.

It is for these reasons that there have been complaints in some of the developing countries that domestic enterprise and initiative is being swamped by U.S. enterprises. Thus, when a domestic company enters a new field of production and opens the market, a U.S. company may enter with more efficient techniques and thereby lower costs. In bidding for domestic resources and cutting costs (and prices), foreign enterprise may edge the domestic producer out of business and stifle that very (domestic) initiative which foreign private enterprise is supposed to foster. . . .

The added demand for resources, resulting in higher factor payments, has not always been welcomed — as in periods of overfull employment in Europe, but it has been eagerly received in most of the less-developed countries.

Factor Payments. The effect of resource shifts is to increase the factor payments when resource supplies in one geographic area or specific category become tight. There is likely to be a gradual increase in payments to *all* domestic factors, including capital! Though it is usually argued that the inflow of capital will reduce the return to capital in the recipient country,[5] the fact that foreign investors increase the demand for domestic capital casts doubt on this conclusion. This is more readily seen when a joint venture is involved, but it is also true for those wholly-owned subsidiaries which borrow on the domestic market for short-term and other capital needs. Thus, there is no immediate reduction of returns to capital; rather, there may be an increase. A partial offset to the increased demand for capital arises from the higher volume of savings generated by the new enterprises, and by the higher level of national income.

Wages are also likely to rise in the long run; short-run increases will occur mainly in the industry which is receiving the inflow of foreign resources, as a consequence of bidding away existing labor and skilled foremen. The availability of unemployed labor will tend to keep general wage rates down, however. Also, the increase in the supply of capital with rising returns will tend to cause a substitution of capital for labor, thus limiting the tendency for wages to rise in the short run. However, in the longer run, as productivity of labor increases in the newly formed industries or in those receiving new technology, wages should rise, supplemented by the general pressure of rising employment. If, in the short run, wages do not rise with productivity, capital formation is faster; the greater use of machinery will raise productivity and wages in the long run. Finally, in many of the less-developed countries, union activities, often with the support of government, assure that wages and fringe benefits are pushed up rapidly even though unemployment remains high....

GNP and Real Income

The increased production arising from introduction of a new product, or the expansion of sales of existing products, and the increase in factor payments, are all reflected in a larger gross national product in the host country. Thus, production outlays and foreign taxes paid by U.S. direct investment enterprises abroad equalled $31 billion in 1957 (excluding imports from the U.S. and depreciation, goods purchased by trading companies and intercorporate sales of petroleum). Of this total, only $1.5 billion was for interest and foreign payments; $4.5 billion was for direct and indirect taxes (60 per cent in petroleum), $18 billion for materials and services, and $7 billion for wages (50 per cent manufacturing). The increase in wages raises consumer demand, widening the market and providing support for further expansion. The expansion is spread to secondary industries serving the U.S. affiliates; this expansion

---

[5] The analysis that leads to the conclusion of diminishing marginal returns to capital in the host country is usually based on static assumptions and does not take into account complementary demands for capital and other factors.

brings internal economies. External economies are gained through rising demand for materials and widening of the market. . . .

International Trade and Payments

The rise in GNP, shifts in resources, and changing factor payments will affect the long-run composition and direction of international trade and the balance of payments.

Trade. The shift in resource use in the host country from relatively labor-intensive enterprises to those which are more capital-intensive brings a realignment of the comparative advantages in international trade. Resource compositions are made more nearly similar as a result of the inflow of foreign capital, personnel, and technology. The basic differences in factor endowments will stem mainly from differences in raw materials and the training of labor (or the attitude of labor and management toward their jobs). These last differences will in time be removed or modified and the differences in raw material availability will be reduced by world trade in these items. It may be expected that the less-developed economies will gradually be enabled to duplicate the pattern of production in the more industrialized countries.

This result will lead to a reduction of trade in items formerly exchanged between these two groups and an expansion in new lines. This has already been seen in the shift in composition of trade among the industrial countries. The developing economies will begin to process their own raw materials, and they will want to export the semi-finished or finished goods, rather than re-importing them from the industrialized countries. Conversely, apart from the flow of basically indigenous commodities, the trade which occurs will probably be among goods producible in many countries but made competitive because of specialization to gain economies of scale through serving a wider market. Comparative advantage will rest less on specialization by entire industrial groupings and more on specialization in production of separate items within an industrial category which permits cost reduction.[6] . . .

Payments. The aggregate payments position of the capital-exporting and capital-importing countries will be altered according to the net change in the exports and imports. . . . Immediately the balance of payments will be affected by imports needed for production by the newly established firms. This is particularly important in the less-developed countries which must import much of their capital goods, but even countries such as Germany require imports for manufacturing production.

[6] Thus, Britain may have an advantage in new ideas and manufacturing costs while the U.S. companies show an advantage in application of ideas prior to the manufacturing stage and in commercialization and marketing. Since the elements of the U.S. advantage can be transferred, manufacturing occurs in Britain. Any loss of this cost advantage will cause a relocation of industrial activity.

. . . The drain on foreign exchange from these demands is, of course, offset by direct exports. . . .

[Also, a] direct charge on foreign exchange earnings arises through the payments for personnel, licenses, and earnings on invested capital. In most countries, there is a fairly close scrutiny of the "burden" of such payments, and contracts for import of U.S. capital and technology will not be approved for dollar payment if the government considers the burden too great. . . . In some instances, however, the gain from exports of the newly introduced product more than offsets the drain from payments to the U.S. investor. . . .

In addition to these direct payments, pressure on the exchanges may arise from a high or rising propensity to import as real and money incomes increase. In many of the less-developed countries there is a fairly high marginal propensity to import (a relatively elastic income demand for imports) so that rising incomes increase imports considerably. The same increase in incomes also tends to withdraw potential exports from the world market.

These trends may be contained by direct and indirect controls, and they may be fully offset through the growth of export capacity and by import substitution. . . .

Impacts on the U.S. Economy

An analysis of the effects of direct investment outflow on the U.S. economy is perhaps more complex and less amenable to empirical investigation than a consideration of the effects of foreign investment on a capital importing country. The discussion in this section is limited to: (1) the direct costs of and returns from sending personnel, capital, and technology abroad; (2) the effects of factor payments in the United States; (3) changes in the pattern and volume of international trade; (4) effects on the balance of payments; and (5) the broader policy implications of these impacts. . . .

Direct Costs and Returns

The direct costs of foreign private investment in subsidiaries or in licenses can be measured according to the value of the real resources transferred. They include personnel, home office time, research and development, and capital; these should be more than matched by the discounted value of the direct returns for the endeavor, to be profitable to the U.S. investor.

The costs of personnel sent overseas are frequently borne by the recipient in that both transportation and salary are paid by the receiving company. But there are also some direct costs in the loss of experienced personnel, both managerial and technical, by the parent company. . . . The shorter the stay abroad, the more readily calculable the costs but the less readily calculable the returns. . . .

The allocation of research and development expenses to foreign operations is equally difficult — in concept and in practice. The familiar problem of joint costs arises vis-à-vis each development forthcoming as well as the division between foreign and domestic uses of research costs "fixed" in accord with the domestic operations of the company. Any allocation of such costs would appear highly arbitrary.

The cost of capital transferred can be more closely determined through comparison with *expected* returns from use of a similar amount in other pursuits. Again, precise calculations are impossible and expectations may be greatly disappointed or fulfilled. . . . If we exclude petroleum, differences in earnings at home and abroad do not appear to be substantial. Over the period 1950–1958, it appears that average earnings were slightly higher for U.S. affiliates in Europe than average earnings in the United States. . . .

Earnings ratios in Canada and Latin America have been consistently lower than average U.S. ratios, since 1955. The Department of Commerce asserts that: "In general, there is much less difference between domestic manufacturing returns, as a whole, and returns on direct foreign investments in manufacturing, than there is between the various categories of manufacturing (chemicals, machinery, etc.) within the United States."[7] This attests to the view that investment abroad is as much induced by an expanding market for a given product line (industry output) as by *differentially* high earnings. . . .

Factor Payments

Although there are sizable transfers of resources overseas, only the use of personnel and capital are lost to the U.S. economy. These "losses" have a significant impact on factor payments. And even the shifts of technology (which involve no "loss" of know-how to the U.S. economy) have an indirect repercussion on factor payments in the United States.

Since there is a reduction in the supply of personnel and a widening of the market for managerial and technical talents, the reward to this factor in the United States should rise relative to other returns. The same result should occur for capital, even if the returns abroad are not greater than at home. The diminished domestic supply and enlarged demand, as the world market is served, should raise the marginal returns in the United States and thus increase the relative share of capital.

If management and capital are to receive higher *relative* shares, labor must accept a smaller *proportion* of the total product. Currently in the United States there is a growing appreciation of the effects of private foreign investment on wages *and* of wages on the movement of capital overseas. . . .

There is little doubt that, in terms of its *relative* share, labor is not benefited from the expansion of direct foreign investment by American business in competitive enterprises abroad. However, labor should not be

[7] *Census, 1957*, p. 51.

concerned simply with its *relative* share, but rather with its *absolute* rewards. With the decline in import prices and the improved efficiency of production which will be required to adjust to changes in world trade, laboring groups could benefit in terms of *real* income, provided there is a net gain in the real national product from the direct foreign investment. This net gain will arise partly from an expansion (or maintenance) of the volume of exports and from income receipts from abroad.

Pattern of Trade

There are four major characteristics of U.S. foreign trade which are being affected by the growing volume of direct foreign investment: aggregate volume, volume compared to domestic production and to production abroad by U.S. associates, composition of trade, and geographic direction of trade.

The volume of U.S. exports is directly or indirectly increased by the capital expenditures of U.S. enterprises operating abroad. A portion of the expenditures may be for capital equipment supplied by a U.S. firm which serves as domestic supplier of similar equipment. Even if the bulk of the expenditures financed by the U.S. capital outflow are made for local labor, materials, and equipment, the added purchasing power will lead to larger U.S. exports. Indeed, if the U.S. capital outflow is to provide additional real resources abroad, other than adding to reserves, the capital must be transferred through an export surplus. On the other hand, the transfer of earnings on the invested capital and payments for services or licenses reduces the host country's capacity to import. . . .

Although the process of continual foreign investment tends to expand trade somewhat, this may be offset by an increase in the production of commodities abroad which are competitive to U.S. exports. . . .

In addition, the composition of trade is likely to change. U.S. trade with highly industrial countries will be dominated more and more by new products and by specialized high-technology items. Exports of consumer goods are decreasing relative to capital goods items to the less-developed countries. The more industrially advanced of the newly developing nations are beginning to produce their own capital goods and durable consumer goods items. As economies diversify and produce domestic substitutes for a wide range of imports, the nature of import demand will change. There will be an increased demand for industrial specialties while exports of standardized commodities will tend to fall. . . .

Considerable specialization among nations will no doubt remain in raw materials. Shifts in domestic production toward industrial items in the newly developing countries may mean a movement in the terms of trade in favor of agricultural commodities. It may be wise for the United States, which has a comparative advantage in production of foodstuffs and cotton, to give increasing attention to exports of agricultural items. . . .

Balance of Payments Effects

A complete analysis of the impact of direct foreign investment on the U.S. balance of payments involves a consideration of not only the relationship between capital outflow and the remittance of earnings, but also of the effects on imports and exports, including the terms of trade. Insofar as the direct balance of payments effects are concerned, direct foreign investment appears to have made a substantial contribution to the U.S. balance of payments position. . . .

This does not mean that if during any particular year the government had halted new direct capital outflow, our net balance of payments position might not have been improved *for that particular year.* However, direct investment must be regarded as a continuous process, and any attempt to shut off the flow of direct investment capital abroad is very likely to redound on earnings within a few years so that, say, over a ten-year period there would be a net loss of foreign exchange from the restrictive action. . . .

When it comes to assessing the indirect impact of direct private investment on the U.S. balance of payments, we run into factors which are difficult, if not impossible, to quantify. As we have seen, direct investment tends to increase the market for certain exports. At the same time U.S. firms operating abroad produce commodities which compete with U.S. exports or are shipped to the United States in competition with domestic production. On the other hand, direct investment in raw materials, of which the United States is in short supply and must import from abroad, tends to improve our terms of trade and, hence, our trade balance. . . . It should also be said that U.S. direct investments abroad frequently provide a market for commodities and services of complementary industries which may be supplied from the United States. Investment in sales and distribution operations and in plants which assemble U.S.-produced components often result in an expansion of the market for U.S. exports. . . . Hence, there is a very close relationship between direct investment and exports, and in many fields the choice between taking orders for shipments abroad and going abroad to participate in some part of the production process is simply not open.

Policy Implications

Assuming no substantial increase in restrictions on foreign investment by capital importing countries, either in Western Europe, Canada, or in the major industrial countries of Latin America, it seems likely that direct investment activity will continue to rise, both in terms of the value of foreign investment and in the number of foreign affiliates. The movement of capital, enterprise, and techniques will not only change the pattern of world trade, but will probably grow at a faster rate than U.S. exports. (Undoubtedly, the increased trade among regional trading associations, such as the European Common Market and the Latin American

Free Trade Area, will be at the considerable expense of imports from outside of the regional groupings.) The United States can do little to stop this development. Even if it should decide to restrict the transfer of direct capital abroad, it would not help its own position because firms from other countries would take the place of U.S. enterprise. The shift in the pattern and character of trade from standardized industrial commodities to high technology and new commodities, and the tendency for movements of capital, enterprise, and technology to substitute for trade in commodities, requires that we maintain as a nation a high degree of flexibility of our industry in order to adjust promptly and efficiently to these dynamic movements. This flexibility must permeate all sectors of the domestic economy — both export and import competing industries — and involves a greater willingness of our producers to make such investments and affiliations abroad as are necessary to maintain or expand their markets. Given these conditions, it does not appear that a case can be made either for subsidizing U.S. investment within Europe or for restricting it. Government assistance which provides better information on market conditions and investment opportunities abroad for U.S. firms would appear to be highly desirable. . . .

47 ..... Foreign Investment and Domestic Employment*

MORDECHAI E. KREININ

Michigan State University

The past decade witnessed an enormous increase in American private investments overseas. . . .

There are many reasons for the growing trend of overseas expansion, not the least of which are lower labor costs, expanding overseas markets, and the erection of tariff barriers against American-made products. These stimulants appear strong enough to counteract the special risks and problems involved. . . . In addition it has been the official policy of the American government to encourage foreign investments by American enterprises. . . .

This official policy does not enjoy the unqualified support of the entire business community. One of the common allegations against the promotion of foreign investments is that the export of capital would result in export of jobs from the United States. . . .

Flaws and Misconceptions

The rationale behind . . . [the foregoing] argument is simple. If our capital is used to increase production facilities overseas, commodities produced there will displace American exports and may even compete with United States products in our domestic market. The major flaw in the argument lies in its over-simplification. It overlooks the crucial fact

* Taken and adapted from "Foreign Investments and Domestic Employment," *Business Topics* (East Lansing, Mich.: Bureau of Business and Economic Research, Graduate School of Business Administration, Michigan State University), Winter 1961, pp. 58–62.

that the increase in overseas production will necessarily be accompanied by rising foreign income and imports.

Most people conceive of international trade as an exchange of manufactured commodities from industrial nations for raw materials and agricultural products from the primary-materials-producing nations. It would follow from this assumption that the latter nations constitute our major export markets, and that these markets would contract as they become industrialized. Nothing, however, can be further from the truth. Contrary to this common misconception, most world trade consists of the exchange of highly specialized manufactured commodities among the industrialized nations.

The Pattern of Trade

Statistical evidence shows that more than half of the manufactured products exported from industrialized countries today go to other industrialized countries. All other countries, accounting for three-fourths of the world population, receive less than half of these exports. Per capita import of manufactured commodities in 1955 amounted to $53 in industrial nations compared to $11 in non-industrial nations. Thus on a per capita basis the industrial countries were almost a five-times-better market for their own manufactures that was the market furnished by the non-industrial countries. The reason for this phenomenon is not difficult to find. Most of the income and therefore the purchasing power in the world is in the hands of industrial nations. They are the only ones able to import industrial commodities, while residents of poorer nations must spend all their incomes on the bare necessities of life, most of which are produced locally.

These figures are consistent with historical data showing that increased production of manufactured goods has normally been accompanied by increased imports of manufactured products. This fact was well documented for a period of half a century preceding the second world war by the League of Nations study *Industrialization and Foreign Trade* (Geneva, 1945). Once industrialization proceeds beyond the early stages, the increased imports consist of consumer as well as capital goods. Countries tend increasingly to specialize in the particular sub-categories of manufacturing in which they enjoy comparative advantages, and to import the rest. And with the increase in their productivity and living standards, they have a greater capacity to import.

These data apply with particular cogency to the export trade of the United States. . . . [The] well-developed industrial countries constitute our major export markets. By helping in the development of underdeveloped nations, we shall contribute to the attainment of higher living standards, and to the expansion of our overseas markets. Our export markets and employment oppportunities at home are thus likely to expand rather than contract in the long run as a result of this process.

This does not mean that the American economy will not have to undergo any adjustments as backward nations develop. The pattern of their demand will undoubtedly shift as they go through the various stages of development, causing changes in the composition of our exports to them. But since foreign trade in general occupies only a minor share in the American economy, it is highly unlikely that the required adjustments will be of significant proportions. . . .

48 ..... Foreign Investment and the U. S. Balance of Payments*

PHILIP W. BELL

Haverford College

... [Some] central findings of this study may be summarized as follows:

1. Shifts in the flow of private capital, in particular in U.S. private capital flowing overseas, have been a major cause of our deteriorating balance-of-payments position since 1956. We do not say that the existing, large outward flow of capital is the source of our difficulties, and therefore corrective action must, of necessity, be taken in this sphere. Any time, positive or negative, can be singled out as the basic source of difficulty, thus necessitating correction — too few exports, too many imports, too much travel, foreign aid, etc. All that we have said is that U.S. private long- and short-term capital outflow increased by over $2 billion between 1952–56 and 1957–61, while the basic balance turned adverse by $600 million, the financial balance by $1.3 billion.

Some of this increased outflow was immediately and directly offset by increased export receipts — a considerable portion of the increase in direct investment (perhaps as much as 20 to 25 per cent) because it went to purchase equipment which was produced in the United States for new plant abroad, as well as probably at least one-half the net outflow of U.S. short-term capital, which went into export credits. Some of the increased outflow began coming back more or less automatically, but only after a delay — in the form of dividends and management fees in the case of

* Taken and adapted from "Factors Affecting the United States Balance of Payments," (Private Capital Movements and the U.S. Balance-of-Payments Position), *Hearings Before the Subcommittee on International Exchange and Payments of the Joint Economic Committee,* 87th Congress, 2nd Session, 1962, pp. 458–466.

direct investment capital, repayments in the case of export finance, and interest on new portfolio securities issued in this country. But at best it would seem that the increased annual outflows of $2 billion a year in 1957–61 were being more or less directly offset by increased inflows on the average of only half that amount, so that the net drain of the private capital outflow on our balance of payments was still far and away the most important cause of our deteriorating balance-of-payments position unless unusually large favorable indirect repercussions were at work in the case of capital outflows, which did not exist for other types of increased outflows. It seems highly doubtful that this was in fact the case.

2. All types of U.S. capital outflow have contributed to the drain, with the exception of transactions in existing private long-term securities. Here the United States has more than held its own in recent years as foreign purchases of U.S. stocks and corporate bonds, mostly by Europeans, have run ahead of U.S. purchases of foreign stocks and corporate bonds, again mostly in Europe. In addition, foreigners have made substantial purchases of U.S. Government securities, some of which should be considered a private capital inflow.

The net 5-year drain of 1957–61 as compared with 1952–56 can be thought of as being split probably more or less equally, among direct U.S. investment outlays less directly related inflows; the excess of net purchases (mostly new issues) of new foreign securities by U.S. residents over and above foreign purchases of U.S. securities, less a small amount of interest receipts; and various types of short-term capital flows. But the timing of these three types of flow differs — new security issues in this country reached a peak in 1958 and then slackened off, direct investment reached one peak in 1957, another in 1960, but has generally continued heavy, while substantial outflows of U.S. short-term capital did not take place until 1960–61.

3. Growth in U.S. direct investment, particularly in manufacturing operations in Europe (which alone comprises one-third of the increase in U.S. direct investment abroad between 1952–56 and 1957–61), has had a serious deteriorating effect on our balance of payments, and the effect will not be recouped for many years if the new, higher level of investment continues to increase, or even simply continues at the present level, which is probably the minimum annual outflow which can be expected. The evidence suggests that it takes 10 to 15 years before the related inflows catch up to a stream of investment outlays in European manufacturing operations, and the investment stream therefore begins to "pay off" in balance-of-payments terms. And if there is substantial substitution of the output of U.S. subsidiaries in Europe for U.S. exports, either to Europe or to the less developed countries, the "catching up" period will be lengthened considerably.

The full balance-of-payments effects of the other types of direct investment which have increased substantially in recent years — petroleum investment (including extensive investment in refineries and distribution outlets in Europe), which amounts to more than one-third of the total outflow between 1952–56 and 1957–61, and investment in mining, trade, and miscellaneous other facilities — cannot be readily measured because little is known of the volume of exports which may be related to this investment. Practically all drilling equipment comes from this country, however, and presumably an extensive amount of refinery equipment also does. Furthermore dividend returns have been relatively high in petroleum. It seems likely, therefore, that petroleum investment produces, net, a smaller drain than investment in manufacturing.

Investment in mining is very much related to U.S. needs. Here, as in the case of petroleum, there may be some substitution of U.S. imports for home production, with attendant adverse effects on the balance of payments — iron ore from Labrador and Venezuela rather than from Minnesota, lumber from Canada rather than from the Northwest, et cetera. In fact, however, it seems likely that most such shifts from domestic production to purchases from abroad would take place with or without the establishment or expansion of U.S. facilities abroad — because of structural considerations (perhaps U.S. resources, for example, are nearing physical or at least economic exhaustion). U.S. production of these products is not expandable, and therefore new demands with U.S. growth must be met from foreign sources. If U.S. facilities are not established overseas, we would be forced to buy from foreign producers. The balance-of-payments drain of such investment in general, then, is outflows less related dividend inflows less related exports (of capital equipment), not this plus imports substituting for home production.

Finally, there has been considerable direct investment in trade outlets abroad. Presumably such investment has a substantial favorable effect on U.S. exports, and therefore the balance-of-payments drain is small, if not negative.

4. Growth in the net outflow of funds between 1952–56 and 1957–61 involving investment in private long-term securities here and abroad was, at least on the surface, about two-thirds as large as the growth in U.S. direct investment. To some extent this net adverse flow was probably offset by an increased net inflow of funds, particularly from Europe but also from Canada, Latin America, and elsewhere, involving private foreign purchases of U.S. long-term Government securities. No information is available on who holds long-term U.S. Government securities abroad, and the Commerce Department simply includes any change in total holdings as a change in U.S. liquid liabilities in balance-of-payments statistics. But some portion, perhaps as much as a quarter, of the increase (between 1952–56 and 1957–61) should be treated as "autonomous" private long-term capital and thus be put "above the line" in balance-of-payments data, offsetting part of the net U.S. outflow reported on private capital account. . . .

5. When we come to short-term capital movements, we find that the substantial growth in the net outflow of funds between 1952–56 and 1957–61 was practically all concentrated in the 2 years 1960–61. As is well known, this 2-year outflow reached astonishing proportions. . . .

When all is said and done, we conclude that only $600 to $800 million of the $2.6 billion of recorded U.S. short-term capital outflow over the 2 years 1960–61 (excluding $175 million in short-term loans by U.S. banks to foreign banks and officials) can be considered as having had an adverse effect on our balance-of-payments position. The rest of the outflow, probably, came directly back to the United States as payment for exports which would not have been purchased had U.S. credit not been made available. What proportion of this $600–800 million outflow was primarily due to the widening of interest rate differentials here and abroad, that is, would not have gone abroad were it not for this factor, is impossible to say. We have been able to uncover evidence suggesting some sensitivity to interest rates in a number of cases, involving more than half of the $600–$800 million outflow. But this does not necessarily imply that taking advantage of higher interest rates abroad was in fact the primary motive involved in the movement. The primary motive may have been tax considerations, or working balance needs, both of which dictated a rising outflow over the period studied. And interest rates appear to explain a relatively small proportion of the deviations about the trend in these outflows. We would expect to find a high correlation in terms of deviations about the trend if the capital flow were very sensitive to interest rates. . . .

6. We come finally to one last consideration. We have tried to analyze as carefully as we could the effects of recorded capital movements on the U.S. balance-of-payments position over the last 10 years. We have suggested that the recorded increase in the outflow of long-term capital over the period, offset in part by increased inflows related to the increase in outflow, has contributed substantially to the deterioration of our balance-of-payments position. Looking at the gross outflow figures alone overstates the adverse effect, but nevertheless there has been, net, an adverse effect.

In the last 2 years the deteriorating effect of outflows on long-term account has diminished, but an enormous increase in outflows on U.S. short-term account has completely swamped the slight improvement shown. We have argued that a substantial part of the 1960–61 short-term outflow, which has continued on into 1962, but on a somewhat smaller scale, has probably not served as a net drain on our position, but rather went to finance U.S. exports which might not have been sold without provision of credit. Nevertheless, at least 20 per cent and perhaps 30 per cent of the $1.2 billion *increase in the annual average outflow* on U.S. short-term account probably has contributed directly, net, to our deficit position. . . .

49..... Foreign Investment and Indigenous Enterprise*

KEITH DAVIS
Arizona State University

ROBERT L. BLOMSTROM
Michigan State University

One way to aid a country is to encourage more locally owned, progressive businesses. Sears, Roebuck and other firms have actively encouraged local suppliers to develop when they move into a country. Sears's program has been especially successful in Latin America, leading to the establishment and growth of hundreds of companies. In the beginning, Sears could purchase within a country only a small percentage of the merchandise it sold there, but now in Latin-American countries, such as Mexico and Brazil, over 90 per cent of its merchandise is made within the country.

The United Fruit Company encourages local owners and suppliers through its Associate Producer Program. This program helps develop native supply services and tries to bring natives into partnership in various aspects of the banana business. Company properties — farms, stores, restaurants, bakeries — are gradually being sold to natives. United Fruit helps arrange financing, provides technical help, and otherwise assists native producers. The far-reaching effect of this program is shown by the fact that all United Fruit's commercial banana acreages in Colombia, Ecuador, and the Dominican Republic have been sold to natives.[1]

* From *Business and its Environment* by Keith Davis and Robert L. Blomstrom, p. 303. Copyright 1966 by McGraw-Hill, Inc. McGraw-Hill Book Company. Used by permission.

[1] Thomas E. Sunderland, "Foreign Trade and Foreign Policy: An Uneasy Coexistence," *Michigan Business Review*, May 1965, pp. 2–11.

In addition to encouraging suppliers and commercial associates, businesses may also work directly to develop new enterprises in unrelated business areas, thereby helping upgrade the general community in which they operate. In Venezuela, Creole Petroleum Corporation has formed a subsidiary investment firm to supply new risk capital to stimulate local investment and expand opportunity. Creole limits its interest to less than 50 per cent to make clear that its purpose is to support local enterprise rather than dominate it. Other Standard Oil affiliates are taking similar steps in other countries.[2] The purpose is strictly to supply risk capital in new areas of business. This objective is entirely different from the common practice of forming a joint venture with a native firm for business purposes in product areas where the two firms normally conduct business.

[2] Robert H. Scholl, *International Business and the Community*, New York: Standard Oil Company (New Jersey), 1963, pp. 1–10.

PART FIVE ....

POLICY ISSUES ON INTERNATIONAL BUSINESS

In Part Four, we turned our attention to international business — what it is and what it does. In the broadest terms, we saw that activities under this heading both "contribute to" and "draw upon" the international economy. But, also, we saw that special problems attach to this category of activity. Accordingly, in Part Five, we turn to the problem aspects — to key *policy issues* that bear on international business.

The issues with which we concern ourselves are of a few main types; of whatever relevance to other regions, each has importance for one or another form of private-sector activity of United States derivation. The first relates to the environment in locales abroad. Is it favorable for the entry of goods, for import-marketing activity, for the entry of investment funds, for new or added production activity? And once an investment (or other commitment) has been made, what, for it, should be regarded as "fair" treatment?

The second issue relates to the environment at home. Are the various ingredients of official policy, as currently in effect, conducive to new or continuing activity abroad? Are legitimate ways available, not already invoked, to assist further?

The third issue relates to a special problem: the standards applied by host countries for ascertaining the merit of proposed new investment. On hand is the matter of when foreign-sponsored investment is to be regarded as "good," and when not.

The gist of a survey of representative literature is that the "answers" to many issues are not easy to come by. What appears reasonable and "right" often depends simply on where one stands as one views a situation. Indeed, nowhere is this fact more true, or more dramatic, than in business (and economic) relationships within a *multi*-country setting.

We follow consideration of the foregoing issues with a section on the *subject* of international business. Since international business is a new academic field, of uncertain future content and direction, it seems appropriate to ask — To what and to whom should it be addressed? And what form should its research projects take?

A ..... Issues in the External Environment

A number of "policy issues" (of relevance to international business) are rooted in the environment of *foreign* areas. The record attests, to be sure, that international business proceeds even in the absence of resolution of these issues; yet, international business stands to be served better if at least some of them are resolved.

The role of nationalism is a foremost issue. It is, of course, altogether fitting that a sovereign country and people be imbued with the spirit of nationalism — if by this we mean a sense of identification as a cohesive unit, along with a feeling of self-pride. In fact, it may well be, as in the case particularly of development-bent underdeveloped countries, that a meaningful forward push requires the popular sharing of nationalist sentiment. However, nationalism is not always expressed in constructive ways. It can, as readily, serve to underwrite isolationist measures and tactics inimical to an economy's full, or satisfactory, incorporation within an international context.

A pertinent fact is that much of what occurs in national conduct is premised essentially on a nineteenth-century "ideology" that runs counter to the demands, as measured in terms of good economics, of twentieth-century reality. Very simply, the practice of autarky (self-sufficiency in its various forms) stands in opposition to current pressures for closer economic integration internationally. The big question is *how* nationalism can be retained and directed toward useful ends, freed of unwarranted resistance to forces favoring international interdependence.

Among the specific "autarkical" actions that countries sometimes take and that prove disturbing to international business, whether business is already on the scene or merely considering entry, the foremost — or certainly the most drastic — is expropriation. Others include exchange controls that limit profit remission and that, also, restrict the import of goods; regulations on labor usage (e.g., laws requiring that a certain percentage of a company's labor complement or of its payroll be strictly domestic); discriminatory application and/or enforcement of, say, tax provisions; and so on.

The foregoing — the frequent presence of an anti-foreign feeling and its venting in various restrictive and inhibiting ways — has deep implications for international business. And deep implications, whether recognized or not, for the host countries in terms of their current and future economic well-being.

Actually, of course, some of the risks of doing business abroad are insurable — via the Investment Guaranty Program, in the case of new American direct investment abroad (applicable to expropriation, inconvertibility, and war loss). Perhaps more basic, however, is the question of whether it is even reasonable, or desirable, to seek to eliminate every condition or factor that business thinks inhibiting. To illustrate, the presence of exchange control in, say, an underdeveloped country may well prove a thorn-of-sorts in the side of a foreign (American) company pursuing operations there; yet, this reliance on exchange control may make good sense from the standpoint of the subject country on the grounds that developmental effort can be aided by means of a deliberate pro-development allocation of available foreign exchange.

The present section includes two selections that treat the foregoing type of subject matter. The first, by Professor Fayerweather, is about nationalism, per se. The content of his presentation is reflected by the title of his original article: "19th Century Ideology and 20th Century Reality." This is followed with a selection by Professors Hess and Cateora who concern themselves with certain "manifestations of nationalism." Specifically, they enumerate and discuss a number of risks that individual businesses face abroad: expropriation, controls on money flows, import restrictions, tax controls, labor problems, and so forth.

50..... Nationalism and International Business*

One of the more distressing features of our day is the continuing conflict between two of the strongest and potentially most constructive forces in modern society: nationalism and the multinational corporation. From time to time the conflict erupts in spectacular form in expropriations of property — electric utilities in Brazil and Castro's sweeping takeover of U.S. investments in Cuba. But more common and actually of greater overall importance are a multitude of lesser points of conflict — over the share of capital and control a foreign company may hold in a local venture, the degree of regulation foreign governments exercise over foreign operations and many other facets of overseas business.

While each of the points of conflict has some specific logic in itself, underlying them all is the massive sentiment of nationalism limiting the ability of sincere men on both sides to act dispassionately. For example, the question of how much profit a foreign company should be permitted to repatriate is debatable in rational economic terms. On the one hand, there are the rights of the contributor of capital to a payment for the use of his money. On the other, there are pressing demands in the host country for importation of capital equipment and the materials needed for economic development. But to any one who observes negotiations on this issue it is readily apparent that emotional value judgments are often controlling. The foreign investor is not just receiving "a payment for the use of his money," a cold, economic-legal concept. Rather he "is draining the

* Taken and adapted from "19th Century Ideology and 20th Century Reality," *Columbia Journal of World Business*, Winter 1966, pp. 77–84.

host nation of its wealth," a phrase emanating from a politically sensitive mentality attuned to the feelings of the general populace. As often as not, in developing nations with colonial pasts, there are further under-tones of "the obligation" of the west to finance development regardless of reward, in order to compensate for excessive profiteering and failure to support development in earlier periods.

Thus, no matter how effectively we may deal with the cold logic of the problems confronting the multinational corporation, we cannot hope for a major breakthrough on many of the critical issues unless the na-tionalistic component of the conflict is resolved. This is no simple prob-lem, and there is little indication that we are yet even close to solving it. It is the purpose of this article to try to clarify the character of the prob-lem. I propose to look carefully at the nature of both nationalism and the multinational corporation, defining the elements in each which are perti-nent to the problem and considering the direction in which each might evolve to reach some greater accommodation with the other.

What lies at the heart of the conflict between nationalism and multi-national business? To answer that question we had best look at the essen-tial characteristics of each.

Nationalism as we know it is of quite recent origin. While it had as-sorted early forebears, it was not firmly established until the beginning of the 19th century. Prior to that time patriotism, i.e., loyalty to one's country and its monarch, existed. But nationalism goes a good deal be-yond patriotism and did not emerge until the majority of the populace achieved a real identification with the state through the middle-class revolutions. A citizen might admire, respect, and love his king and feel emotional ties to his country, but feelings of a quite different order were tapped when the people felt that the nation and its government were truly theirs.

Although nationalism is relatively new, its psychological roots are not. Nationalism is a new manifestation of a fundamental human trait. The key motivation at work is the quest for security, reinforced by other social satisfactions which come from participation in a group. From earliest times these feelings have brought people together into groups with a high degree of internal cohesion and sharp separation from external elements. Social scientists use the term "we-group," which aptly describes the atti-tudes of the participants. They feel a strong identification with the group, thinking of it and acting in it on a "we" basis and treating those who are not in the group as a distinctly different category: "they," "outsiders," "foreigners." The individual is raised in the traditions, culture, and values of the we-group. He is expected to and generally does willingly accept them and give them strong emotional loyalty and support. Doing so contributes greatly to his own security, for he gains both emotional and physical security from the sense that his group is good and right and strong.

Basis of New Nationalism

For centuries these feelings found their main expression in groups which lived in relatively close physical proximity — the family, the clan, the tribe, the village, and even the city-state. These were units in which the individuals could effectively share in a common life and have a sense of participation in the group. There were larger government units to be sure, but the mass of people were too poorly educated to have much knowledge of or sense of unity with "countrymen" beyond their immediate community, and they had too little participation in the government to feel full identification with it. But there was nothing in the psychological forces involved which inherently limited we-group attitudes to small units, and two important changes, reinforced by other developments, brought forth the new nationalism: mass education and popular government.

As literacy became more common, facilitated by the printing press, people became better acquainted with the world around them and found in this knowledge an identification with the language, traditions, literature, culture, and often religion of their national group as distinguished from the foreigners of other peoples. Concurrently the rise of the middle class was being fostered by economic growth and by the new social structure associated with the industrial revolution and large-scale manufacturing. The middle class soon developed a strong interest in the functioning of the national government and a capacity to participate in it which superseded that of the feudal-landowning aristocracy.

These limited observations, of course, gloss over a quite long and difficult transition. But in broad outline we can see how and why the we-group psychology was elevated to the national level. From its middle-class base in Europe and North America, nationalism has now spread, in this century of popular government, mass communications and independence movements, to every part of the globe and deep into the ranks of the lower classes, leaving only the more primitive tribal groups outside its influence.

This historical review has two implications for the future. First, since the underlying psychology of nationalism is basic, it will not disappear. Second, changes in the way in which this psychology is manifested may occur. We must look therefore at the developments under way in the world today to see where they may be leading.

Following this train of thought, one's instinct is to look for signs that we are moving toward a yet broader span of we-group structure — the family, the tribe, the nation, now an international cohesion. And, indeed, there are numerous things we can point to which seem to fit the requirements for such a transition. Mass communications media are making people all around the world aware of each other and familiar with their ways of life. There has been a steady growth of what might be called international subcultures. Teenagers, for example, in virtually all countries share tastes in hair styles, music, and the like. To at least a limited degree they show a mutual identification rising above national affiliation. We have similar trends among international businessmen, scientists, chess players, radio hams, and assorted others.

The increasing integration of the world economy is also an encouraging sign. Just as the emergence of nationalism coincided with, and apparently was related to, the economic suitability of the nation-state as the industrial revolution got under way, our modern economy seems to require a cohesion and cooperation among nations. The International Monetary Fund (IMF), the General Agreement on Tariffs and Trade (GATT), the European Economic Community (EEC), the Latin American Free Trade Association (LAFTA), and similar mechanisms rising above national sovereignties are critical to world trade and thus to the welfare of people in all nations.

The Threat That Binds

But despite these favorable elements, there are some reasons for doubting that we are on the threshold of a true international we-groupism. First, if we look at the past, we find that no we-group has ever existed without a "they." The need for security is generally accepted as a critical motivation in the individual's commitment to the we-group. While a person may need security in relation to the unknown or in isolation, his concern about tangible external threats is strong and its absence removes a significant support of any we-group affiliation. The communist threat has created a degree of cohesion in the free world, but these ties are limited by the affiliation of large portions of the populations of many countries to communism. It is hard therefore to visualize the peoples of the world being drawn together tightly in the absence of a threat from outer space.

Likewise, for all the development of international subcultures, the differences among the nations are still very great and in important respects show little sign of diminishing appreciably. In such vital respects as language, religion and cultural values the Indian, the Japanese, the German and the American are still a very long way apart. One cannot therefore readily conceive of the rise of an international we-groupism strong enough to rival the national variety.

Nationalism is especially strong in the area of business, chiefly because of the heavy influence external business has exerted on the internal social and political affairs of many nations, especially the less-developed ones. This is the dominant theme in Richard Robinson's searching historical analysis of the effect of western investment.[1] Animosity toward foreign

---

[1] Richard D. Robinson, *International Business Policy*, Holt, Rinehart and Winston, New York, 1964, pp. 1–44.

investment is therefore part of the nationalistic tradition which binds these peoples together. Thus we start at a tremendous handicap in proposing that multinational business affairs become disassociated from nationalism.

Hope from History

On the other hand, it is hard to ignore the historical indications that government policies have always tended to synchronize with the basic economic system and business which was desirable for the effective use of the technology of the day. Throughout history, business institutions and political structures have evolved in constructive directions both independently and in their mutual relations. New forms of business units have appeared which were effective in utilizing the technology of the times, and political systems have developed which were appropriate to prevailing economic conditions.

In the Middle Ages, for example, the simple manufacturing technology which for the most part functioned effectively within quite limited geographic areas was satisfactorily utilized by the artisan system. The city, supplemented by the guild, provided adequate social services and control for the artisan economy. As wealth and regional interchange grew, the great trading companies appeared, and at the same time national governments capable of such complementary roles as protection of shipping emerged. The industrial revolution brought with it the large, publicly owned corporation, with its capacities for bringing together large amounts of capital and operating huge production facilities serving major marketing areas, and the parallel evolution of stronger national governments which built the essential infrastructure and maintained broad controls over business.

If the multinational corporation is in fact beneficial economically, there is a supposition here that government policies and the national sentiments behind them will in some way be adjusted to accommodate it. In speculating about ways in which this might happen another feature of past history is worth observing. Throughout the prenationalistic eras, various forms of internationalism have existed. There have been administrative unifications like the Roman and Ottoman empires in which bureaucracies recruited locally served what were for those times truly international systems, despite the gulf between their masters and the local we-groups to whom they had an initial loyalty. Likewise, in the Renaissance period in Europe the elite, the intelligentsia, were in a sense a distinctive we-group unto themselves, separate from the masses. They spurned localism in favor of a common mission in a unified Catholic society. Can international business and the government officialdom that must work with it around the world achieve such a sense of unity and disassociation from nationalistic patterns? At the moment we can only speculate. But the prospects will certainly be influenced greatly by the extent to which the multinational corporation proves of benefit to the world community.

In examining the benefits conferred by the multinational corporation, we are of course focusing on the social utility of the organization, not on its business efficiency. This distinction is important, for what is profitable for the company, even in a sound long-term view, is not necessarily beneficial to society as a whole. We hope it may be, but we have to prove it.

Is the multinational corporation socially useful, and if so, in what form? Some people have suggested that the hope for the future of international business lies in the creation of a "supranational" corporation chartered by the United Nations, with its headquarters in some center with minimal national character (like Luxembourg), owned by stockholders of a broad range of nationalities and managed as a true world enterprise without partiality to any country. While this is an appealing ideal conceived in conjunction with a transition from nationalism to internationalism, its inadequacy as a means of minimizing the conflict with nationalism is readily apparent. It is effective in removing the impact of the nationalism of the home country of the multinational corporation, but it really does nothing to alter relations with other countries. The supranational corporation is still an outsider, still a "they," whether it be of United States origin or United Nations origin. If and when the peoples of the world start to transfer their we-group emotions to the United Nations in substantial measure, then the device may be really meaningful. But we have seen that this is not a promising outlook, and in its absence I would suggest that the idea has to be viewed with considerable skepticism. Moreover, the change may amount in large part to a fiction, if as seems likely, the capital and management of the corporation still come from a limited number of major industrial countries. Furthermore, for all their negative comments about foreign capital, many nations may have considerably more confidence in the beneficence and responsibility of highly developed business communities than in the qualities of a floating corporation chartered by a very weak government institution and presumably virtually free of overall government control. This is not to say that the concept may not in fact prove sound, but only to emphasize that at the moment it is unduly favored by the age-old advantages of "the grass in the next pasture."

Can the Ties Be Loosened?

I think therefore that we should more logically look in the other direction; namely, whether to minimize the conflict with nationalism, the multinational corporation could evolve into a system of national units whose external ties are nonexistent. This is a contradiction in terms and is an unlikely, if not definitionally impossible, outcome. External ties are basic to the concept of the multinational corporation. They are the channels along which benefits flow. One can legitimately ask whether these ties can be reduced or severed without at the same time diluting the benefits. Yet since any progress along these lines would cut down on nationalistic antagonisms, it seems worthwhile to consider the extent to which we may move in this direction.

The multinational corporation's external ties may for convenience's sake be subsumed under four main headings, representing the basic flows within a business organization: product, finance, technology and management.

Product Flow

The social utility of the flow of products from one country to another scarcely needs defense. A host of scholars since Adam Smith and Ricardo have so established the concept of comparative advantage that the fact of the flow of goods into a country is thoroughly accepted.

The identification of products with the external multinational corporation by trade names and brands is another matter. In the less-developed countries and to a degree in more advanced industrialized areas like Europe, U.S. companies have found that their brand names are profitable assets because United States industry in general and they in particular have a reputation that attracts consumers. This is seemingly inconsistent with the "anti-they" attitude of nationalism. Suffice it to say that foreign nationals tend to be ambivalent: as practical consumers they want the specific brands, but as nationalists they feel constrained to attack their entry. Polish hams in the U.S. may be a reverse example.

Do multinational brands serve a socially useful purpose? This is a difficult question that cannot be answered clearly. On the surface the value is not apparent. But digging deeper one may suggest that the consumer acceptance the brands achieve is an important vehicle for market expansion and economic development. We enter here into the question of whether a number of aspects of aggressive commercial marketing make significant contributions to the expansion of a national economy. Theory in this regard is still crude and inconclusive, so all we can do is leave it as an open question.

A final question is whether control of the marketing process must remain in the hands of the home office. It should be noted that the marketing function is one which traditionally has been most readily transferred to independent local businesses. That is, multinational companies both at home and abroad have turned over a large part of their distribution to local wholesalers, import merchants, dealers, and the like. However, we also observe that corporate efficiency motives have led many firms to withhold the marketing of at least the first level of distribution in foreign markets from local firms. Their objectives have been to sell more aggressively, to provide better direction of dealer organizations and other ends which add up to "better" distribution. Thus, in judging whether these penetrations into foreign nations have social value, we are back again to the unanswered question of the contribution of marketing to economic development.

Finance Flow

The input of capital and the return of earnings are fundamental to private business interest in foreign operations. In Europe and other highly industrialized areas, it is doubtful whether the imported capital is of significant value to the host nation, but in less-developed areas it has an acknowledged beneficial role. Indeed, both the U.S. government and the receiving nations have made major efforts to increase the flow of capital. There is the theoretical possibility that capital needs might be supplied by indirect investment; for example, by purchase of stock of local companies by U.S. investors. The practical prospects in this regard are not good, however, as portfolio investments in the less-developed areas are still living down the adverse experience in the interwar period.

The chief vehicle for inducing a capital inflow but moderating the nationalistic reaction against it is the joint venture — a partnership of foreign and national capital. This may be a partial answer but it appears to dodge the issues, especially when, as most new nations prefer, the foreign company interest is limited to less than 50%. First, any arrangement which uses local capital to substitute for part of the investment a foreign company might make reduces the net inflow of needed external capital. Second, in the opinion of the majority of multinational companies a joint venture is managerially less effective than one with single control and may thus weaken the contribution to industrial growth. This is another complex subject which we can only leave as an open question.

It seems reasonable to conclude that the industrialized nations can manage without large capital infusions from abroad. The policies of Japan in the postwar era have followed this general line with success. But in the less-developed countries the social value of inputs of capital tied to managerial control to assure their effective use seems beyond question.

Technology Flow

The flow of research-derived technology for use in products and production processes would seem to provide the strongest basis for the multinational corporation, both in business terms and in terms of social value. Certainly it is in the fields where technology counts most that international firms have been strongest — chemicals rather than textiles, office machines rather than bread, etc.

The economic efficiency of doing research in a limited number of centers rather than duplicating it in every country of the world appeals to simple logic. We may have a cross flow of technology between developed areas, as we do between Europe and the United States. But since it seems almost certain that the less-developed nations will lag behind in technology for many years, the technological flow between the developed and developing will be predominantly in one direction.

Can this flow be severed from ownership through licensing agreements? The existence of a vast number of such arrangements is ample proof that it can be done. But we are again confronted with a practical block and a theoretical question. Most large companies would prefer to control the operations rather than turn their technology over to others. They feel that they can do a better job, especially in the developing countries where many of the potential licensees are at a generally lower level of managerial competence than their own organizations. This leads to the same type of question we encountered in the marketing area. If the multinational corporation can do a better job of implementing the technology, is it not the more desirable vehicle for development of the national economy?

Managerial Flow

The substance of this part of the multinational business is hard to describe in concrete terms, especially to the antagonistic nationalist. Yet it has a real meaning. The ability to blend a group of people together into an efficient business organization and to formulate and execute effective policies is recognized as one of the main strengths of the industrialized economies. The application of this competence in foreign countries has given many multinational corporations a basis for superiority well beyond what their products, capital or technology could provide. The social value of inflows of this managerial skill is certainly attested to by the way all countries have sought to draw on the management skill of the more developed. Consider, for example, the multitude of invitations to U.S. management professors and consultants to work in other countries, as well as the activities of the International Executive Service Corps. And while there is the possibility that the inflow might be provided by individual contributions rather than through the organizations of multinational corporations, there are so many proponents in government and academic circles, as well as business, of the thesis that an integrated, going organization is the best transmission device for managerial know-how that one must accept this as a strong presumption.

After we have looked at each of the components of the multinational corporation's activities, there is still something more to be considered in appraising the value of a unified business organization. Just as there is a historical evolution toward large we-groups, there is steady progression toward larger business organizations in which capital, technology and management are integrated with varying degrees of vertical control in the acquisition and distribution of products. We know that this progression has not excluded the existence of smaller enterprises and that a number of enterprises can coexist. It is not impossible therefore to conceive a world in which all corporations would be confined to their own national borders, but would engage in exchanges of products, capital, technology and management skills by arm's length bargaining. But this conception runs counter to the trend of history. It is far easier to accept what we see today as the natural evolution — great corporations efficiently accomplishing these flows through their own integrated operations spreading across national borders.

These views of the component flows and integrated character of the multinational corporation give us a basic perspective on its capacity to accommodate to nationalism. The outlook does not appear highly promising. This is not to say that the corporation cannot act in ways which minimize the effects of nationalism. Much has already been written by this author and others about the practical actions which companies may take to meet nationalistically motivated desires, including the use of local nationals in management, employment of local capital and sympathetic relations with foreign governments.[2] While the details of these actions involve numerous questions, I am here accepting them as obvious and sound basic policies. The present analysis has been pitched to a different level. My concern is that even after we have implemented these basic policies to the point which is typically sound from a business efficiency point of view, we find that the external ties remain so significant that the conflict with nationalism retains a solid core of substance.

Is Conflict Permanent?

My purpose has been to examine the fundamentals of the structure of the multinational corporation to see whether a quite different concept could be conceived which would achieve both business efficiency and social utility. The picture as I have drawn it does not suggest this to be the case. But it should be cautioned that we do not have the type of well-documented, thoroughly analyzed research we need to reach considered conclusions on many aspects of this subject. My primary aim has not been to reach conclusions but to outline the character of the issues and the ways in which we may usefully think about them. As a conclusion it is adequate therefore to observe that there is a very hard core of conflict between nationalism and the character of the multinational corporation and that it is difficult to see how this conflict can be ultimately eliminated.

Where does this leave us? Will the conflict be a permanent one or will a pattern of mutual accommodation evolve? No one really knows. Taking a final look backward, however, we can find encouragement in the way other conflicts within society have found resolution, at least to a fair degree. For example, there is an apparent conflict between the acquisitive, materialistic character of modern industry and the tenets of

2 For example, see my article, "LRP for International Operations," *California Management Review*, Fall 1960, pp. 23–29.

Christianity. Yet, the two have been effectively married in Western Europe and Anglo-Saxon countries by the Protestant Ethic, which in giving religious sanction to hard work encouraged industrial productivity and justified the rewards of industry on this earth. John D. Rockefeller could thus feel no basic conflict in being a good Baptist and making millions of dollars. Likewise, the conflict between job security and the advance toward higher productivity has been always with us, whether in the English Luddites, who smashed textile machinery in the 1810's, or the railroad featherbedding issues of the 1960's. Yet labor has increasingly recognized the social utility and ultimate benefit to itself in more productive industrial methods. In a few notable cases it has even provided leadership in introducing labor-saving devices, e.g., John L. Lewis in the coal industry.

The proposition that the activities of the multinational corporation within various nations have social value has not been proved here, but it does appear to have strong support. If it is valid, then our historical perspective gives encouragement that a resolution of the conflict with nationalism will evolve. Although the change may come through some broad movement from nationalism toward political internationalism, it is more likely to occur through a mutual recognition of self-interest on the part of businessmen and business-oriented government officials around the world, a decline in the nationalistic preoccupation with business affairs, and a reduction of the external ties of the multinational corporation in each nation to the minimum that is clearly socially useful.

51 ..... Expropriation and Other International Deterrents*

JOHN M. HESS
PHILIP R. CATEORA
University of Colorado

The kinds of risks resulting from the political implications of a company's activities can range from expropriation, the most severe, to many lesser but still important government activities such as exchange controls, import restrictions, price controls, and labor policy. Each of these politically and/or economically inspired sanctions against foreign business is sufficiently important and occurs with enough frequency to require . . . special consideration. . . .

Expropriation

The most severe consequences of a hostile political environment faced by a foreign investor is the acquisition of his property by the host country. Expropriation of foreign business, with or without reimbursement, is probably the most crucial politically induced risk of foreign business. Modern economic history is replete with cases of expropriation: some better known examples are Mexico's take-over of the foreign-owned railway system in 1937 and the oil industry in 1938; Guatemala's take-over of foreign-owned banana plantations in 1953; Iran's attempted nationalization of British-owned oil interests in 1952;[1] and the more recent Cuban expropriation of all industry, as well as Brazil's take-over of United States-owned electrical power plants.

* Taken and adapted from *International Marketing*, Homewood, Ill.: Richard D. Irwin, Inc., 1966, pp. 135–139.

[1] Walter Krause, *International Economics* (Boston: Houghton Mifflin Company, Inc., 1965), p. 266.

The motivation of a country that expropriates foreign investment is frequently couched in deep sentiments of nationalism. Why does a nation feel that it must seize foreign investment? Many reasons are given, but basically such action stems from the belief (whether or not correct is immaterial) that the country's national goals and self-interest can best be served by government ownership rather than by foreign control of a particular industry.

Expropriation is typically justified on the grounds that the industry is critical to national defense, national sovereignty, national wealth and/or national economic growth, and thus, the nation's interests require that the industry not be controlled by a foreigner. Consequently, certain industries are more susceptible to expropriation than others. Public utilities are a frequent target since it is universally held that they are critical to economic growth, as well as being instrumental in defense capabilities. Mining, oil, and other natural resources are also especially vulnerable since the nation's wealth is at stake. Other kinds of industries can be as defenseless as these above if the industry is the primary basis for the country's economy. Another justification for expropriation is the strong feeling held by many that foreign businesses have typically exploited the national wealth of the host country, taking everything from the country and giving nothing in return.

Expropriation does not always mean total loss for the foreign investor. In some cases, the investment is nationalized and the government reimburses the investor for the value of his losses; the reimbursement is seldom felt to be "equitable" to the foreign owner, but there is less stigma attached to such government action if some payment is made. Confiscation is especially alluring to the underdeveloped country; as one observer noted, confiscation ". . . is easy and all it requires is a decree. It is dirt cheap, for it costs nothing at all, and it seems to transfer national wealth and property from foreign hands to their own."[2]

Some authorities believe that the risks of expropriation will be less in the future for three important reasons. One is that countries are coming to realize that foreign investment is necessary to the achievement of desired growth potential and that expropriation, whatever the reason, typically dries up much needed investment capital. Furthermore, past experience has shown that government ownership does not always yield the desired results. In fact, in some cases, experience has shown that after expropriation of an industry, the industry has faltered and its contribution to the national economy has decreased. A second fact which may alter future attempts at expropriation is the more stringent economic pressure being levied against the offending nation by the country of the exploited firm when equitable reimbursement is not made. The third reason is derived from the activities that investing firms are taking to

[2] Frank Tannenbaum, *Ten Keys to Latin America* (New York: Alfred A. Knopf, 1962), p. 65.

make themselves indispensable and less vulnerable in a host country. Such activities include encouraging nationals to invest in the business venture, employing nationals in important management positions, and generally attempting to erase the constant suspicion that the foreign firm is somehow exploiting the host country.

Although the threat of expropriation may be abating, it still persists and is of prime importance as a political risk in doing business abroad. More common and frequent risks come from the multitude of minor but nonetheless costly harassments often encountered when . . . doing business in another country.

Other Risks Faced by Foreign Business

Expropriation of a foreign business with or without restitution is an extreme course for any government. Instead of expropriation, most businessmen abroad are faced with less drastic, but nevertheless troublesome risks of politically condoned or inspired controls and pressures exerted against foreign operators. Political objectives under the banner of national security and/or the protection of infant industry are demanded despite the cold economic facts involved.

Exchange Controls

Exchange controls stem from shortages of foreign exchange held by a country. A recurrent problem of the foreign investor is that of getting his profits and investments into the currency of his home country. When a nation faces shortages of foreign exchange, controls may be leveled over all movements of capital or, selectively, against the most politically vulnerable companies in order to conserve the supply of foreign exchange for the most essential uses.

Exchange controls are also extended to products by applying a system of multiple exchange rates to regulate trade in specific commodities classified as necessities or luxuries. Necessary products are placed in the most favorable (low) exchange categories, while luxuries are heavily penalized with high foreign exchange rates.

In countries with an especially difficult balance-of-payments problem, earnings as well as principal have been frozen for considerable periods of time.[3] Such extreme measures are infrequent, as are those cases of some countries limiting profit remittance to a small, fixed percentage of net assets.[4]

Currency convertibility is becoming less of a problem than it has been, but most countries maintain regulations for control of currency. In the event that an economy should suffer a setback or foreign exchange re-

[3] Krause, *op. cit.*, p. 267.
[4] Harold H. Whitman, "Financial Problems and Risks Operating Abroad," *International Management Series No. 1*, p. 30.

serves suffer severely, the controls on convertibility can be imposed rapidly.[5]

Import Restrictions

Selective restrictions on the imports of raw materials, machines, and spare parts are a fairly common strategy to induce foreign industry to purchase more of its supplies within the host country, and thereby create markets for local industry.[6] Although this is done in an attempt to support the development of domestic industry, the net result is often to hamstring and sometimes interrupt the operations of established industries. The problem then becomes critical when there are no adequately developed sources of supply within the country.

Tax Controls

Taxes must be classified as a political risk when they are used as a means of controlling foreign investments. In such cases they are often raised without warning and in violation of formal agreements. A squeeze on profits is affected by raising taxes significantly as a business becomes established; oil companies have found this a frequent problem. There are cases where initial agreements have called for specific tax rates, only to have them increased considerably after some degree of success. Venezuela boosted the taxes on United States oil companies to 65% of net income and, in addition, placed a ceiling on the prices of the company's oil. Despite a Chilean law passed in 1955 guaranteeing no new tax increases on the copper industry, a new tax was levied, and Kennecott's Chilean subsidiary was required to pay taxes amounting to 82% of the 1961 income.[7] In those underdeveloped countries where the economy is constantly threatened with shortages of funds, unreasonable taxation of successful foreign investments frequently appears to be the handiest and quickest means of finding operating funds.

Price Controls

Essential products that command considerable public interest, such as drugs and medicines, gasoline, and tires, are often subjected to price controls. These controls are generally applied during inflationary periods, and when inflation is particularly rampant, the consequences of price ceilings can be extremely costly. The problems of a company faced with price ceilings during the two years that the value of the cruzeiro in Brazil decreased by as much as two-thirds were almost insurmountable.[8] Since periods of inflation are not restricted to only a few countries, this type of risk must be considered for most areas. Between 1953 and 1961, for

---

[5] Alexander O. Stanley, *Handbook of International Marketing* (New York: McGraw-Hill Book Company, Inc., 1963), p. 139.

[6] Whitman, *op. cit.*, p. 29.

[7] "Special Report: Latin America," *Business Week*, September 22, 1962, p. 168.

[8] "World Business," *Time*, January 25, 1963, p. 89.

example, the percentage increase in the cost of living for France was 44%. The figure was 66% in Mexico, and Bolivia's cost of living increased 2,470% during the same eight-year period.[9] Rampant inflation itself can be very costly under any circumstances; but when coupled with stringent price controls, the result is often disastrous.

Labor Problems

In many countries labor unions have strong government support that they effectively use in getting special concessions from business. Layoffs may be forbidden; profits may have to be shared; and an extraordinary number of services may have to be provided. In fact, in many countries foreign firms are considered to be fair game for the demands of the domestic labor.

In France, the belief in full employment is almost religious in fervor; layoffs of any size, especially by foreign-owned companies, are looked upon as national crises. When, as a result of cutbacks in demand, both General Motors and Remington Rand attempted to lay off workers in their French plants, the French Minister of Industry reprimanded them and stated that he would not allow "certain isolated enterprises to practice an irresponsible policy that does not respect the social contract linking a financially powerful enterprise to the labor it employs."[10] Although both General Motors and Remington Rand were privately assured that the minister's remarks were only for public consumption, the reaction is indicative of the role between government and labor in many countries. An interesting sidelight is that the same conditions that forced General Motors and Remington Rand to lay off workers were affecting domestic French industry as well so that they too were laying off personnel; but apparently this situation went unnoticed by the government. In Mexico, not only is the freedom to fire restricted, but recent amendments to the constitution legally obligate companies to share profits with their employees. A "national committee" has been set up to determine the amount of a firm's profits and the extent to which they must be shared with labor. The committee is composed of representatives of government, management, and labor, each with equal representation. It is felt that the representation is not balanced fairly since labor unions are regarded as, in effect, arms of the Mexican government. As a consequence, many believe that management will be outnumbered two to one.[11]

Another labor problem is the restriction sometimes placed upon the entry into a country of key technicians. In order to force the hiring of nationals, some countries will not provide work permits to technically trained personnel regardless of whether or not men with similar talents are available within the country.

9 "World Business," *Time*, September 7, 1962, p. 42.
10 "Freedom to Sign France," *Business Week*, September 22, 1962, p. 96.
11 "World Business," *Time*, September 21, 1962, p. 50.

While no one of these risks is sufficiently detrimental to ruin a venture, they can separately or collectively cause trouble and seriously affect the profitability of a firm's operation. Obviously, it takes more than risks of this nature to deter foreign investment. This is expressly borne out by the increased investments that continue to pour into so-called "risky" countries. One reason that foreign capital can still be found, despite the risks involved, is that the United States Government encourages American investment abroad by offering protection against certain political risks.

B..... Issues in the
Domestic Environment

Along with issues in the foreign environment go issues grounded in the *domestic* environment (of capital-supplier countries). A short list of issues relevant to the United States includes, for example, the following. How far should the home country go in "opening doors" abroad for its exporters and investors? How should foreign-earned income be taxed? If the home country is to offer insurance against risks abroad, what risks are to be regarded as fit for coverage? What should the home country do to lessen possible adverse balance-of-payments impact for its economy? Should foreign aid be viewed as an instrument of business-and-investment promotion on behalf of home-country companies?

The present section is devoted to these and other questions. A first selection, by Professor Blough, cites and examines a number of policy factors that have a bearing on the foreign-investment decision: home-imposed restrictions on investment, tax policy, investment guarantees, the use of diplomacy on behalf of investors, and so forth.

In the next selection, Professor Behrman turns to recent-day restrictions by the United States on new foreign investment, imposed to lessen balance-of-payments pressure. His appraisal is critical of these restrictions.

A third selection, by Emilio G. Collado, takes up the relationship between foreign aid and the promotion of private direct investment abroad. The gist of his argument is that the United States should give more attention in its foreign-aid program to what can be accomplished through "private development."

A final selection, by Emilio G. Collado and Jack F. Bennett, raises the question of *who* — the supplier country or the host country — bears the greater responsibility for the promotion of investment incentives. Their conclusion is that the burden of responsibility is primarily on the host country.

52..... Supplier-Country Policy Toward Foreign Investment*

ROY BLOUGH
Columbia University

If the government's policy is to promote private foreign investment, businessmen's awareness of investment opportunities abroad and willingness to undertake them can be increased through educational and promotional activities. The prospective financial return can be increased through tax exemptions, favorable tax rates, and other provisions of the tax laws, or through other financial subsidies. The risks of investment can be reduced through investment guaranties and insurance. The probability of acceptance and favorable treatment of the investment by host countries may be increased through diplomatic action. If the government's policy is to channel investment into some industries or geographical regions and away from others, appropriate promotional and restrictive measures may be combined.

Governmental Requirements and Restrictions

A legal requirement that an investor or business shall invest overseas is rarely a practical measure. Under Western law individuals and private corporations cannot be compelled in times of peace to deploy their property to particular purposes, except as it can be taken through taxes and spent by government.

There are a few types of cases in which a governmental "suggestion" might have the effect of lawful requirement. For example, an interna-

* From *International Business: Environment and Adaptation* by Roy Blough, pp. 254–261, 263–264. Copyright 1966 by McGraw-Hill, Inc. McGraw-Hill Book Company. Used by permission.

tional airline that was heavily dependent for diplomatic and other support might find it expedient to agree to a governmental request to invest in the local airline of some less developed country and give it technical assistance and managerial aid. While all international businesses are heavily dependent on the home government for protection and general services, it would be politically unacceptable for government to try to compel an expansion of foreign investment through a threat of withholding normal diplomatic assistance or other general aid. Business firms ought not to be expected by government to take investment initiatives that appear unwise from the business viewpoint, at least when legal requirements cannot be imposed and applied without discrimination on all firms.

The power of government to forbid or constrain foreign investment through exercise of due process of law is well established. The method used would depend on the purpose to be achieved. If it was considered important that certain types of machinery should not be sent to any or particular foreign countries even in the form of business investment, the restraint could be applied directly to the export of the goods in question. If, on the other hand, it was desired to restrain financial investment, the prohibitions undoubtedly would be applied to financial transactions.

If financial capital outflows were to be entirely prevented, the form of the restriction would almost certainly be that of exchange control. Great Britain, for example, used this method during the difficult years after World War II. . . .

A less general form of prohibition that might reduce capital outflows sufficiently in a given situation would be to prohibit nationals from purchasing foreign securities or lending funds to foreign borrowers. Violations by individuals would presumably be hard to control, but the activities of banks, investment houses, and stock exchanges would be relatively easy to regulate and might be sufficient if the law were of short duration. . . .

Voluntary cooperative action to reduce or cut off the outflow of new foreign investment by banks and businesses, taken at the urging of the government, has advantages over compulsory measures in that it does not require new laws, can be more flexible, and is more acceptable to those being restrained. If it is truly voluntary, it suffers from the disadvantages that it requires a high sense of public responsibility on the part of those agreeing to the restraint, together with continued confidence that everyone is complying. . . . Quasi-voluntary action, where the government can impose sanctions of one type or another, has a better chance of success. In the United States voluntary program to limit capital outflows, introduced in 1965, sanctions were available that could be applied to banks, but in the case of other businesses the absence of comparable sanctions made it necessary to rely on organized business support and a continuing effort to achieve mutual understanding by government and business of their respective dilemmas.

Tax Measures and Subsidies

A profound difference between governmental requirement and financial incentive . . . is that the former denies the right of private choice in the context of the market while the latter changes the relative attractiveness of various alternatives while preserving the right of choice. . . .

If the desired policy is to discourage foreign investment, tax measures can readily be designed to accomplish that result. An excise tax could be placed on the investment of capital abroad. The allowance of a credit for foreign income taxes paid on income from foreign sources against United States taxes on the same income could be repealed with respect to income from foreign investment. Higher tax rates could be imposed on income from foreign investments than on other income. Deductions and other tax provisions intended to stimulate investment, such as accelerated depreciation, percentage depletion, and investment credits could be denied to foreign investment. A country that had in effect an exchange control system could impose taxes on the purchase of foreign exchange destined for capital export. . . .

Examples of tax provisions intended to discourage foreign investment have only recently appeared in the United States tax laws. The Revenue Act of 1962 ended the deferral of taxes on the income of certain foreign subsidiaries of United States corporations. Such action was proposed by the Treasury to attain tax neutrality between domestic and foreign investment, but it was interpreted by many of the businesses affected as a tax penalty on foreign investment. The investment credit of the 1962 Act was not applied to investment outside the United States. The interest equalization tax, proposed in 1963 and passed in 1964, was definitely intended to discourage long-term portfolio investments abroad by American residents and corporations. The rate structure of the tax was calculated to increase the cost of money secured by foreigners in the United States by approximately 1 per cent (of the principal) for each year of the life of the security, in order to help equalize the rates of interest in the United States with those prevailing in foreign financial markets, and thus to help end the balance-of-payments deficit of the United States.

Since taxation operates to repress activity, it is not difficult to discourage investment abroad through tax measures; but the use of such measures to encourage investment abroad is a more difficult and less certain operation. The usual method of using taxation to encourage a particular activity is to exempt that activity from taxation while imposing full taxes on alternative activities. Various types of measures resulting in partial or total tax exemption have been adopted or proposed for stimulating private business investment abroad. Some countries do not tax business corporations on income from "foreign sources" if it already has been subject to some taxation abroad. The United States has never been prepared to waive its right to tax foreign-source income, but has provided partial exemption of such income in a number of ways.

The strength of the incentive provided by tax exemption cannot be greater than the restrictive effect of the tax on activities subject to it. There would be no incentive at all in case no income was anticipated on the investment. The limits to the effectiveness of exemption as an incentive to foreign investment has persuaded some businessmen and government officials that positive subsidies will be required to achieve the desired amount of private investment in less developed countries. Presumably a sufficiently large financial subsidy can make attractive the most risky and unprofitable venture. One of the proposals that has been made along these lines is to grant a tax credit against the total income tax of the corporation. The credit would be equal to some percentage (30 per cent has been proposed) of new investment made by an American investor in a less developed country. For companies with taxable income from sources other than the new investment this is the equivalent of a cash subsidy that does not appear as such in the budget.

Investment Guaranties and Other Security Measures

All investments carry some risk that hoped-for income will not be realized or that part or all of the capital will be lost. The extent of the risk differs widely among investments. The greater the risk appears to be, the higher must be the anticipated rate of return on a successful investment if the investment is to be undertaken. Accordingly, if the expected risk can be reduced, investments with lower anticipated rates of return will become attractive. It will be noted that it is the expectation, not the realization, that influences the making of the investment. The major factor that determines the expectation of risk is uncertainty, which is of two general kinds. First is uncertainty regarding the adequacy and accuracy of knowledge of the existing state of affairs; this can be overcome through improved "intelligence" services. Second is uncertainty regarding what changes will take place in the future; this can be reduced through more thorough and sophisticated forecasting but can never be fully overcome. Risks are commonly classified into business risks and political risks. Business risks involve the correctness of judgment regarding current and future demands, costs, and competition. Political risks are inherent in judging the outlook for actions on the part of governments — the host government, the home government, perhaps intergovernmental organizations — that might impair or destroy the profitability of the venture or the value of the capital, or make it impossible to transfer or otherwise realize profits.

Uncertainty about the existing situation is likely to be greater regarding foreign than domestic investment because of the greater difficulty in securing adequate information. Risks of unfavorable future business developments may be either greater or less abroad than at home, but the difficulty of assessing such risks is likely to be greater in the foreign environment. Political risks in particular are likely to be greater in most other countries than in the United States, and in some sense the foreign political risk is added to whatever may be the domestic political risk.

The abilities of business firms to live with risk differ widely. A multinational corporation doing business in many countries may have such a broad spread of risks that it can absorb losses in one or more countries without undue financial strain. Smaller or geographically less diversified corporations, however, may be unwilling to invest their capital in a country in which they believe, rightly or wrongly, political risk is substantial.

Most of the major capital-supplying countries make some provision for "insuring" the business against political risks. The United States government through the Agency for International Development (AID) has provided insurance for new investments against three types of risks: foreign exchange, expropriation, and war risks. The insurance cannot be written unless the host country has entered into an agreement with the United States government. One reason for requiring such an agreement is to give the United States a solid legal position in the country, since upon payment of a claim to an insured investor the United States takes over the claim and seeks to recover from the host country. To provide insurance without such an agreement might constitute an encouragement to the host government to behave in an irresponsible manner toward United States business.

The foreign exchange risk that is covered is the risk that greater restrictions will be placed on the transfer of profits and capital than existed at the time the investment was made and the insurance undertaken. Problems of interpretation arise when certain restrictions were in effect when the investment was made, while different restrictions came into effect later. The insurance does not cover the risk of the devaluation of the currency of the host country despite the fact that a company might lose heavily from such devaluation. One reason for not covering this risk is that the extent of loss due to devaluation depends largely on how the company's profits were affected by the inflation that usually precedes devaluation, and in what forms the company's assets have been held. The net effect of inflation and devaluation may be almost incalculable, and is influenced greatly by the competence of the management, making this more of a business risk than a political risk.

The coverage of war risks includes destruction of property in the host country due either to foreign war or domestic revolution. The insurance against expropriation provides reimbursement to the investor in case of nationalization without adequate compensation. It does not cover the risks of harassment in the form of price fixing, punitive taxation, or regulations that make the carrying on of business more difficult and costly. If such harassment is a prelude to nationalization, it may be intended to reduce the value of the nationalized property.

The guaranties are available to United States citizens, partnerships, and corporations and to wholly-owned foreign subsidiaries. . . .

The United States program of guaranties for new investment was initiated in 1948. The annual premiums charged are a percentage of the investment for each of the risks involved. During the early years the insurance was not much used, in part because some of the less developed countries in which investment was greatest, for example, Brazil, had not yet entered into the necessary agreements. Also, many firms did not consider the risks substantial or the coverage adequate. In some cases so much of the investment was old and would not qualify for insurance that there seemed little advantage in covering the new investments. . . . In recent years more use has been made of the insurance; however, in some of the countries with high political risks, the host government has not been willing to enter into the necessary agreement. Reasons given for such unwillingness usually have been that it was an insult to suggest that political risks existed in their countries and that the agreement for the United States to take over private claims involved a violation of sovereignty. An increasing number of countries have been persuaded to enter into the necessary agreement, but some still refuse. . . .

Treaties and Diplomacy

The home government of the business firm can assist it abroad by influencing the action of the host government directly and through participation in international organizations. Two levels of action may be distinguished: the negotiation of an advantageous arrangement applying to business firms in general, and case-by-case activity on behalf of specific firms. A necessary foundation for business investment and operations in a host country is the bilateral treaty of friendship, commerce, and navigation between that country and the home country. These treaties usually include provisions to assure equal treatment in each country for the nationals and business firms of the other country, and cover various topics that may in the past have been a cause of mutual concern. A second type of treaty that is relevant here is designed to reduce double taxation and fiscal evasion. Hundreds of such treaties are in force. The central problem with which they deal is the double or multiple taxation of the same income or transaction by the two countries. . . .

Some intergovernmental arrangements are necessary if the incentives offered for foreign investment by the home country itself are to be effective. Reference was made above to the necessity for agreements with the host countries before making investment guaranties under the United States AID program. Another example of this kind is the provision for lending to United States businesses in a country of up to 25 per cent of local currency derived by the United States from sales to the host government of surplus agricultural products (the "Cooley funds" under the P.L. 480 program). Such loans cannot be made unless the beneficiary country agrees in the contract of sale.

The provisions of treaties and of international law in general are not self-enforcing, and one of the tasks of diplomacy is to ascertain that business firms are receiving the promised treatment. Diplomats also have the task of learning and reporting to Washington what is going on in the area of their assignment. A great deal of the information made available for businessmen interested in importing, exporting, or investing abroad comes from this source. The value of this information is indicated by the efforts made by businessmen to increase both the promptness and the extent of the release of such information. . . .

The question arises concerning how much our government should "represent" our businesses abroad. Formerly the strictures against such representation discouraged intervention. Revised directives of the Department of State in 1961 have broadened the scope for ambassadorial initiative. Activity to secure reduction of trade barriers is encouraged. It is normal procedure for the embassy to make introductions and arrange interviews, if requested to do so. As in the matter of claims, the degree of effort and cooperation by diplomatic personnel is largely a matter for the judgment and discretion of the ambassador and the embassy staff. When there is inadequate implementation, the reason may be that the concept of the diplomat regarding his proper function does not include salesmanship for private businesses. There is moreover always the question whether efforts in this field may make the broader problems of international relations more difficult. Again, in many cases the business firm seeking assistance has actual or potential competition from other American firms. When this danger arises, the United States official would find his position highly embarrassing if he were to assist one against the others. . . .

Complaints thus continue to be heard that there is inadequate cooperation by American diplomats abroad in promoting the interests of specific businesses. There is another view, however, doubtless a minority view, that the relations of an American firm in the host country will be more cordial and less likely to be disrupted by unfavorable action in future years if the firm neither seeks nor receives diplomatic aid in its negotiations. . . .

53 ..... Policy Toward Foreign Investment: The U.S. Case*

JACK N. BEHRMAN
University of North Carolina

For most of the postwar period the U.S. Government was an eager promoter of private foreign investment while the business community maintained a go-slow attitude. Despite the institution of a government program of investment guarantees in 1948, private U.S. direct outlays averaged only $700 million a year during 1947–1955, mostly to Canada and Latin America. This was well below the desired level of $2 billion. In 1956 and 1957 the outflow soared to $2 billion and to $2.5 billion, respectively — mainly as a result of European recovery and the purchase of Venezuelan oil concessions — only to drop back to just over $1 billion in 1958.

By the early 1960's, however, business began a mild scramble to "go foreign," and direct investment, buoyed by substantial European outlays, climbed sharply. Yet just as the effusion began to approach the postwar target levels, the signals were changed: the business community was in effect told to adopt two poses — to concentrate its investment in the developing nations and restrain itself in the industrialized countries. The principal avowed reason for this switch: the stubborn balance-of-payments problem.

It is characteristic of the Government's approach to the question of direct investment that little thought was given to whether this Janus-like attitude is really viable. In point of fact it is not, and won't become so even if Congress passes the proposed 30% tax credit on investment in less-developed areas.

* Taken and adapted from "Foreign Investment Muddle: The Perils of Ad Hoccery," *Columbia Journal of World Business*, Fall 1965, pp. 51–59.

Few U.S. manufacturing companies begin their foreign operations in the developing countries; they get their feet wet in safer water. Dampen the initiative to enter or expand operations in industrialized nations and you reduce the volume of funds potentially available for outlays in the less-developed countries. On the other side of the coin, the willingness of governments of developing countries to permit expansion in their private sectors, as well as to welcome foreign investors, may be cooled by the recent posture of the U.S. Government. Opponents of private investment in the host countries can now attack more freely, asserting that U.S. investors cannot be counted on to continue to assist in development after the economy is no longer classified as "less developed." While such arguments may not be logical or supportable, they can be effective. Constraint on investments in one area, therefore, will undoubtedly have repercussions in other areas.

Misinformation Is Rife

This basic inconsistency in the government approach to overseas investment should surprise no one. We can hardly expect all policy makers to understand the relationship between investment in the developed and less-developed worlds when many have failed to grasp the connection between overseas investment as a whole and the nation's international balance sheet. Despite incessant exhortations from those intimately involved and better informed, many in Congress, the Executive, the press and elsewhere persist in regarding foreign investment as a kind of dispensable luxury. Cut down the capital outflow and you can just about eliminate the deficit and, as a side benefit, stop the drain of U.S. jobs overseas, runs the argument in its most extreme form. And while only the most naïve offer such a patently absurd comment, many who should know better share something of this psychology.

In point of fact, these people may have other reasons for seeking to cut down foreign investment, but they have seized on our adverse payments situation as a major "cause célèbre." Instead of bothering to establish the preconditions (including the filling-in of yawning lacunae in the data) for an intelligent and long-term policy toward a key debit item — the capital outflow — and a key credit item — the return of earnings — they are reacting *ad hoc* with proposals that are often dangerous and self-defeating.

It is therefore appropriate to reemphasize two oft-stated but little-understood truths: (1) investors often do not choose to move abroad; they go because they have to if they wish to preserve their markets; and (2) foreign direct investments pay their way in a balance-of-payments sense — over the long term, to be sure, but often in the short range as well.

The available evidence suggests that American manufacturers try to hold on to foreign markets by exporting to them for as long as possible.

Few enjoy the risks and the high initial cost of establishing operations abroad. When the manufacturer decides to move abroad it is usually because changes in relative costs, political conditions, foreign exchange controls or import quotas, among other things, make it impossible for him to continue to service his overseas market through exports.

Why Companies Go Foreign

Say that the foreign market has grown large enough so that it is now economic to set up a plant there. Say further that the local citizens would more readily accept the product if it were produced in their own country and that they are anxious to avail themselves of the income- and employment-generating benefits of local production. Add that the foreign country may now be part of an economic union that has sharply pared tariffs among its members while maintaining barriers against outsiders. And note finally that the host country may be experiencing balance-of-payments difficulties that force it to conserve precious dollars by slicing so-called unnecessary imports for some time to come. Weigh all these considerations and you form an idea of why "going foreign" is practically an imperative for many American companies. It is not a question of going or not going but of getting there and establishing oneself ahead of the competing German, British or French firm.

Reflows Start Immediately

Once having established itself overseas to service a market that has become relatively inaccessible to similar U.S. exports, the subsidiary immediately starts to offset the unfavorable payments effects of the initial outflow by purchasing U.S. capital equipment, raw materials, components, management and technical services, etc. And although some of these goods and services are available locally, particularly in industrialized countries, most have to be imported from home.

According to an extrapolation from a representative sample of companies by the U.S. Department of Commerce, it would appear that domestic firms sent about $5 billion worth of goods to foreign affiliates of U.S. companies in 1963 — 23% of all U.S. exports.[1] U.S. manufacturing firms accounted for $4.4 billion of this total, of which $3.2 billion went to overseas manufacturing facilities. On the other hand, direct overseas outlays amounted to only $1.9 billion in 1963, and investment in manufacturing facilities totaled $700 million. If we confine ourselves to the data reported by the sample companies without extrapolation, we find that U.S. exports to all overseas affiliates in 1962 and 1963 were 50% greater than the total capital drain to these companies.

[1] Fred Cutler and Samuel Pizer, "U.S. Trade with Foreign Affiliates of U.S. Firms," *Survey of Current Business,* December 1964, pp. 20–26.

However, these figures do not tell the whole export story. It is well known that foreign investment stimulates the economy of the host country, raising incomes and consumption. Part of the resulting additional sales are made by U.S. subsidiaries, but an undetermined amount undoubtedly represents increased U.S. exports that are not channelled through overseas affiliates.

Offsetting these export advantages is the fact that foreign subsidiaries may produce goods that (1) displace U.S. exports in third markets and (2) are imported into the United States to compete with domestic production. The impact of point 1 is not fully known and may be substantial, but it is also clear that when exports to former U.S. markets are made by or through a subsidiary, it is not because the parent *wishes* to give up the market. It would, in the main, prefer direct sales for U.S. dollars and will permit a subsidiary to service a third market only under economic or political pressure.

Little Competition with Domestic Goods

The effect of the second point is often greatly overstated. Of the $31.3 billion in foreign manufacturing affiliate sales in 1963 only $1 billion worth was sold to the U.S.,[2] and 80% of this consisted of semi-finished products for further processing (mostly from Canada and Latin America). The $1-billion figure is about the same as in 1962 (despite the fact that overall foreign manufacturing affiliate sales rose 13%) and was not much different from the 1957 amount. Moreover, domestic producers probably would not have been able to service the market supplied by these U.S. foreign subsidiaries, and, in consequence, many of the orders for goods produced by U.S. foreign affiliates may well have been filled by foreign firms if domestic companies had not set up operations abroad. This is so even for the finished manufactured imports of $200 million, of which half were automobiles. Given the growing American preference for European-type cars, it is doubtful whether American-built autos could have been able to hold this market in the face of vigorous competition from European-owned producers. In addition, many imports are noncompetitive with U.S. production, while others (e.g., parts and components) may help the U.S. export effort by lowering the cost of production of final products.

Besides stimulating exports, foreign investment contributes significantly to a positive payments balance by repatriation of earnings. From 1950 through 1963, repatriated earnings exceeded net new direct foreign investment by over $12 billion. There are two principal reasons for these favorable returns: (1) foreign investments have been profitable (earnings

---

[2] Fred Cutler and Samuel Pizer, "U.S. Firms Accelerate Capital Expenditures Abroad," *Survey of Current Business,* October 1964, pp. 5–12.

on manufacturing investment in Europe averaged 12% of total book value of investment in 1962 and 1963, but were 17% in the 1957–1960 period and about 19% in 1954 and 1955) and (2) over half of these earnings (in the developed countries) have been returned to the parent.

Combining the earnings and export effects of foreign outlays, we obtain the following interesting balance. In 1957, receipts (i.e., remittances, royalties and direct exports received from U.S. firms) accounted for by foreign manufacturing affiliates exceeded payments (i.e., imports into the U.S. and capital outflow) by $1.2 billion; by 1963, the positive balance had doubled — to $2.4 billion.

The Payout Problem

While it seems incontrovertible that foreign investment pays for itself in the long run, one is reminded of J. M. Keynes' famous remark: "In the long run we are all dead." Obviously it makes a great deal of difference to the stability of the U.S. dollar whether the "payout" period on a given foreign investment is five, ten or twenty years. As long as the financial transfer inherent in a capital outflow exceeds the flow of real resources and the reflow of foreign remittances, the possibility exists that a super-abundance of dollars will find their way to foreign central banks to be presented to the U.S. for payment in gold.

The U.S. Treasury constructed a number of models in 1961 and 1962 to demonstrate its case that foreign investment in European manufacturing facilities has an unconscionably long payout period. The first models maintained that the payout period was about fifteen years, but after subsequent refinements, this was reduced to seven years. Data on company operations published late last year by the Department of Commerce enable us to take a fresh look at these calculations and the results are startling, to say the least. Let us consider the payout period (so far as the balance of payments is concerned, *not* in terms of the company's own accounts) on a $10 million investment in Europe.

If the venture is an entirely new one, the actual U.S. dollar outflow may be as much as 40% of the total investment, with the rest financed through overseas borrowing; if merely an expansion of an existing investment, the outflow is likely to be about 20%-25% of total capital expenditures and the remainder will be financed through retained earnings and depreciation allowances, as well as foreign-source borrowing.[3] Thus, at the worst, we get an initial debit item of $4 million on the $10 million investment. Since company practice indicates that something like 15% of European subsidiary purchases of capital equipment, which normally total about one-half of the overseas investment, are made in the U.S., there is an offset of about $0.8 million (15% of 50% of $10 million) even

3 *Ibid.*

before production abroad actually begins.[4] This reduces the outflow to about $3.2 million. According to Commerce figures, annual U.S. exports of materials, parts and finished goods (other than capital goods) to foreign affiliates in Europe average close to 5% of affiliate sales, and these, in turn, are usually about 2½ times total investment. Thus 5% of $25 million (2½ × $10 million) gives us a $1.25 million export credit each year. Adding annual repatriated earnings of $240,000 (6% of investment — as noted, European investment earns 12% of book value and at least half is remitted home), we get a balance-of-payments return of close to $1.5 million of the initial investment.

Within about two years, therefore, the capital outflow will have been paid for in a balance-of-payments sense, even assuming a 40% initial contribution of U.S. funds. (Of course, in these calculations we have made no mention of the additional export sales that may be made during the "start-up" period either because of intensified company efforts to widen the market or because foreign customers become less uneasy about purchasing imports when they know that a domestic source of supply will soon be available. Also, we have not included the indirect export stimulus resulting from the income-generating effects of the affiliate's presence in the host country, although this may amount to about 1% of the affiliate's sales. Nor, have we counted, on the debit side, the effects of imports sent back to the U.S., since such sales from U.S. European subsidiaries have not risen significantly, despite expansion of U.S. investment to this area.)

A Self-Defeating Policy

The foregoing suggests that the Government's policy of discouragement of foreign outlays in the developed world rests on a somewhat tenuous factual foundation. Obviously, if one excludes the less-developed countries, the maximum conceivable benefit of a restrictive investment policy would be the discontinuance of the outflow to the industrialized countries, or about $1.5 billion — equal to nearly half the payments deficit. But once the outflow dries up, overseas subsidiaries would slow down the repatriation of earnings and employ them instead for expansion. This, together with a drop in exports associated with new overseas ventures, would probably wipe out the entire benefit. Even if it did not, a partial restriction, i.e., of outflows to only industrialized countries, is almost impossible to administer, requiring not only the licensing of capital but also control of export proceeds and the cooperation of foreign governments. Moreover, since exporting leads to licensing or investment when the foreign market is sufficiently developed, any constraints on investment would adversely affect the Government's export drive. Support of the drive can

---

[4] If the investment is an expansion of old facilities, the *initial* return is greater in relation to the dollar outflow, e.g., an outflow of $2 million is offset by immediate purchases of nearly $1 million.

be expected to wane to the extent that businessmen feel they are developing markets that would only have to be given up later — either to indigenous or to other foreign producers.

Instead of moving to choke off foreign investment in developed nations, the Government would do well to take a more constructive tack to the payments problem — one that would take full account of the long-run strength of the U.S. position. Such an approach should aim at making U.S. business fully competitive with its overseas counterparts and guaranteeing that its contributions to the balance of payments are maximized. If this approach is to be adopted, the Executive must make sure that the policies of various governmental agencies are subordinated to the overriding exigencies of foreign economic policy. Let me note some problem areas and offer a few remedial suggestions.

A continuing complaint by U.S. business has been that its interests are not adequately represented abroad by our embassies. . . . Only in exceptional cases is there a close working relationship between embassy officers and U.S. businessmen overseas. Nor have U.S. ambassadors in general gone far in supporting U.S. business in difficult negotiations or discussions with foreign governments — contrary to the practice of governmental representatives of other countries. While governmental help is more important in the developing countries, the pressures in some of the industrialized nations make official counterpressure at times essential.

To obtain a better understanding of how business views opportunities and obstacles overseas, all appropriate embassy officials should establish a close, day-to-day working relationship with local U.S. businessmen. Such an understanding would facilitate the satisfactory handling of conflict situations overseas and provide guidance for business-government cooperation in the foreign country.

A second sore point is industrial property rights (patents, trademarks, trade secrets, know-how, etc.). The Government's general support of these rights in industrialized countries is weakened by its position on commercial exploitation by companies developing those rights under government contract. Until recently, the Government has usually retained title, even when the invention or development has commercial uses; it then has given the rights away to foreign governments for exploitation by a foreign company, thus destroying normal commercial relations. The foreign company, in turn, is free to move into a third market without paying royalties to the U.S. It is estimated that we have lost something over $100 million a year on our balance of payments through this giveaway. And although this situation has been partially corrected (the Department of Defense and other agencies are now permitting the contracting U.S. companies to retain some rights to commercial exploitation), more needs to be done to support fully the export of military-type items and licensing or investment arrangements for foreign production and sale in third markets.

Export controls also have a constraining impact. The Government requires companies to obtain either a validated license from the Department of Commerce or assurances from their overseas licensees that neither certain technical data nor the direct (and sometimes the second) product thereof shall be shipped to prohibited destinations. The constraints impose a burden on the licensor (not borne by his competitors) in that he must either delay decisions to come to the Government or insist on commitments which his licensee is often reluctant to make. Also, it is difficult for the licensor to police the commitment, and he may find himself betwixt and between on occasions, as was one U.S. company that licensed a Japanese manufacturer who was found to be selling to Red China in violation of U.S. laws. But the American firm would have been in violation of Japanese law if it had cancelled the contract — a felony. It required diplomatic action to untangle the situation, and in the end the Japanese firm ceased trading with China. Although the result in this case was salutary, the overall impact of such actions is to make foreign companies wary of technical tie-ups with U.S. companies — to our detriment and theirs.

The Administration would do well to admit the conflict of export controls with the competitive position of U.S. companies licensing abroad. Once admitted, business and government could then settle down to devising the most effective exchange of information and a system of regulation which at the same time minimizes interference with competitive objectives.

The Separate World of Antitrust

Another problem area is antitrust. Antitrust regulations have been administered as though they were not part and parcel of the foreign economic policy of the U.S. Government. To my knowledge, such an attitude of separateness is not accepted in any other area of governmental control. Communications-landing rights, shipping, exports, etc., are all subject at times to overriding economic or political necessities. But only in the rarest of cases have antitrust positions given way to overriding political objectives, and only by statutory exemption (the not-so-effective Webb-Pomerene Act) to overall objectives of foreign economic policy.

The Justice Department takes the position that it must enforce the courts' dictum that competition is an end in itself and that other supposed benefits from combinations or anticompetitive acts are less important than those resulting from greater competition. Enforcement can, however, have detrimental effects on the balance of payments.

For example, one U.S. company was anxious to license a British company to use its know-how for the manufacture of electronic equipment, with machinery and components to be exported from the U.S. Since under U.S. antitrust laws the licensor could not exclude the resulting products from the U.S. market (no patent or trademarks were involved), he decided to forego the arrangement. The result: a loss of both export income and royalty returns; no consequent gain! Similar cases can be cited in Japan and other countries. Foreign companies are under no such constraints.

Alternatively, the U.S. licensor may feel that his licensee constitutes a sizable market for materials and components, and that he would like to get the licensee to agree, as a condition of receiving the license, to purchase these items exclusively from him. At present, such a tie-in sale is looked on unfavorably by the Justice Department on the grounds that it is discriminatory to other U.S. firms producing these components — though it is common elsewhere and its absence may merely lose sales to other countries.

The inhibiting effects of antitrust regulations are further illustrated by the example of a U.S. company which found that the only Italian firm suitable as a promoter of its exports to Italy already had arrangements that would have put the U.S. firm in violation of the law had it proceeded with an agreement. Again, foreign companies are under no such constraints.

Prerequisite to action in the antitrust area is a change in the attitude of the Justice Department, which has hitherto assumed that "there is no problem." While the Department's view that it is "merely implementing the law" may be technically correct, it is also the responsibility of the executive branch to propose changes in existing laws. There is ample evidence from Congressional hearings and business complaints that supports a call for close and candid examination of the impact of the law as implemented. To some, including the present writer, the "rule of reason" in antitrust cases should not necessarily be the same when applied abroad as when applied within the United States.

Need for Harmonization

A study should be undertaken to consider whether to broaden the "exemptions" from antitrust regulations or liberalize the interpretation of "reasonable behavior." Such a study might also seek to determine what modifications are necessary to bring U.S. law and EEC regulations more into line, removing some of the worst conflicts that a U.S. company faces in operating under two or more jurisdictions. Out of these deliberations might well come some proposals to amend the law, but there are some experts who consider that amendments are not necessary and that sufficient authority now exists to operate in the fashion more consistent with the requirements of foreign economic policy.

In the tax field it is impossible at this time to repeal some of the most intricate and burdensome provisions of the Revenue Act of 1962, one of the objectives of which was to restrict overseas investment by taxing the profits of certain types of foreign subsidiaries when earned rather than when distributed.

Conquest through Complexity

. . . [Many] of the provisions of this law are undesirable and unnecessary to achieve the stated objectives, but obviously extended comment on this point is beyond the scope of this paper. Suffice it to note that if the overall objective of making U.S. business competitive abroad is accepted, it is possible for Treasury to work with business in drafting the regulations so as to impose as small a burden as possible on accounting and tax departments of business firms and to make certain that the impact of the Act is no harsher than that intended by Congress. The Act is at present so complicated that one businessman commented: "I did not think that the provisions would deter foreign investment, but I think Treasury has achieved its objective by making them so complex and confusing that it simply takes too much expert and executive time to unravel them and make an investment decision."

To review the impact of its regulations, Treasury should establish a consultation program with business in order to review any complaints of inequity or injustice before they fester into acrimony or seriously interfere with the pursuit of overall overseas objectives. The Treasury should also be instructed to look carefully into the tax systems of other countries to assess the competitive position of U.S. industry abroad. This examination might shed some light not only on the situation within a second country, but also on the ability of a U.S. company to serve a wider market from the second-country base, just as its local competitor abroad is able to do. Out of these deliberations could come appropriate amendments to the Revenue Code; but until such an analysis is made (coupled with evidence as to the balance-of-payments impact), it is unlikely that Congress will see the reason for amendments.

On its part, business should proceed to develop information on its overseas operations which will answer the questions posed by Government — not only precise data on the balance-of-payments effects but also on the tax and antitrust effects. The need for information was recognized by the panel on "Foreign Investment and Exports" at the White House Conference in 1963, which urged business to support a study being undertaken by the National Industrial Conference Board on foreign operations. Other studies are under way. . . . Business assistance in these independent analyses should help provide much of the evidence required for informed policy decisions.

In the meantime, business should take immediate steps to reorganize its overseas operations to maximize the return flow of funds to the United States and minimize the dollar outflow *without* losing any opportunity to compete in world markets. There is evidence in the data for 1963 and 1964 that greater reliance is being placed on internal financing and foreign borrowing, relieving the outflow of funds. In addition, more ways could be found to increase purchases in the United States. Finally, business should realize that 100% acquisition of a majority-owned operation overseas *may* add little to the U.S. balance of payments and that the ill-timed or ill-considered actions of a few may redound to the harm of all, through changes in government regulations here and abroad.

. . .

There is little new in the above suggestions, nor is novelty needed. What is needed now are means to bring them to fruition. This will require some institutional changes in both the Government and business.

The executive branch must establish a line of authority for reconciling differences within the Administration on business problems. Each of the major departments has now become more or less directly concerned with international activities, and some are attempting to gain more control over those activities that fall within their purview. While this closer attention is itself desirable, it will lead to complex jurisdictional problems unless a mechanism is established to achieve coordination. A singe center of coordination is needed, and it logically should be the post of Undersecretary of State for Economic Affairs. . . . A variety of separate inter-agency committees, each with different terms of reference, means that no one looks after overall policy or makes certain that decisions are consistent. . . .

In order to back up the process of decision making and bring the White House in at appropriate times, as well as to prevent the meetings from becoming merely a rubber stamp for State Department positions or simply a "hearing" prior to a State Department decision, a Special Assistant to the President should be appointed with responsibility for foreign economic policies. . . . At present, . . . there is no procedure for bringing such matters through the agency maze, save on specific issues where *ad hoc* committees exist: balance of payments, trade negotiations, and export expansion. None has the scope necessary for the problems now discussed.

These are the organizational steps recommended for Government, but the business community itself has some reorganizing to do if it is to contribute to an effective dialogue on foreign investment problems. To date there is no single channel through which business interests may be heard on the issue discussed here. The Business Council speaks on some problems, but not necessarily on these or to all relevant officials. The NAM and U.S. Chamber are not sufficiently representative of all interested in international problems, and there are still divisions within their ranks as to priorities on domestic and international issues — reflecting a similar division within corporations themselves. Nor are any of the business groups that direct their attention to one foreign area or to one type of activity able to speak authoritatively for all. None in fact fits the particulars required or begins to match the type of close consultation and continuing dialogue provided by the appropriate organizations in Germany or England. The problem of how business should organize to speak effectively to Government is not easily solved, and a careful assessment of alternatives is needed. But the assessment should begin now.

If business can develop appropriate mechanisms and if the Government organizes its channels of authority effectively, laying the responsibility for *direct* contact with business on the relevant operating departments and establishing proper interagency coordination, the various decisions affecting international business should be more consistent and appropriate. The positions should then fit into an overall objective, founded on sound data, clearly discernible to business and foreign governments, and hopefully reflecting confidence in the role of business in promoting the economic growth of the free world.

54 ..... Foreign Aid and Private Foreign Investment*

EMILIO G. COLLADO

Standard Oil Company of New Jersey

. . . [Policy] discussions in the United States . . . focus on how our aid may best contribute to development when taking into account the effects of that aid on the developmental efforts of the countries concerned. The desirability of aid has not been at issue. Despite differing views on how large our aid appropriations should be, there does seem to be a consensus in the United States that it is wise for our Government to assist selectively the less developed areas of the world. There seems to be agreement also that among the objectives of such development are a broader distribution of rising economic benefits through planned measures for the improvement of "conditions of rural living and land use," "of housing and community facilities," "of public health" and of "the equity and effectiveness of existing tax schedules" — to use the words of the 1960 Act of Bogota. . . .

In my opinion, these measures are in most cases desirable and necessary. Yet . . . I have joined others in expressing a fear that their success was being jeopardized by two trends — both relating to the use by the developing nations of their own resources — which the United States aid program may unwittingly have been encouraging. Fortunately, the problem is increasingly recognized and some corrective steps have been taken. It is the purpose of this article to discuss the problem and the remedies.

. . .

* Excerpted by special permission from "Economic Development Through Private Enterprise," *Foreign Affairs*, July 1963. Copyright by the Council on Foreign Relations, Inc., New York, pp. 708–720.

The first of the disturbing trends of recent years has been the growth of an excessive preoccupation with the direct introduction of measures for social improvement and a consequent neglect of the bases for economic development on which such social improvements must fundamentally depend. The second trend has been the increasing introduction of governmental activity and control into fields of economic activity which could be more productively pursued by private initiative and which, when undertaken by governments, divert their limited administrative and financial resources from social development programs.

These tendencies have been commented upon not only by observers in the United States but also by responsible businessmen and political figures in the developing nations. Certainly one should expect some opposition in these countries to specific measures of reform, such as higher taxes affecting particular groups, but the concern expressed goes beyond this. In some countries private businessmen so far despair about the prospects for private initiative that at times the flight of capital has exceeded the inflow of public assistance from abroad. In these circumstances, it is not pleasant to be told by citizens of developing nations that our programs are contributing to the destruction of private enterprise and initiative in their economies.

Many changes in economic organization and past practices are required if these countries are to develop modern economies consistent with the best in their traditions and yet incorporating the flexibility and efficiency necessary to produce the rising standards of life demanded by their citizens. And reforms are needed to improve the social distribution of economic benefits. We must remember, however, that increases in a nation's output cannot be just legislated. They must be earned.

There are, of course, differences — both philosophical and practical — in the approaches to development followed by various countries. In some areas, however, so much attention is being paid to procedures for dividing the national output that there is a danger of not even maintaining the present size of the total output — and this in the face of the expanding requirements of rapidly growing populations.

Preoccupation with measures for social improvement schemes has been evident in many ways. A glance at the resolutions adopted at Bogota, at Punta del Este, and in the gatherings of the United Nations and its regional and specialized agencies, for example, shows that attention has been devoted primarily to detailed exhortations in the fields of social welfare and planning. At these and other international economic gatherings the prerequisites for optimum growth have occasionally been presented with force. Yet the typical speeches of the representatives both of foreign governments and, until recently, of the United States have stressed the need for more and more government activity. At the same time the neglect of the basic conditions conducive to private economic activity has been painfully apparent to businessmen, both local and foreign, who have attempted to operate in many of the less developed areas. Outright expropriation aside, unreasonable exclusions, controls and exactions have drastically limited the opportunities and incentives for private economic endeavor.

These tendencies have not been unrelated. They have all to some extent reflected a widespread intellectual belief that government should conduct an increasing part of a nation's economic activity. . . .

. . .

Even those less developed nations now embarking on widescale programs of government enterprise normally produce the bulk of their economic output by private enterprises. It would seem clear that the road to economic advancement would be through building upon this existing base rather than adopting measures which stunt its performance. In many instances, then, the most helpful thing our Government could do to promote the economic future of a less developed nation would be to bring home to the leaders of that nation the need to preserve and build upon the private enterprise base which the nation already has. Yet in recent years there were times when the actions of our own Government seemed to display no conviction in the productive superiority of private enterprise.

The public speeches of our officials laid great stress on the right of every country to choose its own form of economic organization; but they did not couple such remarks with any recognition of the likely results of unwise choices upon economic growth. Our spokesmen concentrated on land reform, tax reform, planning and the alleged need for government action to push economies to an assumed "take-off." There was virtually no reference to measures to preserve the health of the productive private sector that already existed. There was no concerted effort to ensure that our aid loans and grants did not in practice serve to diminish the opportunities for private enterprise in the developing countries. There were, to be sure, commendable procedures to see to it that contracts for construction, supply and sometimes initial operation of aid projects were open to private bidders on an equitable basis, but there is a vast distinction between a contract for a "turnkey" job and a true equity interest in a continuing venture.

In recent years the international investor has been given somewhat more attention than the local private entrepreneur. The United States investment guaranty program has undoubtedly brought some newcomers into the foreign field and has resulted in the adoption of some beneficial projects which would not have been undertaken without this kind of insurance. At the same time the United States Government has adopted some oversimplified doctrines which have tended to discourage private investment in the developing areas. One of these doctrines is that strong preference should be given to joint ventures, and that normally aid should be considered for a project originated by a U.S. investor only if he takes in a local partner. Superficially this policy might seem designed to build up local enterprise, and this may have been the result in some instances; but the reverse has also been true. Private investment from abroad has a strong incentive effect in encouraging independent local firms to become suppliers and processers, further manufacturers, and sellers of the product of the foreign-financed venture. If limited local resources are forced into the ventures initiated by a foreign investor, there is less available for the truly independent and complementary local enterprise, and the nation's scarce foreign exchange resources may be depleted. The availability of a local partner may sometimes encourage an investment from abroad, but in other circumstances a prospective investor may wish to avoid the managerial problems, financing difficulties, disagreements on dividend and reinvestment policies, tax burdens and political favoritism that are sometimes involved in joint ventures. Each project needs to be judged on the basis of its own special circumstances. It is, therefore, unfortunate that the Government seems to have adopted such a hard and fast stand in support of joint enterprises. This policy has encouraged other governments to impose rigid requirements for local participation which have served to deter investment from abroad. . . .

. . .

Despite the difficult times through which investors have been living in many parts of the less developed world, the death notices on private investment are premature. Statistically this is easier to demonstrate for foreign than for local private investment, even though the latter is far greater in magitude. . . .

. . .

The tasks ahead are still staggering. Economic progress must be spread not only among nations but also among the regions within nations — not only to Paraguay but also to the northeast of Brazil. Stratified societies and rigid economies must be "unfrozen" and rendered flexible. In this task private enterprise can be both a prime agent of productive change and a beneficiary of more liberal opportunity. Competition among private firms with their many different approaches can be a mighty engine for change and development. A good climate for private investment cannot be created just by a stroke of a pen; a consistent pattern of fair treatment by government must be established over time, but success in removing traditional barriers to enterprise will lead to ever-increasing commitment of private resources for further development. . . .

The efforts of our Government to arrange a judicious distribution of aid and to negotiate reductions in trade barriers must continue; they can contribute much to the economic development of the free world. But at the same time we should recognize that the potential for the most dramatic contribution lies in creating opportunities for the citizens in the developing nations to apply their own skill and resources productively without unjustifiable interference and restraint by governments. We can yet demonstrate the great force of private enterprise for creating conditions for human opportunity and dignity, and the evolution of stable and democratic institutions.

55 ..... The Responsibility
For Promotion of
Investment Incentives*

EMILIO G. COLLADO
JACK F. BENNETT
Standard Oil Company of New Jersey

. . . [We] must not be blind to the influence of our own Government, whose actions can strongly affect the level of private investment abroad, both directly by measures it takes itself and indirectly through its influence on investment climates abroad. In determining what economic opportunities are open to United States citizens and companies, and in advancing United States foreign policy interests, it is essential that a proper relation be established between Government actions and the international private investment process. . . .

[While] the United States Government has the power to take actions that would facilitate investment abroad, . . . the analogy applies that it is easier to pull a string than to push it. The climates created by foreign governments and foreign communities will remain the principal factor determining the levels of private foreign investment.

There is reason to hope that foreign officials anxious to further the welfare of their countries will observe and take heed of the accumulating evidence of what private investment can accomplish in the field of economic development. Among the clear-cut results available for observation are the examples of Canada, Venezuela and Peru, which are largely free from obstacles to investment. . . .

The potential for [investment] growth is large. The basic factors are present to create the indispensable economic opportunity; there is a

* Excerpted by special permission from "Private Investment and Economic Development," *Foreign Affairs*, July 1957. Copyright by the Council on Foreign Relations, Inc., New York, pp. 639, 644–645.

408

growing demand for raw materials and for sources of power in developed countries and for manufactured goods in the underdeveloped areas. That investors are making use of this opportunity is shown by the rapid growth in the total statistics on foreign investments, and is also borne out in the day-to-day experience of law firms and banks that assist new investors in going abroad.

Private investment abroad should continue to expand geographically as well as in total volume. This is not to say that the need for economic assistance programs will abruptly end. In the years to come there may well be political developments and emergency situations justifying such assistance. There is a clear relation, however, between increased private investment and reduced need of public assistance for general economic development abroad. Even in those countries with which we have important military obligations, and in which external assistance is now large in relation to the domestic economies, growth in private investment can reduce the need for assistance. Also, many of those countries now receiving only economic aid have excellent opportunities to attract sizable amounts of private investment, thereby reducing their reliance on public assistance. . . .

There is no reason beyond human remedy why all countries — to the immense benefit of their citizens — could not partake fully of the burgeoning of international investment which we believe possible, and likely, in the next few years.

C ..... Host-Country
Investment Standards

Americans contemplating investment abroad often are surprised when they learn that, as a condition preceding entry, they must secure approval for their projected investment from a "screening committee." They are surprised that anyone should doubt the automatic desirability of new investment and new enterprise. Why, they ask, should prospective investors from abroad even be questioned, let alone be turned down on occasion?

The facts are as follows. Some countries, particularly underdeveloped countries, suffer persistent balance-of-payments stringency — a constraint, for them, in their developmental efforts. Accordingly, they want to assure themselves that new investment not only can contribute to desired development, but, in all likelihood, can do so without concurrently inducing undesirable balance-of-payments pressure. Let us illustrate. If a foreign investor were to establish a gambling casino, the casino might prove ever so profitable in a business way, yet (in the absence of a tourist trade of the requisite sort) earn no foreign exchange whatsoever. The investor expects eventually to remit profits to his home country, even though his business earned none of the foreign exchange needed for the remittance. If the investor, at this point, is denied foreign exchange for remittance purposes, he is unhappy — in fact, he may even complain at his embassy. If he is granted the needed foreign exchange, the country ends up with that amount less of this scarce item — an amount that might, alternatively, have been used on behalf of its developmental effort. Contrast this situation with investment in a production facility which, in addition to proving profitable in a business way, helps to add to the country's foreign-exchange holdings (either via access to more foreign exchange as exports rise or via savings of foreign exchange as new domestic output substitutes for goods previously imported). In this case, the presence of the investment provides, also, the basis for servicing the investment externally. Everyone now is happy, and development is not choked off because of the investment.

As the foregoing suggests, some investment from abroad is worth having, while some is better done without. It is because investments differ in impact that countries concern themselves in their development planning with investment priorities (whether investment is from abroad or strictly domestic), and have chosen to back up the matter of investment choice with "screening committees" (relative to the admittance of foreign investment).

A pressing question in development planning, however, is — *What* is the proper priority? (In the absence of enough capital to do everything, an order of preference seems desirable.) The "answer" is bound to be very important: important domestically because developmental progress hinges on it, and important to the prospective investor from abroad because his "value" to the country hinges on it.

A number of "answers" have been suggested. The present section examines three. Raúl Prebisch makes use of "import substitution" as an investment criterion. Import-substitution industries are those that yield products previously imported. Not only does the output of such an industry save foreign exchange for a country (by removing the need for equivalent imports), but the prospect of success for the firm is good because of assurances inherent in the market situation (namely, previous imports prove the existence of a ready market, while subsequent exclusion of customary imports removes competition for the new domestic output).

A second selection features "foreign-exchange impact" as the relevant investment criterion (for industry). New industries that are foreign-exchange-"earning" or foreign-exchange-"saving" are to be preferred. The logic is that a new industry has special merit if its presence leaves undiminished, or adds to, the total supply of scarce foreign exchange on the basis of which *other* investments can be contemplated.

A final selection presents the views of Professor Hirschman. According to him, "imbalance" in an economy paves the path of progress; development occurs as an economy readjusts to disequilibrium situations within it. By pushing ahead on a strategic front, other fronts, influenced through "forward and backward linkages," also respond — either under pressure or through inducement. The moral of the Hirschman version of the development process is that many investments are good — that, in anticipating the merit of a given action, one needs to take into account its secondary as well as direct effects.

56..... Import Substitution as an Investment Criterion*

RAÙL PREBISCH

Secretary-General, UNCTAD;
formerly with ECLA

Historically, the spread of technical progress has been uneven, and this has contributed to the division of the world economy into industrial centers and peripheral countries engaged in primary production, with consequent differences in income growth. We are now at a transitional stage, in which this division is being gradually weakened, but it may take rather a long time to disappear. As the spread of technical progress into the periphery — limited originally to exports of primary commodities and related activities — is advancing more and more into other sectors, it brings with it the need for industrialization.

Indeed, industrialization is an inescapable part of the process of change accompanying a gradual improvement in per capita income. In response to differences in the income elasticities of demand and in rates of increase in productivity, the active population is tending to shift — chiefly through the distribution of its increment — from occupations with a relatively low income elasticity of demand — principally primary production — to industry and other activities where this is relatively high.

This process has characterized the development of the industrial centers and is now advancing into the periphery. Industrialization of the centers is not a matter of dispute: it seems quite obvious that industrial countries should continue to industrialize. On the other hand, industrialization of the periphery has always been a controversial subject, not only in the centers, but also in the peripheral countries themselves.

* Taken and adapted from "Commercial Policy in the Underdeveloped Countries," *American Economic Review*, May 1959, pp. 251–256.

Although the opposition is receding, there are still some who consider industrialization to be a harmful diversion of productive resources from primary activities. Those who promote industrialization of the periphery are still credited with odd or ill-founded motives: the belief that industry makes nations wealthy while agriculture is a source of poverty; animosity towards the countryside, reasons of prestige, or the desire to achieve self-sufficiency or to imitate the centers.

Let the peripheral countries increase productivity in their primary activities through much-needed technical progress and thus expand their exports. Their rate of development will then be accelerated on a sound basis. So runs the argument.

Technical progress in export activities of these peripheral countries has undoubtedly been a great stimulus to their growth. But if this process is extended to other primary activities for internal consumption, where productivity is usually very low, and industry is not developed to absorb redundant manpower, then the inevitable outcome will be more disguised unemployment or downright unemployment.

Thus the plea for technical advance in primary production as an alternative to industrialization in order to improve standards of living defeats its own purpose, as some of the fruits of such technical advance will usually be transferred from the peripheral countries to the outer world, unless it is buttressed by a vigorous process of industrialization and increasing productivity in industry. The greater the inelasticity of demand for peripheral exports, the larger the proportion of the fruits that is so transferred.

Industry and technical advance in primary production are thus complementary aspects of the same process. And in this process, industry plays a dynamic role, not only in inducing technical progress in primary and other activities, but in the new attitudes fostered by industrial development.

. . .

Import substitution (defined here as an increase in the proportion of goods that is supplied from domestic sources and not necessarily as a reduction in the ratio of imports to total income) is the only way to correct the effects on peripheral growth of disparities in foreign trade elasticity. Let us take a numerical example to clarify this aspect of our problem. For the sake of simplicity, we shall assume that there is only one center and a periphery, having equal rates of population growth. Assuming that the center's rate of income growth is 3 per cent yearly and the income elasticity of demand for imports of primary commodities is 0.80 and that there is no import substitution, then the rate of growth of these imports will be 2.40 per cent (3 per cent × 0.80 per cent) per year.

Suppose now that at the periphery income elasticity of demand for industrial goods from the center is 1.30. If, in a balanced development process, the rate of growth of these imports is to be no higher than that of exports, then peripheral income cannot increase faster than 1.84 per cent per year. This is the rate which, combined with that coefficient of elasticity, gives the limit of import growth — that is to say a rate of 2.40 per cent, the same as that for exports.

Should peripheral income grow at a rate, say, similar to the 3 per cent of the center, its demands for imports of industrial products would grow at the rate of 3.90 per cent (3 per cent × 1.3 per cent) while exports of primary commodities would increase at the rate of only 2.40 per cent. To bridge the gap between these two rates, either the rate of increase of demand for imports would have to fall by 1.50 per cent, by means of import substitution, or industrial exports would have to be added to the primary ones, or a combination of the two.

We have assumed the same rates of population growth at the center and periphery. If the rate is higher at the latter . . . [Latin America being a case in point], industrialization has to be intensified in order to have the same per capita rate of income growth as the center. This is particularly necessary if the present differences in per capita income are to be gradually narrowed down.

We have seen that import substitution tends to correct the disparity in income elasticities of demand for imports and for exports. This does not mean that industrialization is not necessary in the exceptional cases . . . where there is no such disparity. It has been shown that industrialization also responds to internal disparities of demand. If exports of a particular country grow faster than its demand for imports, industry will still have to grow, but its contribution towards meeting total demand for industrial goods will decline while that of imports will increase. By contrast, when demand for imports tends to grow at a faster rate than exports, import substitution is necessary to correct this disparity, and then imports constitute a declining proportion of total demand for industrial goods.

On the other hand, a country whose exports grow at a very fast rate and constitute a relatively high component of its aggregate product is in a better position than others to accelerate its rate of economic growth; but this acceleration may induce a rate of increase in the demand for imports higher than the increase in exports, requiring import substitution to correct the disparity.

* * *

Let us . . . clarify one important point. Industrial costs higher than import prices do not necessarily mean that an industry is not economic for a country. . . . Of course the smaller the difference the better.

The problem has to be considered from another angle. It is not really a question of comparing industrial costs with import prices but of comparing the increment of income obtained in the expansion of industry with that which could have been obtained in export activities had the same productive resources been employed there.

I am afraid that it is not possible to arrive at the optimum solution of this problem if market forces are left unrestricted. The classical mechanism of the free play of market forces, either in its original form of wage adjustments or in its contemporary version of price adjustments through exchange rate movements, does not bring about that optimum solution. On the contrary, the periphery transfers to the outer world a greater part of the fruits of increased productivity than if the market forces had been contained at a certain point, either through customs protection or some other form of interference in the process. . . .

57 ..... Foreign-Exchange Impact as an Investment Criterion*

WALTER KRAUSE

University of Iowa

The primary rationale for placing foreign-exchange impact in a pivotal position [as an investment test] is that the immediate bottleneck handicapping industrial development in the typical underdeveloped country is found in foreign-exchange stringency, and that, therefore, the effect of any new industrial enterprise upon total foreign-exchange supplies logically represents a core consideration.[1] The contention is that an enterprise has special merit if it helps ease the foreign-exchange situation, since added development then becomes easier, not harder; on the other hand, an enterprise loses in merit if its presence serves to impair the foreign-exchange situation further and thus automatically precludes additional development.[2]

Beyond this primary rationale, a major secondary rationale also exists: tests based on foreign-exchange impact are held to be practical, especially in the sense of being easy to apply. Some persons are convinced that tests rooted in comparative advantage are likely to prove impractical; attempts to judge new enterprises on this basis serve to raise a great many ques-

---

* From *Economic Development* by Walter Krause, pp. 138–142. © 1961 by Wadsworth Publishing Company, Inc., Belmont, California. Reprinted by permission of the publisher.

[1] Other deterrents to industrial development are not thereby ignored; the point is simply that *the* shortcoming that forges to the forefront to inhibit the "very next step" in the course of industrial development tends, with almost uncanny regularity, to be foreign-exchange stringency.

[2] Typically, a major rationale for establishment of a screening committee proceeds in terms of the need for control over the evolving investment pattern so as to assure beneficial foreign-exchange impact from new investments (or to preclude adverse foreign-exchange effects).

tions, both of theory and fact, so that over time the performance record is in danger of becoming one of "much talk and little new industry." These persons are inclined to regard action as much more probable when tests are based instead on foreign-exchange impact. They contend that greater action is fostered because only problems of immediate consequence are pivoted into a central position, with other issues left for later argument — presumably when industrial development is well underway and a country can afford the luxury of the debates likely to be associated with efforts toward the refinement of testing techniques. In essence, as these persons see the matter, what underdeveloped countries need is some new industry *now* — whenever such can be had on a workable basis; absolute perfection is not necessary all along the line.

The key consideration, then, is foreign-exchange impact. Stated briefly, any enterprise that is *foreign-exchange-earning* or *foreign-exchange-saving* is regarded to have merit in terms of this approach (and the more foreign exchange earned or saved, per given amount of investment, the more meritorious an enterprise is presumed to be). But what, precisely, is a foreign-exchange-"earning" or "saving" enterprise? A foreign-exchange-earning enterprise is one whose output enters export markets, and whose presence has the net effect of adding to a country's foreign-exchange-earning capacity, so that the country's foreign-exchange reserves are increased by virtue of the new enterprise. Outstanding examples of foreign-exchange-earning enterprises include those devoted to the processing of raw materials prior to export. On the other hand, a foreign-exchange-saving enterprise is one whose output substitutes for previous imports. In order to "save" foreign exchange, new domestic production must cost less in associated foreign-exchange outlays than did imports displaced by it. Foreign exchange is not saved if the volume of domestic production is expanded to such an extent that associated foreign-exchange outlays exceed those previously made on imports of the product in question (or if any expansion in volume is not offset by substitutions in import composition such that total foreign-exchange outlays on the product and its substitutes are held below those previously made on the product and its substitutes). During early stages of industrial development, foreign-exchange-saving enterprises tend especially to be those concerned with articles of widespread domestic consumption, e.g., textiles, soap, and cigarettes.

Numerous advocates of industrial development are inclined to favor foreign-exchange-saving enterprises over those in the foreign-exchange-earning category — meaning that they prefer production for the domestic market to production for export. The explanation for this preference appears rooted, for the greater part, in a fear that reliance upon foreign-exchange-earning enterprises will give a country nothing better than some elementary processing of raw materials prior to exportation, which frequently is regarded as a "low" form of industrial development at best, and, at worst, just more colonialism in operation. Significantly, however, foreign-exchange-saving enterprises can save foreign exchange only insofar as imports occurred previously. Therefore, developmental potential in the foreign-exchange-saving category is limited by the size of the existent balance-of-payments configuration. On the other hand, foreign-exchange-earning enterprises are not limited in this manner; their earnings are not circumscribed within some previous or current balance-of-payments framework, but occur *outside* and beyond any such balance-of-payments framework. Therefore, developmental potential in the foreign-exchange-earning category is limited only by a country's capacity to produce and to secure foreign markets.

Always, however, an eased foreign-exchange situation — whether a result of foreign-exchange supplies being freed-up through the saving of foreign exchange or increased outright through the earning of foreign exchange — helps a country to sustain additional foreign-exchange commitments associated with further development, so that the process of growth is fostered. Foreign-exchange-earning and foreign-exchange-saving enterprises represent new development, in and of themselves, and, in addition, they "open the door" for further development in that they help ease the foreign-exchange situation. This is the essential appeal. As proponents, drawing upon the old adage that "the proof of the pudding is in the eating," like to put the matter (in support of basic tests related to foreign-exchange impact): industry ordinarily results thereby, and industry now is preferable to industry later (or maybe never).

Point of Controversy

As evidenced by the foregoing, a basis exists for controversy as between two distinct goals: maximization of *efficiency* versus *extrication* from a balance-of-payments straitjacket. Under terms of the first, the problem is seen as one of how to allocate resources and effort so as to maximize productive efficiency, i.e., of how to secure maximum output per given input. According to its proponents, pursuit of this goal requires each country to concentrate on activities in compliance with the law of comparative advantage, or some interpretation of it. Under terms of the second, the problem is seen as one of "how to get things moving" — or, "moving faster." According to its proponents, pursuit of this goal requires that special attention be given foreign-exchange impact. Given the differing points of emphasis, criticism and counter-criticism readily emerge. On the one hand, advocates of efficiency as the basic consideration fear that demotion of it as a test, in favor of tests related to foreign-exchange impact, is likely to result in the foisting upon an economy of enterprises that are destined to prove inefficient over the long-run, and hence prone to prove a drag upon the economy. On the other hand, advocates of foreign-exchange impact as a test question preoccupation with efficiency, particularly when underemployment is widespread (representing, perhaps, the greatest source of inefficiency of all); as they view the matter, even "inefficient" activity is defensible, if the only alternative is activity of even lesser caliber, or no activity at all.

The issue, as outlined, is a much-discussed one in certain quarters (e.g., within those US Government agencies concerned with the flow of official capital to underdeveloped countries), but discussion seems more often to lead merely to greater precision in the statement of divergent views than to a reconciliation of those views. In practice, no great conflict springs from the status of export-type enterprises. Foreign-exchange-earning enterprises must be able to compete in an international market in order to survive; hence, tests of efficiency, stemming from some interpretation of the law of comparative advantage, are not entirely precluded. Clashes of viewpoint, insofar as they arise, tend to show up more particularly in reference to enterprises oriented to the domestic market. There individual positions tend typically to divide on whether, or how, to take the following three factors into account. First, does one allow for, or disregard, the presence of underemployment or of unemployment? Second, does one allow for, or disregard, implications attributable to the presence of exchange control and to the "artificial" exchange rates that typically exist and serve to distort international price relationships? Third, does one permit, or disallow, new enterprises catering to new domestic demands, i.e., demands of a type that place the new enterprises in the position of being neither foreign-exchange-earning nor foreign-exchange-saving? To say the least, the situation is made to order for disagreement. And disagreement there is!

A Statement of View

Achievement of a world situation in which reasonably high real per-capita income and near-full employment are realized represents an "ideal" that many persons — including this author — are prepared to view as a worthy goal. But if the global environment thus envisaged as a goal is to be achieved, a transition period of some duration needs to be undergone. Seemingly, one should inquire what policies are appropriate when the ideal situation prevails, and what policies are appropriate during the transition period preceding its attainment; perhaps the two differ.

Significantly, the traditional law of comparative advantage assumes an environment that conforms more to the one pictured here as a goal than it does to the one actually prevailing or reasonably to be expected during the transition period preceding attainment of the goal. Accordingly, in the opinion of this author, the traditional law of comparative advantage is subject to important shortcomings as a guide in determining the types of industries a present-day underdeveloped country might reasonably contemplate in the course of its efforts to achieve development. Some deviation from, or modification of, the law of comparative advantage (in this form) seems warranted to help ease and speed the transition — as many persons have maintained in times past and as is much in evidence, for example, in infant-industry-type arguments. Yet, it seems inadequate simply to recognize a shortcoming in the law of comparative advantage and to condone deviation from it; some standards in terms of which basic decisions can be made still seem needed. Thus, the important question is what tests might prove workable during the transition. It is in this connection that "foreign-exchange impact" as a test acquires special relevance.

The central argument for foreign-exchange impact as a test — with which this author is in basic agreement — is that it "makes sense" in the here and now; it offers meaningful guidance for underdeveloped countries in the selection of the specific industries that can hope to survive and prosper, and that industries that can hope to survive and prosper, and that hence can help in the transition to that now-distant global environment in which conditions are reasonably akin to those assumed for the traditional law of comparative advantage — at which time the law of comparative advantage can well be looked to for the guidance its framers intended. In short, foreign-exchange impact is viewed as a meaningful test for the *short-run*, pending that time when evolution of an environment akin to that assumed by the law of comparative advantage serves to give meaning to its application as the *ultimate* test.

58..... Unbalanced Growth and Investment Criteria*

ALBERT O. HIRSCHMAN

Harvard University

. . . If we look at an economy that has experienced growth at two different points in time, we will of course find that a great many parts of it have pushed ahead: industry and agriculture, capital goods and consumer goods industries, cars on the road and highway mileage — each at its own average annual rate of increase. But surely the individual components of the economy will not actually have grown at these rates throughout the period under review. Just as on the demand side the market can absorb "unbalanced" advances in output because of cost-reducing innovations, new products, and import substitution, so we can have isolated forward thrusts on the supply side as inputs are redistributed among users through price changes, and at the cost of some temporary shortages and disequilibria in the balance of payments or elsewhere. In fact, development has of course proceeded in this way, with growth being communicated from the leading sectors of the economy to the followers, from one industry to another, from one firm to another. In other words, the balanced growth that is revealed by the two still photographs taken at two different points in time is the end result of a series of uneven advances of one sector followed by the catching-up of other sectors. If the catching-up overreaches its goal, as it often does, then the stage is set for further advances elsewhere. The advantage of this kind of seesaw advance over "balanced growth," where every activity expands perfectly in step with every other, is that it leaves considerable scope to *induced* investment decisions and therefore economizes our principal scarce resource, namely, genuine decision-making. . . .

* Taken and adapted from *The Strategy of Economic Development*, New Haven: Yale University Press, 1958, pp. 62–63, 65–70, 76–81, 83–86, 88–90, 98–102.

421

Development as a Chain of Disequilibria

. . . [The] balanced growth theory results from comparing the initial point of underdevelopment equilibrium with another point at which development will practically have been accomplished. A certain impatience with the process that lies between these two points — i.e., with the process of development — is shown by the following quotation from a well-known article by Scitovsky:

> Profits are a sign of disequilibrium; and the magnitude of profits under free competition may be regarded as a rough index of the degree of disequilibrium. Profits in a freely competitive industry lead to investment in that industry; and the investment in turn tends to eliminate the profits that have called it forth. Thus far, then, investment tends to bring equilibrium nearer. The same investment, however, may raise . . . profits in other industries; and to this extent it leads away from equilibrium. . . . The profits of industry B created by the lower price for factor A, call for investment and expansion in industry B one result of which will be an increase in industry B's demand for industry A's product. This in turn will give rise to profits and call for further investment and expansion in A; and equilibrium is reached only when successive doses of investment and expansion in the two industries have led to the simultaneous elimination of investment in both. It is only at this stage that . . . the amount of investment profitable in industry A is also the socially desirable amount. The amount is clearly greater than that which is profitable at the first stage before industry B has made its adjustment. We can conclude, therefore, that when an investment gives rise to pecuniary external economies, its private profitability understates its social desirability.[1]

To my mind, the first part of this passage is a most pertinent portrayal of how development is set and kept in motion, but Scitovsky, considering the proceedings he describes unnecessarily laborious, proposes to short-circuit them and to reach in a single jump a new point of equilibrium where the "elimination of investment" has been accomplished. But, actually, development is a lengthy process during which interaction of the kind described by Scitovsky takes place not only between two industries, but up and down and across the whole of an economy's input-output matrix, and for many decades. What point in such a virtually infinite sequence of repercussions are we supposed to shoot at? Which intermediate expansion stages ought we to skip, and which ordinarily successive stages ought we to combine? Some skipping or combining may be possible, but with no more than the modest objective of speeding up development here and there. In general, development policy must concern itself with the judicious setting up of the kind of sequences and

[1]Tibor Scitovsky, "Two Concepts of External Economies," *Journal of Political Economy*, April 1964, pp. 148–149.

repercussions so well described by Scitovsky, rather than with any attempt to suppress them. In other words, our aim must be to *keep alive* rather than to eliminate the disequilibria of which profits and losses are symptoms in a competitive economy. If the economy is to be kept moving ahead, the task of development policy is to maintain tensions, disproportions, and disequilibria. That nightmare of equilibrium economics, the endlessly spinning cobweb, is the *kind* of mechanism we must assiduously look for as an invaluable help in the development process.

Therefore, the sequence that "leads away from equilibrium" is precisely an ideal pattern of development from our point of view: for each move in the sequence is induced by a previous disequilibrium and in turn creates a new disequilibrium that requires a further move. This is achieved by the fact that the expansion of industry A leads to economies external to A but appropriable by B, while the consequent expansion of B brings with it economies external to B but subsequently internal to A (or C for that matter), and so on. At each step, an industry takes advantage of external economies created by previous expansion, and at the same time creates new external economies to be exploited by other operators.[2]

In Scitovsky's example, these external economies are essentially caused by production complementarities of one type or another. . . .

Technical complementarity in the strict sense is usually defined as a situation where an increase in the output of commodity A lowers the marginal costs of producing commodity B. This will happen typically as a result of the following situations:

a. because A is an input of B and is produced under conditions of decreasing costs;

b. because B is an input of A and is itself produced under conditions of decreasing costs;

c. because A and B are joint products (or because B is a by-product of A) and are produced under decreasing costs.

Because situations such as these have long been familiar to economists, complementarity is usually associated with economies of scale.[3] But there is no need for so restrictive an interpretation. We can define complementarity as any situation where an increase in the demand for commodity A and the consequent increase in its output call forth an increased demand for commodity B at its existing price. This happens not only when the connection between the two commodities is via the production process. The connection between A and B may also arise because the increased *use* of A leads to greater demand for B. We are not thinking

[2] Note that the private profitability falls short of the social desirability of any venture only when its "output" of external economies exceeds its "input" derived from other ventures.

[3] W. Fellner, *Trends and Cycles in Economic Activity* (New York, 1956), pp. 199–200. N. S. Buchanan and H. S. Ellis, *Approaches to Economic Development* (New York, 1955), pp. 279–280.

here of situations where A and B *must* be employed jointly in fixed proportions. In this case it would not make much sense to say that demand for A and the subsequent increase in its output provide an incentive for the production of B, as it is rather the demand for the good or service into which A and B enter jointly which explains the demand for both products. This is the familiar case of derived demand. But there are many situations in the course of economic development where the increased availability of one commodity does not *compel* a *simultaneous* increase in supply of another commodity, but *induces slowly*, through a loose kind of complementarity in use, an upward shift in its demand schedule. The phenomenon has been described under the apt heading "entrained want";[4] Veblen observed it long ago and effectively summed it up when he said that "invention is the mother of necessity" rather than vice versa.

An example of the rigid type of complementarity in use (best treated as derived demand) is cement and reinforcing steel rods in the construction, say, of downtown office buildings. Examples of the looser, "developmental" type of complementarity (entrained want) can be found in the way in which the existence of the new office buildings strengthens demand for a great variety of goods and services: from modern office furniture and equipment (still fairly rigid), to parking and restaurant facilities, stylish secretaries, and eventually perhaps to more office buildings as the demonstration effect goes to work on the tenants of the older buildings. Here again, failure to arrange for all of these complementary items from the start could be denounced as "poor planning" which ought to be avoided by centralized decision-making. But, just as in the case quoted by Scitovsky, an attempt to telescope the whole process would be futile because of the virtually infinite number of complementarity repercussions, and because of the uncertainty about a good many of them; moreover, such an attempt would miss the point that the profitable opportunities that arise as a result of the initial development move constitute powerful and valuable levers for subsequent development which are to be carefully nursed, maintained at some optimum level, and if necessary created consciously rather than eliminated.[5]

The common feature of the various complementarity situations is that, as a result of the increase in the output of A, the profitability of the pro-

---

[4] The term is used by H. G. Barnett in *Innovation: The Basis of Cultural Change* (New York, McGraw-Hill, 1953), pp. 148–151, with the exact meaning we have in mind here: "The fulfillment of one need establishes conditions out of which others emerge . . . In most instances it is impossible for people to foresee [these emergent wants] even if they try . . . Entrained wants are a consistent feature of motivational stresses for cultural change" (p. 148).

[5] This does not mean that when new buildings are put up one should refrain from planning for new parking facilities. Development itself constantly extends the range of complementarities that are rigidly compelled and necessarily simultaneous: the optional equipment of one period becomes the standard equipment of the next, as a result of social and cultural pressures and needs, rather than because of purely technological factors. . . .

duction of B is being increased because B's marginal costs drop, or because its demand schedule shifts upward, or because both forces act jointly.

Put even more generally, complementarity means that increased production of A will lead to *pressure* for increasing the available supply of B. When B is a privately produced good or service, this pressure will lead to imports or larger domestic production of B because it will be in the *interest* of traders and producers of B to respond to the pressure. When B is not privately produced, the pressure does not transmute itself into pecuniary self-interest, and will take the form of political pressure for the provision of B. This is the case for such public services as law and order, education, satisfactory monetary and banking arrangements, highways, water, electric power, etc. Complementarity then manifests itself in the form of complaints about shortages, bottlenecks, and obstacles to development. Action in this case does not take place through the operation of the profit motive, but through group pressures on public authorities and agencies. . . .

Efficient Sequences Versus Investment Criteria

We can now begin to consider one of the most crucial problems in development theory and policy: that of investment choices.

Development requires the undertaking of a series of projects producing favorable effects on the flow of income, in a wide variety of fields: public administration, education, health, transportation, power, agriculture, industry, urban development, etc. The limitation of resources, be they savings available for investment or our "ability to invest," compels a choice among these projects. In traditional economics, the market performs this function by equating the productivities of the various projects at the margin. It is recognized, however, that in any economy a substantial proportion of funds must be devoted to projects (in education, health, some public utilities, etc.) whose output has no readily assigned or fully recoverable market value. Moreover, underdeveloped economies tend to exhibit certain systematic discrepancies between private costs and social costs, and in such cases reliance on the market would lead to misallocation of resources.[6]

These considerations and the practical needs of development planners have led to elaboration of *investment criteria*. The problem that has been discussed in this connection can be formulated as follows: given a limited amount of investment resources and a series of proposed investment projects whose total cost exceeds the available resources, how do we pick out the projects that will make the greatest contribution relative to their

---

[6] There are at least three important areas in which such systematic discrepancies are apt to occur: the wage rate (because of disguised unemployment), the exchange rate (because of overevaluation of the currency), and the interest rate (because of rationing of loan funds on the part of the banks). See J. Tinbergen, *The Design of Development* (Baltimore, 1958), pp. 39ff.

cost? In answering this question, economists have ordinarily interpreted "contribution" as *direct contribution to output* once the project has been completed. This is only natural if growth is visualized as depending exclusively on aggregate output and income which, via the propensity to save, secretes the means for further growth. On these premises, the measurement of what has been called the "social marginal productivity" (SMP) of different projects — essentially a more or less sophisticated benefit-cost ratio — becomes the instrument that should in theory permit us to rank different projects in the order of their expected contribution to output and therefore to further growth.[7]

Recently, a far more elaborate concept has been proposed by Leibenstein: In addition to the output stream, investment criteria ought to take account also of the differential effects of the proposed ventures on the supply of entrepreneurship and of savings, on consumption habits, population increases, and a variety of other factors affecting further growth.[8] Leibenstein admits that a criterion embodying all these repercussions (in addition to SMP proper) would be of unusually difficult application.[9] In practice, his criticism seems likely to result in an agnostic "it all depends" attitude since it seriously impairs the usefulness of the SMP criterion without replacing it by a manageable new instrument.

In attempting a different approach, we shall first draw a distinction between substitution choices and postponement choices. Consider any choice between project A and project B: If the decision favors A, this may mean either that B is *discarded permanently* or that it is *postponed*. In the former case, the choice is between technical substitutes such as alternative means of providing a city with power or water supply. Many important choices are of this kind. They relate to the best means of attaining a given end or to the best design of a project whose output itself is needed beyond question. In deciding such choices, the usual investment criteria retain considerable usefulness. Nevertheless, we feel that in underdeveloped countries additional considerations must be introduced. . . .

Let us suppose for the time being that all substitution choices have been made and that we have before us a series of useful projects which are ideally designed to accomplish their respective purposes. In this situation, we are only faced with postponement choices.[10] We no longer

---

[7] A. E. Kahn, "Investment Criteria in Development," *Quarterly Journal of Economics,* February 1951, pp. 38–61; H. B. Chenery, "The Application of Investment Criteria," *Quarterly Journal of Economics,* February 1953, pp. 76–96; J. Ahumada, "Preparación y evaluación de proyectos de desarrollo económico," *El trimestre económico,* July–September 1955, pp. 265–296.

[8] Leibenstein, *Economic Backwardness and Economic Growth,* Ch. 15.

[9] *Ibid.,* p. 268.

[10] In an earlier paper, "Economics and Investment Planning: Reflections Based on Experience in Colombia" in *Investment Criteria and Economic Growth,* ed. M. F. Millikan (Cambridge, Mass., M.I.T., 1955, multilithed), I argued essentially that economists ought to confine themselves to the making of substitution choices. I still believe that the most urgent task of development planners usually consists in arriving

choose A instead of B; rather, we choose the sequence AB instead of the sequence BA. What is the possible rationale for such a choice? If we suppose that our goal is to have both A and B, but that "now" we can undertake only either A or B, leaving B or A, respectively, for "later," then it is clear that the only conceivable reason for preferring AB to BA is that B will be possible sooner once A is in place than vice versa. In other words, our choice depends entirely on the pressure that the existence of A exerts toward the coming into existence of B as compared to the corresponding pressure that would emanate from B toward A. Once the problem is formulated in this way it becomes quite clear that the comparative productivity of A and B which will both have to be undertaken is likely to be a rather minor factor in the decision assigning the priority.

Although our reasoning has been drastically simplified, it takes hold of an important aspect of the development problem. Essential tasks always abound in underdeveloped countries since backwardness has so many different interrelated facets. From this interrelatedness we do not draw the balanced growth conclusion that a simultaneous attack is essential. But what might be called a sequential or chain solution is indeed required. In other words, isolated progress in one area is possible, but only for a limited period; if it is not to be choked off, it must be followed by progress elsewhere. Therefore to compare the productivity increases that result from two projects in, e.g., education and transportation, is an insoluble problem not only in practice but conceptually. Such comparisons must be made on the *ceteris paribus* assumption that progress is being achieved in only one of the areas; and on this assumption the longer-term productivity of both undertakings is simply *zero* since the improved transportation facilities will serve little purpose and will fast deteriorate if education is not also improved in due course and vice versa. Therefore, the question of priority must be resolved on the basis of a comparative appraisal of the strength with which progress in one of these areas will induce progress in the other.[11] In these basic types of development decisions, it is therefore not sufficient to supplement, qualify, and otherwise

---

at correct substitution choices; but I realize now that postponement choices cannot be evaded. They must be made at two different stages of the process of development planning: first before it is decided in which sector or sectors substitution choices are to be studied, for the decision seriously to study alternative means of fulfilling a given need usually already implies a decision to give priority to this need; and secondly, after substitution choices have been completed in several different sectors.

[11] It may be objected that indivisibility could not be such as to prevent us from investing our resources partly in education and partly in transportation. However, the point we are making does not depend on indivisibility in the sense of "lumpiness." Let us assume that we have identified n essential and interrelated projects, costing 200 million dollars, but that we have only 100 million dollars at hand. Suppose that out of the n projects we can put together various collections of $m<n$ projects costing 100 million dollars. Then again the criterion for picking any particular collection of m projects would be the strength with which their execution would induce the remaining projects. Thus indivisibility is assumed only in the trivial sense that some projects will necessarily be undertaken ahead of others.

refine the usual investment criteria. We must evolve entirely new aids to thought and action in this largely uncharted territory of efficient sequences and optimal development strategies.

There is no doubt that the task that we have set ourselves is extremely complex. Let us suppose that we know which are the *n* steps that need to be taken to, say, double a country's per capita income. Then there exist in principle *n!* possible sequential arrangements of these *n* steps! Of course, there can be no question of neatly deducing, through a series of syllogisms, *the* most efficient sequence. Rather, we will strive to "sub-optimize"[12] and to develop a few guideposts, principles, and illustrative models.

To begin with, there was a great deal of exaggeration in our statement that there exist *n!* sequences in which the *n* steps may be undertaken. Many sequences are unavoidably "one-way" for purely technical reasons (a road must be built before it can be paved); one also feels that other one-way sequences are imposed not because they are technically determined but because they are necessary if development is to be properly planned, i.e., is to proceed in an "orderly" fashion. But here there may be some doubt as to how far it is advisable to go. Observation tells us that rapid growth of countries, cities, industries, and individual firms hardly ever proceeds in a completely orderly fashion, but that an excess of disorderliness may exert an inhibiting and demoralizing influence on further growth. Can we then perhaps define an optimum degree of orderliness in development? To illustrate this problem, let A, B, C, and D in Figure 1

FIGURE 1

The Optimum Disorderliness Model

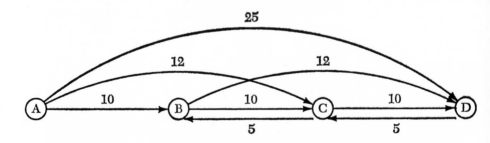

represent a group of development steps we wish to take and that ought to be taken in this order if ideal "orderliness" is to be achieved. Let us also suppose that step A *must* be realized before B, C, or D can possibly be undertaken, but that with A accomplished the sequence is no longer

12 Charles Hitch, "Sub-optimization in Operations Problems," *Journal of the Operations Research Society of America*, May 1953, pp. 87–99.

imposed. In the absence of limiting factors, the sequence ABCD would be chosen because it provides the smoothest transition from state A to state ABCD. But we now introduce a limited resource, such as decision-making or organizational ability, or simply time, and assume that different amounts of this resource are spent in going from one point to another. We want to minimize the use of this resource. If, say, ten units of this resource are spent in going from A to B, from B to C, and from C to D, then it is natural to think that to go from A directly to C will take a somewhat larger (say 12 units) and from A to D perhaps a much larger amount (say 25 units), because of the absence of the intermediate preparatory stages. On the other hand, less than ten units (say 5) should be needed to "fill in" B or C after C or D, respectively, because once the later steps have been realized the lack of the intermediary ones makes itself felt in so pressing a manner that the decision to undertake them requires far smaller quantities of the scarce ability or time than when they represented genuine forward steps.

If we apply the foregoing illustrative figures, then the expenditure of our scarce resource that is involved in the various possible sequences is as follows:

A to B to C to D	30 (10 + 10 + 10)
A jump to C then fill in B, then D	27 (12 + 5 + 10)
A to B then jump to D, then fill in C	27 (10 + 12 + 5)
A jump to D, then fill in B and C	35 (25 + 5 + 5)

In this example the figures have been selected so as to show that a limited amount of "putting the cart before the horse" may be efficient as compared to both maximum orderliness and maximum disorderliness.

It may be helpful to attempt a translation of this model into more familiar terminology. Let us assume two ventures, m and n, which require equal amounts of capital and have a yield of 10% and 8% respectively. At the beginning of period 1 the interest rate stands at 9%, hence only venture m is undertaken. At the beginning of period 2, with venture m in existence, the expected yield of venture n has risen to 10% and is now also launched. But we are free to suppose that, if n were undertaken first, m would be urgently required and that its expected yield would rise to 14% at the beginning of period 2. In this eventuality, investors would maximize income by selecting in period 1 the investment with the lower yield! Besides they would do everything to rush m to completion. Such strange results are avoided in traditional theory by the implicit assumption which we chose to discard here, that the profitability of different ventures is invariant with respect to the order in which they are undertaken.

The preceding examples are highly artificial as they imply that development proceeds along a single path. Nevertheless, they embody a number of concepts that are recurring throughout this essay: the difference between "permissive" and "compulsive" sequences, the possible rationality of violating "first things first" norms and the fact that the difficulty of taking a development decision is not necessarily proportional to the amount of capital it requires. . . .

Social Overhead Capital versus Directly Productive Activities

Definitions and Biases

The distinction between Social Overhead Capital (SOC) and Directly Productive Activities (DPA) is a recent one. Like all such classifications it must be judged not by its logic, which is far from compelling, but by its theoretical and practical usefulness, which has been considerable. SOC is usually defined as comprising those basic services without which primary, secondary, and tertiary productive activities cannot function. In its wider sense, it includes all public services from law and order through education and public health to transportation, communications, power and water supply, as well as such agricultural overhead capital as irrigation and drainage systems. The hard core of the concept can probably be restricted to transportation and power. Thus limited, SOC can be operationally defined as comprising those activities for the financing of which the International Bank for Reconstruction and Development shows a pronounced preference, just as the behavioral sciences have been said to comprise all those endeavors which manage to obtain financial support from the Ford Foundation. The conditions for including an activity under the category of SOC are probably at least the following three:

1. The services provided by the activity facilitate, or are in some sense basic to, the carrying on of a great variety of economic activities.

2. The services are provided in practically all countries by public agencies or by private agencies subject to some public control: they are provided free of charge or at rates regulated by public agencies.

3. The services cannot be imported.

The difference between the wide and the narrow meaning of SOC depends on whether one adds a fourth condition, namely:

4. The investment needed to provide the services is characterized by "lumpiness" (technical indivisibilities) as well as by a high capital-output ratio (provided the output is at all measurable).

This last condition clearly focuses attention away from, say, health and education, toward port installations, highways, hydroelectric projects, etc.

Statistical and historical research has shown the importance of SOC in the total investment picture as well as the large share of foreign investment that went into SOC, particularly railroads, during the nineteenth and early twentieth centuries.[13] As a result, economists, and particularly the

---

[13] A. K. Cairncross, "The Place of Capital in Economic Progress," in L. H. Dupriez (ed.), *Economic Progress*, Louvain, 1955; Ragnar Nurkse, "International Investment

"developers" among them, have become acutely SOC-conscious. It is widely assumed that enlarged availabilities of electric power and of transportation facilities are essential preconditions for economic development practically everywhere. Here, at least, we have a field where economists have given full recognition to the principle of "efficient sequence." Investment in SOC is advocated not because of its direct effect on final output, but because it permits and, in fact, invites DPA to come in.

The trouble with investment in SOC — or is it its strength? — is that it is impervious to the investment criteria that have been devised to introduce some rationality into development plans. The computation of capital-output ratios often presents almost insuperable statistical difficulties (as in the case of highways) and is moreover considered to be misleading anyway because of the igniting effect SOC investment is expected to have on DPA. As a result, SOC investment is largely a matter of faith in the development potential of a country or region.

The fact that there is so little possibility of evaluating objectively how much investment in SOC is really indicated in any given situation should give us pause. Such a situation implies at least the possibility of wasteful mistakes.

The absence of ex ante criteria is compounded by the weakness of sanctions when mistakes have actually been made. Underutilized port installations, highways, and even power plants do not present nearly the same administrative and public relations problem as a factory that is idle or suffers losses because of insufficient demand.

Perhaps it is this absence of criteria and of sanctions that has endeared SOC so much to the developers. Development planning is a risky business and there is naturally an attraction in undertaking ventures that cannot be proven wrong before they are started and that are unlikely ever to become obvious failures.

It must be conceded that, to some extent, investment in SOC is "safer" than investment in DPA, not only on this account but also in a real sense: it is diversified investment in the general growth of the economy rather than in the growth of one specific activity. This is the case, for instance, of improvements in a country's *principal* port, of modernization of an *integrated* railroad system, and of additions to the capacity of an *interconnected* electric power production and distribution system. But many SOC investments do not represent similarly diversified risks, and are rather narrowly tied to the anticipated rising fortunes of one city, one valley, or one traffic route; in such cases, it is questionable whether SOC investment is less risky than, for example, investment in an industry whose products might have a nationwide market.

Today in the Light of Nineteenth Century Experience," *Economic Journal*, December 1954, pp. 744–758, and *Problems of Capital Formation in Underdeveloped Countries*, Oxford, 1953, pp. 152–154. . . .

There is another important reason for which the importance of SOC investment may have been overstressed in recent years. In the countries outside the Soviet orbit, directly productive activities in industry, agriculture, and commerce are generally in the hands of individuals or private firms. Therefore, development programs, although often claiming to lay down comprehensive patterns of resource use for the future, are concerned primarily with the allocation of public investment funds among those activities that are considered to be the responsibility of public agencies. The provision of transportation and communications facilities, the production and distribution of electric power, the construction of irrigation and drainage systems are now widely agreed to be appropriate fields of governmental economic activity in addition to the more traditional ones of law and order, defense, education, health, etc. Since economic planners are then spending most of their time on SOC projects, it is only natural that they should claim for them overriding and fundamental importance. This in itself would be innocuous enough were it not for the fact that a combination of taboos, opposing interests, and self-restraint makes it difficult for public investment to enter the DPA sectors. Therefore SOC investment is not only being overadvertised; it also risks being overdone since alternative and possibly more desirable uses of public funds are simply not within the horizon of the planners.

Development Via Shortage and Via Excess Capacity of SOC. There can be no question whatever that SOC investment is "essential" for economic development. The sizable percentage of total investment occupied by SOC investment in all countries testifies to this fact. But all we know from such statistics is that SOC investment is a most important ingredient of economic development. *They cannot tell us to what extent SOC investment leads or follows DPA investment,* and that is the question we are interested in.

There is no simple answer. Either sequence is conceivable and we must look toward economic analysis and history for indications of the advisability of one or the other under given conditions.

Some SOC investment is required as a prerequisite of DPA investment. Access to an area by sea, road, rail, or air is indispensable before other economic activities can unfold there. But within rather wide limits, the relationship between SOC and DPA is not technologically determined. Within these limits, the cost of producing any given output of DPA will be the higher, the more inadequate the SOC of the economy. . . .

But it is one of the paradoxes of development that poor countries cannot always afford to be economical. Our principal assumption throughout this essay is that the real scarcity in underdeveloped countries is not the resources themselves but the ability to bring them into play. We shall now apply this notion by stipulating:

1. that SOC and DPA cannot be expanded at one and the same time; and

2. that preference should go to that sequence of expansion steps which maximizes "induced" decision-making.

As a result of the first condition, we can immediately visualize two types of sequence: one that starts expansion through increases in the supply of SOC . . . and one where the initial expansionary step is always taken by DPA. . . . The first sequence may be labeled *"development via excess capacity"* (of SOC) and the latter *"development via shortage"* (of SOC). . . .

Suitability of the Various Sequences. The principal characteristics of the two varieties of unbalanced growth which we have described is that they yield an extra dividend of "induced," "easy-to-take," or "compelled" decisions resulting in additional investment and output. Excess capacity of SOC, "building ahead of demand," is expected to create this demand by making a country, region, or city attractive to DPA investors. If, on the other hand, DPA is allowed or is made to run ahead of SOC, strong pressures are set up for the provision of SOC in a subsequent period. Development via shortage is an instance of the "disorderly," "compulsive" sequence discussed earlier in this chapter. Development is speeded up because an intermediate stage that is being jumped over can be filled in with comparative ease as pressures and needs arise from the already realized stages. The absence of the intermediate stage is now felt as a shortage and the decisions to remedy it are more readily taken than before the shortage arose. For instance, fiscal measures and utility rate changes which are needed to secure the funds for expansion and whose adoption was out of the question prior to the shortage are suddenly accepted as inescapable.

Thus balanced growth of SOC and DPA is not only unattainable in underdeveloped countries; it may not even be a desirable policy because it does not set up the incentives and pressures that make for this "dividend" of induced investment decisions. . . .

Backward and Forward Linkage

. . . Our search for efficient sequences and for mechanisms that tend to maximize "induced" investment decisions must now move on to the directly productive activities themselves. Here we meet with such well-known development alternatives as agriculture versus industry, export promotion versus import substitution, heavy versus light industry, etc. Rather than examine in isolation each one of these specific problems we shall attempt to sketch a generalized method of attack.

In our discussion of SOC versus DPA we made two assumptions:

1. that within certain limits the proportions in which investment must be divided between these two categories are variable (this assumption resulted in the possibility of excess or shortage of social overhead capital); and

2. that in case of a shortage, the remedy of imports was not available (this is fairly realistic in the case of transportation and power, not to speak of more basic SOC activities such as education and law enforcement).

Both assumptions will now be reversed; insofar as relations among various directly productive activities are concerned, we shall operate on the assumption, familiar from input-output analysis, that input coefficients are fixed or at least that needed inputs increase monotonically with outputs. In other words, while it was conceivable that an economy is inadequately or overgenerously equipped with technical training facilities, port installations, roads, and electric power stations relative to its endowment of manufacturing capacity, it is plausible to suppose (at least with given techniques) that an increase in the output of cotton yardage requires a larger input of raw cotton. Flexibility is restored, on the other hand, by the assumption that if a required input is not supplied from domestic sources it can be imported.

The pattern of pressures, incentives, and repercussions is therefore likely to be quite different from the one that was characteristic of the SOC-DPA relationship.

In discussing the latter, the concepts of SOC shortage and excess capacity emerged as the principal agents of further development. With our new assumptions, a specific shortage of goods and services required as inputs for a certain newly established economic activity is inconceivable. If the required inputs are not available, the activity will simply not take place. If it does take place, the inputs must already be forthcoming — either as a result of domestic production or through imports. Thus it seems that there is little room here for the kind of direct and strong pressure that leads from one productive activity toward another. But important stimuli result nevertheless from the fact that the setting up of an industry brings with it the *availability of a new, expanding market for its inputs* whether or not these inputs are supplied initially from abroad.

Similarly with what we called excess capacity. At first it would seem that this concept has little place within the DPA sector. An industry must sell its output. It will come into being only if it anticipates being able to do so; if the anticipation turns out to be a miscalculation, the industry will have to close its doors. Thus the coming into existence of an industry must be the result of some pre-existing demand, but can it be held to induce new activities and demand? Such repercussions are less obvious than the road which permanently encourages new traffic flows. Nevertheless, the domestic availability of a product whose output will ordinarily be expanded if necessary does have some features in common with the availability of a basic service.

It may seem that, given our assumption that DPA products can be imported, there is no reason why domestic availability of a new product should prove a better spur to further economic activity involving the product as an input than availability from foreign sources of supply that existed all along. In pure theory, this may indeed be so, but in practice three important considerations make domestic availability a considerably more effective spur to further development:

1. Importing requires special skills and therefore reduces the number of potential entrants.

2. Importing is subject to special balance-of-payments uncertainties, and production largely based on imports is therefore particularly risky; if inflation is expected to proceed more rapidly at home than abroad and adjustment of the exchange rate is held back, quantitative import restrictions become likely; if, on the other hand, the exchange rate is allowed to depreciate freely, it is likely to do so faster than the domestic purchasing power of the country's currency and there would be a long-run cost advantage in relying as much as possible on domestic inputs.

3. Finally and perhaps most important, the fact that a certain product is produced domestically is likely to result in efforts on the part of the producers to propagate its further uses and in their financial participation in such ventures. The domestic availability of a product thus brings into being active forces that make for its utilization as input in new economic activities catering to newly "entrained wants." In this respect, it is therefore a less purely permissive inducement mechanism than the existence of a road which merely "invites" more traffic.

Thus, in close analogy to the alternative between development via shortage and development via excess capacity which we described for the SOC-DPA situation, two inducement mechanisms may be considered to be at work within the DPA sector:

1. The input-provision, derived demand, or *backward linkage effects*, i.e., every nonprimary economic activity, will induce attempts to supply through domestic production the inputs needed in that activity.

2. The output-utilization or *forward linkage effects*, i.e., every activity that does not by its nature cater exclusively to final demands, will induce attempts to utilize its outputs as inputs in some new activities.

Development policy must attempt to enlist these well-known backward and forward effects; but it can do so only if there is some knowledge as to how different economic activities "score" with respect to these effects. Ordinarily economists have been content with general references to the advantages of external economies, complementarities, cumulative causation, etc. But no systematic effort has been made to describe how the development path ought to be modified so as to maximize these advantages even though the existence of input-output statistics supplies us with a few tools for an analysis of this kind.

First, a further note on the linkage concept itself. What do we imply when we speak of the linkage effects emanating from industry A toward industry B? Language can be quite ambiguous here, for we may have in mind the potential *importance* of the linkage effect in terms of, say, the net output of the new industries that might be called forth; or we may mean the *strength* of the effect, i.e., the probability that these industries will actually come into being. The total effect could be measured by the sum of the products of these two elements; in other words, if the establishment of industry W may lead, through linkage effects, to the establishment of n additional industries with net outputs equal to x_i ($i = 1,2...n$) and if the probability that each one of these industries will actually be set up as a result of the establishment of industry W is p_i ($i = 1,2...n$), then the total linkage effect of industry W is equal to

$$\sum_1^n x_i p_i.$$

The probabilities can be interpreted as measuring the strength of the stimulus that is set up. For backward linkage, this strength can be roughly measured as follows: suppose industry W requires annual inputs of $y_1, y_2...y_n$ and suppose that the minimum economic size (in terms of annual productive capacity) of firms that would turn out these inputs is equal to $a_1 a_2...a_n$; then the strength of the stimulus or the probability that the setting up of industry W will lead to the setting up of industries producing the inputs is equal to the ratio of the y's to the a's.[14] Minimum economic size is not a technical concept, but is defined in economic terms relative to normal profits and efficient foreign suppliers. In other words, it is the size at which the domestic firm will be able both to secure normal profits and to compete with existing foreign suppliers, taking into account locational advantages *and* disadvantages as well as, perhaps, some infant industry protection. In this way comparative cost conditions are automatically taken into account.[15]

In the case of forward linkage, an interpretation of the p's is less straightforward. The concept of economic size is not helpful here, since the size of the market for the industries that might be brought into being through forward linkage does not depend on their suppliers. A clue can perhaps be found in the importance of the articles produced by industry W as inputs for the output of the to-be-linked industry. If these inputs are a very small fraction of the industry's eventual output, then their domestic availability is not likely to be an important factor in calling forth that industry. If, on the other hand, these articles are subjected to new

[14] The ratio is to be defined as having a ceiling of 1, i.e., the value of the ratio is equal to unity, whenever the y's are equal to *or larger than* the a's. Note also that the y's are equivalent to the gross output of the new industries or firms in physical terms whereas the x's are their net outputs in value terms.

[15] Data on the economic size of plants in different industries would be the starting point for determining minimum economic size in different countries. Research in this area in relation to economic development is surprisingly scant, except for the pioneering article of K. A. Bohr, "Investment Criteria for Manufacturing Industries in Underdeveloped Countries," *Review of Economics and Statistics*, May 1954, pp. 157–166. Some basic data for small and medium plants are available in a series of Industrial Reports issued by the . . . International Cooperation Administration. For data on optimum plant size in U.S. industry, see J. S. Bain, *Barriers to New Competition* (Cambridge, Mass., 1956), Ch. 3.

further manufacturing operations, then the strength of the forward stimulus is likely to be substantial, provided demand is sufficient to justify domestic production.

In these cases, then, importance and strength — the x's and the p's — of the linkage effect are inversely correlated. Industries where the x's are small and the p's large are sometimes aptly called "satellite" industries. They are almost unfailingly established in the wake of industry W but are of minor importance in comparison to that industry. Thus defined, satellite industries can be established through backward or forward linkage. In the case of cement, for instance, the manufacture of multi-wall bags for packing purposes represents backward linkage while the establishment of a cement block industry represents satellite formation through forward linkage. . . .

D..... Research on
International Business

International business, as we have observed earlier, is a relatively new, but rapidly growing, field. With the field in something of a state of flux, legitimate question exists as to what it should cover, for whom its "message" should be geared, what the content of its "message" should be. The present section offers a selection, by Professors Robock and Simmonds, that deals with this general matter — a survey of the field and speculation on its future.

Minimally, two groups legitimately have a high interest in international business: businessmen and students contemplating business careers. An immediate interest of the businessman is in the substance of research findings. In contrast, the student is interested in training *preparatory* to a career. His need is a dual one: (a) a stock of "know-how," plus (b) a mode of thinking. Relative to (b), the manager of the future should have a good understanding of the *context* within which international business operates, in addition to an understanding of matters inside a going concern. Unquestionably, a premium attaches to greater appreciation of what it is reasonable for a business to expect, or not to expect, within a given environment — an environment that varies widely geographically and over time. True, business can hope to affect the world about it; but, also, it must live *within it* — and, about this facet, and all that it entails for business, the manager of the future should have a keen sensitivity.

59..... The Subject of International Business*

STEFAN H. ROBOCK
Indiana University

KENNETH SIMMONDS
Manchester Business School

The tremendous growth in international business represents one of the most dramatic and significant world events of the last decade. International business operations have become massive in scale, are expanding rapidly, and are influencing patterns of political, economic, and social development throughout the world.

At the same time this phenomenon has confronted the business executive with new and unique management problems. He must deal with new elements of risk, of conflict, of environmental adjustments, and of influence over social and economic change — elements he has not been facing in purely domestic operations. And, until recently, the international business executive was not able to look to the academic centers of business research and education for much help.

Although an educational lag still persists, a significant new trend has been gaining momentum in American business education — to give explicit attention to the international dimension of business. The new trend is supported by the view that existing theories, generalizations, principles, methods, and techniques, developed in response to norms in the United States, are neither general nor universal and that the international dimension of business involves unique aspects that need to be explicitly treated in business education.

This new emphasis on international business studies has important implications for the businessman, because he can utilize both the knowledge being developed and the personnel being trained. How the field of

* From "What's New in International Business?" in *Business Horizons,* Indiana University, Winter 1966, pp. 41–48.

439

international business is being defined, what materials and ideas are being developed, and how the international dimension of business is altering the business school curriculum are issues that should be of interest to the businessman.

The Field of International Business

The label "International Business" covers the evolving multidimensional pattern of international activities by business firms. As a field of study, it supersedes and extends beyond the traditional field called "Foreign Trade." Until recently, because the international dimension of business consisted mostly of importing and exporting, courses in foreign trade were the mainstay of the international dimension in business education. But since the end of World War II, investment has begun to displace trade.[1] Many firms have established industrial and commercial operations in a number of different countries. These operations involve direct foreign investment and direct managerial responsibility. Furthermore, much of the import and export activity of multinational corporations depends directly upon having business operations in many countries.

Business firms differ significantly in their degree of direct and indirect international involvement. The international dimension for some firms may be limited to importing or exporting; other firms may be purely domestic but subject to considerable foreign competition. At the end of the spectrum is the multinational business firm that has its home in one sovereign national state but operates and lives under the laws and customs of other countries as well.[2] The multinational corporation may operate on a world scale without a dominant commitment to a particular country, but it is more common at present for the international firm to have close ties to its home country. Although few, if any, business firms are isolated from the effects of international business activity, the field of international business gives major, but not exclusive, attention to the role of the multinational corporation.

Business firms operating within only one country, whether it is the United States or a foreign country, are generally covered by the concepts and ideas being taught in the functional fields of marketing, finance, production, and control. And where necessary, the substance of those fields may need to be adapted to the peculiar conditions of different foreign environments. Yet, where the operations of a domestically owned company or a foreign subsidiary influence or are influenced by a relationship with a foreign firm or institution, problems arise that fall within the scope of the international business field.

---

[1] For an interesting discussion of why investment is displacing trade see Emile Benoit, "Interdependence on a Small Planet," *Columbia Journal of World Business* (Spring, 1966).

[2] David E. Lilienthal, "The Multinational Corporation," in Anshen and Bach, eds., *Management and Corporations 1985* (New York: McGraw-Hill Book Co., Inc., 1960).

In a broad sense, then, the field of international business focuses on unique problems that arise when the business firm crosses national boundaries — whether through the movement of goods, services, investment capital, money flows, or personnel. The field also includes problems of decision making by public officials who must understand the effects of government policies and actions on international business activities and take such effects into account in the formulation and implementation of public policies. These problems all require special concepts, theories, ways of thinking, and methods of analysis not developed in existing areas of business concentration.

Separate Identity of International Business

Although unique variables and considerations of business have fostered the development of the field as a separate entity in the business area, not everything concerning international business must be studied separately under that heading. Some aspects of international business may be covered most effectively by extending existing fields; others can be better developed as a unified whole than as segmented appendages to existing fields. For example, an understanding in depth of cultural differences as they affect international business operations is more likely to develop when the subject is treated as a unified whole than if the scholars of finance, marketing, production, and management were each to study separately the adjustment of their function to different cultures.

These are four aspects of international business activity around which new types of thinking are beginning to emerge. These four aspects overlap to some degree and do not exhaust the potential for new approaches that may evolve. But each stems from unique problems that develop when business crosses national boundaries, and each gives rise to a new body of study and concepts.

International Risk Elements

The special risk elements confronted in international business activity include financial, political, regulatory, and tax risks. They arise from causes such as the existence of different currencies, monetary standards, and national goals, but they are all measurable through their effect on profitability or ownership.

The financial risk elements involve balance-of-payments considerations, varying exchange rates, differential inflation trends among countries, and divergent interest rates. In the political area, the risk of expropriation or lesser harassment directed toward the foreign firm must be considered for many years ahead when heavy capital investments are being contemplated. The regulatory risks arise from different legal systems, overlapping jurisdictions, and dissimilar policies that influence such conditions as the regulation of restrictive business practices and the application of antitrust laws. In the tax field, unforeseen changes in fiscal policies can significantly affect the profitability of the multinational corporation. Furthermore, uncertainty as to application of tax laws frequently creates a risk of double taxation.

International economics provides essential tools for understanding the risks arising from balance-of-payments considerations, foreign exchange regulation, problems of international liquidity, tariff policies, and trade restrictions. Political theory is developing new insights into nationalistic tendencies and the preferences of different societies for varying mixes of public and private sector activities. Legal research on international business transactions has been expanding, and a growing amount of international tax research is enlarging the general understanding of different tax systems and practices.

But the coverage in these related fields does not yet meet many of the major needs of international business. For example, the emphasis in international economics is still predominantly on international trade rather than on international investment. Also, the extension and application of the materials and concepts in the related fields to multinational business operations has been slow. Public policy has been even slower to adopt ideas and analysis that recognize the implications to international business activities of international economic and political variables.

The vigorous business and academic criticism of recent U.S. policies to restrict direct foreign private investment in order to improve the balance of payments suggests that the international business effects of such policies must be better identified in the formulation of governmental policies.[3] In the case of foreign investment controls, the recipient countries need to examine more rigorously the effect of such controls on international business and the question of how much and what kind of outside investment benefits the country.

The international risk elements are beginning to be identified and evaluated.[4] Some work is under way on the prediction of these risks. And the need is becoming recognized for a continuing business intelligence activity of considerable complexity to identify and predict international risks. Ideally, international risks should be analyzed for underlying causal forces, and projections into the future should be formulated in terms of probabilities and quantified in terms of potential costs.

Multinational Conflict Elements

Of major concern to international business are the conflicts that arise because of different national identities of owners, employees, customers,

[3] For example, Judd Polk, Irene W. Meister, and Lawrence A. Veit, *U.S. Production Abroad and the Balance of Payments* (New York: National Industrial Conference Board, 1966).

[4] John G. McDonald, "Minimizing the Risks of Moving Abroad," *Business Horizons*, IV (Spring, 1961).

and suppliers and because of divergencies between national interests and the business goals of multinational corporations.[5] Some of the conflicts occur within the international firm, and others involve the firm's relationship to the external environment.

An extremely troublesome area of external conflict concerns profit maximization decisions that result in the transfer of funds, types of production, and employment from one country to another. The results of these decisions may at times run contrary to the national economic policies of one or all of the countries involved. For example, extension of credit to foreign subsidiaries at times when the foreign nation is attempting to dampen purchasing power through monetary restrictions and exchange controls can undermine national objectives as well as place local firms at a competitive disadvantage.[6] The list of areas in which conflicts occur also includes such matters as contribution to local exports or reduction of imports, national interests in strengthening local research and management, or the country's international competitive position.

External conflicts frequently arise in decisions concerning a firm's allegiance to national defense policies. A recent example is the French subsidiary of an American computer manufacturer, which, in deference to American allegiance, did not solicit computer sales from Eastern Europe. Another recent example resulted from the different national security policies followed by the United Kingdom and the United States in dealing with Cuba. As a result of this difference, a British subsidiary of an American firm was persuaded to maintain American allegiance and not sell motors that would be installed in passenger buses going to Cuba. Conflicts on defense matters are likely to increase with the growing numbers of foreign-owned subsidiaries in technically advanced fields.

Within the international corporation the mixture of national allegiances raises further issues. Better preparation of Americans for business posts tends to perpetuate American management abroad, and expansion from a parent organization in a developed country tends to retain research and administration functions in the developed countries. Disparity in wage and salary rates has also led to widely practiced discrimination on the basis of nationality. A number of nations have already placed restrictions on the numbers of foreign expatriates they will allow in local operations.

The conflict aspect of international business requires thinking that will relate a multiplicity of interests, each with different objectives and different criteria for evaluating potential outcomes. Specific attention to the development of this way of thinking can be a valuable contribution

---

[5] Howe Martyn, "Multinational Corporations in a Nationalistic World," *Challenge Magazine* (November–December, 1965).
[6] See, for example, Raymond Vernon, "Saints and Sinners in Foreign Investment," *Harvard Business Review* (May–June, 1963), p. 157.

of international business study. No other business field covers this very successfully. The international businessman, trained to identify each conflicting interest and to think through the possible actions and reactions from each viewpoint, will be better prepared to plot his own best strategy in a complex situation. One of the functions of international business study should be to erase any tendency to make blindly nationalistic decisions or revert to pure economic arguments. There is currently a gradual emergence of an international framework for establishing legal validity of claims and actions of different parties involved in these conflict situations.[7]

Multiplicity of Environments

The most pervasive distinction between international and domestic business lies in the environmental framework. As business activity transcends a national setting, its environmental framework becomes more complex, more diverse, and more significant in influencing the effectiveness of business operations.[8] Aside from its relationship to the elements of risk and conflict discussed above, the multiplicity of environments in international business creates a wide range of operational problems that require new tools, concepts, analytical methods, and types of information. The wider the scope of the firm's international activities, the greater become the environmental diversities and the more crucial becomes the task of identifying, evaluating, and predicting environmental variables.

The environmental framework must be enlarged to include forces operating at a supranational level — such as the European Common Market — and forces involving relations between pairs of countries. Variables associated with different national settings must also be included. The need to understand the effect of environment on international business activity in both business decision making and public policy formulation has begun to produce analytical approaches peculiar to international business.[9]

One important category of environmental variables relates to business activity open to the international business firm and the form of business organization that must be used. The field of public utilities, including electric power, communications, and transportation, is not open to private enterprise in many countries. Business activity in the natural resource field, such as petroleum and mining, is restricted by many nations to

[7] W. G. Friedmann and R. C. Pugh, eds., *Legal Aspects of Foreign Investment* (Boston: Little, Brown and Co., 1959); A. A. Fatouros, *Government Guarantees to Foreign Investors* (New York: Columbia University Press, 1962).

[8] Roy Blough, *International Business: Environment and Adaptation* (New York: McGraw-Hill Book Company, 1966).

[9] Richard N. Farmer and Barry M. Richman, *Comparative Management and Economic Progress* (Homewood, Ill.: Richard D. Irwin, Inc., 1965).

domestic private enterprise or public enterprises. In some situations, the options open to international business firms require joint ventures with majority local ownership or joint ventures with government.

A second major category of environmental variables involves the diversity of the institutional settings. Labor unions, for example, are organized on different philosophical foundations and play different roles from country to country.[10] Patterns of national, regional, and local economic planning vary greatly in scope and in their influence over business activity. Capital markets and financial institutions are in different stages of development and, in some cases, are evolving along different paths.

Another broad environmental variable involves cultural differences that affect business management. International business needs to know how cultural differences influence the behavior of customers, suppliers, and employees, and how these influences on behavior will change. This aspect of international business involves the full range of communication problems arising out of different languages, different customs, and different values.[11]

International business has begun to develop its own body of cultural analysis following the functional division of business, with marketing questions receiving most attention. Considerable management literature has focused on the cultural adjustment of expatriate management and on the differences in foreign management and work force that might require adjustment of organization or procedures.[12] While concern for specific problems initially channeled cultural analysis along these functional lines, the common need throughout many business functions to understand cultural factors is leading toward a more unified approach, which might be titled "Cultural Analysis for Business Decisions." In the same way, other customary segments of environmental study such as educational, political, economic, and legal aspects can be explored in a unified manner.

International Business and Development

International business is frequently a major change agent and a key force in the economic and social development of a nation. This can be true for developed countries, such as those of Western Europe, as well as for underdeveloped countries. Thus, international business needs new concepts that provide an understanding of what can and cannot be achieved by the change agent and what are the potential contributions that international business can make to development.

[10] Arthur M. Ross and Paul T. Hartman, *Changing Patterns of Industrial Conflict* (New York: John Wiley & Sons, Inc., 1960).

[11] Edward T. Hall, "The Silent Language in Overseas Business," *Harvard Business Review* (May–June, 1960).

[12] John Fayerweather, *The Executive Overseas* (Syracuse: Syracuse University Press, 1959).

In the case of the underdeveloped countries, the need to identify and justify the contribution that a proposed international business activity will make to the country has been forcefully stated by Richard Robinson as follows:

> The reason for attempting at least a semi-rigorous analysis of what a firm proposes to do in an underdeveloped country within the context of the national interest of that country lies in the near certainty that the host government will analyze the project in similar terms — if not at first, then later. The Western businessman must be prepared to defend the utility of his local enterprise in terms of sustained economic growth and political modernization.[13]

The large diversified international corporation that has flexibility in its selection of countries and products to offer within those countries is much in need of a body of expertise to guide its global operations. Although economists have given some attention to the divergence between social benefit and the firm's profit maximizing alternative, they have stopped far short of the specific calculations needed by the international business decision maker. Although economists have also given some attention to the costs and benefit to a country from foreign private investment, they have not yet developed an adequate and objective framework for decision making on such questions by the host countries.

One facet of the contribution of international business to development that requires more attention is its role in encouraging indigenous entrepreneurship. On the one hand, the international firm may create new entrepreneurial opportunities external to the firm for local suppliers and merchants. On the other hand, it may attract much of the entrepreneurial potential in a country and thereby inhibit the possibilities for development of other national enterprises.

The role of international business in development also raises moral and ideological issues. It is frequently true that profit maximization will keep the firm away from the less developed markets. Yet the opportunity for the greatest long-term good from the viewpoint of both the corporation's home country and the developing nations may well be to enter the developing countries.

Once a corporation has entered a developing market, a whole new range of considerations arise that are beginning to draw attention in international business studies. One such issue is the degree to which the firm should become involved in the community and undertake expenditures normally the function of the public sector.[14] As a number of studies

---

[13] Richard D. Robinson, *International Business Policy* (New York: Holt, Rinehart and Winston, 1964), p. 100.

[14] Clifton R. Wharton, "Aiding the Community: A New Philosophy for Foreign Operations," *Harvard Business Review* (March–April, 1954), pp. 64–72.

have demonstrated, the paternalistic firm, which provides much of the normal functions of the public sector, can foster animosity among the local population.[15]

International Business Training

The Student

International business training has advanced most in the United States at the postgraduate level and in programs leading to the master of business administration degree. Some steps have been taken in undergraduate business programs and in executive development programs to include the international dimension of business. In addition, some business schools have programs at either the undergraduate or the graduate level for the student to complete part of his course work in a foreign university. The approach may internationalize the student by exposing him to a different foreign environment, yet foreign study per se does not necessarily include specific consideration of the substantive aspects of international business.

At the M.B.A. level, the kinds of students and their training needs will vary greatly. Most business schools structure their programs on the assumption that they are training future top business executives. In reality, however, many, if not most, of the M.B.A. students will make their careers as specialists in particular functional activities of business or as second-level managers.

Some students will want to study international business as a field of concentration; others will want international business courses as a supplement to their concentration in the traditional fields of accounting, marketing, finance, and so on. Some students specializing in international business hope to follow a career working in foreign countries. Others will take positions in the headquarters operations of a multinational firm that uses nationals for operating foreign subsidiaries. In schools with a sizable graduate program, courses and study programs can be designed to satisfy the international business training needs of the varied student body.

Having identified the kinds of concepts and materials required for international business as well as the different training needs of the students, a business school must develop an appropriate strategy for preparing these students to deal effectively with the international dimension of business. Ideally, the approach adopted should endeavor to achieve two goals: to internationalize the student as an individual so that he develops special sensitivities, attitudes, flexibility, and tolerance, and to make available the body of knowledge on international business.

[15] Stacy May and Galo Plaza, *The United Fruit Company in Latin America* (Washington, D.C.: National Planning Association, 1958), pp. 240–43.

Ethnocentrism and personal parochialism can be attacked in several ways. Living and working experience in a foreign environment through student exchange programs such as that of AIESEC (Association Internationale des Etudiants en Sciences Economiques et Commerciales), which arranges summer internships in foreign countries for students in commerce and business, can provide some of the necessary personal reconditioning. Recruiting a good mix of students from various countries will expose the international business student to other cultures and values through class discussion and through team projects, where the teams are composed of different nationalities.

In a personal and emotional sense, the international businessman must have a special kind of radar that alerts him to situations where specific values and ways of action that he takes for granted in his own environment are different in other cultures and nations. The businessman must develop enough flexibility to understand what underlies these differences, and he must have enough tolerance to recognize that types of behavior and sets of values different from his may be valid for other people.

The Curriculum

To inject the substantial materials of international business into a curriculum, one line of attack is to enlarge the international experience of members of the business school faculty, in the hope that increased international content of existing courses will result.[16] Attempts simply to tack international content onto existing courses are doomed to failure if the faculty is not convinced of its merit and if this addendum fails to mesh with the real purpose of the course.

Addition of specialist courses in international aspects of existing fields, such as international finance and international marketing, is another alternative. However, these courses usually require a number of prerequisite courses in the same field. Without this requirement a course in international marketing, for example, can degenerate into a course in marketing taught with international examples. Prerequisite requirements naturally limit the number of international courses a candidate without prior business training could take in a two-year master's program.

The more direct approach is to introduce courses, not necessarily tied to existing fields, that are aimed specifically at emerging concepts in international business. Such an approach offers more opportunity to those students with special international interests, and enables the faculty to concentrate both their teaching and research directly on international problems.

All of these approaches for internationalizing the business school can be complemented by making greater use of international study resources

---

[16] Borje O. Saxberg, "International Business and Economics Faculty Internship Exchange Programme," *The Quarterly Journal of AIESEC International,* II (February, 1966).

in other parts of the university. Languages, social sciences, history, law, and area studies all can be used fruitfully in building specific dimensions for the individual business school student. Specialist business graduates will be increasingly needed in work such as prediction of social unrest and resulting risk to international business or changing cultural attitudes and their long-run effect on demand.

. . .

Only a few years ago, American business schools did not recognize the international dimension of business except through traditional courses on foreign trade. Now the teaching of international business is growing rapidly, and considerable discussion is underway as to what the field should embrace, how international business can be developed as an academic discipline, and how the subject matter should be included in the business school curriculum.[17]

New concepts, theories, ways of thinking, and methods of analysis needed in multinational business operations and public policy formulation are becoming identified. A small but growing amount of research is under way. The results are finding their way into the curriculum of American business schools and executive development programs through a variety of patterns. The field is in an early stage of development and the opportunities for contributions by business educators are immense. . . .

[17] Stefan H. Robock and Lee C. Nehrt, eds., *Education in International Business* (Bloomington: Bureau of Business Research, Indiana University, 1964).

PART SIX ....

PROSPECTS FOR THE FUTURE

To complete our survey of the international economy, it is only fitting that, having viewed the past and present, we now try to "preview," to some extent, the future.

From an overall standpoint, the dual forces of diversity and inter-dependence, to which we referred in our introduction to Part One, appear destined to remain. Their interaction points to continued stress and further problems for the world; yet a growing technology may act as a counter-force which, if we can channel it wisely, may spell enormous opportunity and unprecedented well-being. In a first selection in this section, Professor Kuznets discusses these several forces, and comments on their possible impact and significance.

If proof is needed that the interaction of diversity and interdependence makes for conflict, we can find it in the present-day clamorings of under-developed countries, where dissatisfaction with the rewards assigned by the traditional pattern of world production and trade is widespread and where the cry is for economic development *now* (meaning, generally, a lessening dependence on raw materials through the greater acquisition of new industry). The foremost spokesman of the underdeveloped countries, Raúl Prebisch, is the author of their "official" indictment and reinforcing rationale. He has the distinction, also, of being the prime mover of a global conference — the UNCTAD Conference of 1964 — that witnessed a direct confrontation between the underdeveloped countries and the developed countries on trade and development issues. The conference looms large because it may stand as the prototype for others, all part of an attack on the "established" order of things.

In our second selection in this section, we read a Prebisch statement, expressly prepared as background material for the cited UNCTAD Conference. Included there, too, are excerpts from the final report of the conference, along with a brief appraisal of the conference.

Reinforcing the thesis that a more even spread of industrial develop-ment is essential in the world for the realization of general prosperity, our

451

third selection — by Professors Kerr, Dunlop, Harbison, and Myers — pictures industrialism as the "wave of the future" which will level differences between widely-separated regions and vastly-varied ways of life. Our final selection concerns the future of international business. Three views are presented there. Professor Robinson addresses himself to a trend of growing internationalism within which, he suggests, international business should be prepared to assume an increasingly "global" attitude. Professor Fayerweather points to a rising volume of business at the international level, characterized by the evolution of a markedly altered pattern of commodity flow. The final view (by Thomas Aitken, Jr.) is that of a businessman. He raises a question: With American business' activity expanding in the international economy, should businessmen not envisage themselves as invested with a "diplomatic" responsibility?

60..... The Forces of World Change: Diversity and Interdependence*

SIMON KUZNETS

Harvard University

. . . [The] diversity among nations with respect to size, economic level and structure, and political organization, combined with interdependence stemming from economic exchange and competition, universal possession of a stock of knowledge and other creative attainments useful to all mankind, and divisive attitudes and policies of hostility and aggression, are productive of many stresses and problems, accompanying the substantial economic advance that has undoubtedly been attained in recent decades. We conclude by brief observations on: (a) the recent trends in diversity and interdependence; and (b) the relations between these aspects of world structure and the basic forces underlying modern economic growth.

(a) If to give us some perspective we shift our view of the world economic structure from today to a past period, say to the last half century but with emphasis on recent decades, the picture suggests that the range of several aspects of diversity among nations has widened, while the ties of interdependence have become stronger. And, as a result, the problems and strains that the combination of diversity and interdependence generates may have been intensified.

While we cannot document these observations here, and they must therefore remain tentative conjectures, some supporting illustrations are at hand. Thus, the contrast in per capita income between developed and underdeveloped countries must have widened appreciably over the last

* Reprinted by permission of the publishers from Simon Kuznets, *Postwar Economic Growth*, Cambridge, Mass.: Harvard University Press, Copyright, 1964, by the President and Fellows of Harvard College, pp. 22–28.

half century — at least between the group of non-Communist countries classified as developed . . . and all less developed countries in Asia and Africa, including the Communist countries (the latter comprising something like two-thirds of world population today). Half a century ago the per capita income of the developed group was already much above that of the underdeveloped areas in Asia and Africa (that is, all except Japan); since that time per capita product grew at rates well over 10 per cent and often over 20 per cent per decade in the developed group while it grew much more slowly in the underdeveloped areas. Indeed, the contrast must widen by definition for any dichotomy in which we compare currently developed countries with currently underdeveloped areas — since any sustained participation in modern economic growth over a substantial period (say half a century) should shift a country from the underdeveloped to the developed group. A classification based on *present* levels and economic structure limits the underdeveloped group to countries that, by definition, grew more slowly than the units in the developed group; and widening of contrast in per capita income (over the long period as a whole) automatically follows. But even if we start with a dichotomy based on levels and structure at the *beginning*, not at the end, of a fairly long period such as half a century the contrast may still widen, *if* entry into modern economic growth, sustained industrialization, affects only a limited proportion of the initially underdeveloped group of countries (or, rather, population). And this is what happened: if we consider Japan and the U.S.S.R. as the two countries that shifted over that period from the underdeveloped to the developed group (admitting the U.S.S.R. into the latter category to strengthen the case) the population accounted for by this shift is only 0.3 billion out of a total of close to 2 billion in the underdeveloped parts of the world (outside of Latin America and Eastern Europe).

The trend (over the past half century) in diversity among nations by size is somewhat less certain, if we deal with nation-states, largely because of the major change from colonial status and dependency to political independence. A classification of the earlier colonial empires as single political units would reveal a decline in the number of huge political entities that would have been represented by the British, French, Japanese, and even the Dutch empires. But this trend would not have affected significantly the size of such giant nations as the United States, the U.S.S.R., and Mainland China; and, on the other hand, would show large additions to the number of small formally independent nation-states. In the skewed distribution of nation-states by size, the group at the small-size end of the range . . . was thus much increased; and the magnitude of diversity . . . must have risen sharply. This was particularly true of the most recent decade, when political independence was attained by so many small units in Africa.

This recent growth in number of nation-states and the emergence of the Communist bloc within the last half century suggest that diversity in political organization has widened, in comparison with the time before World War I, and increasingly so in recent decades. True, in the past there were differences in political organization not observed today — for example, among absolute monarchies, constitutional monarchies, republics, and the like. Yet, at the danger of being dogmatic, one may argue that in their bearing upon economic structure and growth, the differences in political organization that have developed recently . . . represent a widening of diversity among nation-states.

In particular, we should note the increase in the number of large countries that managed to tap the potential of modern economic growth. If we consider the United Kingdom, France, Germany, and the United States as the large developed countries early in the period, the emergence of Japan and the U.S.S.R. as developed countries meant a substantial *proportional* increase. And in view of the different historical background of these newcomers, the likelihood of strains in their relations with each other was all the greater.

In recent decades the widening diversity among independent nation-states in size, per capita economic product, economic structure, and political organization has been accompanied by significant strengthening or intensification of interdependence among nations. First, and most obvious, continuing innovations in transportation and communication have increased accessibility, and thus permitted far closer interdependence than would have been possible otherwise. Second, if we set aside the difficult question whether international trade and related flows have kept pace with the growth of total world output, and *allow* for the restrictive effects of the autarkical Communist bloc, the very widening of diversity in per capita product, combined with the intensified drive toward economic adequacy and growth, increased the dependence of at least the underdeveloped countries upon the developed. Third, the strains of hostility and aggression introduced by the newly emergent lines of political organization have also made for greater interdependence among nations. Clearly under conditions of a cold war the ties among the participants, either on one side or among those on both, are much closer than under conditions of relative isolation and indifference. The closer interdependence between, say, the United States and the U.S.S.R. than that between this country and some distant developed non-Communist nation (like Australia), or than that between the United States and Czarist Russia before World War I, is a phenomenon too obvious to need stressing, even though the dependence is one of mutual watchfulness and sensitivity to security.

It would seem, then, that the trends toward widening diversity and more intensive interdependence may have induced the greater stresses and perturbations that characterize life today. We may now ask whether these trends have been associated with the forces and drives that underlie much of the economic growth in modern times.

(b) Before answering this question we must recognize the magnitude and source of modern economic growth. . . . But, forestalling this . . . discussion, we mention here that the major source of modern economic growth, with its high rates of aggregate increase and rapid structural shifts, lies in the vast increase in the stock of useful knowledge. Much of this knowledge is based on science and connected with widespread changes in the attitude of human beings to material welfare and in their capacity to exploit effectively the world around them to useful ends. Yet, the potential of ever-increasing economic achievement, permitted by the growth of science and technology, requires, if it is to be exploited, many social adjustments — rearrangements of the old established pre-modern social and political institutions — to generate the necessary capital, to permit adequate investment in the education and training of human beings, to facilitate the movement of individuals to the places of greatest economic opportunity, and to provide sufficient motivation and return so that growth becomes self-sustaining rather than self-limiting, because of bottlenecks resulting from monopolization of opportunities or resistance of obsolescent industries, occupations, and so on, to the necessary transition.

It is in this connection that the nation-state . . . plays a major part by introducing and facilitating the essential adjustments in the social and economic institutions inherited from the past; and does so by means of its dominant power grounded in a social consensus that tolerates within the society the decline of some groups and the advance of others. Thus, the spread of the nation-state and its growing role in setting the conditions for economic growth may be viewed as a function partly of the greater potential of economic growth provided by the ever-growing complex of modern material and social technology; partly of the uneven spread in the utilization of this potential among nations which, while widening current diversities in economic level and structure, makes for an ever-increasing strain of backwardness. In a sense, the intensification of nationalism, with the resulting pressure to set up divisive self-centered nation-state units, is the price paid for the potential ability to channel the energies of societies so organized to the task of exploiting the promise of modern economic growth — exploiting it on the basis of a consensus stemming from some common bonds that sustain the society despite the disruptiveness of modern economic change. Modern economic growth is revolutionary in the rapidity of its structural shifts, the changes in relative position among various groups in society; and the modern nation-state is the mechanism usually employed to channel and contain such a revolution. I am not arguing that this is the only mechanism, or that all its current manifestations are indispensable to the task;

but in the light of modern developments, the basic relevance of the nation-state to the task of economic growth seems patent.

From these observations it follows that the increasing diversity among nations with respect to size and political organization may well be a result of the extension of modern economic growth to many areas, and of the rapid growth of the potential power provided by modern technology — employable internally or externally. All of this makes adjustment to the increasing gap in economic, and hence political, power more and more difficult. Of particular importance may be an aspect only briefly noted above — the increase in the number of *large* nations that have managed to secure the power bestowed by modern economic growth, nations that almost inevitably are affected by different historical backgrounds and heritage. This increasing diversity among large and relatively developed nations themselves, in addition to diversity in size, is a potent source of increasing international strains and tension. And it is in this connection that the spread of modern economic growth and the striking rise in the potential of modern technology are productive of major dangers in the world structure of today; and, if these dangers can be avoided or damped, of great opportunities.

61..... Attack on the Old Order[*]

RAÙL PREBISCH
Secretary-General, UNCTAD;
formerly with ECLA

This second world trade Conference [the United Nations Conference on Trade and Development, 1964], convened by the United Nations, is meeting under a star very different from that under which the first one met at Havana[1] sixteen years ago.

The first conference was clearly influenced by experience of the events that preceded the great depression of the 1930's, experience of a system reaching back to the nineteenth century. At that time, the remarkable expansion of world trade, with multilateralism in full swing, acted as a powerful catalyst of spontaneous development in the peripheral countries, which provided the industrial centres with food and raw materials.

The great depression precipitated the break-down of this old order, already undermined by the political impact of the First World War. In view of all this and of the consequences of the Second World War, it is out of the question to think of restoring the old order now. In the not too distant days of Havana it might have been possible to harbour illusions of doing this, but the subsequent course of events has finally dispelled these illusions once and for all.

It is imperative to build a new order with a view to solving the serious problems of trade and development that beset the world, especially the problems that affect the developing countries.

From the standpoint of the developing countries, the Conference will be particularly concerned with a phenomenon that was a subject of controversy until recently, but which is today a matter of understandable general concern: the persistent tendency towards external imbalance

[*] Taken and adapted from UN, *Towards a New Trade Policy for Development,* New York, 1964, pp. 3–10, 107–108.

[1] The Havana Trade Conference, whose central proposal for the creation of an International Trade Organization (ITO) subsequently failed to win the requisite multi-country approval needed for activation — *Editors.*

associated with the development process. The phenomenon is already well known. While primary commodity exports are, with a few exceptions, expanding relatively slowly, demand for imports of manufactured goods is tending to grow rapidly, at a pace that increases with the rate of development. The resulting imbalance creates a serious external bottleneck which makes development difficult. The imbalance must be rectified if development is to be accelerated in conditions of dynamic equilibrium.

One of the main objectives of the United Nations Development Decade is the attainment of a minimum annual growth rate of 5 per cent in the income of the developing countries by 1970. This is certainly a rather modest target and not much higher than the average rate of 4.4 per cent registered in the 1950's. Nevertheless, it will be extremely difficult — if not impossible — for many of the developing countries to achieve and maintain this rate of growth unless the present Conference brings about a policy of international co-operation that would make it possible to eliminate the imbalance in trade.

What are the implications of the 5 per cent minimum growth target for international trade? First and foremost, it should not be expected that, if the income of all developing countries is to rise at the minimum by 5 per cent every year, their imports can increase at a rate much less than 6 per cent. One of the main reasons for this is that any acceleration in the rate of growth requires additional investment; and the import content of this investment is normally much higher than that of income as a whole. Consequently, it is not going too far to conclude that imports would have to rise at a rate somewhat higher than that of total income. This view is supported by estimates based on the experience of developing countries.

The second implication of the 5 per cent growth target is that exports of the developing countries would also have to rise at the rate of 6 per cent *per annum,* in order to maintain balance-of-payments equilibrium. More precisely, a volume of exports should rise at a rate which, after allowing for changes in the terms of trade, would pay for a volume of imports increasing each year at a rate of 6 per cent.

As we all know, experience during the 1950's was highly unsatisfactory in this respect. The annual rate of growth in export volume of the developing countries during that decade was only 4 per cent *per annum,* and, if the petroleum-exporting countries are excluded, the average is significantly lower. At the same time, the terms of trade deteriorated, so that the purchasing power of exports over imports rose more slowly still, by under 2 per cent *per annum.*

Thus, even at existing rates of growth there is a widening gap in the balance of payments of the developing countries; at higher rates of growth consistent with the objectives of the Development Decade, the gap would be even greater if the trends of the 1950's continued.

This, then, has to be the starting-point of the Conference. One cannot posit a 5 per cent rate of development without accepting also all the consequences that this implies for the rates of growth of imports and exports.

There are many ways, of course, in which the external resources of the developing countries could be increased: through additional exports of primary products, through more exports of manufactures, or through greater external aid. To some extent, each of these possible solutions is a substitute for the others. To the extent that one fails in solving the problem under one heading, one increases the burden to be borne under other headings. For example, in so far as one fails to secure any significant improvement in the rate of growth of exports of developing countries, recourse must be had to a greater inflow of international finance. And within any given target rate of increase in exports as a whole, the less that is done to widen market opportunities for foodstuffs and raw materials, the greater need will there be to open up new markets for manufactures. A combination of interdependent elements is involved; and it is an essential condition for success that the various measures adopted should be integrated within an over-all policy for achieving the desired result.

Unless these measures are adopted, the trade gap of the developing countries will be immense; available estimates show that, if the factors responsible for the present trend in world trade continue, the trade gap may reach an order of magnitude of about $20 billion[2] by 1970 if the growth rate of 5 per cent is to be achieved. This gap is potential and not real: if the means of bridging the gap are not found, the developing countries will be forced to reduce their rates of growth unless they are prepared to achieve higher rates at an excessive economic and social cost involving serious political consequences.

The rate of growth of 5 per cent *per annum*, set as an objective of the Development Decade, can in no sense be considered fully satisfactory. It would mean an annual rate of increase of only 2.6 per cent in the average per capita income of the peripheral countries in view of the rapid rate of population growth, which is higher than in any previous era and makes it all the more difficult to expedite development.

Nearly half of the capital invested in the developing countries is needed to provide for the increase in population, thereby limiting the resources available for substantially and steadily raising the over-all level of living. Unless the present tempo of population growth slows down,[3] it would take eighty years at an annual rate of growth of 5 per cent for the developing countries to reach the current average per capita income level of western Europe, and approximately forty years more for them to reach

[2] This figure has been calculated on the basis of a 5 per cent *average* rate of income growth. If a *minimum* growth rate of 5 per cent is used, the figure for the potential trade gap will be higher.

[3] During the 1950's, the annual growth rate of the population of the developing countries as a whole was 2.2 per cent. It is estimated that it will rise to 2.4 per cent between 1960 and 1980.

that of the United States. For the least advanced countries, accounting for one half of the population of developing areas, the period required to reach the present western European level would be of the order of two hundred years.

A 5 per cent annual rate of growth could therefore be considered acceptable only for a short transitional period in which to create the internal and international conditions required for accelerated development.

On the other hand, even if a fall in the rate of population growth were to help in alleviating certain problems and tensions, it would in no sense be an excuse for slackening rather than intensifying the domestic development effort or for narrowing the scope of international co-operation; rather should it provide an opportunity for accelerating development so that its basic objectives may be attained in a shorter period of time, a period that is politically and socially acceptable.

The potential of modern technology is so enormous that the developing countries should not have to wait as long as the present industrially advanced countries had to wait to develop their technologies step by step and use them for the eradication of poverty and its inherent evils. Indeed, they cannot wait as long, because the acceleration of their development is an absolute necessity that brooks no delay. The pressure exerted by the masses for real improvements in their levels of living has never been as strong as it is now, and in the years to come it will become a growing source of internal and world-wide tension if it is not met by a vigorous policy of economic and social development in which international co-operation must play a decisive role.

The obstacles which the economic and social structures of the peripheral countries place in the way of development policy are well known. It is quite clear that important decisions must be taken to bring about structural changes, as has been indicated in previous reports of the United Nations and its specialized agencies. Suffice it to state here that, without such structural changes, and without a determined political effort to promote development and remove the internal obstacles from its path, measures of international co-operation, however good in themselves, will be very limited in their effect.

The Old Order

The imposing code of rules and principles, drawn up at Havana and partially embodied in the General Agreement on Tariffs and Trade (GATT), does not reflect a positive conception of economic policy in the sense of a rational and deliberate design for influencing economic forces so as to change their spontaneous course of evolution and attain clear objectives. On the contrary, it seems to be inspired by a conception of policy which implies that the expansion of trade to the mutual advantage of all merely requires the removal of the obstacles which impede the free play of these forces in the world economy. These rules and principles are also based on an abstract notion of economic homogeneity which conceals the great structural differences between industrial centres and peripheral countries with all their important implications. Hence, GATT has not served the developing countries as it has the developed ones. In short, GATT has not helped to create the new order which must meet the needs of development, nor has it been able to fulfill the impossible task of restoring the old order.

In the context of the nineteenth century and the initial decades of the twentieth, as we see it, there was no place for this idea of rationally influencing and so modifying the course of events. The course of events had merely to be followed and anything that obstructed it eliminated. Development in the periphery was a spontaneous phenomenon of limited scope and social depth; it came about under the dynamic influence of a unique combination of external factors which have since ceased to exist.

The situation can be presented simply in the following terms. During the last quarter of the nineteenth century, the United Kingdom, as the world's leading dynamic centre, accounted for 36 per cent of world exports of manufactures and 27 per cent of the imports or primary commodities. Since the historical accident of the industrial revolution happened in the United Kingdom before it did in other parts of the world, that country, with its limited resources and given its level of technology at the time, had to grow outwards and there emerged the classic pattern of exchanging manufactured goods for primary commodities. Imports of primary goods and other commodities by the United Kingdom grew apace, as did their share in the national income: the over-all import coefficient rose from approximately 18 per cent in 1850 to the very high figure of almost 36 per cent in 1880–84, as a result of free trade. This phenomenon influenced the rest of Europe, although not to the same extent, and its effects on the development of countries on the periphery of the world economy were striking.

Actually the process was the opposite of that which has gradually come into existence since the end of the First World War and especially since the great depression: the substitution of imports of food and raw materials for domestic production and not *vice versa*.

There was another factor which encouraged the growth of consumption and primary commodity imports: these imports were not yet subject to the adverse effects of technological progress as they would be in later years. Per capita income was still able to sustain an active demand for foodstuffs, synthetic production of raw materials had not yet begun on a large scale, and European farmers still clung to their traditional methods.

The Great Depression and World Trade

It is sufficient to mention these facts to emphasize the radical change which was ushered in during the First World War as a result of political and economic factors and which grew in scope and intensity as a result of the world depression of the 1930's.

The United States displaced the United Kingdom as the leading dynamic centre. This was more than a mere change of hegemony; it had a far-reaching influence on the rest of the world. The enormous natural resources of the vast territory of the United States and the resolutely protectionist policy it pursued from the start of its development were apparent in the steady decline of its import coefficient. In 1929, on the eve of the world depression, this coefficient was barely 5 per cent of total income and the restrictive measures resulting from the depression reduced it still further. In 1939, at the beginning of the Second World War, it had fallen to 3.2 per cent.

The effects of these developments on the rest of the world were of enormous importance. With the advent of the great depression, the order that dated back to the nineteenth century, and which the First World War had seriously shaken, now disintegrated. The trends towards agricultural self-sufficiency were encouraged to an extraordinary degree in the industrial countries, which were striving to cut their imports in order to cope with the violent contraction in their exports. Bilateralism and discrimination emerged as means of mitigating the intensity of this phenomenon. This movement spread throughout the world and forced many developing countries to adopt even more drastic restrictive measures, since the value of primary exports was declining more sharply than that of industrial goods.

The precipitous fall in the import coefficient of the United States, the leading dynamic centre, and the slow recovery in the level of its activity, compelled the other countries of the world to lower their import coefficients too by all kinds of restrictive expedients. Under the most-favoured-nation clause, the restrictions ought to have been applied to all countries alike, but the discrimination fostered by bilateralism allowed them to be directed mainly against the United States, as a means of remedying the acute dollar shortage.

This problem recurred after the Second World War. As in the 1930's, recourse was then to bilateralism but this phase was very short-lived. Western Europe decided to attack its difficulties boldly, not just by adopting negative and defensive attitudes but by positive action of enormous scope: the modernization of its economy, which boosted its export capacity, and the policy of integration, which promoted its reciprocal trade to the particular detriment of imports paid for in dollars. While this attitude contributed to over-all equilibrium, it had a serious effect on some developing countries. So it was that the European Economic Community (EEC) and the European Free Trade Association (EFTA) came into existence.

Thus ended the long period of structural imbalance vis-à-vis the United States, which not only unreservedly welcomed the formation of the Community but also offered it its firm support.

In their turn, eight socialist countries[4] formed their own grouping, the Council for Mutual Economic Assistance (CMEA), in order to integrate certain important activities, plan them jointly, and impart greater fluidity to the reciprocal trade of the participating countries.

A new order is thus emerging among the more advanced industrialized States and the next few years will reveal its ultimate significance more clearly: it remains to be seen whether this new order will be one in which vast regions withdraw into their shells and isolate themselves with a minimum of trade between them, or whether it will be one in which they take advantage of a closer economic link involving new forms of the international division of labour.

Hence the vital significance of the massive cut in tariffs proposed by the late President Kennedy for the next round of GATT negotiations. The success of these negotiations among the advanced countries which conduct their trade relations mainly by means of tariffs will thus have a considerable influence on the future development of the world economy.

The EEC authorities have repeatedly affirmed the outward-looking character of their economic policy, a position which coincides with that of the United States. There has been a gradual relaxation of that country's traditional protectionism and it is to be hoped that this new policy can now enter upon a very broad phase.

The socialist States of CMEA have also repeatedly expressed their support of the principle of the international division of labour. The success of the Kennedy round and the improvement in the international political atmosphere could considerably facilitate the adoption of formulae which would enable the socialist countries to play an active part in world trade by removing the obstacles which obstruct their participation. This refers not only to relations between them and other industrially advanced countries, irrespective of the differences in their economic and social systems, but also to relations with the developing countries, in view of the interdependence of world trade.

The Disintegration of the Old Pattern and the Developing Countries

All this is highly important for the developing countries, but it is far from enough. . . . What was happening in those countries after the great depression, while such significant changes were taking place in the industrial countries?

The break-down of the old pattern of trade created new problems for the developing countries. The persistent trend towards external imbalance began, first, as a result of the contraction of their exports during the

---

[4] For the sake of brevity, the term "socialist countries" in this report refers to the countries designated as "countries with centrally planned economies" in United Nations publications.

great depression and, later, as a result of their slow rate of growth. From the outset, a number of countries tried to counteract this imbalance by means of import substitution, i.e., by inward-looking industrialization, without foreign markets, and later, after the Second World War, by continuing this policy without interruption and by drawing on the international financial resources made available to them.

The external imbalance was thus covered, but in a precarious manner in the countries which at that time were pushing ahead with their industrialization. As time went on, the consequences of this system became increasingly apparent. Industrialization encounters growing difficulties in the countries where it is pursued furthest. These difficulties arise from the smallness of national markets and also from the following peculiar fact. The further substitution proceeds in respect of some imports, the more other imports grow because of the heavier demand for capital goods and, subsequently, because of the effects of higher income. In addition to this pressure, the adverse effects of the decline in the terms of trade in recent years have weakened the effectiveness of financial contributions from international sources.

Furthermore, these contributions entail a heavy burden of servicing which is mounting rapidly, mainly owing to the amount of amortization in respect of relatively short-term credits. Thus servicing competes with an active demand for imports for the relatively scanty supply of foreign exchange earned by exports.

This phenomenon has no historical parallel. The old pattern of international trade, as it existed in the nineteenth century, was characterized, as has already been pointed out, by a strong and steady growth in exports, which provided the means for servicing debts. Any difficulties which arose were due not to structural defects, as now, but rather to financial misbehaviour or short-term cyclical contractions. In addition to all this, there is the mounting burden of external payments for maritime freight and insurance. The developing countries own only 6 per cent of the world maritime tonnage and this creates a series of problems. Moreover, while the system of shipping conferences may be explained by the very nature of sea transport, it involves combines that restrict competition and affects the developing countries as regards both the cost of services and the impact of this cost on various products depending on their degree of processing. The desire to extend import substitution policy to these services is therefore very understandable, but the information so far available in support of this policy is very meagre. All this necessitates further inquiry, and it is to be hoped that the information needed for the purpose will be forthcoming.

This is a characteristic picture of many of the developing countries, especially those where industrialization has made most headway. None of the others, however, is, over the short or long term, immune to the persistent tendency towards imbalance, except in certain exceptional

cases; and what is now happening in the more industrialized developing
countries foreshadows what will happen in the others unless a conscious
and deliberate effort is made to influence the course of economic events
and to apply the enlightened policy which those events have made imperative. . . .

External Bottlenecks Obstructing Development

There is one dominant note in this report. On the international economic scene we are faced with new problems, new in kind, in some cases,
and new because of the magnitude they have acquired, in others. We
therefore need different attitudes from those prevailing in the past, and
these attitudes should converge towards a new trade policy for economic
development.

The problems that beset the developing countries are very grave indeed. They have to assimilate modern techniques swiftly in order to raise
their levels of living. But new techniques, while they bring enormous
advantages with them, are fraught with dangerous consequences, because
we have not yet learnt fully to control the forces of development in a
rational way.

The direct and indirect effects of technological progress are responsible
for the fact that world demand for primary commodities is growing so
slowly, to the detriment of the developing countries. The effects of the
protectionism prevailing in the industrial countries are an added factor.
Even though access to the markets of the latter countries is facilitated,
the primary production of the developing countries should adjust to this
slow tempo of demand, but structural difficulties prevent it from doing
so to the extent necessary to prevent primary commodity prices from
deteriorating in relation to those of manufactures. The further modern
techniques permeate primary production, the stronger may be the tendency towards such a deterioration. Action by Governments is therefore
imperative to deal with this paradox of development.

Such action is also essential for rapid industrialization to become the
dynamic factor in the development of the world periphery, just as primary exports were the dynamic factor in the development of the world
periphery in former times. But in those days development had no social
depth. Today it must. This makes the problem of development more
complex and pressing.

The circumstances in which industrialization must proceed are, moreover, very adverse. The developing countries are still suffering the consequences of the disintegration of the world economy that followed upon
the great calamity of the 1930's. They do not export industrial goods,
except in very small quantities. Since their primary commodity exports
are growing so slowly and their terms of trade tend to deteriorate, they
lack the resources necessary to import, on an adequate scale, the goods
required for a satisfactory rate of development.

These imports are mostly industrial goods, and only part of them have been or could be produced domestically on an economic basis owing to the smallness of national markets. They must export in order to enlarge these markets. But it is usually difficult to increase exports because costs are high, and costs are high because of the difficulty of realizing economies of scale in the absence of exports. Here, too, a policy is needed, action by Governments to break this vicious circle by providing reasonable access to the markets of the industrial countries for manufactures from the developing countries, and a decided effort to promote the exports of such manufactures.

The developing countries should also form their own groupings in order to plan and develop their industries in wider markets. In some cases they have only just embarked on this policy and they should be given firm international support in the technical and financial fields, within a more favourable institutional framework than now exists. Such cooperation is needed to help import substitution within the groupings with respect not only to goods but also to services, since maritime transport and insurance, for example, represent very substantial external payments.

Among the growing imports necessary for development, capital goods stand out prominently. Such imports have been financed in part by international financial resources. But, in addition to being inadequate, these resources present a further problem. The burden of servicing them grows heavier and heavier, and in some cases the situation is becoming very critical, again because the exports which must provide the necessary funds for servicing are expanding very slowly and losing their purchasing power, while the demand for imports continues to grow.

All these factors that are so unfavourable to the developing countries converge in the persistent trend towards external imbalance that stifles economic development. As was seen at the beginning of this report, it has been estimated that the potential trade gap in goods and services will amount to some $20 billion by the last year of this decade if the present course of events continues unchecked. This is a staggering figure from the standpoint of the developing countries, but not from that of the industrial countries, since the amount by which the former would have to increase their exports of primary commodities and manufactures in order to bridge this gap, to the extent that it is not covered by international financial resources, represents only an insignificant fraction of the latter's consumption.

The problem must therefore be cut down to its proper size. The remarkable development of the industrial countries has given them a high foreign trade potential. Everything depends on ensuring that part of this potential is translated into practical measures that would bring about a significant increase in imports from the developing countries.

Appendix A. The UNCTAD Conference Report*

*With two matters of special concern to underdeveloped countries —
"trade" and "development" — central to its agenda, the now-famed United
Nations Conference on Trade and Development was convened in Geneva
during March–June 1964. There, the confrontation between delegates
from some 120 countries, developed and underdeveloped, proceeded in
terms of, essentially, "underdeveloped countries versus developed countries." Reproduced below are major statements from the "Final Act,"
approved at the close of the sessions, June 16, 1964.*

General Principles

General Principle Four

Economic development and social progress should be the common
concern of the whole international community and should, by increasing
economic prosperity and well-being, help strengthen peaceful relations
and co-operation among nations. Accordingly, all countries pledge themselves to pursue internal and external economic policies designed to accelerate economic growth throughout the world, and in particular to help
promote, in developing countries, a rate of growth consistent with the
need to bring about a substantial and steady increase in average income,
in order to narrow the gap between the standard of living in developing
countries and that in the developed countries. . . .

General Principle Six

International trade is one of the most important factors in economic
development. It should be governed by such rules as are consistent with
the attainment of economic and social progress and should not be hampered by measures incompatible therewith. All countries should co-operate in creating conditions of international trade conducive, in particular,
to the achievement of a rapid increase in the export earnings of develop-

* Taken and adapted from UN, *Proceedings of the United Nations Conferences on
Trade and Development* (Final Act and Report, Vol. I), New York, 1964, pp. 10–13.
(Italics supplied.)

ing countries and, in general, to the promotion of an expansion and diversification of trade between all countries, whether at similar levels of development, at different levels of development, or having different economic and social systems.

General Principle Seven

The expansion and diversification of international trade depends upon increasing access to markets, and upon remunerative prices for the exports of primary products. Developed countries shall progressively reduce and eliminate barriers and other restrictions that hinder trade and consumption of products from developing countries and take positive measures such as will create and increase markets for the exports of developing countries. All countries should co-operate through suitable international arrangements, on an orderly basis, in implementing measures designed to increase and stabilize primary commodity export earnings, particularly of developing countries, at equitable and remunerative prices and to maintain a mutually acceptable relationship between the prices of manufactured goods and those of primary products.

General Principle Eight

International trade should be conducted to mutual advantage on the basis of the most-favoured nation treatment and should be free from measures detrimental to the trading interests of other countries. However, *developed countries should grant concessions to all developing countries* and extend to developing countries all concessions they grant to one another *and should not, in granting these or other concessions, require any concessions in return from developing countries.* New preferential concessions, both tariff and non-tariff, should be made to developing countries as a whole and such preferences should not be extended to developed countries. *Developing countries need not extend to developed countries preferential treatment in operation amongst them.* Special preferences at present enjoyed by certain developing countries in certain developed countries should be regarded as transitional and subject to progressive reduction. They should be eliminated as and when effective international measures guaranteeing at least equivalent advantages to the countries concerned come into operation. . . .

International Commodity Problems

In order to deal with the problems facing the primary commodity trade of developing countries, the Conference has recommended . . . provisions . . . [for] increasing the export earnings of the developing countries by general measures as well as by specific measures related to individual commodities. . . .

Trade in Manufactures and Semi-Manufactures

The Conference recognizes the urgent need for the diversification and expansion of the export trade of developing countries in manufactures and semi-manufactures, as a means of accelerating their economic development and raising their standards of living. . . .

The Conference has noted both the agreement, signified by *all* developing countries and a great majority of the developed countries, with the principle of assisting the industrial development of developing countries, by the *extension of preferences in their favour*, and the opposition to this principle expressed by *some* developed countries. . . .

Appendix B. The UNCTAD Conference in Perspective*

WALTER KRAUSE

University of Iowa

Implications for the Future

With the UNCTAD sessions now history, what can one say in appraising apparent impact on world affairs? Certainly no great and abrupt change, politically or economically, is to be noted as having followed swiftly upon adjournment. Nevertheless, there is good reason to believe that the conference, a momentous event in and of itself, continues to hold major meaning for developments yet to come during the years ahead.

First, great significance attaches to the fact that the conference *did* occur. A global conference, convened under United Nations auspices, at which "trade and development" matters are up for discussion within the avowed context of "underdeveloped countries *versus* developed countries" is — in terms of the standards of pre-UNCTAD days — a landmark of high order. Presumably, with the firm precedent of UNCTAD now on hand, follow-up conferences, possibly even more hard-hitting, become easier to arrange.

Second, the conference revealed that a "united front" among underdeveloped countries is possible (at least when some major matters are at stake). By and large, the underdeveloped countries remained a solid bloc in the support of their initial basic position. This was no small test, and the resultant cohesion surprised many observers (who, perhaps, did not expect this degree of tactical sophistication from a membership embracing, among others, some countries only recently freed of a colonialist tie). And, especially this cohesion seemed remarkable with the realization that the developed countries, on their part, were *unable* to retain a fully consistent posture throughout.[1] Thus, with one demonstration of

---

* Taken and adapted from Walter Krause (ed.), *The Economy of Latin America,* University of Iowa, 1966, pp. 171–173; new material added.

[1] For example, in reference to the proposal for higher tariffs by developed countries on manufactured-goods trade among themselves [as a means by which the developed

471

cohesion among underdeveloped countries on hand, a willingness by them to stand up in the future in a direct confrontation on other scores may be enhanced.

Third, the underdeveloped countries did not leave the conference entirely empty-handed. To illustrate, the United States offered a conciliatory policy statement to the effect that: "The industrialized nations should provide ready access to the products of the underdeveloped nations by reducing tariffs and other barriers, *without necessarily expecting full reciprocity for their own exports.*"[2] This was a far cry from the multilateralist, reciprocal-type approach to which this country had always tenaciously clung previously, and to which it had long urged other countries to subscribe. Certainly, it would prove much more difficult in the future to withstand tangible requests for action in this direction, given the fact that the statement now was on the record as a policy concession.

All in all, the UNCTAD sessions represented a direct confrontation in which, clearly, the developed countries did not stand firm (or united) on all points. A reasonable presumption, thereafter, was that with a "crack in the dike" on hand for all to see, some subsequent set of circumstances of the "right" kind could well trigger the unleashing of a flood. While changes in basic ground rules typically come about only slowly, a far more tangible basis now existed for thinking that "something will have to give, sooner or later."

Current Action

Not everyone, to be sure, was confident that a "united front" attitude among Latin America, Africa, and Asia would survive to follow up on the achievements of the UNCTAD meeting. Illustrative of this, one view current . . . [in areas such as Latin America] was as follows (in substance):

> The idea of a united front between Latin America, Africa, and Asia is based on political, if not economic, unreality. We, in Latin America, see our destiny in terms of *working arrangements with the United States primarily*, just as the underdeveloped countries of Africa and Asia are logically obliged to seek their destiny in relationships geared primarily to

---

countries might raise funds to "retransfer" back to the underdeveloped countries as a form of redress for the alleged long-range deterioration in the terms of trade of primary commodities — all in line with Prebisch argumentation for a "retransfer" of income], a British delegate chose to voice opposition in terms of "unfairness." He contended that those countries whose imports comprise a high percentage of GNP — Britain being a case in point — would be forced to bear a disproportionately heavy burden in the "retransfer" process. Significantly, he did *not* argue that the retransfer idea was, in itself, ill-advised (as some other developed-country groups believed). He merely questioned how the costs of the retransfer were to be shared. To onlookers, the reaction could only have been one of "something less than a united front" within the developed-countries camp.

[2] Italics supplied.

Western Europe. Moreover, it isn't a simple case of the underdeveloped countries *versus* the developed countries (or, of Latin America *versus* the United States). Many of the raw materials of Latin America are also domestic raw materials in the United States (e.g., wheat, corn, cotton, copper, petroleum, etc) — so that even in the problem-ridden raw-materials realm there is a substantial community of interest between Latin America *and* the United States.

However comforting such a view may be for those who frame United States foreign policy, a final answer seems slated to await the passage of some more time. Meanwhile, a pertinent fact is that the World Bank — representing, with only few exceptions, the same countries that participated in the UNCTAD meeting — is actively engaged in a number of studies triggered by the UNCTAD sessions [and certainly needed in the event of a further confrontation]: the external debt burden of developing countries; the use and terms of suppliers' credits; the influence of fluctuations in export earnings on orderly economic development and multilateral investment insurance; the transference internationally of capital assistance on "soft" terms; etc.[3] . . .

By 1966, considerably earlier than one might reasonably have conjectured at the close of the 1964 sessions, official releases of the continuing UNCTAD organization (within the United Nations) indicated that preparatory arrangements were in progress for a *second* UNCTAD meeting, tentatively scheduled for 1968.

[3] IBRD, *Press Release,* February 15, 1965.

62..... Industrialism and World Society[*]

CLARK KERR
University of California

JOHN T. DUNLOP
Harvard University

FREDERICK HARBISON
Princeton University

CHARLES R. MYERS
Massachusetts Institute of Technology

If we watch the way the world is industrializing day by day, we are likely to get a confusing and bewildering picture. There seems to be little consistency in the multitude of patterns followed by various nations, except that the underdeveloped ones are trying to catch up, and the developed ones are trying to stay ahead. Long-range predictions about the future of industrial man seem impossible.

But if we stand back from the day-to-day news picture and take a broader, more historical perspective, we find that there *is* a pattern to all the apparent chaos. From Southeast Asia to Western Europe and from Chile to the Congo, the forces making for uniformity — especially uniformity in the all-important relations between labor, management, and government — tend surely to become stronger than the forces perpetuating diversity. The imperatives of industrialization cause the controlling elites to overcome certain constraints and to achieve objectives *which are the same in all societies undergoing transformation.* . . .

[*] Taken and adapted from "Industrialism and World Society," *Harvard Business Review,* January–February 1961, pp. 113–115, 122–126.

How Development Starts

Most of the nations of the world are on the march toward industrialism. They aspire to higher living standards. They yearn to throw off economic backwardness, illiteracy, and disease. The economically underdeveloped countries are dedicated to a rapid reduction of the inequalities that have been growing in the past century between the few rich Western nations and the poor countries which comprise the mass of humanity. They know they face desperate tasks, and they must run twice as hard to narrow the large gap since the other, more advanced countries continue to make spectacular gains. Their leaders preach dedication and hard work. They are committed to an industrial future, and they have high expectations. They are launched on a long course that they realize is certain to change their communities into new societies.

In the 1850's the world had essentially one model of successful industrialization: that led by middle-class capitalists in Western Europe and the United States. Today the newly industrializing countries have a wide variety of prescriptions, a range of political and economic forms, and a growing body of industrializing experience from which to choose. The experimentation with methods of achieving the industrial society continues to grow, as the recent history in India, Yugoslavia, China, Brazil, and Egypt illustrates. This diversity of experience not only enriches the policy-making process within countries and international agencies, but it also affords a growing body of material well suited to the comparative study of the industrialization process and of the interrelations of workers, managers, and governments.

Pioneering Minorities

Industrialization is always introduced by a minority group. It cannot come into full bloom overnight, except perhaps in small societies with unusual natural resources which attract external capital, like Kuwait, Arabia; but even there an initiating human agent is requisite. Usually industrialization starts in a restricted geographical area or sector of a society, as a small subculture initiated by a subordinated group, which then spreads into new areas and new sectors until it is the dominating system of production affecting almost all the relations of men within the society.[1]

The subordinated group initiating the industrialization process is, of course, a product of the particular culture existing in the preindustrial society. The range of issues which confront this industrializing elite is

---

[1] See Everett E. Hagen, "The Process of Economic Development," *Economic Development and Cultural Change*, April 1957, p. 206, and "How Economic Growth Begins: A General Theory Applied to Japan," *Public Opinion Quarterly*, Fall 1958, p. 373.

similarly shaped by both the cultural and economic constraints. As individuals, members of the industrializing elites do make choices, but these choices are affected by their values and by the fact that the culture and the economic environment have thrown them up as leaders.

At his juncture in world history there are five types of elite that customarily and variously take the leadership of the industrialization process:

1. A dynastic elite.
2. The middle class.
3. The revolutionary intellectuals.
4. The colonial administrators.
5. The nationalist leaders.

Each of these elite groups may have associated with it, or indeed may be composed of, several elements — political leaders, industrial managers, military officers, religious figures, top civil servants, and leaders of labor organizations, among others. Accordingly, when we speak of a certain type of elite, we refer more to the character of its central orientation than to the specific individuals who constitute it at any moment of time.

Each group has a strategy by which it seeks to order the surrounding society in a consistent and compatible fashion. An internal conflict between the old culture and the new culture, with its dominant theme set by the industrializing elite, is inevitably fought on many fronts — the economic, political, religious, and intellectual. And an external conflict, between alternative ideologies of industrialism, tends to be fought on all fronts at once. Each industrial system becomes a "way of life," no matter what its specific form, and a "way of life" demands internal acceptance and external protection if it is to function successfully in the long run. . . .

The Road to Similarity

We have seen that the natural, historical tendency of each of the five types of elite is to change — sometimes completely. Will these changes keep on occurring in the future as in the past and, if so, in what direction? This brings us to some important — and unconventional — conclusions about the strength of pressures for uniformity.

It will help us to appreciate these forces all the more if we keep in mind that the sources of diversity are great, too, and are all the time working in the world, even if with not quite so much effect. Thus:

(1) *The differing elites each want to organize the process of industrialization in a different fashion.* Once structured, the institutions and the ways of doing things tend to develop a life and a persistency of their own, provided the ruling elites are reasonably successful in handling industrialization and other problems of the nation. There are, after all, several

possible ways of organizing an industrial society. Furthermore, the slogans, the heroes, the vested interests that collect around an ideology and a strategy for organizing society give any system considerable tenacity and are a great source of diversity in an industrializing world.

(2) *The culture of a nation and the degree of its continual adherence to that culture also create world-wide diversity.* The family and the class carry on, particularly under the dynastic elite. Education often adapts quite slowly from its traditional forms, again particularly under the dynastic elite. But other national traits carry on as well. Take, for instance, the discipline and energy of the Germans, the individualism of the French, and the easy-going approach of the Indonesians.

(3) *The stage of development makes for variation.* Early industrialization, regardless of the overall strategy, has its own special problems, its own special attitudes, its own special approaches. Mature industrialization, with its well-developed institutions and web of rules, its full complement of industries and services and trades, its settled labor force, its greater consensus, is a different phenomenon regardless of the organizing forces. Degree of development, of course, relates both to the date of the start and the rate of the change.[2]

(4) *The special character of the basic resources and the central industries causes variations from one country to another.* Plantation agriculture, crude oil production, heavy industry, light industry, and so on, each give a tone to their society. Some industries are more prone to industrial unrest than others; some are more likely to engage in paternalistic practices; some are occupationally more highly stratified; some are more subject to a system of norms; some have more large-scale enterprises. Each industry has its own character — the waterfront, coal mining, banking — and these cast their reflections on the surrounding society. A small or a newly industrialized economy is more likely to reflect the special character of one or a few industries than is a large and mature economy. Thus oil gives a special flavor to Iraq, much as textiles and coal mining once did to England.

(5) *The demographic aspects of a nation impart to its industrialization continuing characteristics.* A relatively empty country, like Australia, has quite a different course of development than a heavily populated one, like India. Wages tend to be higher, recruitment more difficult, a significant increase in the standard of living more possible, a high evaluation of the worth of the individual worker and the attention he deserves more likely, and so forth.

But time moves along and, as it does, many a battle is joined between the forces of perpetuating diversity and those prompting uniformity. Many of these battles are the impersonal clashes of old ways and new facts, and in any case they are fought under many banners and in a myriad of places. But the more we look at these battles collectively, in some kind of time and intercontinental perspective, the more impressed

[2] See W. W. Rostow, "Economics for the Nuclear Age," *Harvard Business Review,* January–February 1960, p. 41.

we become with the power of the forces for uniformity. What are the most striking ones?

History and Homogeneity

The passage of history itself is a force. Each industrializing nation moves farther from its introduction into the industrial world, from its pre-existing forms, from its original leadership. The early elites bring in new recruits from other strata. The elite group grows in size and becomes less identifiable, merging into each successively lower level in the new hierarchy. The second, third, and fourth generations of leaders and the led alike are different from the first.

The age of ideology fades. When man first entered the irreversible journey into industrialization, there were innumerable views about the best way to organize society. Some of them have largely disappeared from the scene: anarchism, syndicalism, communalism, cooperativism. Others of them have been blunted and revised from their original form, particularly capitalism and socialism. The age of utopias is past. An age of realism has taken its place — an age in which there is little expectation of either utter perfection or of complete doom. One of the results of the past century is the accumulation of experience about the realistic alternatives.

Thus the conflict of ideologies is blunted and fades between societies. Consensus develops wherever industrialization is successful. The labor force becomes committed to and settled into industrial life. It accepts the pace of work, the web of rules, the surrounding structure. The sense of protest subsides. The business managers, left to their own devices, push less hard. Society provides more of the amenities of life. Men learn from experience how better to do things, and the rough edges are evened off. Industrialization is accepted.

Finally, as the elites become less differentiated and the ideological controversies become more barren, the cultural patterns of the world intermingle and merge. These changes are in evidence although the majority of nations in the world have been in the active throes of industrialization only two generations or less.

Technology and Society

Technology is also a unifying force. At one moment of time there may be several best economic combinations or social arrangements, but only one best technology. The technology can be up-to-date or antiquated, but there is no question which is which, and the modern is constantly replacing the ancient. The same technology calls for much the same occupational structure around the world — in steel, in textiles, in air transport. The occupational role of a man gives him a place in society and affects his behavior in many ways. Also, there comes to be a growing diversity of occupations and of levels of management, and no really clear-cut dividing lines visible to all. The occupation takes the place of the class.

The technology is dynamic and it calls for change. Men change their locations and their occupations. A labor market must be created with substantial mobility within it. A fully paternalistic system at the plant level becomes less possible. Mobility calls at least for the semi-independent rather than the dependent worker.

The skill level rises. Men are given responsibility for more expensive equipment, more essential processes. Their consent becomes more important. The need for their consent gives them influence. It may even give them organized power, for there is a tendency to organize around the occupation. True, only scientists may be given this right at first, but the pressure will always exist to spread professional and occupational organization.

Push of Progress

The thrust of progress also serves the cause of uniformity. The industry mix, country by country, becomes more balanced and thus more like that elsewhere. There is insistent pressure to obtain a rough balance of supply and demand in the labor market.

The development of consumer-goods industries and service trades requires the creation of markets — in spite of the addiction to plans (the market mentality and the planning mentality are quite different). The rising standard of living and increasing leisure create the capacity to read and travel and compare. They also encourage an aggressive materialism on the part of people. Progress brings the great metropolitan center and the city as the natural habitat of man. The city has been the home of variety and of freedom throughout the centuries.

Education and Equality

An industrial society must educate its people. There are at least two imperatives: (1) The vast bulk of the population must be literate in order to receive instructions, follow directions, and keep records. (2) Managers, engineers, and civil servants must be trained to operate the new productive system. Beyond that are the needs for doctors, lawyers, scientists, and university professors. Education becomes a leading industry.

Out of education come several results. Education is intended to reduce the scarcity of skilled persons, and this after a time reduces the wage and salary differentials they receive. It also pulls people out of the least skilled and most disagreeable occupations and raises wage levels there. It conduces to a new equality which has nothing to do with ideology; in fact, it may come faster and more fully in a middle-class society than in a society under the revolutionary intellectuals who proclaim equality as a primary goal. This equality is at first economic, but it also affects class status and political outlook.

Out of education may also come a new call for freedom. This call will be most insistent at the highest levels in the educational pyramid, for knowledge knows no geographical boundaries; but it may spread down through many of the ranks of society. Education and personal independence have usually walked the road together. With an educated labor force, jobs tend to change or be changed. On the average, more responsibility adheres to them; they are made more interesting; and their incumbents are treated more individually and humanely.

Government and Business

The state, everywhere, becomes an important instrument in society. It becomes responsible for the general rate of growth, the level of economic activity, the distribution of power in society, the settlement of conflicts, and the prevention of economic or other sabotage of the economy by special interest groups. It may, of course, do much more. But at least it must set the many basic rules for the economy, *and it inevitably becomes a partner, if not the sole partner, in labor-management relations.*

At the same time, the productive enterprise, whether public or private, becomes a large-scale organization in many industries. It comes to be run by professional managers, recruited and trained through the educational system, separated from ownership and protected from power politics. These enterprise managers must be placed under the constraints of the market or planning budgets to assure their suitable performance, and the structuring of these pressures and controls is an essential task in society. The professional administrator has great power, but it is power subject to checks and balances in all developed industrial societies.

The managers are basically responsible for the web of rules in the plant and industry which relate them to the managed, although they share this responsibility with the state and the organized workers. Basically, this web of rules must spell out the authority of the managers and how far they may go, for economic enterprise is always essentially authoritarian under the necessity of getting things done, and the limits to executive authority must be specified.

Compulsion of Comparisons

Man everywhere wants progress and participation. The two are substitutes for each other, and often progress will be accepted for a time in lieu of participation; but in the end industrial man wants both and will keep pressing for both. Progress means a higher standard of education, better health, more consumer goods and services; participation means choice of jobs, choice of consumer goods, a chance to influence the web of rules, and even an opportunity to influence those who guide society itself. These same pressures develop regardless of culture and ideology.

The pressures for progress and participation are enhanced by the worldwide character of industrialization, by international trade, by travel, and by the exchange of ideas. Generally the impact will be to bring greater uniformity in the nature of the societal product which people widely judge to be the best. People may not be willing to settle for much less in their own systems than the standards and performance of competing systems.

Pluralistic Industrialism

Men attempt to peer ahead, to understand the structure of history, and to alter the process of history, if possible, in accord with their preferences. The future they appear to be choosing and pressing for is what might be called *pluralistic industrialism.* We use this term to refer to a society which is governed neither by one all-powerful elite (e.g., the monistic model) nor by the impersonal interaction of innumerable small groups with relatively equal power (e.g., the atomistic model in economic theory). The complexity of the fully developed industrial society requires, in the name of efficiency and initiative, a degree of decentralization of control, particularly in the consumer-goods and service-trades industries; but it also requires a large measure of central control by the state and conduct of many operations by large-scale organizations.

As the skill level rises and jobs become more responsible, any regime must be more interested in consent, in drawing forth relatively full co-operation. For the sake of real efficiency, this must be freely given. The discipline of the labor gang no longer suffices. With skill and responsibility goes the need for consent, and with consent goes influence and even authority. Occupational and professional groups, of necessity, achieve some prestige and authority as against both the central organs of society and the individual members of the occupation or profession.

Education brings in its wake a new economic equality and a new community of political outlook. This, in turn, along with many other developments, helps bring consensus to society. The harsh use of power by the state is no longer so necessary to hold society together at the seams. Education also opens the mind to curiosity and to inquiry, and the individual seeks more freedom to think and to act. It brings a demand for liberty, and can help create conditions in which liberty can safely be granted. It leads to comparisons among nations with respect to progress and participation.

Industrialism is so complex and subject to such contrary internal pressures that it never can assume a single, uniform, unchanging structure; but it *can* vary around a general central theme, and that theme is pluralism. While it will take generations before this theme will become universal in societies around the world, the direction of the movement already seems sufficiently clear.

Unwithering State

The state will be powerful. It will, at the minimum, have the responsibility for:

The economic growth rate.

The over-all distribution of income among uses and among individuals.

The basic security of individuals (formerly the family was the basic security unit).

The stability of the system.

Providing the essential public services of education, transportation, recreational areas, cultural facilities, and the like, which will become more important as the standard of living rises, leisure increases, education improves, and men multiply in numbers.

Providing a favorable physical environment for urban man.

In addition, any pluralistic society is subject to three great potential internal problems, and the state is responsible for handling each:

1. *Conflict among the various power elements.* The state must set the rules of the game within which such conflict will occur, enforce these rules, and act as mediator. Conflicts between managers and the managed are the most noticeable, but by no means the only ones.

2. *Collusion.* The state must control collusion by producers against consumers, by any profession against its clients, and by labor and management against the public. Undue aggrandizement of sectional interests is always endemic if not epidemic in a pluralistic society; in fact, one of the arguments for monism and for atomism alike is the avoidance of such sectionalism.

3. *Organizational rules.* The state will come generally, under pluralistic industrialism, to set the rules relating members to their organizations — who may get in, who may stay in, what rights and obligations the members have, what the boundaries for the activities of the organization are, and so on. It will, almost of necessity, be against too much conflict among, or collusion between, or domination of the members by the subsidiary organizations in society.

All these responsibilities mean that the state will never "wither away"; that Marx was more utopian than the despised utopians themselves. The state will be the dominant organization in any industrial society. But it may itself be less than fully unitary. It may itself be subject to checks and balances, including the check of public acceptance of its current leadership and its policies.

Crucial Role for Business

The productive enterprise, whether private or public, will be in a dominant position under pluralistic industrialism. It will often be large, and it must always have substantial authority in order to produce efficiently. But there will be no "managerial revolution," as James Burnham suggested, with the manager reigning supreme over all of society.

The distinction between the private and public manager will decrease just as the distinction between the private and public enterprise will diminish; and the distinction among managers will be more according to the size, the product, and the nature of their enterprises. The controlled market and the controlled budget will bring more nearly the same pressures on them. The private enterprise, however, will usually have more freedom of action than the public enterprise.

Battles in the Corridors

The occupational or professional association will range alongside the state and the enterprise as a locus of power in pluralistic industrialism; and there will be more occupations and particularly more professions seeking association. Group organizations around skill and position in the productive mechanism will be well-nigh universal. These organizations will affect output norms, comparative incomes, access to employment, and codes of ethics in nearly every occupational walk of life. Their containment within reasonable limits will be an all-enduring and all-pervading problem; and some of the groups will always seek to invade and infiltrate the government mechanisms which are intended to supervise them. Class warfare will be forgotten and in its place will be the bureaucratic contest of interest group against interest group. The battles will be in the corridors instead of the streets, and memos will flow instead of blood.

Uniting the state, the enterprise, and the association will be a great web of rules set by the efforts of all the elements, but particularly by the state. Persuasion and pressure and manipulation will take the place of the face-to-face combat of an earlier age. Executives in industry and government will pore over narrower, more technical issues than in earlier times when there was real disagreement over the nature of and the basic arrangements in industrial society.

Labor organizations will not be component parts of class movements urging programs of total reform, for the consensus of a pluralistic society will have settled over the scene. Nor may they be very heavily identified by industry, particularly with the increasing multiplication and fractionalization of industries; rather, they may tend to take more the craft or, perhaps better, the occupational form. With skills more diverse, at a generally higher level, and obtained more through formal education, and with geographical mobility greatly increased, professional-type interests should mean more to workers than industry or class ties. . . .

Conclusion

Pluralistic industrialism will never reach a final equilibrium. The contest between the forces of uniformity and for diversity will give it life and movement and change. This is a contest which will never reach an ultimate solution. Manager and managed will struggle all up and down the line of hierarchies all around the world; quiet but often desperate little battles will be fought all over the social landscape.

The uniformity that draws on technology, and the diversity that draws on individuality; the authority that stems from the managers, and the rebellion, however muted, that stems from the managed — these are destined to be the everlasting threads of the future. They will continue in force when class war, and the contest over private versus public initiative, and the battle between monistic and atomistic ideologies, all have been left far behind in the sedimentary layers of history.

63..... International Business in the Days Ahead: Three Statements

I. Growing Internationalism*

RICHARD D. ROBINSON

Massachusetts Institute of Technology

... One can predict with some confidence that in the last decades of the twentieth century, Western business will constitute a powerful pressure in the direction of *internationalizing* the process of political socialization, through the institutional relationships it creates and the flow of communication inherent in them. Even Communist societies may be included, for the private ownership of the actual machines of production is not a necessary prerequisite in this relationship. In many countries joint public-private ownership of large sectors of production is already occurring, and in some of these situations private Western enterprise is participating in the manner suggested above.

It is relevant to point out that a number of foreseeable technical developments will likewise push in the direction of *international* — rather than national — development. Reference is made to such innovations as submarine mining, weather control, supersonic transport flight, world-wide television networks, arctic exploitation, and the like. . . . Already, certain leaders within the international business field are transcending national frontiers in their willingness to undertake anything, anywhere, in association with anybody, so long as it promises a reasonable long-run return. By legally elevating the transmission of those business services suggested here to the international level, the business organizations involved would be, at least in part, insulated from use by nationalist politi-

* Taken and adapted from Richard D. Robinson, *International Business Policy*. Copyright © 1964 by Holt, Rinehart and Winston, Inc., Publishers, pp. 223–224.

cal authorities to further the ambitions of any state against another. One can sense that already there exists an international business community, the members of which have ceased being emotionally committed to the perpetuation of particular cultures and value systems. This community has members in both developed and underdeveloped worlds.

The significance of this development may be enormous. Political scientist Hans J. Morganthau once wrote, "When the national state will have been replaced by another mode of organization, foreign policy must then protect the interest in survival of that new organization." He then suggested that such organization come into existence only by conquest or by "consent based upon the mutual recognition of the national interests of the nations concerned."

The author suggests that there is perhaps a third path which has been largely overlooked — specifically, the expansion of internationally constituted private groups (that is, business) whose mutual interests are contrary to the continued existence of national sovereignty as presently constituted. One can look forward perhaps to the day when these groups will become so large and powerful as to have a significant impact on national foreign policy itself. It is also conceivable that they will of themselves create a supranational interest possessed of not insignificant power. . . .

The distinguishing characteristic of the international business approach to international relations is that it envisages institutional, functional, nonpolitical, multinational relationships that are conducive to the weaving of an ever larger fabric of common interest and loyalty, thereby eroding the concept of national sovereignty and conflicting national interests. In the end it is possible even to imagine the appearances of privately owned supranational corporations, registered, controlled, and taxed by an international organization. . . .

II. Trends of Trade

JOHN FAYERWEATHER
New York University

International business is highly beneficial to the United States. Through exports and overseas investments we are able to participate in the economic expansion of other nations. Imports bring to our shores essential foods and raw materials as well as manufactured goods which other countries can make more economically than we. But these benefits cannot be fully realized unless we are adept in handling the difficult problems of adjusting our own industry to increased imports, keep our international payments in balance, and make our overseas operations acceptable to host nations. In the past we have repeatedly fallen into difficulties in our international business through failure to foresee the nature of these problems and to meet them realistically and constructively as they arose.

It is well worth our while, therefore, to look ahead . . . to see what sort of problems we can expect in the next decade and what we must do to resolve them in the best interests of our country. It seems certain that the economies of the world will make great forward strides in the next ten years. Major increases are being forecast in the gross national products of all areas: 71 per cent for Japan, 73 per cent for Canada and Mexico, 63 per cent for South America, 55 per cent for Western Europe, and 42 per cent for the United States.[1] Although these figures are certainly crude guesses, rates of growth of comparable magnitude are currently being experienced by these areas and there is every reason to assume they will continue. This growth will cause an expansion and diversification of demand for the tremendous range of products which American industry can provide. At the same time, the expansion of the American economy and the drain on our domestic raw-material resources will create ever-greater demand for imported goods.

---

* Taken and adapted from Richard D. Robinson, *Facts and Fallacies of International Business.* Copyright © 1964 by Holt, Rinehart and Winston, Inc., Publishers, 1962, pp. 165–167.

[1] Thomas Aitken, *A Foreign Policy for American Business* (New York: Harper & Brothers, 1961), p. 31.

Specifically we may expect these developments affecting our international business. First, as standards of living rise abroad, markets for consumer goods will continue to broaden. The trend toward overseas production . . . will continue, with foreign manufacture displacing United States exportation of more products in still more countries.

Second, the parallel expansion of American exports of specialized products . . . will also continue pushing our total exports ever higher.

Third, we should be able to increase our exports of agricultural commodities. One of the tragic inequities of our current world economic situation is the maldistribution of food supplies. The United States has a major problem of excess agricultural output. Other nations, such as India and Pakistan, are struggling to produce enough to keep their populations fed at a bare subsistence level. We may hope that as one of the consequences of economic progress these underfed nations will be able to produce enough so that they can export more manufactured goods and be able in turn to buy more of our agricultural excesses.

Fourth, on the import side we will clearly have increased our purchases of raw materials, but, more important, it will be economically sound to import a greater volume and variety of manufactured products. With the earnings from our expanded exports of specialized industrial products and agricultural commodities, we will be able to benefit from the low costs which foreign mass production of consumer items will permit.

One can readily visualize the outcome of these trends. By the 1970's American companies will have overseas factories with double or more their present productive capacity. Exports of mass-consumption items will have dwindled to a low level. At the same time, exports of machinery, specialized chemicals, and similar products will have increased and the expanded outflow of grains, cotton, and other farm produce will be drawing off the productive surpluses of our land. We will, in turn, be importing vastly greater quantities of petroleum and minerals, and imports of basic consumer goods, from textiles to electrical appliances to simpler mechanical products, will have taken over a greater share of the American market.

What does all this require of us? Clearly the heart of the whole process is change, and the key to success must be flexibility — the ability to foster and benefit from changes, not to resist and suffer from their effects. We must be ready and able to expand our investments abroad to keep pace with the rate of expansion in each country. We must give continuing attention to the problems of overcoming the fears of exploitation and American control among the people of other nations. We must be alert to the new export opportunities which will open up for specialized products and agricultural goods at the same time that our exports of mass-produced manufactured products decline. Finally, we must leave the door open to the expansion of imports of manufactured goods, giving thoughtful attention to the problems of adjustment of industries which are hurt by competition from imports.

If we demonstrate wisdom and flexibility in our business and government policies in dealing with these changes as they come along, then as a nation we will be able to reap the great rewards which international business proffers us.

III. Business and Foreign Policy*

THOMAS AITKEN, JR.

Vice-President,
McCann-Erickson Corporation

New responsibilities are being thrust upon American business overseas. Speakers, writers, educators, and government leaders have been saying that American business abroad represents the people and the government of the United States as well as its own stockholders. They have pointed out that the contacts of our businessmen with their foreign counterparts, overseas suppliers, consumers, labor, and observers, affect foreign opinions of our country. Hence, American business has been charged with an ambassadorial obligation, but has not received the rank or prestige that would aid in its fulfillment.

This new concern with a field of business operations that formerly went almost unnoticed has been confusing not because of the suddenness of its appearance, but because it obscures a deeper issue. It is increasingly apparent that American business is becoming an instrument of this country's foreign policy. Its movement into such a role follows no plan but is the result of combining sets of circumstances. Businessmen do not seek to play this part, nor has government designated it as theirs, but history and economics are setting the course like currents carrying a rudderless craft.

* Taken and adapted from "Can Business Carry the Flag?," *Business Horizons*, Indiana University, Winter 1962, pp. 101–102.

The trend is now too important to leave its outcome to chance; events are following each other too rapidly to permit further hesitation. At today's pace, the point of no return is very close to the starting line. The relationship between our business performance abroad and our commercial health at home is now vitally significant, and it has become most urgent, therefore, that American business take a stand regarding its posture in international affairs.

03122